The Parthenon Marbles and International Law

Catharine Titi

The Parthenon Marbles and International Law

Springer

Catharine Titi
French National Centre for Scientific
Research and CERSA
University Paris-Panthéon-Assas
Paris, France

ISBN 978-3-031-26356-9 ISBN 978-3-031-26357-6 (eBook)
https://doi.org/10.1007/978-3-031-26357-6

This Springer imprint is published by the registered company Springer Nature Switzerland AG
The registered company address is: Gewerbestrasse 11, 6330 Cham, Switzerland

For Anna

Foreword

Over the years, innumerable arguments have been rehearsed in favour of returning to their place of origin the fragments of marble that once formed part of the Parthenon temple in Athens, and equally many have been rehearsed against it. The aim of this book is not to collect and assess all these arguments (though it provides a vigorous overview), but to focus on the essential legal question: were these pieces legally acquired, and if not, is there a mechanism under current international law by which their return can be enforced?

The legal case does not constitute the most important argument for return, but it is fundamental to the debate. The overwhelming reason for return is that these exquisite specimens of marble carving, seen by many as the most beautiful products of ancient Greek art, form an integral element of a decorative programme of which only part can be seen in London. Above all the frieze, which once wrapped round the interior of the Parthenon temple, forms a continuous narrative, originally 160 m in length, with an unbroken depiction of the religious procession which was the high spot of the religious year of the cult of Athena Parthenos, the Virgin Goddess. Part of this frieze is in Athens, now housed in a purpose-built museum close to the Acropolis. There it can be seen in the bright Mediterranean light which shows it to best effect and displayed the right way round, as it was on the temple itself, not inside-out as in London's dull light. The overwhelming argument is that these uniquely important fragments belong together. It goes against all contemporary understanding of the importance of context to artworks to divorce them from their context, location and adjoining fragments.

Some would argue that all works of art, whether legally or illegally acquired, belong back in their country of origin. This viewpoint is extreme and highly questionable and risks the disintegration of the great museum collections of the world, which themselves represent high cultural values. It is not necessary to adopt this point of view to demand the return of the Parthenon marbles, nor would their return imply that this argument was valid. Historically, artworks have frequently established their validity in new contexts: the porphyry sculptures of four emperors at the corner of St Mark's in Venice, once looted from what was then

Constantinople, now ‘belong’ in Venice not Istanbul and their return would be pointless vandalism. But the Parthenon marbles are not like the porphyry tetrarchs, the original context of which no longer exists. They are an integral part of a still standing monument, itself regarded as one of the finest, if not the finest, examples of Greek architecture; and while returning them to that monument is no longer practicable, reuniting them with their sisters in Athens is indeed now practicable, and the long-standing desire of the Greek government which constructed a new museum to enable this move.

The problem is that such ‘moral’ arguments for restitution run up against a thicket of legal obstacles. The British Museum, which houses them, claims that it is not allowed to deaccession its holdings and insists moreover that they were legally acquired and cannot be legally removed. Such legal questions can only be resolved by legal experts, and it is therefore of critical significance that in this book Professor Titi, an international lawyer based in Paris, examines these issues with the scrupulous thoroughness which is needed to convince sceptics. Her argument is that the acquisition of the marbles was demonstrably illegal and admitted to be such by Elgin himself in billing the British government for the money spent in illegal bribes; and that recent developments in international law affecting such objects mean that there is now a very strong case to be brought before the appropriate international authorities, in her view the International Court of Justice. Whether or not the Greek government is prepared to take such a step, rather than pursuing the diplomatic channels which it has always preferred, awareness on the part of both the British Museum and the British government of the legal weakness of the case for retention must make them more open than they have been in the past to a diplomatic approach.

This is a book that must be read with attention by all parties to this debate; and it is my hope and belief that it will accelerate the process by which an art-loving and philhellenic Britain finds a consensual way to return to its ancient ally a collection of broken and decontextualised fragments which illuminate a moment two and a half millennia ago when the city that pioneered democracy created a monument of transcendent beauty which embodied the values that inspire us still.

University of Cambridge
Cambridge, UK
November 2022

Andrew Wallace-Hadrill

Acknowledgements

I am grateful to many people who have taken the time to read drafts of the book or discuss my ideas as they developed, and those who have helped me access crucial information that has made this a better book. I am indebted to museum curators who agreed to discuss with me, answered questions and shared material with me: Raphaël Jacob and Stamatia Eleftheratou, archaeologists at the Acropolis Museum; Peter John Higgs, acting keeper of the department of Greece and Rome at the British Museum; Cécile Giroire, director of the department of Greek, Etruscan and Roman Antiquities at the Louvre; Stine Schierup, curator at the National Museum of Denmark. I am deeply thankful to Vasiliki Eleftheriou, director of the Acropolis Restoration Service (YSMA) at the Greek Ministry of Culture and Sports; Artemis Papathanasiou, senior legal adviser at the Greek Ministry of Foreign Affairs; Christos Psaltis from the British Embassy at Athens; Augusta-Maria Kaloudi from the Greek Ministry of Culture and Sports; Dimitris Kourkoumelis-Rodostamos, director of the *Mentor* shipwreck excavations, from the Greek Ministry of Culture and Sports; Anna Koulikourdi from the General State Archives (Greece); and Thomas Dermine and Katia Dewulf from the Belgian Ministry of Economics and Employment. For permission to reproduce images, I am very grateful to the Acropolis Museum (cover image and plates) and Theodore Theodorou (Robert Adair's draft letter). Further words of thanks must go to my editor, Anja Trautmann, from Springer, for her enthusiasm and work on this project from the very beginning, as well as to the Springer production team: Estelle Rigaud, Pradeep Kuttysankaran, Akshayadevi Arivazhagan, and Periyanayagam Leoselvakumar. I would also like to thank the following friends and colleagues: Elisa Baroncini, Marc Bungenberg, Maria Rosaria Calamita, Guido Carducci, Hilary Charlesworth, David Collins, Emily Crawford, Federica Cristani, Tony Cole, Edhem Eldem, Katia Fach Gómez, Derek Fincham, Elizabeth Key Fowden, Anastasios Gourgourinis, Antonis Karampatzos, Petros-Orestis Katsoulas, Mark Knights, Ursula Kriebaum, Joanna Lam, OM Lewis, Antonio Musolesi, Roger Michael O'Keefe, Stavros Pantazopoulos, Elisabetta Pellini, John Picton, Mauro Politi, José Àngel Rueda García, Hélène Ruiz Fabri, Arman Sarvarian, Tullio Scovazzi, Calliope M Sudborough, Seyyed Mohammad

Taghi Shariat-Panahi, Attila Tanzi, Marlen Taffarello Godwin, Geir Ulfstein, Güneş Ünüvar, Giovanni Urga, Timothy Webb, Wen Xiang, and Ganna Yudkivska. I am profoundly grateful to Paul Cartledge for reading closely drafts of this book and for his detailed and insightful comments. My particular thanks must go to Andrew Wallace-Hadrill for his sharp comments, and for his unwavering enthusiasm, encouragement and support.

I am also indebted to my extended family and, in particular, to Alex McDowell, for sharing important information; Marina Savvidou and Yannis Savvides, for spending hours with me in the Acropolis Museum on repeated occasions, discussing ancient Greek temple polychromy and many other topics; Dane Van Dyck for his encouragement and support; my parents for helping me access research material, for providing me with practical feedback, and, above all, for being my most patient audience; my partner, Alain Pirotte, for bearing with me while working on this project and for doing everything possible to allow me to focus on it. Last and certainly not least, I would like to thank my sister, Anna Van Dyck, for reading draft chapters and providing sharp comments, and most of all for her constant and unconditional support over the years with my reasonable—and my less reasonable—projects and for her support and encouragement with this book in particular. For this, and for all the other reasons, I wish to dedicate this book to her.

Contents

Abbreviations

ARPA	Archaeological Resources Protection Act
CAfA	Court of Arbitration for Art
DSU	Understanding on Rules and Procedures Governing the Settlement of Disputes (Annex 2 of the Agreement Establishing the World Trade Organization—WTO)
ECHR	European Convention on Human Rights
Hague Convention of 1954	Convention for the Protection of Cultural Property in the Event of Armed Conflict
ICJ	International Court of Justice
ICOM	International Council of Museums
ICPRCP (or Intergovernmental Committee)	Intergovernmental Committee for Promoting the Return of Cultural Property to its Countries of Origin or its Restitution in case of Illicit Appropriation
ICSID Convention	Convention on the Settlement of Investment Disputes between States and Nationals of Other States
ILC	International Law Commission
ITLOS	International Tribunal for the Law of the Sea
NDPB	Non-departmental public body
NGV	National Gallery of Victoria
NSPA	National Stolen Property Act
PCA	Permanent Court of Arbitration

PCIJ	Permanent Court of International Justice
UN Charter	Charter of the United Nations
UNCITRAL	United Nations Commission on International Trade Law
UNCLOS	United Nations Convention on the Law of the Sea
UNESCO	United Nations Educational, Scientific and Cultural Organization
1970 UNESCO Convention	Convention on the Means of Prohibiting and Preventing the Illicit Import, Export and Transfer of Ownership of Cultural Property
UNGA	United Nations General Assembly
UNHRC	United Nations Human Rights Council
UNIDROIT	International Institute for the Unification of Private Law
UNIDROIT Convention	Convention on Stolen or Illegally Exported Cultural Objects
UNSC	United Nations Security Council
V&A	Victoria and Albert Museum
WHO	World Health Organization
WIPO	World Intellectual Property Organization

Chapter 1
Introduction

1.1 Background

1.1.1 From Verres to Elgin

All roads, it is said, lead to Rome, and it is not unusual to consider the dispute about the Parthenon marbles in light of another case that arose more than two millennia ago in the late years of the Roman Republic.[1] Yet if the indictment against Caius Verres in the Roman Extortion Court in the seventieth year BC invites parallels to the Parthenon marbles dispute, the similarities between the two cases are nothing short of striking. The prosecution of Verres was of course a famous case. Verres was a Roman magistrate who, having become governor of Sicily, caused the once prosperous island to fall into ruin and desolation.[2] Roman officials were reputed for treating their governorships as opportunities to amass private wealth,[3] and Verres' Sicilian stint took gubernatorial covetousness to altogether new heights. For three years, between 73 and 71 BC, Verres abused his office ravaging the province he was sent to govern.[4] He was arraigned on charges of plunder of temples and statuary, thefts of private works of art, extortion of taxes, torture and execution without trial of Roman citizens—all in all a lengthy repertoire of crime complete with sex offences and bribes.[5] Verres' crimes were surely memorable. But if history remembers the indictment as vividly as it does, this is not only on account of its ignominious

The original version of this chapter has been revised with few text corrections. A correction to this chapter is available at https://doi.org/10.1007/978-3-031-26357-6_13

[1] E.g. Byron (1832) Note 6 to Canto II, 67. For other examples, see Robertson (2019) preface and Chap. 8; Miles (2011) 32.

[2] Cicero, *In Verrem* 1.13. The book relies on various translations of *In Verrem*. The modern-day publication is identified when a word-for-word quote is used.

[3] Cicero, *In Verrem* 2.4.53.

[4] Cicero, *Divinatio* 11; Cicero, *In Verrem* 1.12.

[5] Cicero, *Divinatio* 11; Cicero, *In Verrem* 1.13, 1.14, and *passim*.

C. Titi, *The Parthenon Marbles and International Law*,
https://doi.org/10.1007/978-3-031-26357-6_1

protagonist but also for engaging and confirming the politician who was to become Rome's foremost orator, Marcus Tullius Cicero.[6]

The Sicilians solicited Cicero's assistance, for they knew and appreciated him from his time as quaestor on the island.[7] Little more than a provincial backwater,[8] still largely Greek, Sicily stood united behind the indictment.[9] Cicero must have immediately recognised the case as an opportunity, both on account of the unprecedented scale of Verres' crimes and for political reasons,[10] seeing that the defence would be presented by the highly-acclaimed Quintus Hortensius, who was to be consul the following year. To enter the fray of this unexampled trial, Cicero had to abandon his traditional role of defender and act as prosecutor.[11] But he explained that this pleading of his that seemed to be an accusation was in effect not so much an accusation as a defence; a defence of 'many men, many cities, the whole province of Sicily'.[12] If he prosecuted one man, it was to defend the many whom he had wronged.[13]

Verres stole, and he stole on a grand scale. Cicero dedicated the fourth book of his second speech to the plunder. In it we learn that, besides stealing from many a private citizen, including a king, Verres despoiled Greek temples, monuments, and statues all over Sicily.[14] Agrigento, Catania, Centuripe, Marsala, Segesta, Syracuse, Tindari are some of the cities that bore witness to his heists.[15] Remarkably, by the time he became governor of Sicily, Verres had already accumulated a string of spoliations.[16] His earlier track record included the looting of temples at Delos, Samos, and Athens.[17] We are told that he stole a considerable amount of gold from the Parthenon

---

[6]It is debated whether the Verres case would have been one of 'the minor events of the period' instead of 'the scandal of the century' without Cicero's involvement, Gruen (1971) 12; Alexander (2005) 60. The case was also a milestone in the history of Roman law, since it was the last to be decided by a jury composed only of senators. The senatorial monopoly on juries ended with the *lex Aurelia*, passed shortly afterwards, Balsdon (1938) 99, 106; Spencer (1916) 839; Vasaly (2009) *passim*.

[7]Cicero, *Divinatio* 2; Cicero, *In Verrem* 2.1.16-2.1.17.

[8]Sicily's modest claim to importance was that it served as the granary of Rome, Cicero, *In Verrem* 2.2.5.

[9]Cicero, *Divinatio* 11. Some doubt is permitted as to how united Sicily was, e.g. Cicero, *In Verrem* 2.4.136.

[10]Miles (2002) 29.

[11]Cicero, *Divinatio* 1.

[12]Cicero, *Divinatio* 5; Cicero, *In Verrem* 2.4.82, describing himself as 'the defender of the Sicilians'. The translations used here are taken from Yonge (1903).

[13]Cicero, *Divinatio* 5. See also Cicero, *In Verrem* 2.4.2.

[14]Cicero, *In Verrem* 2.4.

[15]Cicero, *In Verrem* 2.4.

[16]Cicero, *In Verrem* 2.1.

[17]Cicero, *In Verrem* 2.4.71.

at Athens[18]—the same Parthenon in whose despoliation Elgin's men would join in so enthusiastically all these centuries later.

Verres is certainly not a unique figure in the history of art plunder. But probably no man's actions rivalled his in the way Elgin's did. Like his Roman counterpart, Thomas Bruce, 7th Earl of Elgin, was a public official going about state business when he set in motion the machine to dismember the Parthenon. A Scottish representative peer, Elgin was appointed British ambassador to the Ottoman government and took up his position in 1799.[19] This was a time when British influence over the Ottomans was at its apogee, for, after the defeat of the French in the battle of the Nile the previous year, the Sublime Porte looked to Britain to protect its interests against France.[20] Finding himself in a position of incomparable opportunity,[21] Elgin claimed to have obtained an authorisation, a firman, from the Ottoman authorities allowing him to engage in an act of large-scale vandalism and plunder, stripping the Parthenon on the Athenian Acropolis of its most beautiful (and best preserved) sculptured marbles—and this before he had ever set foot in Ottoman-occupied Athens. The collection that he sold to the British government some years later included about fifty slabs of the frieze of the Parthenon, that is, 75 m (247 ft) of the original frieze,[22] fifteen metopes,[23] and seventeen pedimental figures (for the position of the frieze, metopes, and pediments, see Fig. 2.1).[24] In the course of removing parts of the ancient temple, Elgin caused the monument to suffer serious damage.[25] Frieze slabs were sawn through to have their back cut off, which would make for easier transport, the cornice was removed to allow the metopes to be detached, and the entablature that held the metopes was broken.[26]

Although we tend to associate Elgin with the destruction of the Parthenon, much like with Verres, his rapacity went further. He engaged in frenetic pillaging: everything he could lay his hands on must become his. Besides the Parthenon, Elgin stripped treasures off other monuments on the Acropolis, including bas-reliefs from the Temple of Athena Nike, a caryatid and part of the frieze of the temple known as

---

[18] Cicero, *In Verrem* 2.4.71.

[19] Smith (1916) 163-164.

[20] Browning (2008) 11.

[21] Browning (2008).

[22] British Museum, 'The Parthenon Sculptures' https://www.britishmuseum.org/about-us/british-museum-story/objects-news/parthenon-sculptures.

[23] Although Elgin is often said to have removed fifteen metopes from the Parthenon, it appears that he removed fourteen metopes. The fifteenth metope, which he sold to the UK government, appears to have originally belonged to Auguste de Choiseul-Gouffier, the former French ambassador. The catalogue of what Elgin sold to the UK government lists only fourteen metopes, see Select Committee (1816) Appendix No 11, Catalogue of the Elgin Marbles, Vases, Casts, and Drawings xxix.

[24] Select Committee (1816) Appendix No 11, Catalogue of the Elgin Marbles, Vases, Casts, and Drawings xxviii-xxxii.

[25] See Sects. 3.5.1 and 6.3.1.2. See also St Clair (1998) 102-103, 110.

[26] Smith (1916) 202; Browning (2008) 11-12.

the Erechtheion, a colossal statue from the Theatre of Dionysos, plus various columns and capitals.[27] Later, he deplored not having more time and deeper pockets to be able to remove yet more treasures.[28]

Much of this hunt for antiquities was orchestrated from Constantinople. His eventual visit to Greece in 1802 afforded him another opportunity to hoard treasures.[29] 'Everywhere he went', we are told, he removed antiquities.[30] He sent a string of instructions to his agent, Giovanni Battista Lusieri, advising him that the 'monasteries round Athens were to be searched, columns were to be taken from Daphne, and excavations were to be started at Eleusis'.[31] He instructed further that 'the feasibility of large-scale excavations at Olympia was to be looked at again'.[32] At Mycenae, Elgin 'was able to obtain some ancient pillars as well as some vases'.[33] On his way back to Constantinople, he 'sailed round to Marathon, where he ordered more digging, and then set off across the Aegean, calling at several islands to pick up antiquities'.[34] Yet even this was not enough. When he was about to leave his post at Constantinople, still he urged Lusieri 'to more removals and more excavations'.[35] When a prisoner in France, he sent again instructions to Lusieri that he must search for more archaeological treasures in Aegina, Argos, Corinth, Eleusis, Epidaurus, Megara, and Salamis.[36] Overall, Elgin removed from Greece a great many items including, in addition to those already mentioned, a large number of architectural fragments, detached heads, pieces of sculpture, marble, bronze and earthen urns, altars, sepulchral pillars, and inscriptions.[37] The objects were so numerous and they had been so carelessly hoarded that sometimes they were not even listed individually—much less were they described. Like bric-a-brac, in one case the items were collectively mentioned as 'hundreds of'.[38]

Such wide-ranging operations required of course assistance. Both Verres and Elgin employed agents to help them amass their collections. With Verres went two brothers, a sculptor and a painter, who assisted him in finding artworks[39]—his

---

[27] Select Committee (1816) Appendix No 11, Catalogue of the Elgin Marbles, Vases, Casts, and Drawings xxxiii-xxxiv.

[28] St Clair (1998) 118.

[29] Smith (1916) 209; St Clair (1998) 107.

[30] St Clair (1998) 108.

[31] St Clair (1998) 108.

[32] St Clair (1998) 108.

[33] St Clair (1998) 108.

[34] St Clair (1998) 109.

[35] St Clair (1998) 118. See Elgin to Lusieri (8 October 1802), cited in Smith (1916) 234.

[36] St Clair (1998) 138.

[37] Select Committee (1816) Appendix No 11, Catalogue of the Elgin Marbles, Vases, Casts, and Drawings xxxiv-xli.

[38] Select Committee (1816) Appendix No 11, Catalogue of the Elgin Marbles, Vases, Casts, and Drawings xxxvii.

[39] Cicero, *In Verrem* 2.4.30ff.

art-hunters, we might call them. We learn from Cicero that Verres became excited not only by the treasures he saw but also by those he was told about,[40] so that whatever pleased his agents was certain to be grabbed.[41] Elgin too had his agents, including the abovementioned Lusieri, a painter, Dr Philip Hunt, a chaplain of all things, and William Richard Hamilton, a fellow Harrovian,[42] whom he had appointed as his private secretary[43]—'finders' Byron would call them.[44] Elgin's men went to Athens with the intention of drawing, modelling, and making casts,[45] but once there, they set covetous eyes on the Parthenon, and it took little effort to galvanize Elgin into changing the plan, with the result that we know. When Elgin visited Greece, the removal of the marbles was already well underway and many had already been boxed for dispatch to Britain.[46]

Both Verres and Elgin had an explanation as to how the artefacts came to be in their possession. Verres claimed that he bought the treasures he had in fact removed by force.[47] Cicero fiercely disputed that he could have bought them. Roman governors were not allowed to make purchases in the provinces precisely because the interests of the provincials needed to be protected.[48] Some Sicilians appeared to have been forced to sell to Verres at significant undervalue.[49] The purchase price was so low, Cicero observed, that the adage was coined 'I had rather buy it than ask for it'.[50] Verres was a governor with a military command, and he claimed to have bought every treasure on the island leaving nothing to anyone.[51] Produce me a list, Cicero thundered, of the treasures you acquired in Sicily, from whom you acquired them and the price you paid for each item.[52] Show me proof that any of the objects in your possession was purchased and you have gained your cause.[53] Verres had no accounts to present.[54]

[40] Cicero, *In Verrem* 2.4.39.

[41] Cicero, *In Verrem* 2.4.31.

[42] Smith (1916) 324.

[43] St Clair (1998) 5-6, 24-25.

[44] Byron (1832) Note 6 to Canto II, 67. In fact, Byron employs the term when comparing Lusieri to one of Verres' men ('At Italian painter of the first eminence, named Lusieri, is the agent of devastation; and like the Greek *finder* of Verres in Sicily, who followed the same profession, he has proved the able instrument of plunder', emphasis in original).

[45] Browning (2008) 11.

[46] St Clair (1998) 107.

[47] Cicero, *In Verrem* 2.1.60-61, 2.4.8ff.

[48] Cicero, *In Verrem* 2.4.9-10.

[49] Cicero, *In Verrem* 2.4.7-14.

[50] Cicero, *In Verrem* 2.4.12. The translation used is from Yonge (1903).

[51] Cicero, *In Verrem* 2.4.8.

[52] Cicero, *In Verrem* 2.4.35.

[53] Cicero, *In Verrem* 2.1.61.

[54] Cicero, *In Verrem* 2.4.36.

And how did Elgin come by 'his' marbles? He claimed that he received a firman allowing him to remove 'some pieces of stone with inscriptions and figures'.[55] As we will see, there is no evidence either that a firman ever existed (although an order or letter addressed to the local officials at Athens possibly did) or that it authorised Elgin's actions.[56] But even if, for the sake of argument, Elgin had obtained a permission allowing him to do what he did, still this does not explain on what grounds this was granted. Elgin's account of what happened is garbled and contradictory. Sometimes he appeared to claim that the marbles were given him as a gift by the Ottomans. As British ambassador to the Ottoman government, Elgin may have been in a position to throw his weight about. But would the Ottomans agree to give him freely what they had denied everyone else?[57] Elgin maintained that he did not procure the marbles by pressing home the advantage of his ambassadorial position.[58] Why then would he be thus singled out? And if the marbles were a gift, why did the Ottoman officials at Athens fear prosecution from the central government?[59]

And again, if the marbles were a gift, why did Elgin need also claim that he *bought* them? He did so in a letter to the prime minister, Spencer Perceval, in 1811.[60] There was but one snag. Like Verres, Elgin was unable to produce any proof of purchase. Conveniently, he maintained that he had destroyed his papers in France, but he was also evasive about what exactly was lost where.[61] When he provided a list of expenses, he did not include a single pound for purchase.[62] Why then would he tell the prime minister that the marbles had been 'sold' to him?

In fact, the answer to how Elgin was able to obtain the marbles lies elsewhere. Elgin's accounts may have failed to corroborate his claim of a purchase, but they did reveal something else. According to the list of expenses he presented to the House of Commons, 21902 piastres was paid for 'presents, found necessary for the local

[55] Select Committee (1816) Appendix No 10, Translation from the Italian of a [Firman] or Official Letter. 'Some pieces of stone' is my translation of the Italian '*qualche pezzi di pietra*'. This is discussed in Chap. 3, text to nn 96-97.

[56] See Sect. 3.3. See also Rudenstine (2001); Greenfield (2007) 74; Fincham (2013) 997-998; Fullerton (2016) Chap. 7.

[57] Browning (2008) 11.

[58] See in general Select Committee (1816). This is discussed in Sect. 4.5.3.

[59] St Clair (1998) 110-111.

[60] Elgin to Perceval (31 July 1811), cited in Hitchens (2008) 44.

[61] Select Committee (1816) 36 and Elgin to Long (1811; with a Postscript added February 1816) reproduced in Select Committee (1816) as Appendix No 5, xv.

[62] E.g. Elgin to Long (1811; with a Postscript added February 1816) reproduced in Select Committee (1816) as Appendix No 5; Elgin to Bankes (13 March 1816), reproduced in Select Committee (1816) as Appendix No 6.

authorities, in Athens alone'.[63] In today's money, this would be £157500 in bribes.[64] The House of Commons was then fully aware that the marbles were obtained by *bribing* the *local* Ottoman officials at Athens[65]—those same officials who were afraid of being prosecuted. No wonder, as soon as the deed was done, Elgin was anxious to remove the marbles from Ottoman territory.[66]

A final point of similarity between Verres and Elgin is their intention to make personal use of the looted artworks. Verres' plundered treasures were used to decorate his house and those of his friends.[67] Elgin's intention too had been to decorate Broomhall, his Scottish mansion,[68] although later he devised loftier, albeit contradictory, motives. Having lived beyond his means for long years, he found himself distressed and unable to afford to run Broomhall, which remained in good part unfurnished.[69] His divorce in 1808 added to his financial troubles, since it deprived him of his wife's sizable fortune.[70] So instead of transporting the marbles to Scotland, he arranged for them to be displayed in his London residence at the corner of Piccadilly and Old Park Lane,[71] which he aimed to convert into a 'private museum, to which the public would be admitted as paying customers'.[72] What eventually put paid to this plan was that it turned out to be uneconomical.[73] Elgin resolved to sell his London house and the marbles were temporarily stored in the enclosure at the rear of Burlington House, then a private residence.[74] Debt-stricken, Elgin became anxious to sell the marbles to the UK government. He now claimed that he had removed them from Athens to improve the arts in Britain. But the stubborn reality remains that he did not donate the marbles to the nation. He made a sale to pay off his debts and he even haggled over the price. It is revealing that, at one moment, for part of his expenses alone, Elgin was asking £23,240 (£2.68 million

[63] Elgin to Long (1811; with a Postscript added February 1816) reproduced in Select Committee (1816) as Appendix No 5, xv; Elgin to Bankes (13 March 1816), reproduced in Select Committee (1816) as Appendix No 6, xix.

[64] CPI Inflation Calculator https://www.officialdata.org/uk/inflation/1816?amount=21902 (information correct as of November 2022). The price is inflation-adjusted using as reference 1816, the year the marbles were purchased by the UK parliament.

[65] E.g. Select Committee (1816) 142-143, 146-147; Elgin to Long (1811; with a Postscript added February 1816) reproduced in Select Committee (1816) as Appendix No 5, xii-xiii.

[66] St Clair (1998) 116.

[67] Cicero, *In Verrem* 2.1.57, 2.4.7.

[68] Elgin to Lusieri (10 July 1801), cited in Smith (1916) 191-192.

[69] St Clair (1998) 142-143, 173.

[70] St Clair (1998) 142-143.

[71] This house, located on 137 Piccadilly, on the west corner of Old Park Lane, was later demolished and a new building was erected in its place, Weinreb and others (2008) 327. In the last fifty years, the address is better known as the home of Hard Rock Cafe London.

[72] Smith (1916) 298-299, 303, 306; Hitchens (2008) 42; Meyer (1977) 175-176; Michaelis (1882) 138.

[73] Smith (1916) 307.

[74] Smith (1916) 313; St Clair (1998) 178-179, 214.

today)[75] for *interest*.[76] Ultimately, failing either to furnish his house, create the 'Elgin Museum',[77] or secure the price he hoped the marbles would fetch, he ensured that the collection that was henceforth to be entrusted to the British Museum would bear his name. The act of parliament passed on the occasion stipulated that the collection was to be referred to as the 'Elgin Marbles' and the 'Elgin Collection'.[78] Elgin himself was made a trustee of the British Museum, a title that was to continue to be bestowed upon his descendants,[79] and the purchase price was set at £35,000,[80] that is, about £4 million in today's money.[81] So much for Elgin's munificence and altruism.

Additional parallels can be drawn between Verres and Elgin. But this narrative of the similarities between the two cases now comes to an end. For the differences between them are no less staggering. And the most startling difference of all is this. Verres' trial was a criminal case. Cicero prosecuted Verres before the Roman Extortion Court—a criminal court with the power to impose capital punishment. Verres fled into voluntary exile shortly after the first hearing,[82] which was regarded as an admission of guilt.[83] An accused man who went into voluntary exile would be found guilty, ordered to make restitution or pay damages, and suffer banishment.[84] And so, Verres was dubbed by history the 'corrupt governor of Sicily', his name becoming a byword for reckless profiteering, rapacity, plunder, and abuse.[85]

And what of Elgin? In contrast to Verres, Elgin never did face any kind of judicial review for the dismantling of the Parthenon. In 1816, a select committee of the House of Commons was convened to inquire into whether the UK government

---

[75] CPI Inflation Calculator https://www.officialdata.org/uk/inflation/1816?amount=21902 (information correct as of November 2022).

[76] Elgin to Long (1811; with a Postscript added February 1816) reproduced in Select Committee (1816) as Appendix No 5, xiv.

[77] Smith (1916) 298-299, 303.

[78] An Act to vest the Elgin Collection of ancient Marbles and Sculpture in the Trustees of the British Museum for the Use of the Public, 56 George III (1816) c 99 (hereinafter British Museum Act 1816).

[79] British Museum Act 1816. This provision was reversed in 1963, see British Museum Act 1963 s 1(1).

[80] British Museum Act 1816.

[81] CPI Inflation Calculator https://www.officialdata.org/uk/inflation/1816?amount=21902 (information correct as of November 2022).

[82] Verres attended only the first two days of the trial, Cicero, *In Verrem* 2.1.20. See further Balsdon (1938) 110; Spencer (1916) 850; Frazel (2004) 132. Little is known about Verres' life in exile apart from the circumstances of his death: he died, like Cicero, during Mark Antony's proscriptions of 43 BC, apparently for refusing to give up some of his Corinthian bronze, Pliny the Elder, *Natural History* 34.3; see also Seneca, *Suasoriae* 6.24.

[83] Livy, *The History of Rome*, 25.4; Smith, Wayte, and Marindin (1890), entry on '*exsilium*, banishment'.

[84] Spencer (1916) 839, 850. See also Plutarch, *Parallel Lives: Cicero* 8.1.

[85] Spencer (1916) 841; Gruen (1971) 10, 12; Miles (2002) 35-36.

should buy the marbles.[86] The committee's investigation into the apparently accessory matter of how Elgin came by the marbles can be described as cursory at best. On the issue of whether Elgin had permission to remove the marbles, the committee essentially relied on the witness statements of Elgin and his immediate entourage (Hamilton and Hunt). The accounts of these witnesses were contradictory and inconsistent. When asked about the content of alleged permissions, let alone their whereabouts, Elgin himself pleaded ignorance.[87] No original proof of the purported authorisation was adduced[88] and no attempt was made to seek information from the Ottoman government, from Ottoman officials, or from any Greeks. It is perhaps revealing that the select committee referred to the Greek population as a 'class of the natives'.[89] Neither was an attempt made to speak to any of the British ambassadors who succeeded Elgin in his post. Had the committee tried to do so, Robert Adair, former British ambassador to the Ottoman government, would have been able to repeat to them what he told everyone who was willing to listen and what he wrote to Elgin in 1811: 'the Porte absolutely denied your having any property in those marbles' (Fig. 3.1).[90]

The select committee took Elgin's *word*—no original evidence of the crucial permissions was presented. Unlike Verres, Elgin made a profit from the marbles, his actions were rubber-stamped by parliament,[91] and in 2019 British Museum director Hartwig Fischer had the temerity to praise his dismantling of the Parthenon as 'a creative act'.[92] He was allowed to lead a comfortable life and, having remarried, he produced more offspring, including a son, James Bruce, 8th Earl of Elgin—better remembered by art historians for the destruction of the Old Summer Palace in Beijing during the Opium Wars.[93] 'Like father, like son', as an author has aptly put it.[94]

History is written by the winners. Cicero, who had been able to deliver only his first speech in court, since Verres fled into exile, published the remaining five

---

[86] Select Committee (1816).

[87] E.g. Select Committee (1816) 36-37, 50.

[88] See also Select Committee (1816) 141.

[89] Select Committee (1816) 114.

[90] Adair to Elgin (draft letter of 31 July 1811) (a scanned image of the letter is reproduced with the permission of the owner as Fig. 3.1 in this book). Abbott (1861) 327 (diary entry of 29 April 1811) ('Mr Adair [. . .] says that he was expressly informed by the Turkish Government that they entirely disavowed ever having given any authority to Lord Elgin for removing any part of his collection'. Notice the categorical tone of both statements: 'absolutely denied' and 'entirely disavowed ever having given any authority'). Upon receiving Adair's letter, Elgin wrote to the prime minister, repeating Adair's words to him, see Chap. 3, text to nn 154-155 and 160.

[91] British Museum Act 1816. See also Fincham (2013) 974.

[92] Mark Brown, 'British Museum Chief: Taking the Parthenon Marbles Was "Creative" – Museum Director Sparks Anger by Saying Removing Sculptures from Greece Was "a Creative Act"', The Guardian (28 January 2019).

[93] Newsinger (2002); Ringmar (2006) 917–933; Ringmar (2013).

[94] Robertson (2019) Chap. 7 (unnumbered page).

speeches that he would have given, had the trial continued.[95] Even allowing for rhetorical hyperbole, there is little question about the basic truth of Cicero's arguments,[96] but we can never know the granular facts. By contrast, most of the facts surrounding the removal of the Parthenon marbles by Elgin are still verifiable—most of course apart from the existence of the permission: you can never prove that something does not exist. At any rate, in law it is the party that invokes a fact—the existence of a permit—that needs to prove it. Had it ever existed, it is clear that Elgin's mutilation of the Parthenon went plainly beyond its assumed terms.

More than two millennia separate us from Verres' famous trial, yet we still remember it as a showcase for art plunder and the punishment for it. If the case seems to be legally irrelevant or, to borrow Cicero's words, 'too ancient, and long ago obsolete',[97] the reader is encouraged to think twice. We cannot brush aside the Verres case as either ancient or obsolete. It is at the origin of some notion of customary international law on the return of cultural property unlawfully taken from its original context. Its relevance to the Parthenon marbles case is arresting. When Cicero addressing Verres declaimed 'Did you dare to lay impious and sacrilegious hands on that temple, so ancient, so venerated, so holy?',[98] he might just as well have been addressing Elgin and his moral successors throughout history.

This book is not an indictment of Elgin—that ship sailed more than two centuries ago. Nevertheless, how Elgin procured the marbles matters, because those who resist their restitution[99] do so, among others, on the ground that they were lawfully obtained. The UK government has been unwavering in its adherence to the view that the marbles were lawfully acquired.[100] In a 1983 debate in the House of Lords,

[95] Gildenhard (2011) 1.

[96] Miles (2002) 32.

[97] Cicero, *In Verrem* 2.1.56. The translation used is from Yonge (1903).

[98] Cicero, *In Verrem* 2.1.47, see also 2.1.48. The translation used is from Yonge (1903). The reference here was to the Delian Temple of Apollo.

[99] Different terms can be used to refer to the return of a cultural object to the context or country from which it was removed. 'Restitution', 'repatriation', 'recovery', 'reunification', and 'return' are some of them. Different legal systems, specific statutes, and different authors treat these terms as distinct, Prott (2009) xxi-xxiv. In international law, 'restitution' presupposes that an internationally wrongful act has been committed, see Articles on State Responsibility of the International Law Commission (ILC) art 35. In that context, restitution is a form of reparation and it means the re-establishment of the status quo ante, the situation that existed prior to the commission of the wrongful act, see ILC Articles on State Responsibility arts 34-35; ILC Articles on State Responsibility, commentary, especially art 35, paras 1-2; Crawford (2013) 510-511. In the *Case concerning the Temple of Preah Vihear (Cambodia v Thailand)* (Merits Judgment) [1962] ICJ Rep 6, the International Court of Justice (ICJ) found that Thailand was under an obligation to 'restore' (as opposed to 'return') to Cambodia a series of objects that had been removed from the temple or the temple area, ibid 36-37. Because of the element of opprobrium attached to the term 'restitution', this book often prefers the more neutral term 'return' to cover both return without the acknowledgement of an internationally wrongful act and restitution following a wrongful act, although other terms, including 'restitution', are also used. For a different discussion on the terminology of 'return', 'restitution', and repatriation, see Kowalski (2001) Chap. 1; Stamatoudi (2011) 14-19.

[100] Greenfield (2007) 73.

Richard Nugent, a member of that House, stated that ‘the legal ownership is beyond all doubt’.[101] Latterly, similar statements were made by Boris Johnson, when he was the UK prime minister,[102] in the House of Commons in March 2020[103] and in the House of Lords in February and in September 2022.[104] But, as Jeanette Greenfield cogently remarked, ‘no legal question is ever beyond all doubt, of course, and certainly not before it has been properly considered by a properly constituted legal authority’.[105] For over 200 years, possession of the marbles has proved to be nine tenths of the law and with the complacency that comes from the knowledge that the law against deaccession limits the British Museum’s freedom of action, the issue of the marbles’ return has been pushed forever to the Greek calends. But possession is *not* a title of ownership and national law cannot serve as an excuse to avoid compliance with an international obligation. The cultural heritage dispute whose origin lies in Elgin’s removal of the marbles persists today because of the continued retention of the marbles in the British Museum. And it is this dispute and the issue of the marbles’ return in light of contemporary international law to which this book is dedicated.

1.1.2 The Parthenon Marbles and the Protection of Cultural Heritage

1.1.2.1 Why the Parthenon marbles?

The Parthenon marbles dispute is the most prominent interstate cultural heritage dispute concerning repatriation of looted antiquities, the Parthenon marbles that form part of the ‘Elgin Collection’ in the British Museum. The case has polarised observers since Elgin’s men hacked the marbles out of the ancient temple at the turn of the nineteenth century in Ottoman-occupied Athens. In 1816, a debt-stricken Elgin convinced the UK government to buy the marbles, which in turn entrusted them to the British Museum, where they have remained ever since under the appellation ‘the Elgin Marbles’. So it was that a dilettante like Elgin[106] managed to link his name to Pheidias, and the *cause célèbre* of cultural heritage disputes was

---

[101] Hansard (1983) cc 399-422, 404. See also Hansard (1996) cc 701-702.

[102] Venetia Rainey and Yannis-Orestis Papadimitriou, ‘Boris Johnson: The Elgin Marbles are Staying in their Rightful Home, the British Museum’, The Telegraph (12 March 2021).

[103] Hansard (2020), intervention by culture minister Caroline Dinenage.

[104] Hansard (2022a), interventions by the parliamentary under-secretary of state for arts, Stephen Parkinson; Hansard (2022b), intervention by Stephen Graeme Parkinson.

[105] Greenfield (2007) 73.

[106] Robertson (2019) Chap. 1 (unnumbered page).

born. As soon as Greece became an independent state, it asked for the return of the marbles and it has not stopped asking for them since.[107]

Efforts have been made to resolve the case at the diplomatic level, but thus far Greece has drawn the line at judicial settlement. An attempt by Greece to mediate the dispute within the Intergovernmental Committee for Promoting the Return of Cultural Property to its Countries of Origin or its Restitution in case of Illicit Appropriation (ICPRCP or Intergovernmental Committee) of the United Nations Educational, Scientific and Cultural Organization (UNESCO) in 2013 was repulsed by the United Kingdom and the British Museum trustees in 2015.[108] At about the time of the British rejection, Greece considered legal action on the basis of international law, but this avenue was eventually not pursued.[109] In 2018, when the issue of the reunification of the marbles was discussed within the UNESCO Intergovernmental Committee, a number of states openly supported the Greek claim for return.[110] Some states did not take a position, but none supported the marbles' retention in the British Museum.[111] UNESCO issued a recommendation that can be interpreted as favouring the Greek request for return.[112] A few months later, in August 2018, the Greek government invited the United Kingdom to engage in negotiations over the return of the marbles, in accordance with the UNESCO recommendation.[113] The response, if any, to this request is unknown at the time of writing. With the Brexit negotiations, speculation started as to whether the Parthenon marbles would be part of the deal,[114] but this opportunity too came and went. Then, in September 2021, the ICPRCP established for the first time that 'the obligation to return the Parthenon Sculptures lies squarely on the United Kingdom Government'.[115]

So what is it that makes this case unique? Why is this 'the ur-text of restitution controversies'?[116] Many an element comes together to make the dispute about the

[107] See Chap. 5.

[108] See ICPRCP, 20th session, 29-30 September 2016, ICPRCP/16/20.COM/Decisions, 4. See Sect. 5.3.2.

[109] Liz Alderman, 'Greece Rules Out Suing British Museum Over Elgin Marbles', The New York Times (14 May 2015).

[110] These were Argentina, Armenia, China, Cyprus, Egypt, Italy, Iraq, Mexico, and Turkey, ICPRCP, 'Final Report', 21st session, ICPRCP/18/21.COM/Report (May 2018), paras 6, 23.

[111] ICPRCP, 'Final Report', 21st session, ICPRCP/18/21.COM/Report (May 2018).

[112] ICPRCP, Recommendation 21 COM 7, ICPRCP/18/21.COM/Decisions (May 2018).

[113] Jon Stone, 'Greece Demands UK Open Negotiations over the Return of the Elgin Marbles', The Independent (21 August 2018). The press release concerning the request for negotiations is available on the website of the Greek Ministry of Culture and Sports (in Greek only) https://www.culture.gov.gr/el/Information/SitePages/view.aspx?nID=2338.

[114] Editorial, 'Opinion: The Guardian View on the Parthenon Marbles: Not Just a Brexit Sideshow', The Guardian (23 February 2020); Bruno Waterfield, 'Greece Demands Elgin Marbles for EU Trade Deal', The Times (19 February 2020).

[115] ICPRCP, 22nd session, 27-29 September 2021, ICPRCP/21/22.COM/Decisions, Decision 22. COM 6, para 7.

[116] Meyer (2006) 89.

Parthenon marbles like no other: the Parthenon, a nonpareil of historical, political, cultural, and artistic significance; the concatenation of circumstances surrounding the removal of the marbles, including the poignant fact that the events took place in the very final years of an almost four hundred centuries-long Ottoman occupation; the controversy over the purported firman; the disfigurement of the ancient temple, which had stood on the Acropolis for more than 2200 years and had not known similar destruction except when a Venetian shell landed on it in 1687; the opprobrium and the public outcry at the removal, Byron's eloquent lament; the botched investigation of the select committee; the 'cleaning' of the late 1930s and the general scandal that Joseph Duveen, an art-dealer of questionable professional ethics, has given his name to the Duveen Gallery in the British Museum; the efforts expended by a great many British people to achieve the return of the marbles to Athens; the buck-passing between the UK government and the British Museum as regards repatriation; the emotive and intense debate that the case has fuelled about the protection of our cultural heritage; and the fact that this dispute has appeared to be on the point of being resolved time and again, including at the moment of writing.

This is the biggest cultural heritage dispute, and it lies deep in every statement about repatriation: from the undercurrent of regret expressed by British-Egyptian novelist Ahdaf Soueif at the British Museum's response to the debate on restitution, leading to her resignation from the museum's board of trustees in 2019;[117] to a 2020 warning sent by the culture secretary Oliver Dowden to top UK publicly funded museums that they must not remove artefacts or they must risk losing taxpayer support.[118] And it has certainly helped dictate the British Museum's riposte that it has 'no intention of removing controversial objects from public display'.[119] While that ministerial missive was triggered by a controversy over the British Museum's display of a bust of Hans Sloane, its slave-owning founding father[120] (the bust was

[117] Ahdaf Soueif, 'On Resigning from the British Museum's Board of Trustees', LRB Blog (15 July 2019); Geraldine Kendall Adams, 'Trustee Resigns from British Museum over its Stance on Sponsorship and Repatriation', Museums Association (16 July 2019).

[118] Letter from the Culture Secretary Oliver Dowden on HM Government Position on Contested Heritage INT2020/19838/DC (22 September 2020) https://www.gov.uk/government/publications/letter-from-culture-secretary-on-hm-government-position-on-contested-heritage. See also Sect. 8.3.1.

[119] 'British Museum "Won't Remove Controversial Objects" from Display', BBC News (28 September 2020).

[120] 'British Museum "Won't Remove Controversial Objects" from Display', BBC News (28 September 2020). In a comment published in The Telegraph, Dowden expressed concern about 'a cancel culture whereby a small but vocal group of people claim to have the monopoly on virtue, and seek to bully those who dare to disagree'. Viewed in this light, the case did not directly relate to the marbles. However, in that same comment Dowden wrote: 'Confident nations face up to their history. They don't airbrush it. Instead, they protect their heritage and use it to educate the public about the past. They "retain and explain", rather than "remove or ignore".' See Oliver Dowden, 'Comment: We Won't Allow Britain's History to Be Cancelled', The Telegraph (15 May 2021). While this may seem appropriate for Sloane's bust, and it was rightly 'retained and explained' (and we may argue about what comes next for the streets and square named after him),

ultimately removed from its pedestal, placed in a glass cabinet, and Sloane was labelled a 'slave owner'),[121] the admonition that museums should not remove artefacts speaks volumes to the Parthenon marbles case, the *most* 'controversial' treasure that the British Museum—or any museum—holds.

1.1.2.2 The protection of cultural heritage

There is an additional reason why the Parthenon marbles case is particularly topical. The dispute falls within an evolving legal framework in international law. Attitudes to the protection of cultural property are changing dramatically and the evolution of customary international law makes some view it as a test case for the return of important cultural property to its place of origin.[122] Loud as the old guard may shout, the inescapable truth is that the nascent customary international law on the return of cultural property means that the retentionists' arguments lie on shaky ground.

To start with, the plunder of cultural property in wartime, including in an occupied territory, had already been illicit according to international law back when Elgin removed the marbles. In the wake of Waterloo in 1815, just a year before the UK government purchased the marbles from Elgin, British foreign secretary Robert Stewart (aka Viscount Castlereagh) and the Duke of Wellington clamoured for and obtained the return to European countries of Napoleon's loot that had adorned the Louvre.[123] The horses of San Marco and the Laocoön were among the masterpieces to make their way back to Italy.[124] The arguments employed by the French to resist restitution at the time are of the same kind as those that the UK

---

the principle is not applicable to the Parthenon marbles. In this case, surely, facing up to history can only mean one thing: facing up to past wrongs and making amends.

[121] Craig Simpson, 'British Museum Removes Bust of Slave-owner Founder Sir Hans Sloane', The Telegraph (24 August 2020).

[122] Robertson (2019) conclusion (unnumbered page).

[123] Note delivered by Viscount Castlereagh to the Allied Ministers, and placed upon their Protocol, Paris, 11 September 1815; and Dispatch from the Duke of Wellington to Viscount Castlereagh, Paris, 23 September 1815, both reprinted in von Martens (1818) 606ff and 616ff respectively. See further St Clair (1998) 22; Miles (2008, 2010) 329; Goodwin (2008) 679-680; de Visscher (1949) 824; Scovazzi (2011) 344, 347. However, not all of Napoleon's plundered treasures found their way home. Some had been scattered across the country, and the French did their best to avoid giving them back, Cohan (2004) 21; Farah Nayeri, 'The Masterpieces that Napoleon Stole, and How Some Went Back', The New York Times (9 June 2021). It appears, however, that other acquisitions were 'legalised' as part of the terms of peace treaties, Quynn (1945) 459. A note of caution: although Napoleon's loot from his European campaigns was to be returned, the 1815 arrangement did not affect Napoleon's Egyptian loot, which had been ceded to the combined British and Ottoman army a few years earlier—think Rosetta Stone. This happened with the French capitulation in 1801, see Articles of Capitulation (30 August 1801), reproduced in Wilson (1803) 346-353, art 16. In addition, while Castlereagh appeared anxious to send Napoleon's loot home, he was helping Elgin import his loot duty-free, see Esther Addley, 'Lord Elgin Paid No British Customs Tax on Parthenon Marbles, Letters Reveal', The Guardian (7 October 2022).

[124] Greenfield (2007) 238.

government has used over the last two hundred years in relation to the Parthenon marbles, notably that the collection was lawfully acquired, that the artworks were removed in order to be rescued for posterity (not least from British travellers!), and that they were better looked after and more accessible to the public in the Louvre than back home.[125] The French also contended that 'the break-up of the unique collection assembled in the Louvre would be an act of vandalism'.[126] However, in 1816, when the issue was no longer one of emptying the Louvre but one of enriching the British Museum, there was a policy shift.

Debates in the House of Commons at the time testify to the unease that some MPs felt at the thought of purchasing the marbles, and a strong appeal was made to return them on *legal* grounds. In a February 1816 debate in the House of Commons on Elgin's petition for an inquiry into the value of the collection, Thomas Babington went on record as saying that 'the mode in which the collection had been acquired partook of the nature of spoliation'.[127] In the June 1816 debate on the purchase, Hugh Hammersley opposed the resolution 'on the ground of the dishonesty of the transaction by which the collection was obtained'.[128] He added that 'he was not so enamoured of those headless ladies as to forget another lady, which was justice'.[129] He called for a different resolution that would allow the British government to buy the collection, not for the British Museum but

> in order to recover and keep it together for that government from which it has been improperly taken, and to which this committee is of opinion that a communication should be immediately made, stating, that Great Britain holds these marbles only in trust till they are demanded by the present, or any future, possessors of the city of Athens; and upon such demand, engages, without question or negotiation, to restore them, as far as can be effected, to the places from whence they were taken.[130]

In the same debate, Serjeant Best, declared that the marbles had been brought to Great Britain 'in breach of good faith. He therefore could not consent to their purchase, lest by so doing he should render himself a partaker in the guilt of spoliation'.[131] He added for good measure that his objection was not based 'on the ground of economy, but of justice'.[132] John Newport too declared that he would vote against the motion 'on account of the unjustifiable nature of the transaction by which the marbles in question were acquired'.[133]

[125] St Clair (1998) 223; Scovazzi (2011) 347.

[126] St Clair (1998) 223. Compare this with David Wilson's comment, see text to n 181.

[127] Hansard (1816a) c 828.

[128] Hansard (1816b) c 1031.

[129] Hansard (1816b) c 1031.

[130] Hansard (1816b) c 1033.

[131] Hansard (1816b) c 1037.

[132] Hansard (1816b) c 1037.

[133] Hansard (1816b) c 1039. See also Hansard (1815).

Ultimately, the MPs opposing the purchase found themselves in the minority and the motion was carried by 82 votes to 30.[134] But parliamentary approval does not turn an internationally wrongful act into one that is lawful. Domestic law is sometimes invoked in the Parthenon marbles case to justify the retention of the marbles in the British Museum,[135] but this book will show that such arguments are nugatory.

If the removal of the marbles was already illicit at the time when it happened, the international law on the protection of cultural property has evolved since then. A growing body of international conventions has been adopted, state and museum practice has been shifting, and tolerance towards the destruction of cultural property has reached an all-time low. The Convention for the Protection of Cultural Property in the Event of Armed Conflict (Hague Convention of 1954), adopted in the wake of the massive destruction of cultural heritage that took place during World War II, is today the most important international treaty focusing on the protection of cultural heritage in times of conflict, including in occupied territories.[136] In 1995, the International Institute for the Unification of Private Law (UNIDROIT) adopted the Convention on Stolen or Illegally Exported Cultural Objects (UNIDROIT Convention), intended to facilitate the restitution and return of stolen or illegally exported cultural objects.[137] Several UNESCO treaties focus on the protection of cultural heritage,[138] and provisions to ensure such protection also exist in additional instruments, including peace agreements,[139] regional conventions adopted under the aegis of the Council of Europe,[140] EU secondary legislation,[141] and a number of resolutions of the United Nations General Assembly (UNGA).[142]

But probably the most important legal instrument on the protection of cultural property against illicit removal is the 1970 UNESCO Convention on the Means of Prohibiting and Preventing the Illicit Import, Export and Transfer of Ownership of Cultural Property (1970 UNESCO Convention), one of cultural heritage law's great

[134]Hansard (1816b) c 1040.

[135]See Sect. 6.4.

[136]Hague Convention of 1954 art 18(2).

[137]UNIDROIT Convention preamble.

[138]See Sect. 9.2.1.

[139]See http://www.unesco.org/eri/la/convention.asp?KO=31038&language=E&order=alpha.

[140]European Cultural Convention of 1954; European Convention on Offences relating to Cultural Property of 1985; European Convention on the Protection of the Archaeological Heritage (revised in 1992).

[141]Regulation 3911/92 on the Export of Cultural Goods, OJ L 395 of 31 December 1992, successively amended by Regulation (EC) No 2469/96, OJ L 335 of 24 December 1996, Regulation (EC) No 974/2001, OJ L 137 of 19 May 2001, and Regulation (EC) No 806/2003, OJ L 122 of 16 May 2003; Directive 93/7 on the Return of Cultural Objects Illegally Exported from the Territory of a Member State, OJ L 74 of 27 March 1993, successively amended by Directive 96/100/EC, OJ L 60 of 1 March 1997, and by Directive 2001/38/E, OJ L 187 of 10 July 2001; Directive 2014/60 on the return of cultural objects unlawfully removed from the territory of a Member State, OJ L 159 of 28 May 2014 and amending Regulation (EU) No 1024/2012 (Recast).

[142]These are discussed in Sect. 10.2.

watersheds.[143] The Convention provides a legal framework for the prohibition and prevention of the unlawful import, export, and transfer of cultural property, with restitution at its heart. In contrast with the relatively narrow membership of the UNIDROIT Convention,[144] the 1970 UNESCO Convention is binding on 143 states, including so-called 'market' countries,[145] such as France and notably the United Kingdom, which had resisted it for a long time.[146] There is but one snag. The 1970 UNESCO Convention, as the abovementioned instruments, is not retroactive. This means that it does not, in principle, apply to any theft or unlawful removal of cultural property that took place before the Convention's entry into force in both state parties and so it cannot apply as such to the Parthenon marbles case.

But if the Convention is not retroactive, restitutions that would have normally fallen within its ambit but for this temporal limitation are increasingly taking place. The return of Nazi looted art is exemplary of the evolution of the law on restitution. The 1998 Washington Conference on Holocaust Era Art called on states to identify art confiscated by the Nazis and encourage its restitution.[147] In 2009, the United Kingdom passed the Holocaust (Return of Cultural Objects) Act, conferring on museums, including the British Museum, the power to return cultural objects 'on grounds relating to events occurring during the Nazi era'.[148] Only a few years earlier, Austria had been ordered to return five Nazi looted Gustav Klimt paintings held in the Belvedere Museum in Vienna to their heir, following a combination of legal action in US courts and arbitration in the famous *Maria Altmann* case.[149] In 2019, France created a task force to track Nazi plundered art in French museums in order to return it to its rightful owners.[150] In response to this, in 2020, the Louvre hired an expert to help it identify such art held in its collections.[151] In February 2022, the French Ministry of Culture passed a law relating to the restitution or return of cultural property to heirs of victims of antisemitic persecutions, authorising the

---

[143] Titi (2017) 539.

[144] See https://www.unidroit.org/instruments/cultural-property/1995-convention/status/.

[145] Merryman (1986) 832.

[146] See https://en.unesco.org/fighttrafficking/1970.

[147] See https://www.state.gov/washington-conference-principles-on-nazi-confiscated-art/.

[148] An Act to confer power to return certain cultural objects on grounds relating to events occurring during the Nazi era, Holocaust (Return of Cultural Objects) Act 2009, c 16.

[149] *Maria V Altmann and others v Austria*, arbitral award (15 January 2006).

[150] Naomi Rea, 'The French Government Is Launching a Task Force Dedicated to Researching and Returning Nazi-Era Loot from Its National Collections', Artnet News (29 March 2019). For more information, see French Ministry of Culture, 'Création au ministère de la Culture de la Mission de recherche et de restitution des biens culturels spoliés entre 1933 et 1945' (Press release, 5 June 2019).

[151] Charles Bremner, 'Louvre Calls in Expert to Hunt for Looted Nazi Art', The Times (14 January 2020).

restitution of fifteen paintings found in public French collections, including a Gustav Klimt painting previously held in the Musée d'Orsay.[152]

Beyond restitutions of Nazi looted artworks, numerous returns of artefacts and other cultural property do not fall within the purview of the non-retroactive conventions. For example, in 1990, in *Autocephalous Greek-Orthodox Church v Goldberg*, Cyprus and the Greek-Orthodox Church of Cyprus won a replevin action in the United States against Goldberg.[153] Goldberg had bought four Byzantine mosaics that had been stolen from a Cypriot church after the 1974 Turkish invasion of the island.[154] Although the US Congress had given its advice and consent to ratification of the 1970 UNESCO Convention already in 1972,[155] implementing legislation was not enacted until 1983,[156] and neither instrument was judged to be controlling in the case.[157] However, the US judges recognised that the 1970 UNESCO Convention foregrounded 'the importance that the United States and other countries have placed on restricting international trafficking in stolen art'.[158] Having regard to the 1983 implementation act, Circuit Judge Cudahy reasoned:

> Nonetheless, the policy that the Act embodies is clear: at the very least, we should not sanction illegal traffic in stolen cultural property that is clearly documented as belonging to a public or religious institution. This is particularly true where this sort of property is 'important to the cultural heritage of a people because of its distinctive characteristics, comparative rarity, or its contribution to the knowledge of the origins, development, or history of that people'.[159]

Another example is the return, from Denmark to Iceland, of thousands of Icelandic manuscripts, including the historically valuable *Flateyjarbók* and *Codex Regius*, between 1971 and 1997.[160] The manuscripts were removed from Iceland at a time when 'a colonial but none the less legitimate political Union' existed between the two states and a good number of the manuscripts had been transferred to Denmark by an Icelander for his own collection and then bequeathed to the University of

[152]Loi n° 2022-218 du 21 février 2022 relative à la restitution ou la remise de certains biens culturels aux ayants droit de leurs propriétaires victimes de persécutions antisémites, JORF of 22 February 2022.

[153]*Autocephalous Greek-Orthodox Church of Cyprus and Cyprus v Goldberg*, 717 F Supp 1374 (SD Ind 1989), aff'd 917 F.2d 278 (7th Cir 1990).

[154]*Autocephalous Greek-Orthodox Church of Cyprus and Cyprus v Goldberg*, 717 F Supp 1374 (SD Ind 1989), aff'd 917 F.2d 278 (7th Cir 1990).

[155]US Senate Rep No 97-564 (1982).

[156]This was the Convention on Cultural Property Implementation Act (19 USC §§2601-2613).

[157]*Autocephalous Greek-Orthodox Church of Cyprus and Cyprus v Goldberg*, 717 F Supp 1374 (SD Ind 1989) n 2; 917 F.2d 278 (7th Cir 1990) (Concurring opinion Cudahy).

[158]*Autocephalous Greek-Orthodox Church of Cyprus and Cyprus v Goldberg*, 717 F Supp 1374 (SD Ind 1989) n 2.

[159]*Autocephalous Greek-Orthodox Church of Cyprus and Cyprus v Goldberg*, 917 F.2d 278 (7th Cir 1990) (Concurring opinion Cudahy), citing 19 USC § 2601(2)(C)(ii)(II).

[160]Greenfield (2007) 13-40.

Copenhagen.[161] The case is especially interesting, in light of the fact that Denmark agreed to return these manuscripts, even though their removal had been lawful.

More recently, in 2017, the French President Emmanuel Macron pledged to return African cultural heritage to Africa, remarking that such heritage 'cannot be a prisoner of European museums'.[162] He added that, while there may be 'historical explanations' for this, 'there is no valid, lasting and unconditional justification'.[163] He commissioned a report, which was published in 2018 and advised that artefacts removed by force or acquired in inequitable conditions should be returned promptly.[164] In December 2020, France promulgated a law to allow the return to Benin and Senegal of artefacts that had been looted in the nineteenth century.[165] In November 2021, France ceremoniously returned the Benin works, which had been looted 129 years earlier.[166] As we shall see later, more Benin bronzes have started to be returned by other countries and museums, although at the time of writing the British Museum still resists the repatriation of the Benin bronzes in its collection.[167]

Museums too have accepted, albeit often grudgingly, to give up looted antiquities whose removal antedated the 1970 UNESCO Convention. An illustration is the return of the famous Euphronios krater, which was held at the Metropolitan Museum of Art (hereinafter the Met) for more than three decades. The krater had been looted from the Etruscan city of Caere (modern Cerveteri) in the early 1970s and was sold to the Met by an art dealer who was linked to an antiquities' smuggling ring.[168] In 2006, after a 'a three-decade tug of war' between Italy and the Met, the two parties entered into an agreement under which the Euphronios krater and other artefacts were returned to Italy.[169]

---

[161] Greenfield (2007) 15, 38-39.

[162] Anna Codrea-Rado, 'Emmanuel Macron Says Return of African Artifacts Is a Top Priority', The New York Times (29 November 2017).

[163] Ruth Maclean, 'France Urged to Change Heritage Law and Return Looted Art to Africa, The Guardian (21 November 2018).

[164] Felwine Sarr and Bénédicte Savoy, 'Rapport sur la restitution du patrimoine culturel africain. Vers une nouvelle éthique relationnelle' (November 2018) 53.

[165] Loi n° 2020-1673 du 24 décembre 2020 relative à la restitution de biens culturels à la République du Bénin et à la République du Sénégal, JORF of 26 December 2020.

[166] 'France Formally Returns Looted Benin Artworks at Élysée Ceremony' France 24 (9 November 2021).

[167] The term 'Benin bronzes' is used to refer to artefacts (not only in bronze but also in other materials, including wood, ivory, brass, and coral, e.g. brass plaques, carved elephant tusks) that were looted from the Benin royal palace in modern day Nigeria by British military forces in a 1897 raid, see British Museum, 'Benin Bronzes' https://bit.ly/3E0DP7A. On the return of the Benin bronzes, see Sect. 10.2.

[168] For a full-length account, see Watson and Todeschini (2007).

[169] Agreement between the Italian Ministry of Cultural Heritage and Activities, the Sicilian Commission for Cultural and Environmental Heritage and Public Education, and the New York Metropolitan Museum of Art (21 February 2006). See further Elisabetta Povoledo, 'Italy and US Sign Antiquities Accord', The New York Times (22 February 2022); Elisabetta Povoledo, 'Ancient Vase Comes Home to a Hero's Welcome', The New York Times (19 January 2008).

Other game-changers in recent years include high-profile cases involving stolen art, such as the conviction in the United States of Frederick Schultz, a prominent New York art dealer found guilty of conspiring to receive purloined Egyptian antiquities;[170] the prosecution in Italy of Marion True, curator of antiquities at the J Paul Getty Museum in Los Angeles, who was accused of participating in a stolen-antiquities ring;[171] or, latterly, the prosecution of the former director of the Louvre, Jean-Luc Martinez, for the alleged laundering of smuggled Egyptian antiquities (he was accused of turning a blind eye to false provenance certificates) that were acquired by the Louvre Abu Dhabi.[172] While the former cases invited scrutiny into how museums built their collections and helped change collecting practices,[173] the latter can probably best be described as a result of this shift in attitudes.

Municipal laws on plunder have toughened too. Under English law, it is now a criminal offence to knowingly deal in a cultural object that is 'removed from a building or structure of historical, architectural or archaeological interest where the object has at any time formed part of the building or structure',[174] irrespective of whether the removal took place in the United Kingdom or abroad.[175] Should the Parthenon marbles be removed today, even British Museum directors could no longer call the disfigurement of the Parthenon 'a creative act'.[176]

But more significantly for the argument in this book, customary international law has been evolving, and a new rule has been emerging that requires the return of some important cultural heritage. The book will show that the two constitutive elements of customary international law, state practice and acceptance as law (*opinio iuris*), now support the view that cultural heritage of particular importance, unlawfully removed from its original context, may be subject to return to its place of origin—and this irrespective of the time of its removal, albeit subject to conditions, all of which are fulfilled in the case of the Parthenon marbles.

---

[170] *US v Schultz*, 333 F.3d 393.

[171] Elisabetta Povoledo, 'Rome Trial of Ex-Getty Curator Ends', The New York Times (13 October 2010); Geoff Edgers, 'One of the World's Most Respected Curators Vanished from the Art World', Washington Post (22 August 2015).

[172] Vincent Noce, 'Former Louvre Director Jean-Luc Martinez Charged in connection with Antiquities Trafficking Investigation', The Art Newspaper (26 May 2022); Editorial, 'L'ancien président du Louvre mis en examen pour blanchiment dans une affaire de trafic d'antiquités', Le Parisien (26 May 2022).

[173] Elisabetta Povoledo, 'Rome Trial of Ex-Getty Curator Ends', The New York Times (13 October 2010); Hugh Eakin, 'Italy Focuses on a Princeton Curator in an Antiquities Investigation', The New York Times (2 June 2010).

[174] Dealing in Cultural Objects (Offences) Act 2003 ss 1(1), 2(4).

[175] Dealing in Cultural Objects (Offences) Act 2003 s 2(3).

[176] See text to n 92.

1.1.3 The Debate and the Dispute

The fate of the Parthenon marbles in the 'Elgin Collection' and the merits of their return have been debated ever since Elgin's agents excised them from the Parthenon on the Acropolis at Athens.[177] Such is the nature of the discussion about the return of cultural property that numerous studies on the topic start with a question purportedly about ownership. Who owns history? Who owns antiquity? Who owns the past?[178] In reality, these questions are often aspirational. What they really mean is: who *should* own antiquity? Or who *should* own the past? While the questions about ownership and return are legal, the answers to them have been built around a debate.[179]

That the issue should be framed in such terms must come as no surprise: the formidable weight of the literature on the Parthenon marbles and the return of cultural property is not written by lawyers. Some of the most influential writings in the field have been penned by archaeologists, classicists, art historians, museum curators, sociologists, journalists, and even poets. Politicians, various personalities, and even a king have taken a position on the case. The debate aims to command the emotions, and feelings certainly run deep. This was undoubtedly the case with Byron's lament in *Childe Harold's Pilgrimage*:[180]

> Cold is the heart, fair Greece, that looks on thee,
> Nor feels as lovers o'er the dust they loved;
> Dull is the eye that will not weep to see,
> Thy walls defaced, thy mouldering shrines removed.[180]

For the British Museum too, it must have been a case of feelings running deep—or tempers running high—when in 1986 David Wilson, then director of the British Museum, contended in a BBC television discussion that '[t]o rip the Elgin Marbles from the walls of the British Museum is a much greater disaster than the threat of blowing up the Parthenon' and went on to compare those who request the return of the marbles to Hitler and Mussolini.[181] At the instigation of the interviewer, he subsequently moderated his statement to excuse Greeks favouring the return of the marbles and redirected his vitriol towards everyone else, namely world opinion and

[177] Fincham (2013) 947.

[178] E.g. Fitz Gibbon (2005); Meyer (2006); Robson, Treadwell, and Gosden (2006); Cuno (2011); Jenkins (2016) Chap. 6 ('Who Owns Culture?'); Robertson (2019); Meyer (1977) Chap. 5 entitled 'Whose Past?'.

[179] cf Fincham (2013), who discusses it both as a debate (e.g. at 947) and as a dispute (at 990ff).

[180] George Gordon Byron, *Childe Harold's Pilgrimage*, Canto II, stanza XV.

[181] Hitchens (2008) 98.

British people who want the marbles to return to Greece, accusing them of 'cultural fascism'.[182]

It is said that 'much of the emotional flailing has been done by those who deny that there is any problem in the first place',[183] and it is certain that not all appeals to sentiment can be taken seriously. Wilson was not the only one to overplay his hand. Notably, when viewed from the standpoint of international law some of the more strongly-voiced arguments against return fail—and not only when expressed by museum curators. On occasion, even legal scholars fall into the trap of the debate and lose sight of the law. A most singular example is that of John Henry Merryman, an art collector and law professor at Stanford University. Merryman wrote well and his writings have had an immense influence on the way we think about cultural heritage law in general and about the Parthenon marbles in particular.

A fervent proponent of 'universal' or 'encyclopaedic' museums, Merryman insisted that the marbles should remain in the British Museum. In an article fraught with factual inaccuracies and legal errors, Merryman declared emphatically that 'the Greeks do not have a legal claim to the Marbles'.[184] His spurious contentions misled international opinion and became an article of faith with many. Yet Merryman was not an international lawyer, and, from the viewpoint of international law, his arguments fail abjectly. Discussing the issue of the marbles' return in 1985, Merryman proclaimed that lawyers have a *déformation professionnelle*: they tend 'to be suspicious of emotionally compelling arguments', because they are often 'weak on the facts or the law or both'.[185] For this reason, Merryman wrote, the resolution of the dispute surrounding the Parthenon marbles should be guided by 'reasoned, principled grounds'.[186] I cannot fully agree with this argument. It appears to me that it is a *déformation professionnelle* of lawyers to be suspicious of legal argument built on 'reasoned, principled grounds' rather than on the law itself. The problem with 'reasoned, principled grounds' is that they can be largely subjective, as Merryman's argument shows. Merryman wanted to decide the dispute on the basis of nonlegal grounds, taking the view that 'there is at present no tribunal competent to consider it. We must therefore supply our own hypothetical supranational tribunal, one charged with making informed, principled decisions concerning the proper allocation of disputed cultural property'.[187] Merryman expounded his self-regarding 'reasoned, principled grounds',[188] but offered no *legal* grounds in favour of or against return.[189] His 'principled grounds' are a rehearsal of the debate viewed through tinted lenses. The passage in question repeats Merryman's positions about

[182]Hitchens (2008) 98-99.

[183]Hitchens (2008) xxvi.

[184]Merryman (1985) 1881.

[185]Merryman (1985) 1883.

[186]Merryman (1985) 1883.

[187]Merryman (1985) 1911.

[188]Merryman (1985) 1910-1921.

[189]Merryman (1985) 1910-1921.

cultural nationalism (compare this with David Wilson's tirade about 'cultural fascism' a year later) and rejects requests for restitution with the argument that they are nationalistic and nationalism is not an acceptable argument. Therein lies a tale. But we'll return to Merryman's theory of cultural nationalism and internationalism and to its doubtful merits.

For now, let's take a moment to consider Merryman's argument from a legal perspective. For a start, Merryman, erroneously or disingenuously, assumed that there is no international court or tribunal that could possibly hear the Parthenon marbles dispute. Contrary to what he seemed to believe, a number of international bodies could be given the mandate to hear the dispute, including the International Court of Justice (ICJ), an arbitral tribunal, and—if one were to opt for a soft mechanism—the UNESCO Intergovernmental Committee. There will be a time and a place to consider the dispute settlement options, and the conditions for accessing them, but for now let us briefly consider the ICJ. The ICJ has decided a small number of cultural heritage cases, including disputes with a restitution component.[190] In 1985, when Merryman wrote his article, the famous *Temple of Preah Vihear* case, in which Thailand was ordered to restore cultural property to Cambodia, including sculptures and fragments of monuments, was already more than twenty years old.[191]

Another flaw in Merryman's reasoning is that, when he proceeded to consider how his hypothetical international tribunal might decide the dispute, he assumed that its decision should be based on 'principled grounds'. Here again his presumption flies in the face of international law. Unless given an *ex aequo et bono* mandate, an international court—much like national courts—must decide on the basis of *law*.[192] 'Principled grounds' simply cannot serve as the basis of a legal decision. At no stage does Merryman suggest what *law* is to be applied by his international tribunal. Nor does he suggest that the tribunal is to decide *ex aequo et bono*. Had an international court decided *ex aequo et bono*, it is improbable that the resultant decision would confirm Merryman's positions. In short, Merryman appeared to believe that an international court or tribunal would decide on the basis of the *debate* rather than on the basis of international law.

That Merryman should not realise that there is an international court that could be called upon to decide the dispute and that its decision would need to be based on law (or an *ex aequo et bono* mandate, if the parties agreed to it) is astounding for someone who had gained scholarly ascendancy. But it is perhaps pardonable—Merryman was not an international lawyer after all. But that flawed reasoning such

[190] See Chap. 7, n 107.

[191] *Case concerning the Temple of Preah Vihear (Cambodia v Thailand)* (Merits Judgment) [1962] ICJ Rep 6.

[192] E.g. Statute of the ICJ art 38; Statute of the International Tribunal for the Law of the Sea (ITLOS) art 23 in conjunction with United Nations Convention on the Law of the Sea (UNCLOS) art 293; Convention on the Settlement of Investment Disputes between States and Nationals of Other States (ICSID Convention) art 42. On *ex aequo et bono*, see Sect. 7.5.2.

as this should have influenced how we understand the legal merits of the Parthenon marbles dispute, *that* is a mistake.

After Merryman, other apologists for 'encyclopaedic' museums, took it upon themselves to prove that the Parthenon marbles are both better off and better appreciated in the British Museum than in Athens.[193] Various arguments have been deployed, such as that more people see the marbles in the British Museum than in Athens—when one presses this argument to its logical conclusion, he or she may be excused for thinking that perhaps the marbles should be removed to the neighbouring Louvre, which claims more visitors than the British Museum or, as an author caustically suggested, Disneyland.[194] The retentionists honed their position, and their arguments evolved over time, so that today they centre on the importance of 'universal' or 'encyclopaedic' museums or, according to the latest terminology favoured by the British Museum, 'world' museums.[195]

While the debate is arresting, and it forms part of the narrative of this book, it is also a diversion from the legal matters in dispute, which are susceptible of a legal answer on the basis of international law. The debate distracts from what is really at issue: are the marbles lawfully possessed by the British Museum and can they be retained on the basis of international law? If they are lawfully possessed, that should be enough to allow the museum to display them in the Duveen Gallery and it would not be necessary to argue that they are seen by more people or, as the British Museum currently claims, that the Parthenon is better off divided in two.[196] (Would anyone argue the same about the Mona Lisa?) If the marbles' lawful home is not the British Museum, then the debate is irrelevant. No one can display in one's home an object belonging to someone else with the argument that it will be viewed by more people or that it is better off seen alongside the Rosetta Stone and Egyptian mummies (an immersive experience enjoyed in one and the same afternoon in Bloomsbury) rather than in the context of its own history in the purpose-built new Acropolis Museum in Athens under the shadow of the Parthenon.

This is also the flaw in the reasoning of former culture secretary Jeremy Wright, when, exalting the logic of world museums and arguing against restitution in 2019, he told The Times: 'Never mind the argument about who owns this thing, let's argue about how it gets to be seen.'[197] This author begs to differ. Aesthetically, the 'thing'

---

[193] E.g. Cuno (2011) 171-172.

[194] Hitchens (2008) 86.

[195] The first linguistic shift was from 'universal' to 'encyclopaedic', see Cuno (2011) 225-226. Now, the British Museum appears to have dropped the term 'encyclopaedic' too, see e.g. https://www.britishmuseum.org/about-us/british-museum-story/objects-news/parthenon-sculptures, mentioning the museum's 'commitment to be a world museum' and https://www.britishmuseum.org/about-us, describing the museum as a 'museum of the world' (information correct as of November 2022).

[196] See annex, 'The Parthenon Sculptures: The Trustees' Statement' (British Museum).

[197] David Sanderson, 'Minister Rules Out Return of Treasures', The Times (22 April 2019). Wright's statement elicited even a reaction from the Director of the Museums Association: 'Just saying "no" is a blunt message to deliver to those seeking information about their cultural heritage,

does not get to be seen better dismembered and torn in two and, legally, the question that matters is *who owns this thing*. We are then back to the original question: whose marbles? This question is a legal question.

That said, this book does not discount the importance of the debate. The debate can be a building block to the resolution of the dispute. But while the debate can be susceptible of no legal solution, the dispute is. This book argues that the answers to the questions of 'who owns the Parthenon marbles' and 'should they be returned' do not hinge on a debate but on international law. These are legal questions susceptible of a legal answer. And so, while the book will address the arguments raised in the debate, it will do so only as far as is necessary to disprove various shades of opinion that have been advanced and which create confusion about the legal resolution of the dispute. Let's debate, but, to do so, let's place the debate on legally sound foundations. It is in the merits of the dispute, in light of the applicable law, that this book is interested. The time for questioning has passed. Now is the time for answers.

1.2 Scope of the Book

1.2.1 Overall Purpose

Much ink has been spilled on the Parthenon marbles. The ethical and cultural merits of their return have been indomitably argued for years. But what has generally not been considered are the *legal* merits of their return in light of contemporary international law. This is where this book comes into its own. The book is the first in legal scholarship to provide an international law perspective of the *cause célèbre* of international cultural heritage law disputes and, in doing so, to clarify the new customary international law on the return of cultural property unlawfully removed from its original context. In contrast with existing studies, the book moves away from the debate about the Parthenon marbles in order to focus on the legal questions hiding behind it and weigh the legal arguments for the marbles' return. To do so, it adopts a dispute settlement perspective: it surveys the facts of the case, it evaluates the dispute settlement options and the conditions for accessing them, and it appraises the substantive international law applicable to the dispute.

---

which has often ended up in UK museums through looting, forced trading or simply because the balance of power was skewed so heavily towards imperial authority', Geraldine Kendall Adams, 'Culture Secretary Rules Out Restitution from National Museums', Museums Association (25 April 2019) https://bit.ly/3qyGy03. It will be recalled that the Museums Association's Code of Ethics for Museums requires museums to '[d]eal sensitively and promptly with requests for repatriation both within the UK and from abroad', point 2.7. A document entitled 'Additional Guidance' mentions, among other factors that need to be taken into account when evaluating a request for repatriation, 'the law' and 'current thinking on the subject'. Both are available here: https://www.museumsassociation.org/campaigns/ethics/code-of-ethics/.

The thrust of this book's argument is that the international legal framework for the protection of cultural property has evolved, so contemporary international law requires the return of the Parthenon marbles to Greece on a number of distinct legal grounds. The most fundamental of these is that a customary international law norm is emerging that requires cultural heritage of particular significance—inalienable, so to speak—illicitly removed from its original context to be returned to its place of origin. While rare authors may have suspected or pointed to this normative shift, this is the first time in legal scholarship that a book sets out to *prove* the emergence of this new customary international law by delving into state practice and acceptance as law. The book demonstrates that state practice on return is widespread and representative, uniform, and consistent, and that it exists because of a sense of legal obligation or legal right. Yet there is still some resistance to restitutions and this must be accounted for too. That said, even the UK government does not dissent from the emerging customary international law rule on the return of unlawfully removed cultural property. When it opposes the return of the Parthenon marbles, it does so with the argument that they were *lawfully* obtained in the first place.

This book shows otherwise. The analysis disproves the contention that the removal and acquisition of the Parthenon marbles were lawful. To bring this point home, the author relies on the available documentary and testimonial evidence, including surviving correspondence from the period and the transcript of the select committee investigation, which she examines in light of the international law of the time. Although ultimately the issue of unlawfulness is treated in the book as a fact,[198] establishing it is important, because the purported lawfulness of the marbles' removal and acquisition is the only legal argument adduced by the UK government in favour of the marbles' retention in the British Museum.

To find that the applicable substantive law favours the return of the marbles is not enough to ensure that the case will be resolved. A forum must yet be found that may actually apply this substantive law. Accordingly, another line of enquiry in the book concerns the practical availability of different methods of dispute settlement. In addition to providing an overview of the likely diplomatic and adjudicative means, the book considers two international courts, the ICJ and the European Court of Human Rights. In contrast with what has been suggested by other authors, this book argues that the European Court of Human Rights is *not* an appropriate forum to hear the Parthenon marbles dispute. Not only will jurisdictional and admissibility hurdles be difficult to pass successfully, but the European Court of Human Rights is also limited by its constitutive treaty to deciding alleged violations of the European Convention on Human Rights (ECHR) and its protocols. Although an application to the European Court of Human Rights may still allow the Greek claim to be vindicated, the fact of the matter is that the Strasbourg-based institution is a human rights court, and the Parthenon marbles case is a 'classic' interstate dispute. Were the case to be submitted to adjudication, *advisory* (as opposed to *contentious*)

[198] This is discussed in Chaps. 3 and 4, which belong to the first part of the book, which examines the facts.

proceedings before the ICJ would be the most suitable and should allow Greece to obtain the restitution of the missing marbles.

However, although the book reviews these two international courts, it also recognises that it is the diplomatic means that are the most appropriate, and the most likely, to resolve the Parthenon marbles dispute, and they are actively pursued at the moment of writing. This does not reduce the relevance of the legal examination of the case. On the contrary, the appraisal of the dispute's legal merits is not only relevant to adjudicative means of dispute resolution. Although only courts and tribunals are mandated to apply substantive law, a good grasp of the relative strength of the parties' legal claims or defences has a tremendous impact on their approach to diplomacy. It may well affect their willingness to negotiate or mediate and the concessions they are disposed to make. This book argues that understanding the legal merits of the case has a profound influence on the parties' attitude towards a potential solution to the conundrum that currently 'keeps' the marbles in the British Museum.

The Parthenon marbles case is the epitome of cultural heritage law disputes, and its resolution will inevitably impact a great many other cultural heritage disputes concerning requests for repatriation and, ultimately, the future of the protection of our cultural heritage. At the same time, the particularities of the dispute also mean that the absence of a combination of the elements that in this case may point to return can be used as arguments against repatriation in others. In the end, even if the Parthenon marbles dispute is resolved, it will still be necessary to clarify the contours of the new customary international law in the interest of all stakeholders. For example, does the new customary international law also cover *lawfully* removed inalienable heritage? (While this book focuses on unlawfully removed cultural heritage, the emerging rule is likely to prove to also cover the return of important cultural property removed under *unethical* circumstances.) Is the receiving state's human rights' record an element to be taken into account? Or does customary international law include a time-bar of 275 years, no more no less, as one author appears to suggest?[199] These questions cannot be answered in the abstract and they are not the focus of this book. But the discussion of the legal aspects of the Parthenon marbles case will still offer better insights into how such questions can be answered in the future.

1.2.2 Coverage of Legal Fields and Dispute Settlement Forums

This book is concerned with the Parthenon marbles and international law. However, it does not purport to cover all of international law. In particular, the book studies the Parthenon marbles case as an interstate dispute. This requires some explanation. The

[199] Robertson (2019) Chap. 8 (unnumbered page).

United Kingdom contests its interstate character—arguably, the dispute may appear to be between Greece and the British Museum, or even between the Acropolis Museum and the British Museum. It is also plausible that an individual application may be filed with the European Court of Human Rights and indeed such an application has been filed—and was dismissed.[200] For reasons explained in Chaps. 4, 6, and 8, the book posits that this is in fact an interstate case that opposes Greece and the United Kingdom.[201] Consequently, it focuses on public international law and the settlement of interstate disputes. It confines itself to diplomatic means of dispute settlement and to the practice of three types of international courts or tribunals: (1) the ICJ; (2) the European Court of Human Rights; and (3) arbitral tribunals. Accordingly, the book examines the law to be applied by these courts or tribunals, especially conventional law (international cultural heritage law and human rights law) and customary international law.

The application of international law sometimes requires us to also consider municipal law and this book turns to domestic legal systems on four occasions in particular: (1) when reviewing the constitutive elements of customary international law, notably state practice and acceptance as law. In this context, the book also has regard to domestic judicial decisions; (2) to the extent necessary in order to make sense of the status of the British Museum as a non-departmental public body (NDPB); (3) in the examination of the ban on deaccession that currently prevents the British Museum trustees from returning the marbles of their own volition; and (4) when having regard to the treatment of corruption in England at the time of the marbles' removal and subsequent acquisition by the UK government.

The book addresses in passing the issue of how the dispute might have been received by English courts, in order to put to rest a specious argument that has been advanced to the effect that Greece has waived its right to pursue the case under international law, because it has not resorted to English courts. However, the book leaves outside its scope the question of how third-party domestic courts might decide the matter. For example, the United States is regarded as one of the best jurisdictions in which to litigate restitution claims.[202] If, for the sake of argument, the marbles were on loan in the United States and Greece litigated the case before US federal courts, would it obtain the marbles? The book leaves such questions aside. Restricting the coverage of the book in this manner may narrow the generality of its conclusions, but it has the merit of allowing an in-depth study of the Parthenon marbles case in light of international law and of its potential reception in the selected international dispute settlement forums.

[200] *Syllogos ton Athinaion v United Kingdom*, App no 48259/15, Decision (23 June 2016).

[201] See especially Sects. 4.5, 6.4, and 8.3.

[202] E.g. Fishman (2010) 355; Kaye (1998) 81.

1.3 Outline of the Book

The book is structured in the following manner. It consists of four parts and comprises 12 chapters. Following this introduction, Part I focuses on 'The Facts' of the Parthenon marbles case. To understand the legal merits of the dispute, the book must return to where it all began, Athens. Chapter 2 takes us on a journey through time to explore the Parthenon as a monument of cultural and political significance, as a temple, and as an emblem of high classical art. The chapter contextualises the creation of the Parthenon in the Athenian golden age, it appraises its iconography, its unique symbolism and importance, and it studies its history from antiquity to the present. The chapter's purpose is both to document the Parthenon's significance for Greece and for world culture and to establish the background against which to assess its despoliation.

Chapter 3 gives an account of Elgin's actions and of the removal and eventual transportation of the marbles to England, and it assesses their lawfulness. The chapter outlines Elgin's plan from conception to execution, it canvasses the contested firman and its purported terms, and it reviews the conditions that made it possible for his agents to prise the marbles off the ancient temple. It argues that Elgin never had any permission from the Sublime Porte, whether prior or ex post, to act as he did. The chapter also turns its attention to the marbles' perilous voyage to the United Kingdom, including the *Mentor* shipwreck, and it considers the reaction of Elgin's contemporaries to the looting. The narrative concludes with the arrival of the marbles in London. The chapter aims to bring home both the scale of the destruction caused to the Parthenon by Elgin and his men and the insouciance with which it was done, and it shows that the removal of the marbles was unlawful.

The following chapter, Chap. 4, surveys the acquisition of the Parthenon marbles by the UK government. The chapter enquires into the summary investigation of the select committee and queries the bona fide nature of the purchase of Elgin's collection by the UK government. It examines critically the international law pertaining to the protection of cultural heritage in occupied territories, the issue of corruption and its treatment under English law contemporary to the purchase, and it discusses Elgin's conduct in the Ottoman empire as the conduct of an ambassador with the potential to engage the responsibility of the sending state. Overall, the chapter suggests that the decision to purchase the marbles was taken regardless of the fact that the unlawfulness of their removal was the elephant in the room—a known fact—and that, consequently, the UK government never acquired legal rights in the marbles.

Chapter 5 documents the Greek demands for the return of the marbles over the years. It is a common misconception that the first official request for the marbles' repatriation was made in the 1980s. In reality, Greece put forward the first formal claim only a handful of years after its recognition as an independent state. The year was 1836. Much of Greece still remained under Ottoman dominion. The chapter chronicles Greece's painstaking efforts to engage diplomacy for the marbles' restitution for two centuries up until the present. This obdurate insistence, while ineffectual, underlines how important the marbles are to Greece, and its obduracy is legally significant: in case of adjudication, the claim for the marbles' return will not be considered time-barred. The chapter lays the groundwork for the later discussion of estoppel, acquiescence, and extinctive prescription.

Chapter 6 turns to the Parthenon marbles and the British Museum. First, the chapter reviews the marbles' custodianship by the British Museum. This part of the chapter includes a discussion of the Duveen scouring scandal, which was kept secret for the best part of 60 years and which resulted in irreparable damage to all the metopes, most of the frieze, and about half the pedimental figures, in a misguided attempt to whiten what remained of the originally polychrome decoration and its centuries-old patina. Second, the chapter delves into the British Museum's arguments against the return of the marbles and examines their gradual metamorphosis over time. Finally, the chapter studies the ban on deaccession that the British Museum has relied upon to explain why legally it cannot return the marbles and questions its relevance to international law.

Part II of the book turns to 'Access to Dispute Settlement'. Chapter 7 enquires into the available dispute settlement options. The chapter assesses the diplomatic and legal means that may be resorted to in order to settle the Parthenon marbles dispute. In particular, it considers the possibility of negotiations, mediation, arbitration, and judicial settlement before the ICJ and the European Court of Human Rights. The chapter continues with some practical considerations, focusing notably on the requirement to exhaust local remedies, the possibility of an *ex aequo et bono* mandate, and the relief sought and its binding force. The chapter posits that, although diplomatic means are preferable by a long way, should the case be submitted to adjudication, advisory proceedings before the ICJ are the most appropriate option.

Chapter 8 canvasses specific issues of jurisdiction and admissibility and establishes the Parthenon marbles case as an interstate dispute. The discussion begins with an enquiry into the nature of the Parthenon marbles conundrum as a legal case raising legal questions, before turning to the issue of attribution. Taking into account the status of the British Museum as an NDPB, including additional issues of funding, the manner of appointment of the museum's trustees, and the ban on deaccession, the chapter argues that the continued retention of the marbles in the British Museum is attributable to the UK government. Furthermore, the chapter considers and refutes the availability of the objections of estoppel, acquiescence, and extinctive prescription against return.

Having examined the modalities of access to dispute settlement, Part III turns to 'The Law Applicable to the Substance of the Dispute'. Chapter 9 explores treaty law. It considers, on the one hand, the existing conventions on the protection of cultural property and their limitations, notably the issue of non-retroactivity, and, on the other, the ECHR, focusing on the right to the peaceful enjoyment of property and the rather uncertain right to cultural identity. The chapter reiterates that, even if technically the dispute can be decided by either the ICJ or the European Court of Human Rights, it is essentially an interstate cultural heritage case and that human rights law is not best adapted to it.

Chapter 10 turns to customary international law. It opens with an analysis of the customary international law on the return of important cultural property. The chapter delves into state practice and acceptance as law and establishes the emergence of a new customary international law rule that stipulates the return of unlawfully removed cultural property of particular significance. The chapter studies the shift in attitudes, evident in the repatriation of numerous objects unlawfully removed before the entry into force of the non-retroactive conventions, and the reasons for which states repatriate these objects. It reviews museum practice on the return of cultural property and asks whether museums too can contribute to 'state' practice. The chapter also questions whether the United Kingdom dissents from the new rule. Subsequently, it considers equity as a source of international law and its relevance to the Parthenon marbles case. In particular, it examines equity as individualised justice and considers the possibility of an intertemporal application of international law in this field where demands for 'cultural justice' thrive. The chapter concludes that the application of equity too would achieve the return of the marbles. Part IV, the book's final part, entitled 'Time Future', is forward-looking. Chapter 11 summarises the book's main findings and concludes with an outlook on the future. Chapter 12 contains the annex.

References

Charles Abbott, *Diary and Correspondence of Charles Abbott, Lord Colchester* (vol 2, John Murray 1861)

Michael C Alexander, *The Case for the Prosecution in the Ciceronian Era* (University of Michigan Press 2005)

JPVD Balsdon, 'The History of the Extortion Court at Rome, 123-70 BC' (1938) 14 Papers of the British School at Rome 98

Robert Browning, 'The Parthenon in History' in Christopher Hitchens, *The Parthenon Marbles* (first publication 1987, Verso 2008)

George Gordon Byron, *The Complete Works of Lord Byron, including his Suppressed Poems* (vol 1, Baudry's Foreign Library 1832)

Marcus Tullius Cicero, *Divinatio in Caecilium*

Marcus Tullius Cicero, *In Verrem*

John Alan Cohan, 'An Examination of Archaeological Ethics and the Repatriation Movement Respecting Cultural Property (Part Two)' (2004) 28 (1) Environs: Environmental Law and Policy Journal 1

James Crawford, *State Responsibility* (Cambridge University Press 2013)

James Cuno, *Who Owns Antiquity? Museums and the Battle over our Ancient Heritage* (Princeton University Press 2011)

Derek Fincham, 'The Parthenon Sculptures and Cultural Justice' (2013) 23 Fordham Intellectual Property, Media and Entertainment Law Journal 943

Joseph P Fishman, 'Locating the International Interest in Intranational Cultural Property Disputes' (2010) 35 Yale Journal of International Law 347

Kate Fitz Gibbon, *Who Owns the Past? Cultural Policy, Cultural Property, and the Law* (Rutgers University Press 2005)

Thomas D Frazel, 'The Composition and Circulation of Cicero's "In Verrem"' (2004) 54 (1) Classical Quarterly 128

Mark D Fullerton, *Greek Sculpture* (John Wiley and Sons 2016)
Ingo Gildenhard, *Cicero, Against Verres 2.1.53-86* (Open Book Publishers 2011)
Paige S Goodwin, 'Mapping the Limits of Repatriable Cultural Heritage: A Case Study of Stolen Flemish Art in French Museums' (2008) 157 University of Pennsylvania Law Review 673
Jeanette Greenfield, *The Return of Cultural Treasures* (3rd edn, Cambridge University Press 2007)
Erich S Gruen, 'Pompey, Metellus Pius, and the Trials of 70-69 BC: The Perils of Schematism' (1971) 92 (1) American Journal of Philology 1
Hansard, 'House of Lords Parthenon Marbles Debate' (8 February 2022) (vol 818, Hansard 2022a)
Hansard, 'House of Lords Repatriation of Cultural Objects Debate' (6 September 2022) (vol 824, Hansard 2022b)
Hansard, 'House of Commons Elgin Marbles Debate' (2 March 2020) (vol 672, Hansard 2020)
Hansard, 'House of Lords Debate' (18 January 1996) (vol 568, Hansard 1996)
Hansard, 'House of Lords Debate' (27 October 1983) (vol 444, Hansard 1983)
Hansard, *Parliamentary Debates 1816* (vol 32, Hansard 1816a)
Hansard, *Parliamentary Debates 1816* (vol 34, Hansard 1816b)
Hansard, *Parliamentary Debates 1815* ('Petition of The Earl of Elgin Respecting His Collection of Marbles', 15 June 1815) (vol 31, Hansard 1815)
Christopher Hitchens, *The Parthenon Marbles* (first publication 1987, Verso 2008)
Tiffany Jenkins, *Keeping their Marbles* (Oxford University Press 2016)
Lawrence M Kaye, 'Art Wars: The Repatriation Battle' (1998) 31 New York University Journal of International Law and Politics 79
Wojciech W Kowalski, 'Restitution of Works of Art pursuant to Private and Public International Law' (2001) 288 Recueil des cours 11
Livy, *The History of Rome*
Georg Friedrich von Martens, *Nouveau recueil de traités d'alliance, de paix, de trêve, de neutralité, de commerce, de limites, d'échange etc. et de plusieurs autres actes: 1814-1815* (vol 2, Librairie de Dieterich 1818)
John Henry Merryman, 'Two Ways of Thinking about Cultural Property' (1986) 80 American Journal of International Law 831
John Henry Merryman, 'Thinking about the Elgin Marbles' (1985) 83 (8) Michigan Law Review 1881
Karl E Meyer, 'Who (Really) Owns the Past?' (2006) 23 (1) World Policy Journal 85
Karl E Meyer, *The Plundered Past* (revised edn, Penguin Books 1973, 1977)
Adolf Michaelis, *Ancient Marbles in Great Britain* (tr Charles Augustus Maude Fennell, Cambridge University Press 1882)
Margaret M Miles, 'Still in the Aftermath of Waterloo: A Brief History of Decisions about Restitution' in Peter Stone (ed), *Cultural Heritage, Ethics, and the Military* (Boydell and Brewer 2011)
Margaret M Miles, *Art as Plunder: The Ancient Origins of Debate about Cultural Property* (Cambridge University Press 2008, 2010)
Margaret M Miles, 'Cicero's Prosecution of Gaius Verres: A Roman View of the Ethics of Acquisition of Art' (2002) 11 (1) International Journal of Cultural Property 28
John Newsinger, 'Elgin in China' (2002) 15 The New Left Review 119
Pliny the Elder, *Natural History* (John Bostock and HT Riley eds, Taylor and Francis, 1855)
Plutarch, *Parallel Lives: Cicero*
Lyndel V Prott (ed), *Witnesses to History: A Compendium of Documents and Writings* (UNESCO 2009)
Dorothy Mackay Quynn, 'The Art Confiscations of the Napoleonic Wars' (1945) 50 (3) The American Historical Review 437
Erik Ringmar, *Liberal Barbarism: The European Destruction of the Palace of the Emperor of China* (Palgrave Macmillan 2013)
Erik Ringmar, 'Liberal Barbarism and the Oriental Sublime: The European Destruction of the Emperor's Summer Palace' (2006) 34 (3) Millennium 917

Geoffrey Robertson, *Who Owns History? Elgin's Loot and the Case for Returning Plundered Treasure* (Biteback Publishing 2019)
Eleanor Robson, Luke Treadwell, and Christopher Gosden (eds), *Who Owns Objects? The Ethics and Politics of Collecting Cultural Artefacts* (Oxbow Books 2006)
David Rudenstine, 'A Tale of Three Documents: Lord Elgin and the Missing, Historic 1801 Ottoman Document' (2001) 22 Cardozo Law Review 1853
Tullio Scovazzi, '*Diviser c'est détruire*: Ethical Principles and Legal Rules in the Field of Return of Cultural Property' (2011) 94 (2) Rivista di diritto internazionale 341
Select Committee of the House of Commons, *Report on the Earl of Elgin's Collection of Sculptured Marbles* (Bulmer 1816)
AH Smith, 'Lord Elgin and his Collection' (1916) 36 Journal of Hellenic Studies 163
William Smith, LLD William Wayte and GE Marindin (eds), *A Dictionary of Greek and Roman Antiquities* (John Murray 1890)
Edward Spencer, 'Verres on Trial for Extortion' (1916) 7 Journal of the American Institute of Criminal Law and Criminology 838
William St Clair, *Lord Elgin and the Marbles* (Oxford University Press 1967, 1998, reprinted 2003)
Irini Stamatoudi, *Cultural Property Law and Restitution* (Edward Elgar 2011)
Catharine Titi, 'International Dispute Settlement in Cultural Heritage Law and in the Protection of Foreign Investment: Is Cross-Fertilisation Possible?' (2017) 8 (3) Journal of International Dispute Settlement 535
Ann Vasaly, 'Cicero, Domestic Politics, and the First Action of the Verrines' (2009) 28 (1) Classical Antiquity 101
Charles de Visscher, *International Protection of Works of Art and Historic Monuments* (US Department of State 1949)
Peter Watson and Cecilia Todeschini, *The Medici Conspiracy* (Public Affairs 2007)
Ben Weinreb and others, *The London Encyclopaedia* (3rd edn, Macmillan 2008)
Robert Wilson, *History of the British Expedition to Egypt* (2nd edn, Egerton 1803)
CD Yonge (tr), *The Orations of Marcus Tullius Cicero* (George Bell and Sons 1903)

Part I
The Facts

Chapter 2
The Parthenon

2.1 Introduction

To appreciate the legal merits of the Parthenon marbles case, the book must return to where it all began, Athens. An emblem of high classical art, a symbol of Athenian supremacy and the triumph of the civilised world over the barbarians, the Parthenon has stood on the Acropolis for two and a half millennia, surviving the slings and arrows of successive wars and occupations, religious shifts, seismic activity, weather conditions, vandals, and even tourists. This chapter will study the history of the Parthenon, from its inception in fifth-century BC Athens, its architecture, and iconography, to its subsequent history until modern times. The chapter will also consider the significance and legacy of the Parthenon, and it will close with a brief overview of the new Acropolis Museum.

2.2 The Athenian Golden Age

2.2.1 Athena's Temple Reborn: The Periclean Building Programme

The Parthenon was not the first temple on the Acropolis to be dedicated to the city's patron goddess, nor was it the first to stand on the current site.[1] After the Athenians successfully repulsed the Persians following their victory in the battle of Marathon, which put an end to the first Persian invasion in 490 BC, they tore down the archaic temple that stood on the site to construct a larger marble temple, the Older Parthenon.[2] During the second Persian incursion of 480 BC, the invading army plundered

[1] E.g. Hill (1912); Dinsmoor (1934); Dinsmoor (1947).

[2] Hurwit (1999) 133.

C. Titi, *The Parthenon Marbles and International Law*,
https://doi.org/10.1007/978-3-031-26357-6_2

and set fire to the Acropolis, razing everything to the ground and reducing the monuments to a sorry state,[3] including the Older Parthenon, which was still under construction.[4] All was destroyed except, as Herodotus tells us, Athena's sacred olive tree from whose burnt stump a shoot miraculously sprang on the day following the devastation.[5] On the eve of the battle of Plataea, in 479 BC, the Greek forces swore an oath that they would not rebuild any of the sanctuaries that had been burnt by the Persians, but they would leave them in the pitiable state in which they stood as a reminder to future generations of 'the impiety of the barbarians'.[6] The battle of Plataea, one of two decisive land battles fought that year against the Persian army, resulted in a resounding Greek victory and the Persians beat a hasty retreat back home.[7] The end of the war marked the beginning of the classical period for Greek city-states and it had a profound political impact.[8] The Persian invasions also had an influence on almost everything to do with the Parthenon, including, as we shall see, its iconography.[9]

The Persian wars were over, but Greek city-states did not know this at the time. The Persians had already raided Greece twice and there was a risk that, after the latest dent to their pride, they would return.[10] After all, their first defeat in 490 BC had not prevented them from coming back with a larger force, and there was no way of knowing that the Persian threat had been eliminated.[11] The upshot was the foundation in 478/477 BC of the Delian league (or Athenian alliance),[12] a military confederacy of Greek city-states, with Athens at the helm.[13] Member city-states would make a contribution to the league in money or ships, and the Athenians received a tribute as league treasurers.[14] Athens was the biggest naval power, and perhaps the alliance was initially meant to bind Athens and ensure that, should the Persians come back, it would assist Ionian Greek city-states, which were both less

---

[3]Herodotus, *The Histories* 8.53.

[4]E.g. Hill (1912) 537; Hurwit (1999) 133-135. For a beautifully illustrated account of the construction of the Old Parthenon, see Korres (2001).

[5]Herodotus, *The Histories* 8.55.

[6]Diodorus Siculus, *Library of History* 11.29.3. For a critical account of the authenticity of the oath of Plataea, see in general Cartledge (2013).

[7]The other one was the battle of Mycale in Ionia, Herodotus, *The Histories* 9.100, 9.106.

[8]Barringer (2014) 196.

[9]See also Beard (2010) 37.

[10]Finley (2008) 16-17.

[11]Rhodes (2010) 18.

[12]Hammond (1967).

[13]Thucydides, *History of the Peloponnesian War* 1.96-1.97, 6.76, 6.82. On the Delian league, see further Hammond (1967); Rhodes (1992); Rhodes (2010) Chap. 2.

[14]Thucydides, *History of the Peloponnesian War* 1.96.

powerful and situated more closely to the Persian threat.[15] Whatever its founding premise, the Delian league ultimately became the basis for Athenian hegemony.[16]

The year 454 BC marked a turning point. The league's treasury, which until that moment had been kept on the sacred island of Delos,[17] was transferred to Athens.[18] Epigraphic evidence shows that, from about that time, a proportion of the tribute paid by league members into the treasury was given as an offering to Athena, just as it is likely that earlier a proportion was offered to Apollo on Delos.[19] With the treasury of the Delian league now safely ensconced on the Acropolis,[20] the Athenians had 'a ready supply' of cash[21] and they were inclined to use it. That said, Athens had large non-imperial domestic revenues—and reserves—on which to draw and was able to tap these other resources, including income from the Laurion silver mines.[22]

Wealth was one of the two important elements that ultimately allowed the rebuilding programme on the Acropolis to proceed.[23] Peace was the other and, arguably, the most important element.[24] The Persian wars were over and, in 451 BC, Athens and Sparta signed a truce,[25] and *c* 449 BC a peace treaty is said to have been negotiated with the Persians.[26] This became known as the peace of Callias, named after the Athenian envoy who led the negotiations.[27]

So it was that the question of the fate of the sanctuaries that the Persians had burnt down re-emerged, and the old promise that they should stand as a reminder of the Persian aggression to future generations was forgotten.[28] An extensive refurbishment of the Acropolis commenced[29] under the building programme of the great

---

[15]Rhodes (1992) 35-36; Kallet (2005) 38.

[16]Thucydides, *History of the Peloponnesian War* 1.97-1.99; cf Kallet (2013).

[17]Thucydides, *History of the Peloponnesian War* 1.96; Plutarch, *Parallel Lives: Aristides* 25.2.

[18]Blamire (2001) 100; Kallet (2005) 44; Finley (2008) 15.

[19]Rhodes (1992) 38, 41.

[20]Connelly (2014) Chap. 3 (unnumbered page).

[21]Barringer (2014) 226; Kallet (2005) 52.

[22]Blamire (2001) 106; Jenkins (2002) 13; Kallet (2005) 37, 49, 56-57; Barringer (2014) 226; cf Jones (1957) 3-20.

[23]Neils (2001) 24.

[24]Neils (2001) 24.

[25]Neils (2001) 24. Sparta was not part of the Delian league but headed instead the Peloponnesian league, centred on the Peloponnesus.

[26]Diodorus Siculus, *Library of History* 12.4; Herodotus, *The Histories* 7.151.1. For a discussion, see Badian (1987).

[27]Diodorus Siculus, *Library of History* 12.4; Herodotus, *The Histories* 7.151.1; Badian (1987) 2.

[28]Plutarch, *Parallel Lives: Pericles* 17.1.

[29]Neils (2001) 24.

statesman Pericles,[30] led by the architects Ictinos and Callicrates[31] and the sculptor Pheidias.[32] Work on the Parthenon began in *c* 447 BC and it was completed in *c* 432 BC,[33] in a mere 15 years. Pericles was instrumental in the building of the Parthenon, as he was in tapping into the treasury of the Delian league, for which he was roundly criticised.[34] Yet, in many ways the Parthenon was also the work product of the citizens of Athens, since the assembly authorised and audited all public expenditure.[35] Construction of one of the most iconic buildings in the world had begun.

2.2.2 Architecture and Iconography

The design of the Parthenon and its execution are 'a mathematical, intellectual, and technical feat of the highest order' and the apogee of high classical art (Fig. 2.1).[36] A Doric temple of Pentelic marble with some Ionic touches, including a continuous frieze above its cella (or inner chamber) walls,[37] the Parthenon does not have any straight lines.[38] The columns taper upwards swelling slightly in the middle, an architectural trick known as 'entasis', which anticipates and counters the optical illusion of a thinning column.[39]

Visitors entering the Acropolis through the Propylaea, would first glimpse the west pediment, depicting the founding myth of the contest between Athena and Poseidon over the patronage of the land of Attica.[40] The gods, so the myth went, presented the Athenians with gifts. Poseidon hurled his trident on the Acropolis and produced a sea (or a well of salt water) and Athena offered the city an olive tree,[41]

[30] Plutarch, *Parallel Lives: Pericles* 13.6; Diodorus Siculus, *Library of History* 12.39.1; Strabo, *Geography* 9.1.12. For a critical assessment of Pericles' role in the building programme on the Acropolis, see Neils (2001) 25-26.

[31] Plutarch, *Parallel Lives: Pericles* 13.4; Strabo, *Geography* 9.1.12. A third architect, Carpion, is mentioned in Vitruvius, *The Ten Books on Architecture* 7.preface.

[32] Plutarch, *Parallel Lives: Pericles* 13.4, 13.9.

[33] Barringer (2014) 227; Browning (2008) 3; Beard (2010) 42.

[34] Plutarch, *Parallel Lives: Pericles* 12 and 14; Diodorus Siculus, *Library of History* 12.38.2, 12.40.2. For a modern account, see Kallet (2005) 56-57; Giovannini (2008); cf text to n 22.

[35] Wycherley (1978) 113; Kallet (2005) 52.

[36] Barringer (2014) 228, 232; Fullerton (2016) Chap. 7; Wycherley (1978) 110-111, 115; Stevens (1940) 1. See further Vitruvius, *The Ten Books on Architecture* 3.

[37] Barringer (2014) 228; Neils (2001) 36-39; Fullerton (2016) Chap. 7; Hurwit (2005) 135; Wycherley (1978) 106, 110; Browning (2008) 6; St Clair (2022) 172.

[38] Barringer (2014) 228; DS Robertson (1943) 115-118.

[39] Vitruvius, *The Ten Books on Architecture* 3.3.13; Penrose (1888) Chap. 5; Wycherley (1978) 110; Fullerton (2016) Chap. 7; Etlin (2005) 367.

[40] Pausanias, *Description of Greece* 1.24.5. See also Barringer (2014) 230.

[41] Herodotus, *The Histories* 8.55; Plutarch, *Parallel Lives: Themistocles* 19; Apollodorus, *Library* 3.14.1; Pausanias, *Description of Greece* 1.24.5; Ovid, *Metamorphoses* 6.70.

that same olive tree that was said to have survived the second Persian incursion after it was burnt.[42] Athena won the contest and became the patron of Attica. Athens was named after her.

The entrance to the Parthenon was on the east side.[43] We know from Pausanias that the east pediment, just above the entrance, featured the birth of Athena,[44] who, according to myth, emerged full-grown from the head of her father, Zeus. The central part of this pediment was destroyed probably when the Parthenon was converted into a church, although it is also possible that it had been damaged earlier.[45]

The pediments depict scenes of the life of Athena and reveal idealised figures.[46] All are similar in size and have the same proportions, and no one is 'old, sick, or unsightly'.[47] Textiles are precisely carved, and the rippling drapery creates the illusion of volume and movement in the figures.[48]

Underneath the pediments and above the architrave, running around the four sides of the temple, were placed the Parthenon's 92 metopes, executed in high relief.[49] The metopes, prominent on the building, commemorate the battles and victories of gods and heroes.[50] On each side of the building, the metopes depict different, mythic or mythological, battle scenes. Those on the east side over the main entrance depict the Gigantomachy, the battle fought between the Olympian gods and the giants for the supremacy of the world[51]—the old guard on its way out, the new guard on its way in, the dawning of a new era. The Gigantomachy was important to the cult of Athena, for she had been instrumental in bringing about the gods' victory, and the theme of the battle was woven into the Panathenaic peplos that was presented to the cult statue of Athena Polias during the goddess's festival.[52] The metopes on the west side represent battle scenes between Greeks and Amazons, a mythical tribe of all-female warriors.[53] When the local Athenian hero Theseus abducted one of them, Antiope or Hippolyta,[54] the Amazons invaded Attica, only to be defeated by the Athenians soon afterwards.[55] (Some readers will be more familiar with Theseus and Hippolyta from

---

[42] Herodotus, *The Histories* 8.55.

[43] Pausanias, *Description of Greece* 1.24.5.

[44] Pausanias, *Description of Greece* 1.24.5.

[45] Barringer (2014) 231; St Clair (2022) 178; cf Wycherley (1978) 121. See also text to n 123.

[46] Barringer (2014) 232.

[47] Barringer (2014) 232.

[48] Barringer (2014) 232.

[49] St Clair (1998) 51; cf Neils (2001) 33; Barringer (2014) 233.

[50] Boardman (1999) 305.

[51] Stevens (1936) 58; St Clair (1998) 51.

[52] Stamatopoulou (2012) 72; Barringer (2014) 233; Neils (1996) 193. See further text to nn 71 and 79.

[53] Stevens (1936) 58-59; St Clair (1998) 51.

[54] The sources reveal some uncertainty as to the name and/or the identity of the Amazon, e.g. see Plutarch, *Parallel Lives: Theseus* 27.

[55] Plutarch, *Parallel Lives: Theseus* 26-28; Herodotus, *The Histories* 9.27.

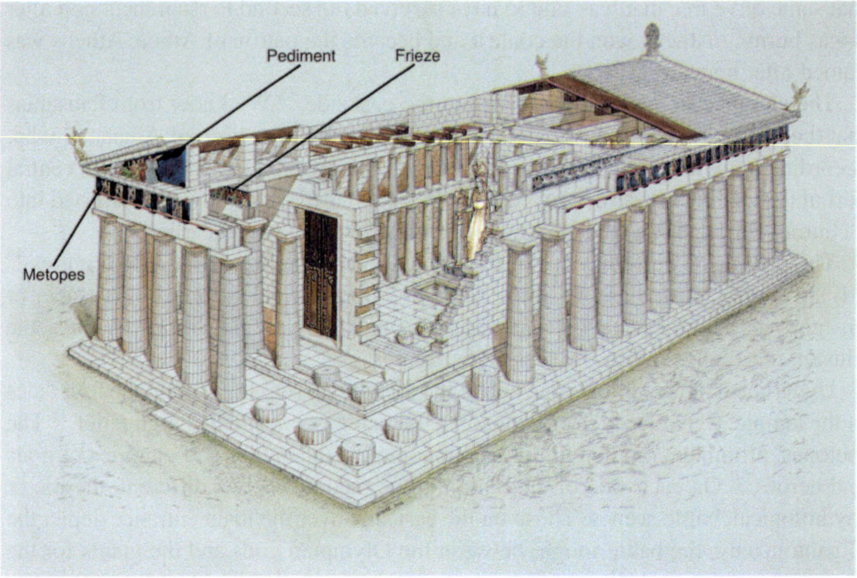

Fig. 2.1 Painted reconstruction of the Parthenon © Acropolis Museum, drawn by A Nikas after A Orlandos. The original image has been modified by the author to show the position of the pediments, metopes, and frieze

Shakespeare's *A Midsummer Night's Dream*, even though the play is more fantasy comedy than myth.) The northern metopes appear to represent scenes from the fall of Troy.[56] Last, the metopes on the south side show battles between Lapiths, a legendary people of Greek mythology, and centaurs, the savage half-men half-horse creatures.[57] Theseus had a role in this myth too.[58] Like the mythological battles with giants and Amazons, the Centauromachy represents the fight of the civilised world against barbarism—Greeks against Persians.[59]

Behind the metopes, hidden underneath the ceiling in the shade of the peristyle, was a continuous Ionic frieze circling the core of the temple.[60] Unlike the metopes, prominent on the temple with their heroic and mythological subjects, the frieze was not so easy to view,[61] but, as was the case with other relief carvings on the temple, additions in metal (horses' bridles and reins, wreaths, etc.) and the application of

[56] Wycherley (1978) 115; St Clair (1998) 51; Barringer (2014) 240.

[57] St Clair (1998) 51.

[58] Woodford (1974); Barringer (2014) 233.

[59] Barringer (2014) 233; duBois (1991) 55, 64, 70.

[60] Boardman (1999) 305; Neils (2001) 33; Barringer (2014) 235.

[61] Osborne (1987); Barringer (2014) 235.

colour helped make the composition clearer.[62] Sculpted in low relief (5 cm deep) and measuring 160 m (524 ft) in length and about 1 m (just over 3 ft) in height,[63] the frieze was primarily reserved for the activities of humans.[64] It depicts a procession with two lines of participants, one moving down the west side of the Parthenon, then down the north, and another progressing along the south side; the two lines converge on the east frieze above the entrance.[65] The frieze includes some 378 figures and 245 animals, and it has been described as 'a tour de force of planning and carving'.[66] The cavalry dominates almost half of the frieze,[67] with a procession of quadrigas (four-horse chariots), often seen as representing the *apobates* contest.[68] The equestrian parade yields to people on foot (elders, musicians, water carriers, women carrying the paraphernalia of sacrifice, officials), with sacrificial animals between them, and gods.[69] The latter are easily recognisable by their superhuman size (they are about one-third taller than the other figures on the frieze) and they can be identified by their carved attributes.[70] Above the entrance on the east frieze, officials and gods frame the central peplos scene, the ceremony that forms the highlight of the narrative.[71] To the viewer's right, pride of place is given to Athena, identifiable by the serpent fringe of the aegis in her lap.[72]

The iconography of the frieze has turned into one of art history's most persistent enigmas.[73] From early on, the frieze was thought to commemorate the Panathenaia, and especially the Great Panathenaia, the religious festival held with pomp in honour

[62] Stevens (1936) 61-62; Neils (2001) 88-93; Barringer (2014) 235; Connelly (2014) Chap. 5 (unnumbered page). St Clair (1998) 51. See also Chap. 6, text to n 31.

[63] Boardman (1999) 305; Neils (2001) 33; Barringer (2014) 235.

[64] Boardman (1999) 305.

[65] Barringer (2014) 235.

[66] Neils (2001) 33; Connelly (2014) Chap. 5 (unnumbered page).

[67] Neils (2001) 132-137; Barringer (2014) 235-237; Jenkins (2005).

[68] Neils (2001) 138-141.

[69] Neils (2001) Chap. 5; Barringer (2014) 235-237.

[70] Wycherley (1978) 118; Neils (1999) 6; Neils (2001) 161-166; Beard (2010) 129.

[71] Barringer (2014) 237; Neils (2001) 166.

[72] St Clair (1998) 52; see also the description of Block V from the east frieze on the British Museum website https://www.britishmuseum.org/collection/object/G_1816-0610-19; cf Neils (1996) 189. Generally, on snakes in Athena's aegis, see Marx (1993) 240; Deacy and Villing (2009) 111-112.

[73] Beard (2010) 132. The interpretation of the frieze is further complicated by the uncertainty surrounding the possible existence of a second frieze, in the pronaos of the Parthenon, running at the same level as the 'first' frieze, below the ceiling and above the entry of the cella. Opinions about this second frieze are divided. According to Manolis Korres, a second Ionic frieze was planned in the pronaos of the Parthenon but we do not know if it was ever completed, and it was destroyed in antiquity, Korres (1994) 94-95, n 28; Mary Beard, possibly relying on Korres, discusses this second frieze in the following terms: 'we now know that there was not just one, but two, friezes on the fifth-century Parthenon, a second whose existence no archaeologist had ever before suspected... It was much shorter and only faint traces survive... Whatever this frieze depicted, it would have been clearly visible, beyond the outer frieze, to any visitor climbing the steps to the main entrance of the building; it is almost bound to have been seen as the continuation of the narrative which ended

of Athena every 4 years.[74] In contrast with the Little Panathenaia, a smaller, local event, the penteteric festival was a big celebration and attracted participants from beyond Athens.[75] The Panathenaia featured musical and dance contests, athletic and equestrian competitions, including chariot racing, and a regatta in the port.[76] Unlike the leading contestants at Olympia who were rewarded with olive wreaths, the Panathenaic victors received choice prizes that included Athena's sacred olive oil (this was presented in the large ceramic jars known as Panathenaic amphorae)[77] as well as gold, silver, or olive wreaths.[78] The celebration culminated in a procession that went up to the Acropolis to present the peplos, a specially woven robe, to the ancient cult statue of Athena Polias, made of olive wood and housed opposite the Parthenon, in the Erechtheion.[79] Another high point of the Panathenaia was the *hecatomb*, the ritual sacrifice of one hundred head of cattle, whose meat was subsequently distributed to the populace of Athens.[80]

The identification of the procession on the Parthenon frieze as the Panathenaia has often been contested. Some have pointed to 'missing' Panathenaic elements, such as the Athenian hoplites (or foot-soldiers) or the ship-on-wheels with the peplos on its mast, which, they have claimed, are made conspicuous by their absence.[81] Other constituents with no role in the Panathenaia are unexpectedly present, such as ranks of horsemen.[82] However, our knowledge about the Panathenaia is mainly based on non-contemporary sources that are not always reliable, the festival was likely not preserved in (the proverbial) aspic but would have evolved over time, the iconography itself may have carried different meanings depending on time, and, in any event, artistic licence could explain the omissions or additions.[83]

The other objection advanced by those who question the dominant interpretation of the iconography relates to the presence of contemporary Athenians on the frieze, since Greek architectural temple sculpture would not depict common mortals

---

(or so, up till now, we have believed) at the scene with the peplos', Beard (2010) 136-137. See also Holtzmann (2003) 119, fig 98.

[74] Stuart and Revett (1787) 12; Wycherley (1978) 117; Neils (2001) 173; Jenkins (2002) 25; Barringer (2014) 237; Shear (2021) 344.

[75] Shear (2021) 35, 314.

[76] Aristotle, *Athenian Constitution* 60.1; Plutarch, *Parallel Lives: Pericles* 13.3; Harris (1995) 8; Neils (2001) 21; Jenkins (2002) 24.

[77] Neils (2001) 21; Hamilton (1996). See also Aristotle, *Athenian Constitution* 60.1.

[78] Aristotle, *Athenian Constitution* 60.1; Harris (1995) 8; Neils (1996) 185; Neils (2001) 21; Jenkins (2002) 24.

[79] Nagy (1992) 64; Harris (1995) 8-9; Neils (1996) 185; Neils (2001) 23, 173; Jenkins (2002) 11; Barringer (2014) 237; Shear (2021) 344. See further Plato, *Euthyphro* 6b; Aristotle, *Athenian Constitution* 49.3 and 60.1.

[80] Neils (2001) 23; Shapiro (1996) 216.

[81] E.g. Holloway (1966) 223; Rotroff (1977); Connelly (1996) 54; Neils (2001) 174; Jenkins (2002) 25; Barringer (2014) 237.

[82] Jenkins (2002) 25; Barringer (2014) 238; Beard (2010) 135.

[83] Neils (2001) 174-175; Ridgway (1999) Chap. 5; Beard (2010) 136; Wachsmann (2012) 238.

participating in a contemporary event.[84] Rather, it would be reserved for mythological and historical themes relating to the temple's divinity.[85]

Joan Breton Connelly and William St Clair have looked for alternative explanations. Connelly has argued that the frieze presents the sacrifice of the daughters of Erechtheus, a mythical king of Athens, and that the 'peplos scene' depicts the dressing before sacrifice, the cloth being a funerary robe.[86] However, fifth-century BC Athens would be unlikely to commemorate a human sacrifice.[87] In addition, the mood of the frieze is one of celebration, and even the gods do not show a solemnity appropriate for a human sacrifice.[88] St Clair has offered a different interpretation. According to him, the frieze commemorates the celebration of the birth of Ion, an Athenian hero and a descendant of Erechtheus.[89] What we should be seeing in the central scene is baby Ion being swaddled. But there's the rub: we do not actually *see* baby Ion or any baby at all. St Clair has pointed out that this is one of the most destroyed parts of the frieze, and the baby's head could have been easily mutilated.[90] Even so, this interpretation would place the baby in an awkward position on the upper edge of the cloth, unnaturally high compared to the man and child holding it (and apparently not looking at the baby). The very idea of the representation of the baby *in the process* of being swaddled seems surprising. The scene would appear to bear no similarity to other images of swaddled babies that have come to us from ancient Greece. Above all, there is no visible baby. So we must fall back to the dominant interpretation and the Panathenaia.

Some have tried to explain the discrepancy between the traditional subjects of Greek temple sculpture and the iconography of the Parthenon frieze with the argument that this is not a procession taken directly from real life.[91] The nudity of many of the figures may also support this interpretation.[92] The scenes could take place in the mythic past,[93] or they could be an idealised representation of the festival,[94] part of 'a discursive environment unconcerned with realism, time, or place'.[95] The latter argument is more compelling. This impression is enhanced by the fact that the frieze shows consecutive aspects of the procession and merges them into one contemporaneous narrative.[96] Some of the procession is in brisk motion and

[84] Neils (2004) 46; Jenkins (2002) 18, 25.

[85] Neils (2001) 174, 197-198; Barringer (2014) 238.

[86] Connelly (2014) Chap. 5; Connelly (1996) 63.

[87] St Clair (2022) 219-220.

[88] St Clair (2022) 221.

[89] St Clair (2022) 235.

[90] St Clair (2022) 211.

[91] Wycherley (1978) 117; cf Martin Robertson (1975) 11.

[92] St Clair (2022) 222.

[93] Wycherley (1978) 117-118.

[94] Martin Robertson (1975) 11; Wycherley (1978) 118; Jenkins (2002) 25.

[95] St Clair (2022) 183, originally used in a different context.

[96] Wycherley (1978) 118.

some of it is not; on the west frieze, many horsemen are still preparing their horses and have not yet mounted; on the east side, the gods have taken their place and the peplos scene is already unfolding.[97] The omitted elements also support the interpretation of the procession as an idealised representation of Athena's festival.[98] In any event, we should be careful not to project too much on the ancients our modern distinction between real life and myth.[99] The obvious interpretations are, as often as not, the correct ones,[100] and the better view, at least until proof of the contrary, is that the frieze represents the Great Panathenaia.[101] If this is an unprecedented representation of the subject, it seems more appropriate to make sense of it as a novelty in sculptural architecture.[102]

Inside the Parthenon itself, pride of place was given to the colossal chryselephantine statue of Athena, another work of Pheidias.[103] Made of gold and ivory,[104] the goddess stood 12.2 m (40 ft) high in sartorial splendour with drapery stretching down to her feet, the whole resting on a wooden framework.[105] The statue is known to us from ancient, albeit not contemporary, writers.[106] Numerous smaller scale replicas have also survived in a miscellany of media, including marble, bronze, terracotta, and on coins.[107] The statue is thought to have been lost in a fire in the second or third century AD.[108]

2.3 The Parthenon over the Ages

If peace and prosperity were essential conditions for the building programme on the Acropolis, the end of peace and prosperity meant the beginning of a new, less glorious era. After the Spartan victory in the Peloponnesian war, Athens knew a period of gradual decline, marked in the fourth century BC by the rise of Philip II of

---

97 Wycherley (1978) 118.

98 Wycherley (1978) 118.

99 Neils (1996) 194.

100 Boardman (1977) 41, originally used in a different context.

101 Neils (2001) Chap. 6; Wycherley (1978) 117-118; Shear (2021) 344; Browning (2008) 6; cf Boardman (1984) 215.

102 Neils (2016) 174; Wycherley (1978) 117.

103 Plutarch, *Parallel Lives: Pericles* 13.9.

104 Pausanias, *Description of Greece* 1.24.5, 1.24.7.

105 Wycherley (1978) 124; Barringer (2014) 238; Beard (2010) 28; Jenkins (2002) 10-12. See also Plutarch, *Parallel Lives: Pericles* 13.9; Pausanias, *Description of Greece* 1.24.7.

106 Plutarch, *Parallel Lives: Pericles* 13.9; Pausanias, *Description of Greece* 1.24.5-1.24.7.

107 Barringer (2014) 238; Beard (2010) 41.

108 Beard (2010) 151; Browning (2008) 7. Contrast Wycherley (1978) 123, who writes that the cult statue was taken to Constantinople and lost. See further Jenkins (2002) 16, according to whom the statue or a later replacement was thought to have been taken to Constantinople where it was destroyed in a fire.

Macedon and later, in the second century BC, by its submission to the Romans. Sulla's sack and destruction of Athens in 86 BC was one of the darkest hours in the city's early Roman history.[109] Soon however the city started to occupy a privileged position as a cultural centre,[110] and Greek evolved into the 'twin language' of the Roman empire.[111] In the second century AD, the emperor Hadrian made a show of bestowing favours on the city, sponsoring an imperial programme of public building that surpassed anything that was granted other provincial Roman towns.[112]

Athens's fate took a new turn in the third century. In 267 AD, it was invaded by the Heruli, a Germanic people, who laid waste to the city and its monuments, reducing part of it to ruins.[113] Things did not look up when, in the century that followed, the emperor Constantine proclaimed Constantinople the new capital of the empire and Christianity its official religion.[114] In 396, a new conqueror arrived: Alaric's Gothic hordes that had invaded the empire decimating everything in their passage reached Athens, but somehow they were persuaded to enter the city peacefully, causing no visible damage to the Acropolis and its buildings.[115] It was about this time that some Athenian treasures were removed to Constantinople.[116] The *coup de grâce* to the traditions of the classical city was finally dealt in 529, when the emperor Justinian ordered the closure of the schools of Athens.[117]

It was probably sometime in the sixth century that the Parthenon was converted into a Christian church.[118] Classical temples have proved curiously adaptable and were repurposed with relative ease by the early Christians, who must have relished the prospect of thus lording it over pagan depravity.[119] The adaptation of classical monuments to Christian use has sometimes guaranteed their survival.[120] Without upkeep, unoccupied temples can become a quarry for construction materials and tend to collapse.[121] On the contrary, Christian use has something to do with ancient monuments that still stand, sometimes 'roof and all'—think of the Pantheon in Rome.[122]

---

[109] Plutarch, *Parallel Lives: Sulla* 12-14; Appian, *Mithridatic Wars* 5.30.

[110] St Clair (1998) 59.

[111] Wallace-Hadrill (2008) 83.

[112] Spawforth and Walker (1985) 92; Browning (2008) 7; Clark (2021) Chap. 8.

[113] Thompson (1959).

[114] St Clair (1998) 59.

[115] Thompson (1959) 66; Frantz (1965) 190. See also Zosimus, *New History* 4.18 and 5.5; cf Clark (2021) Chap. 9.

[116] Thompson (1959) 67, n 39.

[117] Thompson (1959) 70; St Clair (1998) 60.

[118] Beard (2010) 52; Barringer (2014) 231. On the uncertainty of the dating, see Frantz (1965) 201.

[119] Beard (2010) 52.

[120] Beard (2010) 52.

[121] Beard (2010) 52.

[122] Beard (2010) 52.

But, of course, Christian conversion also came at a cost. The scene featuring the birth of Athena on the east pediment could not have been appropriate for the new church and, in the grip of iconoclasm, its sculptures were destroyed.[123] The metope panels would have been harder to remove, so most of the east, north, and west metopes were defaced instead.[124] Yet somehow the rest of the building (the frieze, the west pediment, the metopes that ran along the south side of the temple, a metope at the north-west corner) escaped the early Christian chisel.[125]

For the next six centuries, Athens would remain a provincial outpost of the Byzantine empire, until, in 1204, it was brought to heel and surrendered to the crusaders.[126] As a long succession of catholic rulers followed (Franks, Catalans, and Florentines, with the Venetian and Ottoman threats lurking constantly in the background),[127] the Parthenon became a Roman catholic cathedral and was endowed with a newly-built tower, probably a bell tower.[128] The new church became known as Our Lady of Athens.[129]

When in the fifteenth century, the Frankish garrison on the Acropolis surrendered to the Ottomans (the year was 1458—3 years after the fall of Constantinople), the Parthenon was converted into a mosque and the tower into a minaret.[130] The Acropolis became the Ottoman garrison and the disdar (or military governor) took up residence in the Propylaea, which the earlier Florentine occupiers had turned into a Renaissance palazzo.[131] The Ottomans used the Propylaea as an ammunition store[132] and converted the Erechtheion, which had also been a church,[133] into a harem, leading one observer to remark that 'the famous porch with its line-up of caryatids [was] now doing duty as an advertisement for the delights that lay inside'.[134]

It is said that the most astonishing fact is not the progressive destruction of the Parthenon but its exceptional state of preservation, which was often remarked upon by travellers who visited the Acropolis in the seventeenth century.[135] While the interior of the temple had been altered many times and Athena's cult statue had been

[123]Beard (2010) 55; Barringer (2014) 231; cf Wycherley (1978) 121.

[124]Beard (2010) 55. In fact, it is also possible that some defacement took place under the Ottomans, since we lack detailed drawings from before the Ottoman occupation to document this history, see Beard (2010) 65-66, 74-75.

[125]Beard (2010) 55-57; Fullerton (2016) Chap. 7.

[126]St Clair (1998) 60; Beard (2010) 62; Clark (2021) Chap. 10.

[127]Beard (2010) 63; Browning (2008) 8-9.

[128]Beard (2010) 63-64.

[129]Browning (2008) 9.

[130]Beard (2010) 65, 68; Browning (2008) 9.

[131]Beard (2010) 64, 69; Browning (2008) 9.

[132]Beard (2010) 77.

[133]Frantz (1965) 201-202.

[134]Beard (2010) 69-70.

[135]St Clair (1998) 60.

lost, the building, including its roof and most of its sculptures, remained unscathed.[136] Then, in 1645, the gunpowder store in the Propylaea was struck by lightning and exploded, causing serious damage to the monument and killing the disdar's family.[137] In 1686, the Ottomans demolished the temple of Athena Nike and used the bastion as a position for artillery.[138] It was the thin end of the wedge. Things were about to get a lot worse.

In 1687, Ottoman-occupied Athens was attacked by Venetian forces that had been besieging the Acropolis under the command of Otto Wilhelm Königsmarck and formed part of a Holy league fighting against the Ottoman empire.[139] The Ottomans stored their ammunition in the Parthenon.[140] They also put there their women and children.[141] It is possible that they did so because they trusted the safety of the building,[142] or they did not believe that the Venetians would hit the Parthenon.[143] Whatever their motives, this turned out to be a singularly disastrous decision.

In September 1687, the Venetians started to lob missiles onto the ancient citadel. About 700 shell marks are said to be still visible, and several cannonballs have been found onsite.[144] Inevitably, as one of the shells hit its target, the cache of gunpowder ignited producing a huge explosion.[145] The explosion smashed the centre of the building, irreparably damaging columns, the interior of the ancient temple, parts of the frieze and sculpture, and the roof.[146] As many as 300 people were also killed in the explosion.[147]

When Francesco Morosini, the Venetian commander, entered the Acropolis, he immediately set his sights on the central sculptures of the west pediment, which had survived the attack of his army, and wished to take them home to Venice.[148] But while at work on the pediment, the cables snapped, and the statues plummeted to the ground and shattered.[149] Some fragments of what was left were taken by Morosini's subordinates—a head from one of the pedimental statues, now in the Louvre;[150] two heads from a metope—a centaur and a Lapith—now in the National Museum of

---

[136] St Clair (1998) 60.

[137] Beard (2010) 77.

[138] St Clair (1998) 61; Holliday (2005) 238-239.

[139] Beard (2010) 77; Clark (2021) Chap. 12.

[140] Beard (2010) 77.

[141] Beard (2010) 77; Clark (2021) Chap. 12.

[142] Beard (2010) 77.

[143] Clark (2021) Chap. 12.

[144] Beard (2010) 79-80; Clark (2021) Chap. 12.

[145] Beard (2010) 80; Browning (2008) 10.

[146] Neils (2001) 4; Browning (2008) 10; Beard (2010) 80, 123.

[147] Hurwit (1999) 292; Beard (2010) 68-69, 80.

[148] Beard (2010) 80.

[149] Beard (2010) 80; St Clair (1998) 61.

[150] Hamiaux (2001) 137; Pasquier (2007).

Denmark, in Copenhagen.[151] What was left behind was a 'heap of marble rubble', the debris of destruction.[152] That year, the Venetians damaged the Parthenon more than over two millennia of history had done until that moment.[153]

The Venetians' triumph was short-lived. Some months later, Morosini withdrew his troops from Athens.[154] The Ottomans returned to the Acropolis, which was now reduced to a sorry state.[155] No longer could the Parthenon function as a mosque, and it was at some moment shortly afterwards that a small mosque was erected without foundations in the middle of the ancient temple.[156]

Since the start of the Ottoman occupation of the Acropolis, the site had been converted into a military base under the sole authority of the sultan and the Ottoman government.[157] Locally, the voivode (or governor of the Acropolis) and the disdar were responsible for the site.[158] After the destruction caused by the Venetian explosion, marble fragments that had been detached and were lying on the ground were scavenged for construction materials.[159] The Ottomans were said to break apart marble blocks to access the lead clamps within and burn them into lime.[160] The lead could be used to make bullets, particularly useful in a siege,[161] and lime to make mortar. The marble ruins also served as building material when repair work was needed on the walls of the Acropolis.[162] Not only were marble slabs built into the citadel's walls, but sculptured fragments too were said to be incorporated into the fortifications and in houses in the lower town.[163]

Repurposed ancient building material or antique architectural fragments and sculpture incorporated in newer buildings were in no way unique to the Parthenon and the Acropolis. On the contrary they have been common throughout history.[164] In fact, they are so common that they have a name: *spolia*, a term to which we owe our modern English word 'spoliation'.[165] Roman builders were famous for using ancient

[151] National Museum of Denmark https://samlinger.natmus.dk/as/asset/39613 and https://samlinger.natmus.dk/as/asset/39607 (in Danish). See also St Clair (1998) 61; Clark (2021) Chap. 12.

[152] St Clair (1998) 61; Beard (2010) 80.

[153] St Clair (1998) 61.

[154] Beard (2010) 83.

[155] Beard (2010) 83.

[156] Browning (2008) 11; Beard (2010) 83.

[157] St Clair (1998) 46.

[158] St Clair (1998) 46.

[159] Dodwell (1819) 324; St Clair (1998) 47, 61; Beard (2010) 85.

[160] Dodwell (1819) 324; St Clair (1998) 61-62; Beard (2010) 85.

[161] St Clair (1998) 62.

[162] St Clair (1998) 61.

[163] Dodwell (1819) 324-325; St Clair (1998) 47; cf Connelly (2014) Chap. 3 (unnumbered page), discussing architectural fragments from the Old Temple of Athena that had been built into the north wall of the Acropolis already in antiquity.

[164] E.g. see Brilliant and Kinney (2011); Frey (2015); Brenk (1987) 103.

[165] Frey (2015) 1; Kinney (2011); Kinney (2001) 138; Kinney (1997); Brenk (1987) 103; Esch (2011).

edifices as a quarry for building material.[166] The Colosseum itself did not escape this fate and was treated as a source of travertine (a white sedimentary stone) and metal.[167] This use and reuse means that ancient Rome was 'literally *built into* the modern city that followed it', even though monuments that provided the material may have disappeared.[168] *Spolia* are also present in modern architecture.[169] Repurposing of broken marble blocks certainly took place during the Ottoman occupation of Athens. That said, the damage caused by the Ottomans during this time was exaggerated by Elgin and his party and, while there is no excuse for the destruction that did take place, some of it appears to have been invented.[170]

In the eighteenth century, the Parthenon but also other ancient monuments and antiquities were confronted with a new threat, as western travellers started to flock to Greece—some of them souvenir hunters, keen on getting their hands on antique sculptures.[171] On the Acropolis, successive voivodes and disdars could be bribed to turn a blind eye as ancient fragments were being removed.[172] Besides the pieces taken by Morosini's party, small fragments of the Parthenon removed from Athens at about this time have surfaced in Palermo (this fragment is now permanently returned to Athens),[173] Karlsruhe (now in the British Museum), Padua (now in Vienna), and Paris.[174] Other fragments were found in the Vatican Museum (now in Athens), the Society of Dilettanti (now in the British Museum), and English country houses, such as Chatsworth and Marbury Hall in Cheshire, among others.[175] A piece of the frieze was unearthed in 1902 in an Essex garden.[176] Quite how it made its way there is, frankly, anyone's guess.[177] Three choice fragments, known to have come into the possession of Richard Chandler in 1765, are lost.[178]

Yet, with the exception of the damage caused by the Venetian explosion of 1687, the Parthenon still stood largely intact. Efforts have been made to minimise Elgin's destruction of the Parthenon with the argument that he could not possibly destroy what was already a ruin. This argument was used in a parliamentary debate in

[166] Hansen (2015); Walters (2016); Kinney (2001) 138.

[167] Walters (2016); Hopkins and Beard (2006) 160-161; Gergely (2005) 47.

[168] Hopkins and Beard (2006) 161.

[169] Meier (2011).

[170] See Chap. 6, text to nn 187ff.

[171] Jenkins (1990) 97; St Clair (1998) 62.

[172] St Clair (1998) 62.

[173] This is discussed in Sect. 10.2.

[174] Jenkins (1990) 97-98; St Clair (1998) 63.

[175] Jenkins (1990) 97-98; St Clair (1998) 63; House of Commons (2000), annex IV, para 1.3.

[176] Beard (2010) 87.

[177] For an account of what likely occurred, see Beard (2010) 87. See also Ben Macintyre, 'Piecing Together the Essex Marbles Puzzle', The Times (13 July 2019).

[178] St Clair (1998) 63.

1816[179] and it is now relied upon by the British Museum.[180] But as we shall see, this is not true.

Only a few years after Elgin removed the marbles, Greece gained its independence from the Ottomans. Independence came with strings attached, including a monarchy imposed by the great powers of the time: Britain, France, and Russia.[181] Politically, the newly-minted Greek state was beholden to those powers for its future survival, while most of the Greek world was still under Ottoman dominion. For a short time, it seemed as if the Acropolis might house a royal palace, although, ultimately, in 1834, it was converted into an archaeological site.[182] It was in the same year that a new Greek law came into force, stipulating that all antiquities belong to the nation.[183] Soon afterwards, the recently-founded Greek Archaeological Service (the oldest, national archaeological agency in Europe)[184] took over the site.[185] In the years that followed, the Acropolis was progressively stripped of the traces of the Ottoman occupation: every remnant of the Ottoman garrison was gone, the mosque and minaret were demolished.[186] Alongside them, other accretions of later times, testaments to the hill's foreign occupation that now cluttered the site, had to go: what remained of the Renaissance palazzo and the Frankish tower that loomed over the Propylaea came down.[187] The Byzantine apse that had been built into the Parthenon by the Christians was also cleared away, as were Roman works.[188] Excavations onsite went down to the bedrock and it is said that the appearance of the Acropolis as we know it today is due in no small part to this campaign of 'archaeological cleansing'.[189] Finds from the Acropolis began to be displayed in the first Acropolis Museum, which was built to the east of the Parthenon in the 1860s–1870s.[190]

A major restoration started on the Acropolis in the early 1900s and continued until 1940.[191] Nikolaos Balanos, the chief engineer, was responsible for work during

---

[179] See Chap. 4, text to n 82.

[180] See Sect. 6.3.1.2.

[181] See London Protocol (22 January 1829/3 February 1830).

[182] Beard (2010) 96-99.

[183] Act of 10/22 May 1834 on scientific and technological collections, on the discovery and conservation of antiquities and the use thereof, OJ 22 of 16/28 June 1834, art 61.

[184] Hamilakis (2007) 36.

[185] Beard (2010) 101.

[186] Beard (2010) 101-102.

[187] Beard (2010) 102; Browning (2008) 13; St Clair (1998) 322. For depictions of some of these buildings that no longer exist, see Fowden (2022) 169-174.

[188] St Clair (1998) 321-322; Beard (2010) 102.

[189] Beard (2010) 102.

[190] See YSMA, 'History of Older Interventions' https://www.ysma.gr/en/restoration/history-of-older-interventions/.

[191] YSMA, 'History of Older Interventions' https://www.ysma.gr/en/restoration/history-of-older-interventions/.

this period and it is partly to him that we owe our modern image of the Parthenon.[192] However, notwithstanding that many of Balanos's 'aesthetic decisions' have been applauded, his methods have come in for criticism.[193] Balanos did not care very much about the historical record. He used the famous 'marble rubble' on the Acropolis 'as a common quarry', made little attempt to fit marble fragments in their initial position (anything that fitted would do), and he used cement to fill in missing architectural parts of the temples on the Acropolis.[194] More unfortunate still was the use of iron clamps in the marble blocks, which the wisdom of the day recommended.[195] With the passage of time, the iron oxidised and expanded, resulting in breaks in the masonry.[196] The ancient builders coated their iron clamps in lead to protect against oxidation.[197] In due course, the damage that Balanos's technique caused to the monuments was recognised, as was the impact of a new problem in the 1960s: atmospheric pollution, which was now beginning to eat into the fabric of the Parthenon.[198]

In 1975, the Greek government responded to the problems by setting up a Committee for the Conservation of the Acropolis Monuments, which has planned and supervised the conservation and restoration works on the Acropolis since then. In the most recent decades, it is aided by a twin agency, the Acropolis Restoration Service.[199] These interdisciplinary groups of experts (archaeologists, architects, civil and chemical engineers, among others) now make up this 'flagship programme of Greek archaeology' and they proceed with the utmost care and attention to detail.[200] In 1979, the original sculptures started to be moved from the site to the protected environment of the museum and to be replaced with copies.[201] (Exceptionally, a few original metopes have remained on the west side of the Parthenon, because they

[192] YSMA, 'History of Older Interventions' https://www.ysma.gr/en/restoration/history-of-older-interventions/.

[193] St Clair (1998) 328.

[194] St Clair (1998) 328; Beard (2010) 113; YSMA, 'History of Older Interventions' https://www.ysma.gr/en/restoration/history-of-older-interventions/.

[195] Stevens (1936) 79; St Clair (1998) 329; Hurwit (1999) 299; Browning (2008) 13.

[196] Hurwit (1999) 299; Beard (2010) 113.

[197] Browning (2008) 13.

[198] Beard (2010) 113; St Clair (1998) 329-330; YSMA, 'History of Older Interventions' https://www.ysma.gr/en/restoration/history-of-older-interventions/.

[199] Both are also known by the transliteration of their Greek acronyms, ESMA and YSMA respectively, and are part of the Greek Ministry of Culture and Sports, see https://www.ysma.gr/en/.

[200] Beard (2010) 114. See also ESMA https://www.ysma.gr/en/the-service/organizational-structure/esma/.

[201] E.g. in 1979, the caryatids were moved to the old Acropolis Museum; in 1989, the east metopes of the Parthenon were transferred to the museum; and in 1992-1993, the west frieze of the Parthenon was removed from the site to the museum, see YSMA, 'Timeline of Interventions' https://www.ysma.gr/en/the-service/timeline-of-interventions/; cf Beard (2010) 114; St Clair (1998) 330.

cannot be safely removed.)[202] In the mid-1980s, reconstruction work started on the Parthenon.[203] The Parthenon and the other monuments on the Acropolis have been undergoing a process of dismantling, refitting, and reconstruction.[204] Every stone is inventoried and the history of the buildings over the course of the last 3000 years is minutely documented.[205] The errors of past restorations are corrected, and Balanos's iron clamps are replaced with titanium.[206] The restored blocks are placed in their original position with titanium clamps and white cement mortar.[207] Exceptionally, where ancient parts are preserved in a very fragmentary condition, they may be replaced with new Pentelic marble, in the interests of stability.[208] The interventions conform to the international guidelines for the conservation and restoration of monuments laid down in the International Charter for the Conservation and Restoration of Monuments and Sites of 1964 (Venice Charter).[209] Accordingly, the interventions are reversible, limited to what is strictly necessary (for example, interventions are made to correct damage caused in earlier restorations, and titanium rods are used only if they cannot be avoided), and fragments are not joined together unless they come from the same architectural part.[210] The renovation project has relied on the feedback of '[e]very conceivable expert in the world'[211] and works are carried out with transparency.[212] The effects of pollution (soot deposits and black encrustations) have been removed with the use of purpose-made laser cleaning technology, which is regarded as the most appropriate.[213]

The restoration of the Acropolis monuments has now largely been completed, and the remaining work concentrates on the Parthenon and the Acropolis walls.[214] This

---

[202] E.g. see YSMA, 'The Acropolis Restoration News' (16 September 2016) https://workfun.openabekt.gr/files/items/7696322/P91.30.pdf.

[203] See YSMA, 'Parthenon: Completed Interventions' https://www.ysma.gr/en/monuments/parthenon/completed-interventions/.

[204] St Clair (1998) 330; Beard (2010) 114; YSMA, 'Methodology' https://www.ysma.gr/en/restoration/methodology/.

[205] Beard (2010) 114; St Clair (1998) 330; YSMA, 'Methodology' https://www.ysma.gr/en/restoration/methodology/.

[206] YSMA, 'Parthenon: Ongoing Interventions' https://www.ysma.gr/en/monuments/parthenon/ongoing-interventions/; Ioannidou (2012) 12; Beard (2010) 114; St Clair (1998) 330.

[207] St Clair (1998) 330; YSMA, 'Restoration' https://www.ysma.gr/en/the-service/fields-work/restoration/.

[208] YSMA, 'Methodology' https://www.ysma.gr/en/restoration/methodology/.

[209] Bouras (2012) 3; YSMA, 'Principles of Interventions' https://www.ysma.gr/en/restoration/principles-of-interventions/.

[210] St Clair (1998) 330; Browning (2008) 14; YSMA, 'Principles of Interventions' https://www.ysma.gr/en/restoration/principles-of-interventions/.

[211] Beard (2010) 114; St Clair (1998) 330.

[212] Detailed information on the completed and ongoing restoration work on the Parthenon is available on the website of the Acropolis Restoration Service, see https://www.ysma.gr/en/.

[213] See Chap. 6, text to nn 214-216.

[214] See also YSMA, 'Timeline of Interventions' https://www.ysma.gr/en/the-service/timeline-of-interventions/.

is not to say that everything is perfect. The recent addition of concrete pathways around the Acropolis to improve access for the elderly and disabled has been roundly criticised in Greek media.[215] Despite this, in their current state, the Acropolis and the Parthenon are the closest they have been to their former glory since at least the Venetian explosion of 1687 and stand as proud testaments to the long history of Athens.

2.4 The Unique Significance and Legacy of the Parthenon

> *"Beauty is truth, truth beauty" – that is all*
> *Ye Know on earth, and all ye need to know.*
> John Keats, *Ode on a Grecian Urn*
>
> *The legacy of Greece to Western art is Western art.* Bernard Williams, as quoted in Jenifer Neils, *The Parthenon Frieze* (Cambridge University Press 2001)

In his *History of the Peloponnesian War*, a war that would end with a Spartan victory over Athens, Thucydides has Pericles deliver a stirring encomium of the Athenian polity. This celebrated speech, known as the *Funeral Oration*, served the dual purpose of commemorating the dead at the end of the first year of the Peloponnesian war and boosting the morale of Pericles' compatriots who faced continuing warfare. Shot through with hindsight, it is a moving eulogy to the glory that Athens was. With their halcyon days behind them, embattled Athenians heard about the values that their city represented: democracy, this system that favours the many instead of the few, justice, equality, freedom, a balanced society, cultural refinement, munificence; theirs was a city that served as an example to others.[216] This was stirring stuff—praise pronounced during a war.

Certainly, as some have been quick to point out, Athenian democracy was not perfect, and some aspects of the classical Athenian polity are deeply flawed by today's standards. The Parthenon building programme was financed, at least in part, with the proceeds of empire.[217] Athenian society relied on the labour of slaves, and voting rights were restricted to Athenian-born men.[218] Yet in fifth century BC, Athens was the most advanced political system in existence with no equivalent in

[215] Nick Squires, 'Concrete Pathways Built around the Parthenon Condemned as an Eyesore by Critics in Greece', The Telegraph (2 June 2021).

[216] Thucydides, *History of the Peloponnesian War* 2.36-2.41.

[217] But cf text to nn 17-22.

[218] E.g. Beard (2010) 39-40; Neil MacGregor, 'The Whole World in Our Hands', The Guardian (24 July 2004). It is somewhat ironic that MacGregor should indirectly try to discredit the claim for the marbles' return with the argument that Athens was 'an imperial maritime power', given that the

the world. If we associate Athens with words such as architecture, logic, philosophy, politics, and theatre, democracy has the best claim to be an Athenian coinage.[219] It was Athens that first sought to tackle the great conundrums of how to reconcile 'power with justice, social cohesion with individual freedom, and the pursuit of excellence with equality of opportunity'.[220] Neighbouring Sparta, despite the virtue of its supposed egalitarianism and respect for women,[221] was a military city-state. We remember it for the sacrifice of Leonidas and his 300 at the Battle of Thermopylae during the second Persian invasion, for its victory in the Peloponnesian war, and for its erstwhile queen, Helen of Troy, 'the face that launched a thousand ships', and we associate it with words like 'spartan' and 'laconic'. But it is not of Sparta that we think, when we think of democracy, politics, philosophy, science, or art. It is of Athens.[222] The Parthenon was a product of this society. Culmination of Greek architecture and the apex of high classical art,[223] it has come to represent the classical ideal. Not merely a building, the Parthenon is a symbol.

Its artistic legacy was immediately felt from contemporary art in fifth-century Athens, to Roman art and later the Italian Renaissance.[224] When the marbles arrived in London, they contributed to promoting the neo-classical style.[225] The Parthenon has been replicated many a time. Replicas include full-scale concrete buildings, from the Valhalla in the vicinity of Regensburg in Germany to neo-classical buildings around the world, including US state buildings, banks and museums.[226] In Nashville, Tennessee, a replica of the Parthenon was originally constructed as a temporary pavilion for the 1897 Tennessee Centennial Exposition, but it remained in place long after the event was over and, in the 1920s, it was rebuilt in concrete.[227] In 1990, a 13-m-high recreation of what would have been the chryselephantine statue of Athena in the original Parthenon was added to it.[228]

In contrast with the United States, where the Parthenon inspired both public and private buildings, in Europe features of the Parthenon and other Acropolis buildings were replicated in public monuments and buildings.[229] The façade of the British

---

Parthenon marbles in the British Museum today are a result of British imperialism. For a similar reaction, see O'Neill (2004) 192-193.

[219] Browning (2008) 2-3. For a discussion of Athenian democracy, see Jones (1957); Kallet (2005) 45-51.

[220] Browning (2008) 2-3.

[221] Davies (2017); Millender (2017); Pomeroy (2002).

[222] See further Thucydides, *History of the Peloponnesian War* 1.10.2, famously predicting how Athens and Sparta would be remembered by future generations.

[223] Wycherley (1978) 105; Browning (2008) 6.

[224] Neils (2001) 203.

[225] Neils (2001) 203.

[226] Beard (2010) 5-7; St Clair (1998) 273-275.

[227] Beard (2010) 7.

[228] Beard (2010) 7.

[229] St Clair (1998) 273-274.

Museum, designed in the Greek Revival style is inspired by the Parthenon,[230] as is the neo-classical La Madeleine church in Paris. The Brandenburg Gate in Berlin was partly modelled on drawings of the Propylaea published in James Stuart and Nicholas Revett's book.[231] That said, the Parthenon frieze also provided a motif for Regency wallpaper.[232] The most recent recreation of the Parthenon is the 2022 Temple of Boom in the National Gallery of Victoria (NGV) Garden in Melbourne, Australia. Built to a third scale of the original temple and covered in colourful artwork, the building is meant to serve as an outdoor venue for music and other performances and as a community meeting place.[233]

In 1987, the United Nations Educational, Scientific and Cultural Organization (UNESCO), which chose the Parthenon as its emblem, inscribed the Acropolis on the World Heritage List.[234]

2.5 The New Acropolis Museum

If the Parthenon marbles in the British Museum returned to Athens today, they would be placed in the new Acropolis Museum, which opened its doors in June 2009.[235] Designed by Bernard Tschumi with the collaboration of Michael Photiades, the museum is situated about 300 m (almost 1000 ft) southeast of the Acropolis and stands in the shadow of the Parthenon, just a stone's throw away.[236] The Parthenon Gallery on the top floor houses the temple's sculpture remaining in Greece and offers a panoramic view of the Parthenon itself. The glass walls allow natural light to flood the exhibition space and the gallery rotates from the rest of the building so as to be aligned with the Parthenon.[237] The gallery is arranged around a rectangular core, whose dimensions are the same as the Parthenon's cella.[238] The original sculptured marbles are joint with plaster copies of the marbles in the British Museum and in the

[230] Kelly (2016) 509. The fact that the design of the British Museum drew on the Parthenon was also evoked by the ever-faithful Hamilton in a letter to Elgin, see St Clair (1998) 274.

[231] St Clair (1998) 273.

[232] St Clair (1998) 271.

[233] NGV, 'Temple of Boom Unveiled at NGV International' (Media release, 22 November 2022); Nathan Dunne, 'From Athens with Love: The NGV's Dizzying Recreation of the Parthenon', The Guardian (21 November 2022).

[234] UNESCO, 'Acropolis, Athens' https://whc.unesco.org/en/list/404/.

[235] See Acropolis Museum, 'The Museum Building' https://www.theacropolismuseum.gr/en/museum-building.

[236] Acropolis Museum, 'The Museum Building' https://www.theacropolismuseum.gr/en/museum-building.

[237] See Acropolis Museum, 'The Parthenon Gallery' https://www.theacropolismuseum.gr/en/exhibit-halls/parthenon-gallery.

[238] See Acropolis Museum, 'The Parthenon Gallery' https://www.theacropolismuseum.gr/en/exhibit-halls/parthenon-gallery. See also http://www.tschumi.com/projects/2/#.

handful of other museums that hold Parthenon fragments outside Greece.[239] They are placed looking outward as they did on the Parthenon itself.[240]

2.6 Conclusion

The chapter has offered a brief overview of the history of the Parthenon, from its inception to modern times. It has considered its iconography, its significance, and the new Acropolis Museum. The chapter has not considered one particular aspect of the Parthenon's decorative scheme, its polychromy, which we shall have the opportunity to discuss in Chap. 6. After this short narrative, we are now ready to turn to Elgin and the removal of the marbles.

References

Apollodorus, *Library*

Appian, *Mithridatic Wars*

Aristotle, *Athenian Constitution*

E Badian, 'The Peace of Callias' (1987) 107 Journal of Hellenic Studies 1

Judith M Barringer, *The Art and Archaeology of Ancient Greece* (Cambridge University Press 2014, reprinted 2020)

Mary Beard, *The Parthenon* (Profile Books 2010)

Alec Blamire, 'Athenian Finance, 454-404 BC' (2001) 70 (1) Hesperia 99

John Boardman, 'The Parthenon Frieze, a Closer Look' (1999) 2 Revue archéologique 305

John Boardman, 'The Parthenon Frieze' in Ernst Berger (ed), Parthenon-Kongress Basel (vol 1, von Zabern 1984)

John Boardman, 'The Parthenon Frieze—Another View' in Ursula Höckmann and Antje Krug (eds), *Festschrift für Frank Brommer* (von Zabern 1977)

Beat Brenk, '*Spolia* from Constantine to Charlemagne: Aesthetics versus Ideology' (1987) 41 Dumbarton Oaks Papers 103

Richard Brilliant and Dale Kinney (eds), *Reuse Value:* Spolia *and Appropriation in Art and Architecture from Constantine to Sherrie Levine* (Taylor and Francis 2011)

Robert Browning, 'The Parthenon in History' in Christopher Hitchens, *The Parthenon Marbles* (first publication 1987, Verso 2008)

Charalampos Bouras, 'Thirty-five Years of Restoration of the Acropolis Monuments' in Charalambos Bouras, Maria Ioannidou, and Ian Jenkins (eds), *Acropolis Restored* (British Museum 2012)

Paul Cartledge, *After Thermopylae: The Oath of Plataea and the End of the Graeco-Persian Wars* (Oxford University Press 2013)

Bruce Clark, *Athens: City of Wisdom* (Head of Zeus 2021)

Joan Breton Connelly, *The Parthenon Enigma: A Journey into Legend* (Head of Zeus 2014)

---

[239] Acropolis Museum, 'The Parthenon Gallery' https://www.theacropolismuseum.gr/en/exhibit-halls/parthenon-gallery.

[240] Peter Aspden, 'A Manifesto for the Parthenon Marbles', Financial Times (29 November 2008).

Joan Breton Connelly, 'Parthenon and *Parthenoi*: A Mythological Interpretation of the Parthenon Frieze' (1996) 100 (1) American Journal of Archaeology 53

Philip Davies, 'Equality and Distinction within the Spartiate Community' in Anton Powell (ed), *A Companion to Sparta* (John Wiley and Sons 2017)

Susan Deacy and Alexandra Villing, 'What Was the Colour of Athena's Aegis?' (2009) 129 Journal of Hellenic Studies 111

William Bell Dinsmoor, 'The Hekatompedon on the Athenian Acropolis' (1947) 51 (2) American Journal of Archaeology 109

William Bell Dinsmoor, 'The Date of the Older Parthenon' (1934) 38 (3) American Journal of Archaeology 408

Diodorus Siculus, *Library of History*

Edward Dodwell, *A Classical and Topographical Tour through Greece* (vol 1, Rodwell and Martin 1819)

Page duBois, *Centaurs and Amazons: Women and the Pre-History of the Great Chain of Being* (University of Michigan Press 1991)

Arnold Esch, 'On the Reuse of Antiquity: The Perspectives of the Archaeologist and of the Historian' in Richard Brilliant and Dale Kinney (eds), *Reuse Value:* Spolia *and Appropriation in Art and Architecture from Constantine to Sherrie Levine* (Taylor and Francis 2011)

Richard A Etlin, 'The Parthenon in the Modern Era' in Jenifer Neils (ed), *The Parthenon: From Antiquity to the Present* (Cambridge University Press 2005, reprinted 2010)

Moses Finley, 'The Fifth-Century Athenian Empire: A Balance-Sheet' in Polly Low (ed), *The Athenian Empire* (Edinburgh University Press 2008)

Elizabeth Key Fowden, 'Portraits of Ottoman Athens from Martin Crusius to Strategos Makriyannis' in Elizabeth Key Fowden and others (eds), *Cities as Palimpsests? Responses to Antiquity in Eastern Mediterranean Urbanism* (Oxbow Books 2022)

Alison Frantz, 'From Paganism to Christianity in the Temples of Athens' (1965) 19 Dumbarton Oaks Papers 185

Jon M Frey, Spolia *in Fortifications and the Common Builder in Late Antiquity* (Brill 2015)

Mark D Fullerton, *Greek Sculpture* (John Wiley and Sons 2016)

Rachel Gergely, 'Colosseum (AD 80)' in Melanie Grunow Sobocinski and others (eds), *Detroit and Rome: Building on the Past* (University of Michigan 2005)

Adalberto Giovannini, 'The Parthenon, the Treasury of Athena and the Tribute of the Allies' in Polly Low (ed), *The Athenian Empire* (Edinburgh University Press 2008)

Marianne Hamiaux, *Les sculptures grecques: (I) Des origines à la fin du IVe siècle avant J-C* (Louvre 2001)

Yannis Hamilakis, *The Nation and Its Ruins: Antiquity, Archaeology, and National Imagination in Greece* (Oxford University Press 2007)

Richard Hamilton, 'Panathenaic Amphoras' in Jenifer Neils (ed), *Worshipping Athena: Panathenaia and Parthenon* (University of Wisconsin Press 1996)

NGL Hammond, 'The Origins and the Nature of the Athenian Alliance of 478/7 BC' (1967) 87 Journal of Hellenic Studies 41

Maria Fabricius Hansen, *The* Spolia *Churches of Rome: Recycling Antiquity in the Middle Ages* (tr Barbara J Haveland, Aarhus University Press 2015)

Diane Harris, *The Treasures of the Parthenon and Erechtheion* (Oxford University Press 1995)

Herodotus, *The Histories*

BH Hill, 'The Older Parthenon' (1912) 16 (4) American Journal of Archaeology 535

Peter J Holliday, 'Early Photography and the Reception of Classical Antiquity: The Case of the Temple of Athena Nike' in Judith M Barringer and Jeffrey M Hurwit (eds), *Periklean Athens and Its Legacy: Problems and Perspectives* (University of Texas Press 2005)

R Ross Holloway, The Archaic Acropolis and the Parthenon Frieze (1966) 48 (2) The Art Bulletin 223

Bernard Holtzmann, *L'Acropole d'Athènes: Monuments, cultes et histoire du sanctuaire d'Athéna Polias* (Picard 2003)

Keith Hopkins and Mary Beard, *The Colosseum* (Profile Books 2006)
House of Commons, 'Culture, Media and Sport – Minutes of Evidence' (Culture, Media and Sport Committee Publications 8 June 2000)
Jeffrey M Hurwit, 'The Parthenon and the Temple of Zeus at Olympia' in Judith M Barringer and Jeffrey M Hurwit (eds), *Periklean Athens and Its Legacy: Problems and Perspectives* (University of Texas Press 2005)
Jeffrey M Hurwit, *The Athenian Acropolis: History, Mythology, and Archaeology from the Neolithic Era to the Present* (Cambridge University Press 1999)
Maria Ioannidou, 'Research and Technology' in Charalambos Bouras, Maria Ioannidou, and Ian Jenkins (eds), *Acropolis Restored* (British Museum 2012)
Ian Jenkins, 'The Parthenon Frieze and Perikles' Cavalry of a Thousand' in Judith M Barringer and Jeffrey M Hurwit (eds), *Periklean Athens and Its Legacy: Problems and Perspectives* (University of Texas Press 2005)
Ian Jenkins, *The Parthenon Frieze* (British Museum 2002, reprinted 2019)
Ian Jenkins, 'Acquisition and Supply of Casts of the Parthenon Sculptures by the British Museum, 1835-1939' (1990) 85 The Annual of the British School at Athens 89
AHM Jones, *Athenian Democracy* (Basil Blackwell and Mott 1957, reprinted 1969)
Lisa Kallet, 'The Origins of the Athenian Economic *Arche*' (2013) 133 Journal of Hellenic Studies 43
Lisa Kallet, 'Wealth, Power, and Prestige: Athens at Home and Abroad' in Jenifer Neils, *The Parthenon: From Antiquity to the Present* (Cambridge University Press 2005, reprinted 2010)
Jason M Kelly, 'The Reception of Greek Architecture in Eighteenth Century Britain' in Margaret M Miles (ed), *A Companion to Greek Architecture* (John Wiley and Sons 2016)
Dale Kinney, 'Introduction' in Richard Brilliant and Dale Kinney (eds), *Reuse Value:* Spolia *and Appropriation in Art and Architecture from Constantine to Sherrie Levine* (Taylor and Francis 2011)
Dale Kinney, 'Roman Architectural Spolia' (2001) 145 (2) Proceedings of the American Philosophical Society 138
Dale Kinney, '*Spolia. Damnatio* and *renovatio memoriae*' (1997) 42 Memoirs of the American Academy in Rome 117
Manolis Korres, *From Pentelicon to the Parthenon* (Melissa 2001)
Manolis Korres, 'The Architecture of the Parthenon' in Panayotis Tournikiotis (ed), *The Parthenon and its Impact in Modern Times* (Melissa 1994)
Patricia A Marx, 'The Introduction of the Gorgoneion to the Shield and Aegis of Athena and the Question of Endoios' (1993) 2 Revue archéologique 227
Hans-Rudolf Meier, '*Spolia* in Contemporary Architecture: Searching for Ornament and Place' in Richard Brilliant and Dale Kinney (eds), *Reuse Value:* Spolia *and Appropriation in Art and Architecture from Constantine to Sherrie Levine* (Taylor and Francis 2011)
Ellen G Millender, 'Spartan Women' in Anton Powell (ed), *A Companion to Sparta* (John Wiley and Sons 2017)
Blaise Nagy, 'Athenian Officials on the Parthenon Frieze' (1992) 96 (1) American Journal of Archaeology 55
Jenifer Neils, 'Color and Carving: Architectural Decoration in Mainland Greece' in Margaret M Miles (ed), *A Companion to Greek Architecture* (John Wiley and Sons 2016)
Jenifer Neils, 'Classical Moments—Time in the Parthenon Frieze' in Michael B Cosmopoulos (ed), *The Parthenon and its Sculptures* (Cambridge University Press 2004)
Jenifer Neils, *The Parthenon Frieze* (Cambridge University Press 2001)
Jenifer Neils, 'Reconfiguring the Gods on the Parthenon Frieze (1999) 81 (1) The Art Bulletin 6
Jenifer Neils, 'Pride, Pomp, and Circumstance: The Iconography of Procession' in Jenifer Neils (ed), *Worshipping Athena: Panathenaia and Parthenon* (University of Wisconsin Press 1996)
Mark O'Neill, 'Enlightenment Museums: Universal or Merely Global?' (2004) 2 (3) Museum and Society 190

Robin Osborne, 'The Viewing and Obscuring of the Parthenon Frieze' (1987) 107 Journal of Hellenic Studies 98
Ovid, *Metamorphoses*
Alain Pasquier, 'La « tête Laborde » rendue à elle-même' (2007) 151 (1) Comptes rendus des séances de l'Académie des Inscriptions et Belles-Lettres 125
Pausanias, *Description of Greece*
Francis Cranmer Penrose, *An Investigation of the Principles of Athenian Architecture* (2nd edn, Macmillan 1888)
Plato, *Euthyphro*
Plutarch, *Parallel Lives: Aristides*
Plutarch, *Parallel Lives: Pericles*
Plutarch, *Parallel Lives: Sulla*
Plutarch, *Parallel Lives: Themistocles*
Sarah B Pomeroy, *Spartan Women* (Oxford University Press 2002)
PJ Rhodes, *A History of the Classical Greek World: 478-323 BC* (Wiley-Blackwell 2010)
PJ Rhodes, 'The Delian League to 449 BC' in David M Lewis and others (eds), *The Cambridge Ancient History* (Cambridge University Press 1992)
Brunilde Sismondo Ridgway, *Prayers in Stone: Greek Architectural Sculpture* c *600-100 BCE* (University of California Press 1999)
DS Robertson, *Greek and Roman Architecture* (2nd edn, Cambridge University Press 1943, reprinted 2004)
Martin Robertson, *The Parthenon Frieze* (Oxford University Press 1975)
Susan I Rotroff, 'The Parthenon Frieze and the Sacrifice to Athena' (1977) 81 (3) American Journal of Archaeology 379
HA Shapiro, 'Democracy and Imperialism: The Panathenaia in the Age of Perikles' in Jenifer Neils (ed), *Worshipping Athena: Panathenaia and Parthenon* (University of Wisconsin Press 1996)
Julia L Shear, *Serving Athena: The Festival of the Panathenaia and the Construction of Athenian Identities* (Cambridge University Press 2021)
AJ Spawforth and Susan Walker, 'The World of the Panhellenion (I) Athens and Eleusis' (1985) 75 Journal of Roman Studies 78
William St Clair, *The Classical Parthenon: Recovering the Strangeness of the Ancient World* (Open Book Publishers 2022)
William St Clair, *Lord Elgin and the Marbles* (Oxford University Press 1967, 1998, reprinted 2003)
Zoe Stamatopoulou, 'Weaving Titans for Athena: Euripides and the Panathenaic Peplos (*HEC* 466-74 and *IT* 218-24)' (2012) 62 (1) Classical Quarterly 72
Gorham Phillips Stevens, *The Setting of the Periclean Parthenon* (Hesperia: Supplement 3, American School of Classical Studies at Athens 1940)
Gorham Phillips Stevens, 'The Periclean Entrance Court of the Acropolis of Athens' (1936) 5 (4) Hesperia 30
Strabo, *Geography*
James Stuart and Nicholas Revett, *The Antiquities of Athens* (vol 2, John Nichols 1787)
Homer A Thompson, 'Athenian Twilight: AD 267-600' (1959) 49 Journal of Roman Studies 61
Thucydides, *History of the Peloponnesian War*
Marcus Vitruvius Pollio, *The Ten Books on Architecture*
Shelley Wachsmann, 'Panathenaic Ships: The Iconographic Evidence' (2012) 81 Hesperia 237
Andrew Wallace-Hadrill, *Rome's Cultural Revolution* (Cambridge University Press 2008)
Michael J Walters, 'Reviving Antiquity with Granite: Spolia and the Development of Roman Renaissance Architecture' (2016) 59 Architectural History 149
Susan Woodford, 'More Light on Old Walls: The Theseus of the Centauromachy in the Theseion' (1974) 94 Journal of Hellenic Studies 158
Richard Ernest Wycherley, *The Stones of Athens* (Princeton University Press 1978)
Zosimus, *New History*

Chapter 3
Elgin and the Marbles

3.1 Introduction

In July 1801, the month when his men prised the first metope off the Parthenon, Elgin described to Lusieri his plans for decorating his ancestral seat in Scotland.[1] The matter of his house, he confided, was on his mind constantly, and he wished to place there the 'various things' that Lusieri might be able to obtain for him.[2] He would embellish the hall with columns (the cellars underneath had been 'vaulted expressly' for this reason) and hoped that Lusieri would be able to procure for him marble columns worked in Greece.[3] He wanted, he said, to 'collect as much marble as possible'.[4] Besides the hall, marble was needed in other rooms, for 'one can easily multiply ornaments of beautiful marble without overdoing it; and nothing, truly, is so beautiful and also independent of changes of fashion'.[5] These thoughts, he added, 'only apply to unworked marble. You do not need any prompting from me to know the value that is attached to a sculptured marble, or *historic* piece'.[6]

His other agent in Greece, Hunt, had also been on the lookout for antiquities for Elgin. When at Mycenae, he toyed with the idea of removing the Lion Gate but decided with regret that it was impracticable to transport.[7] The Lion Gate was spared. Then in July 1801, Hunt cast a predatory eye on the Erechtheion with its porch of caryatids,[8] draped female figures that serve as architectural supports in the place of columns for the entablature above their heads. If only Elgin could send to Athens 'a

[1] Elgin to Lusieri (10 July 1801), cited in Smith (1916) 192.

[2] Elgin to Lusieri (10 July 1801), cited in Smith (1916) 192.

[3] Elgin to Lusieri (10 July 1801), cited in Smith (1916) 192.

[4] Elgin to Lusieri (10 July 1801), cited in Smith (1916) 192.

[5] Elgin to Lusieri (10 July 1801), cited in Smith (1916) 192.

[6] Elgin to Lusieri (10 July 1801), cited in Smith (1916) 192 (emphasis added).

[7] St Clair (1998) 101.

[8] Hunt to Elgin (31 July 1801), cited in Smith (1916) 196.

C. Titi, *The Parthenon Marbles and International Law*,
https://doi.org/10.1007/978-3-031-26357-6_3

large Man of War', Hunt wrote, 'that beautiful little model of ancient art might be transported wholly to England'.[9]

Elgin did write immediately to George Keith Elphinstone, naval commander-in-chief for the Mediterranean, to ask for a warship to remove what he called 'a most valuable piece of architecture at my disposal'.[10] He added with glee: 'Bonaparte has not got such a thing from all his thefts in Italy.'[11] But no ship was available, and the damage to the Erechtheion was limited for the time being to a block of the cornice being taken down,[12] although 2 years later a caryatid from the eastern portico would eventually be hacked out and added to Elgin's collection.[13] Elgin's home furnishing and decoration plans were the fateful ingredients that, slowly but surely, masterminded the removal of the Acropolis marbles. Not for Elgin the altruism of a saviour, with which he was later credited.

This chapter considers the chain of events that led to the removal of the Parthenon marbles and other antiquities from the Acropolis, it examines the question of whether Elgin had permission to remove the marbles in the first place or whether he obtained ex post facto permission. It argues that Elgin never had permission to remove the marbles, whether prior or ex post, and that possession of the marbles was not transferred to him through a legal transaction but by means of bribes. The narrative considers the destruction caused by the removal of the marbles and their perilous journey at sea, including the *Mentor* shipwreck, which resulted in a large consignment of marbles lying on the bottom of the sea, some for two long years, before they were eventually salvaged. Finally, the chapter turns to the criticism of Elgin by his contemporaries for the removal of the marbles and closes with the marbles' first years in London, before they were sold to the UK government.

3.2 A Timeline of Looting

Elgin's men arrived at Athens in the summer of 1800 but did not gain access to the Acropolis until the following spring, except to make drawings, on payment of a daily fee of five guineas.[14] Their work must not have been easy, for they were confronted with insults from the soldiers on the Acropolis and the local officials, including the disdar (the military governor of the Acropolis) and his son,[15] something for which the latter would duly pay. During that time, Elgin's men spent more time working on

[9]Hunt to Elgin (31 July 1801), cited in Smith (1916) 196.

[10]Elgin to Keith, cited in Keith (1927) 406.

[11]Elgin to Keith, cited in Keith (1927) 406.

[12]Smith (1916) 196.

[13]Smith (1916) 256.

[14]Select Committee (1816) 33; St Clair (1998) 66, 91.

[15]St Clair (1998) 91.

buildings in the lower city of Athens.[16] *Formatori* (or makers of casts) were employed to work on the Theseum (temple of Hephaestus) and the monument of Lysicrates,[17] but, when they began preparing to take mouldings of the Parthenon, the disdar, who had been given a warning by the cadi (or judge) and the voivode (the governor of the Acropolis and the disdar's superior),[18] barred their access to the Acropolis, and Elgin's agents found that even bribes were no use.[19] The disdar became adamant: nothing but a firman would induce him to let Elgin's men return to the Acropolis.[20] Lusieri explained as much in a letter he wrote Elgin in May 1801, urging him to obtain a firman that would allow his men to continue their comings and goings and other business without interference.[21] His recommendation was backed by Hunt, who, in July 1801, drafted a memorandum, according to which the men at Athens 'in the service of the British Ambassador Extraordinary' should be given free access to the Acropolis and be allowed 'to draw and model with plaster', 'to erect scaffolding, and to dig where they may wish to discover the ancient foundations', and 'to take away any sculptures or inscriptions which do not interfere with the works or walls of the Citadel'.[22]

It appears that on or about 8 July 1801 Elgin obtained a letter from officials in Constantinople relating to the work of his artisans in Athens.[23] The letter reflected the wording of Hunt's memorandum and related to the removal of inscriptions and some pieces of stone with 'figures' that had been lying in the rubble, on condition that such removal should not interfere with the Acropolis works and walls.[24] Hunt himself appears to have taken this Ottoman letter to Athens in mid-July along with an Italian translation.[25] This Italian translation was the one relied upon to prepare the English translation appended to the 1816 parliamentary select committee report. Hunt did not arrive in Athens empty-handed. Besides the letters, he brought with him numerous presents, including chandeliers, telescopes, arms, jewellery, and cloth.[26]

Hunt lost no time in pressing his advantage. No sooner was he in Athens than he made a beeline for the voivode's residence and handed over the 'letters' (no mention of a 'firman' in Hunt's own description of the event).[27] When the voivode had read the 'letters' and understood Hunt's determination, he became extremely submissive.[28] He assured Hunt that he was 'mortified' to learn that the disdar 'had presumed

[16]Select Committee (1816) 33.

[17]Lusieri to Elgin (16 May 1801), cited in Smith (1916) 185-186; see also Smith (1916) 182.

[18]Smith (1916) 179, 195.

[19]Lusieri to Elgin (16 May 1801), cited in Smith (1916) 185-186; St Clair (1998) 66.

[20]Lusieri to Elgin (16 May 1801), cited in Smith (1916) 185-186.

[21]Lusieri to Elgin (16 May 1801), cited in Smith (1916) 185-186.

[22]Smith (1916) 190.

[23]Rudenstine (2001) 1860; St Clair (1998) 91.

[24]For the specific permissions of the 'firman', see text to nn 94ff.

[25]St Clair (1998) 91.

[26]St Clair (1998) 91.

[27]Hunt to Elgin (31 July 1801), cited in Smith (1916) 195-196. See also St Clair (1998) 45.

[28]Hunt to Elgin (31 July 1801), cited in Smith (1916) 195-196.

to treat any Englishman with disrespect' or exact cash 'on any pretext'.[29] When Hunt wished to see the disdar's son, he was initially told that he was absent. But after Hunt insisted that he must get to the bottom of who was to blame for the insults, etc., the disdar's son was made to come in.[30] Hunt must have felt a certain satisfaction recounting the incident to Elgin, describing how 'the poor miscreant', now entirely at Hunt's mercy, 'came in barefooted and trembling'.[31] The voivode announced that the disdar's son would be exiled but when, with apparent magnanimity, Hunt interceded on his behalf 'on promise of his future good conduct', he was forgiven.[32] The meeting did not conclude before the Ottoman officials made a further show of submission accompanied with threats against the disdar's son, in case of a future lapse.[33] The irony of this incident must not be lost on anyone: everything that had been conceded to Elgin's men on the Acropolis was by means of bribes to the disdar.[34] It was the disdar who had allowed them to work on the Acropolis and he barred their access only when he was 'threatened' by the voivode and the cadi.[35] Now the tables had been turned, and the voivode pretended to lay the blame on the disdar.

After this unexpected turn of events, Elgin's prospects looked up. Hunt's meeting with the voivode concluded with the firm assurance that the Acropolis would now be open to all Englishmen from sunrise to sunset and that Elgin's artisans could 'model, dig, or carry away whatever does not interfere with the works'.[36] Local labourers were employed, some of them Greeks ready to throw in their lot with the paymaster[37] (an argument that would later be used to justify Elgin's actions and the indifference of the 'natives'), and men from a ship in the port of Piraeus were brought to oversee the work of the labourers.[38] With the assistance of these labourers, Elgin's men collected every inscription lying around the Acropolis and began zealously to excavate.[39] Then on 31 July 1801, the critical decision was made to approach the Parthenon.[40] The first metope was removed on that very day.[41] A second metope was removed on the following day.[42] Three weeks later, the two

29 Hunt to Elgin (31 July 1801), cited in Smith (1916) 195-196.

30 Hunt to Elgin (31 July 1801), cited in Smith (1916) 195-196.

31 Hunt to Elgin (31 July 1801), cited in Smith (1916) 195-196.

32 Hunt to Elgin (31 July 1801), cited in Smith (1916) 195-196.

33 Hunt to Elgin (31 July 1801), cited in Smith (1916) 195-196.

34 Lusieri to Elgin (16 May 1801), cited in Smith (1916) 185-186.

35 Lusieri to Elgin (16 May 1801), cited in Smith (1916) 185-186.

36 Hunt to Elgin (31 July 1801), cited in Smith (1916) 195-196.

37 Select Committee (1816) 144.

38 St Clair (1998) 92.

39 St Clair (1998) 92.

40 Smith (1916) 196; St Clair (1998) 92.

41 Hunt to Elgin (31 July 1801), cited in Smith (1916) 196.

42 Hunt to Elgin (31 July 1801), cited in Smith (1916) 196.

metopes were unceremoniously boarded onto a ship and sent away.[43] The incident was described by Hunt himself in his testimony to the parliamentary select committee in the following terms:

> I asked [the voivode] permission to detach from the Parthenon the most perfect, and, as it appeared to me, the most beautiful Metope: I obtained that permission, and acted upon it immediately: I had one carefully packed and put on board a Ragusan ship, which was under my orders, from which it was transferred to a frigate, and sent to England. The facility with which this had been obtained, induced Lord Elgin to apply for permission to lower other groupes (*sic*), of sculpture from the Parthenon,[44] which he did to a considerable extent, not only on the Parthenon, but on other edifices in the Acropolis.[45]

The local Ottoman officials continued to genuflect to Elgin's party, and the latter were able to carry on with excavations and removals in the weeks and months that followed. Elgin and his retinue did not arrive in Athens until the following year, in April 1802. For the duration of Elgin's stay in Athens, two British warships remained in port.[46] Many of the marbles had already been packed. Some, as we have seen, had already sailed. Elgin had never yet seen these. In the summer and autumn months of 1802, two more metopes and six slabs of the frieze were removed from the building.[47] A further slab of the frieze was found in excavations.[48] Four slabs of the frieze of the temple of Athena Nike were removed from the fortifications of the Acropolis into which they had been built.[49]

Elgin had given precise instructions that he should have from the Acropolis 'examples in the actual object, of each thing, and architectural ornament – of each cornice, each frieze, each capital – of the decorated ceilings, of the fluted columns – specimens of the different architectural orders, and of the variant forms of the orders – of metopes and the like', as well as 'everything in the way of sculpture, medals and curious marbles that can be discovered'.[50] He returned to Constantinople in early September,[51] but the matter of his collection continued to occupy him greatly. No sooner was he gone than he wrote again to Lusieri:

> you know too well the objects that I desire to make it necessary to repeat them here. But one reflection that I am led to make from my observations in the islands and in Asia is that the least little things from Athens are invaluable. If I had still three years, and all the resources I have had, I would employ them all at Athens. I beg you to convince yourself fully of this impression – especially in relation to objects that can be transported. The first on the list are

---

[43] Hunt to Elgin (3 September 1801), cited in Smith (1916) 196; Lusieri to Elgin (4 September 1801), cited in Smith (1916) 200.

[44] This statement appears to be inaccurate. Hunt was probably thinking of his own informal requests to the voivode. His description is also limited to the removal and shipment of the first metope only.

[45] Select Committee (1816) 142.

[46] St Clair (1998) 107.

[47] St Clair (1998) 110.

[48] St Clair (1998) 110.

[49] St Clair (1998) 110.

[50] Elgin to Lusieri (23 December 1801), cited in Smith (1916) 207.

[51] St Clair (1998) 109.

> the metopes, the bas-reliefs, and the remains of the statues that can still be found. In particular I mention the figures on the pediment of the Parthenon, on the side towards the Propylaea – or at least the figure of the man – as many metopes as you can obtain – to pursue as far as you can the digging all round the temple, to find some further fragments of frieze, and some ornaments. Would it be permissible to speak of a Caryatid? I leave the decision to you, if you have the possibility. Do not forget some capitals on the Acropolis. Nowhere in the world, where we have seen Doric capitals, have we felt the impression that these fine shapes do not fail to produce. I beg you therefore to put some on board ship. To sum up, the slightest object from the Acropolis is a jewel – all the details of the different orders of Architecture. Further, some fragments of Minerva Polias – a capital from these if possible.[52]

Elgin had his will. His artisans collected examples of every architectural detail on the Acropolis, including cornices, capitals, bases, and fragments of columns from the Parthenon, the Propylaea, the temple of Athena Nike, and the Erechtheion.[53] Had Elgin been able to remove the remaining metopes, frieze, and pedimental sculptures, he would have done so. To obtain more of the Parthenon would cause other parts of the temple to collapse.[54] St Clair remarked that to destroy the remaining part of the surviving building further in order to take away some architectural details highlights the 'absurdity of what later became the "saving" claim,[55] as was clear at the time, but evidently Elgin and his agents had intended to go ahead with the help of further "gifts"'.[56] Already, as a result of the removals that did take place, the part of the building that was left standing faced serious stability issues, as will be discussed in Chap. 6.[57]

In January 1803, arrangements were made for Elgin's return home.[58] Lusieri stayed behind in Athens to continue with the removals, but in early 1804, he wrote to Elgin with bad news.[59] He must now cease work, he said, because Louis-François-Sébastien Fauvel, who used to be an agent of the former French ambassador, Auguste de Choiseul-Gouffier, was back in Athens and had convinced the Ottomans that work on the Acropolis must be suspended.[60] And so it happened. Fauvel was able to declare that Elgin would have removed everything, had it not been for the French ambassador Brune in Constantinople.[61] Fauvel, who had reason to resent Elgin (both were collectors and Elgin was, honestly, more successful at 'collecting'), spoke to Brune about Elgin's 'vandalism' and convinced him to obtain an Ottoman order to stop further work on the Acropolis.[62] If any sculptures at all could still be

---

[52] Elgin to Lusieri (8 October 1802), cited in Smith (1916) 234.

[53] St Clair (1998) 110.

[54] St Clair (2022) 430, 671.

[55] See Sect. 6.3.1.2.

[56] St Clair (2022) 671.

[57] See Chap. 6, especially text to n 176.

[58] St Clair (1998) 110.

[59] Lusieri to Elgin (6 February 1804), cited in Smith (1916) 257-258.

[60] Smith (1916) 258.

[61] Fauvel, cited in St Clair (2022) 672.

[62] Fauvel, cited in St Clair (2022) 672.

seen, Fauvel affirmed, it was thanks to this ambassador.[63] This led St Clair to observe caustically that, instead of Elgin 'saving' the Parthenon marbles from the French, it was rather 'the French who "saved" the main part of the Parthenon from Elgin'.[64] The 'firman' with which Hunt put pressure on the voivode to allow the removals on the Acropolis was formally countermanded in 1805, and Elgin's men were ordered to stop.[65]

But although work came to a halt, in Athens Lusieri still stood guard over a voluminous collection of marbles and other antiquities that he had not been able to ship to Britain.[66] And there lay the rub. As of 1806, the Ottomans' good will towards Britain was running low.[67] Lusieri had chartered a vessel to take the collection away and the marbles had been boarded and were about to go, when a government order arrived preventing the ship from sailing.[68] It was at some point soon after that a British warship finally arrived at the Piraeus to receive the marbles, but nothing would avail.[69] The voivode would just not let them go.[70]

Political means were now employed. In Constantinople, Adair, British ambassador to the Ottoman empire until 1810,[71] was at the receiving end of significant pressure from Elgin, Lusieri, and the Foreign Office and applied consequently to the Ottoman authorities asking them to permit the shipment of Elgin's collection.[72] Presents were made to Ottoman officials and the British ambassador found he also needed to give a present to the kaymakam (a title normally used for the acting grand vizier).[73] Ultimately, though, the gifts and pressure did bear fruit, and Adair obtained an order addressed to the voivode of Athens allowing the shipment of Elgin's collection.[74] Most of the remaining marbles were loaded onto a Hydriote ship and, just in case, a British warship was sent from Smyrna to escort them.[75] It did not prove necessary. Another shipment of Parthenon marbles would leave the Piraeus a year later on the *Hydra*.[76] The *Hydra* sailed for Malta in the spring of 1811 carrying a young and as yet little known poet, who was about to acquire fame and notoriety overnight.[77] Byron had just finished writing *The Curse of Minerva*, a poem that

[63] Fauvel, cited in St Clair (2022) 672.
[64] St Clair (2022) 672. See also text to n 129.
[65] St Clair (2022) 430, 670-672.
[66] St Clair (1998) 151.
[67] St Clair (1998) 151.
[68] St Clair (1998) 155.
[69] St Clair (1998) 155.
[70] St Clair (1998) 155.
[71] Bindoff, Malcolm-Smith, and Webster (1934) 167.
[72] St Clair (1998) 155.
[73] Smith (1916) 280.
[74] Smith (1916) 279-280.
[75] Smith (1916) 280.
[76] Smith (1916) 281.
[77] Smith (1916) 281.

would be published only posthumously but would echo down the ages and, like the question of permission and of the dubious ethics of the removals, would plague Elgin and his collection for the foreseeable future.

3.3 The Question of Permission

At the heart of our contemporary retentionists' argument of legality lies the assumption that Elgin had permission to remove the marbles. There has been debate over the years about whether the purported firman authorised Elgin's actions. But if Hunt's Italian translation is a translation of that 'firman', the conclusion is inescapable: Elgin did not have permission to remove the marbles. But more crucial is another matter that is sometimes overlooked: it is the question of whether such a firman actually existed. These are some of the issues that the following paragraphs now set out to address.

3.3.1 A Touch Too Tall? Elgin's Tale of a Firman

Did the firman actually exist? The assumption has generally been that an Ottoman document dated July 1801 that Elgin referred to as a 'firman' was translated into Italian in Constantinople in 1801; that the Italian translation was used to produce the English translation published in the select committee report (this English translation would have been either produced in London in 1816 or forwarded to the select committee by Hunt); and that the document, on its terms, gave Elgin permission to remove the Parthenon marbles from the building.[78] David Rudenstine challenged these 'deeply embedded assumptions' about how these three distinct documents related to one another and disputed the existence of evidence linking the purported Ottoman firman with the Italian translation.[79]

In June 1801, Hunt urged Elgin to ask the Porte for a document describing the activities in which his agents at Athens could engage. In July 1801, Elgin obtained a letter pertaining to the work of his draughtsmen in Athens and addressed to Ottoman officials there.[80] Pisani, the official British dragoman (or interpreter), referred to it as 'a letter' when writing to Elgin with the announcement that he had received it,[81] as did (as we have seen) Hunt.[82] The Italian text too refers to itself as a 'letter'

---

[78] Rudenstine (2001) 1857.

[79] Rudenstine (2001).

[80] Mary Nisbet to William Nisbet (9 July 1801), cited in Nisbet Hamilton Grant (1928) 97.

[81] Pisani to Elgin (6 July 1801), cited in St Clair (1998) 88.

[82] Hunt to Elgin (31 July 1801), cited in Smith (1916) 195.

('*Traduzione d'una lettera*', '*la presente lettera*').[83] This letter was not signed by the sultan, as is often assumed, but by the acting grand vizier (kaymacam).[84] While in western literature it has been claimed that a firman could be authorised by the sultan and signed by one of his ministers,[85] it appears that a firman, in order to qualify as such, had to be signed by the sultan himself. Other irregularities are that the Italian document is undated, and there is nothing to confirm the presence of an imperial cipher on it.[86] Doubts have also been expressed about how some of the terms appearing in the Italian document would have been rendered in Ottoman Turkish.[87] The 1801 document then, if it existed, was unlikely to be a firman but it could have been an order.[88] The trouble is that, firman or order, the original Ottoman document has never been found. Elgin was not able to produce it for the select committee to inspect.[89]

Neither the original July 1801 letter nor any copy has ever been found in the Ottoman archives—nor in any other archive.[90] Surprisingly enough, not even an 1801 reference to the document has been discovered in the Ottoman archives.[91] Yet other permissions from July 1801 have surfaced: travel permissions for Hunt and Elgin's dragoman.[92] It is also reported that, a year later, when Elgin and his party arrived in Athens, Elgin's wife 'ordered Lusieri to put about a *false* story that she had powerful new firmans'.[93] The mystery remains complete.

3.3.2 If the Firman Existed, did it Authorise Elgin's Actions?

The purported permission acknowledged the fact that Elgin engaged five painters 'to examine and view, and also to copy' the figures and stipulated that they should 'meet no opposition in walking, viewing, or contemplating the figures and edifices they may wish to design or copy'.[94] The document authorised Elgin's five draughtsmen

[83] For a transcript and facsimile of the Italian text, see St Clair (2022) 662-669.

[84] The kaymakam was the official deputising for the grand vizier during the latter's absence from the capital, Eldem (2011) 284. See further Chap. 4, text to nn 68-69.

[85] E.g. Greenhalgh (2019) 65.

[86] Eldem (2011) 285.

[87] Eldem (2011) 285.

[88] Edhem Eldem, in '200 + 20 Years in Captivity: The Parthenon Sculptures from Elgin to Boris', webinar organised by Culture through Politics on 11 April 2021 (speaking notes on file with the author).

[89] See Sect. 4.3.1.

[90] Rudenstine (2001) 1860; Eldem (2011) 287.

[91] Rudenstine (2001) 1860.

[92] Eldem (2011) 287.

[93] St Clair (1998) 135 (emphasis added).

[94] Except as otherwise indicated, the translation used is the one reproduced in Select Committee (1816) as Appendix No 10, Translation from the Italian of a [Firman] or Official Letter.

to erect ladders around the Parthenon, to make casts, take measurements, and dig the foundations to search for stones with inscriptions lying in the rubble.[95] By the same token, the said men could remove 'some pieces of stone with inscriptions and figures'.[96] The English translation published by the select committee ingeniously (or disingenuously, depending on one's viewpoint) used the term 'any' pieces of stone. But the Italian document's '*qualche pezzi di pietra*' translates as 'some' or 'a few' pieces of stone, as opposed to '*qualsiasi pezzo di pietra*', which would actually translate as 'any' pieces of stone. As we shall see later, this wording is mirrored in the 1810 order allowing what part of Elgin's collection remained in Athens to be shipped.[97] As Harold Nicolson aptly observed, '[e]ven the most free and lavish translation of the Italian tongue cannot twist these words into meaning a whole shipload of sculptures, columns and caryatides'.[98] According to the same document, Elgin's men could do all of the above, '*particularly as there is no harm in the said figures and edifices being thus viewed, contemplated, and designed*'.[99]

On its terms then this document did not authorise *any* removal from the buildings. It did not give Elgin permission to interfere with the structure of the buildings, break off architectural details and take them away. It is evident that the purported firman meant, on the one hand, to allow ladders (or 'scaffolding' in the English translation of the select committee report) to be placed around the Parthenon, so that Elgin's men could study, make casts and drawings of the buildings and, on the other hand, to authorise them to take some pieces of marble lying in the rubble. Moreover, the document did not authorise Elgin to employ hundreds of workmen on the Acropolis (as he did).[100] The letter specifically referred to *five* painters. Could five painters have been as 'efficient' in denuding the Parthenon as Elgin's labourers were?

It is abundantly clear that the letter, if it had the authority to grant any permission, allowed Elgin's men only to dig and take away what they found in the rubble around the Parthenon. This is exactly how Elgin and his party understood the document at the time.[101] In a letter to Lusieri, Elgin gleefully announced: 'you have now the permission to *dig*, and there a great field is opened for medals, and for the remains both of sculpture and architecture'.[102] Had he believed for a moment that he had permission to remove part of the building still standing, he is certain to have

[95] Select Committee (1816) Appendix No 10, Translation from the Italian of a [Firman] or Official Letter.

[96] Select Committee (1816) Appendix No 10, Translation from the Italian of a [Firman] or Official Letter.

[97] Text to nn 146ff.

[98] Harold Nicolson, 'The Byron Curse Echoes Again', The New York Times (27 March 1949). See also Rudenstine (2002) 459.

[99] Select Committee (1816) Appendix No 10, Translation from the Italian of a [Firman] or Official Letter.

[100] Select Committee (1816) 4; see also Hunt to Elgin (31 July 1801), cited in Smith (1916) 198, referring to 'a train of thirty men' being employed to bring down one single statue; contrast St Clair (2022) 57.

[101] St Clair (1998) 89-90.

[102] Elgin to Lusieri (10 July 1801), cited in Smith (1916) 192 (emphasis added).

'celebrated that extraordinary power, not the prospect of tedious speculative excavations'.[103]

Merryman too could not help but concede that the reference to taking away pieces of stone appeared to be 'incidental, intended to apply to objects found while excavating' and that the purported firman provided 'slender authority for the massive removals from the Parthenon'.[104] It is clear that the assumption that the Ottoman authorities granted Elgin permission to remove part of the Parthenon must rely on a different document, one that must countermand the 'firman''s express stipulation that 'no harm' be inflicted on the buildings.[105] This is why Merryman, who did not find such a document, based his argument of the legality of the operation on an ex post facto approval (discussed in the following section).

The assumption of Elgin's prior permission also implies that when he asked for this permission, he already had in mind that he should remove the marbles from the Parthenon walls, but the evidence contradicts this.[106] Elgin neither had the intention of removing the marbles from the Parthenon, nor did he ask the Ottomans permission to do so. It was Hunt and Lusieri who started to remove the marbles in his name, while Elgin was in Constantinople, unaware of what was going on. Hunt and Lusieri sent him reports of their activities at Athens at the end of July and the beginning of August 1801,[107] and Elgin announced his 'infinite pleasure' at the news that now seemed 'to promise a success beyond our most ardent hopes'.[108]

If Elgin did not understand the Ottoman document to allow his men to remove parts of the Parthenon, neither did Hunt. In a letter to Lusieri, dated 8 July 1801, he wrote: 'I shall carry a [firman] to enable our Artists to prosecute without interruption their researches in the Acropolis of Athens'.[109] The fact that Hunt, despite the 'firman' in his possession, had to specifically ask the voivode for permission before removing the first metope, shows that he did not believe that the 'firman' actually granted him such permission. When the select committee asked Hunt whether the 'firman' gave Elgin permission to remove the marbles from the walls of the Acropolis temples, he explained that the document did not give a 'right to displace and take away whatever the artists might take a fancy to'.[110] However, this 'was the interpretation which the Voivode of Athens was *induced* to allow it to bear', just as he was '*induced*' (the same verb again) to 'extend' the permissions of the firman.[111]

[103] Rudenstine (2002) 457-458.

[104] Merryman (1985) 1899. See also Bartholdy (1807) 45.

[105] Rudenstine (2002) 456.

[106] Rudenstine (2002) 460.

[107] Hunt to Elgin (31 August 1801) and Lusieri to Elgin (6 August 1801), see Smith (1916) 196.

[108] Elgin to Lusieri (8 October 1801), cited in Smith (1916) 201.

[109] Hunt to Hamilton (8 July 1801), cited in Smith (1916) 194.

[110] Select Committee (1816) 142.

[111] Select Committee (1816) 146 (emphasis added).

But this was not a case of 'mission creep', an extensive interpretation of a permission; rather, it was taking away without the central government's permission.[112]

The select committee itself did not believe that the 'firman' authorised Elgin to remove the marbles. Its report made great play of Hunt's claim that 'no remonstrance was at any time made, nor any displeasure shown by the Turkish government, either at Constantinople or at Athens, against the extensive interpretation which was put upon this [firman]'.[113] By relying upon the absence of opposition to legitimise Elgin's actions, the parliamentary committee indirectly recognised that the 'firman' itself did not give Elgin permission to remove the marbles.[114]

Whether the firman did not exist or whether it existed (and was countermanded), Elgin's actions were unauthorised. Adair said as much and Lusieri, addressing Elgin in October 1802, more than a year after the supposed firman, wrote: 'I advise you, my Lord, to procure a firman for the Disdar, in which everything that he has done for your Excellency is approved. It is a paper that you promised him before you left Athens.'[115] Lusieri here clearly asked for ex post facto approval: his letter makes it clear that the removals that the Ottoman officials at Athens had permitted were not approved by the central government. The connivance of these officials proves that, firman or no firman, Constantinople had not approved the denuding of the Parthenon.

3.3.3 Ex post facto Approval?

Merryman admitted that, on the basis of the terms of the 'firman', Elgin would not have acquired property rights in the marbles.[116] But he argued that the Ottoman authorities ratified ex post the removals. He wrote that 'an act in excess of the authority originally granted can be ratified, expressly or by implication from conduct indicating acquiescence'.[117] Acquiescence could indeed have been an important legal consideration, and it will be considered below in a different context.[118] However, acquiescence presupposes that the central Ottoman authorities had knowledge of what was happening in Athens. There is no evidence that they did. Not even the British Museum claims that they did.[119] Quite the contrary seems to be the case.

More specifically, Merryman suggested that the Ottoman government ratified Elgin's actions on two occasions. First, Elgin 'caused the Sultan to issue additional

[112] Robertson (2019) Chap. 3.

[113] Select Committee (1816) 4.

[114] Rudenstine (2002) 459.

[115] Lusieri to Elgin (4 October 1802), cited in Smith (1916) 233.

[116] Merryman (1985) 1899.

[117] Merryman (1985) 1899.

[118] See Sect. 8.4.3.

[119] The museum argues that others knew, see Sect. 6.3.3.4.

firmans' addressed to the Athens officials, in which he 'generally sanctioned what these local officials had done for Elgin and his party'.[120] Second, when the voivode refused to allow the shipment of the marbles that had been added later to Elgin's collection, the Ottoman government issued an order for the local authorities to allow the remainder of the collection to embark.[121] Taken together, Merryman argued, 'these two events make a strong case for ratification of the removal, even if it exceeded the authority given in the original firman'. If the removal was ratified, then it was lawful under international law, and Elgin would be able to transfer property rights in the marbles to the UK government and the British Museum.[122]

3.3.3.1 Ratification by subsequent firmans?

The first claim of ex post facto ratification of Elgin's actions relies on official documents that Elgin allegedly obtained sometime in the autumn of 1802. They were not, it seems again, firmans signed by the sultan, as Merryman assumed, but letters.[123] These are the documents that would have been issued in response to Lusieri's request to reassure the disdar.[124] Elgin and his men at Athens were aware that the removals from the buildings were made possible with the connivance of the local officials at Athens, and that for that very reason these officials feared for their lives.[125] According to St Clair, the letters would provide some measure of protection to these officials, such as that 'they would not be blamed, dismissed, imprisoned, sent to the galleys, summoned to Constantinople for public beheading, or quietly done away with by official assassins'.[126] The fact that the local officials were relieved to receive the letters or documents shows that they must have offered some reassurance.[127]

How many were the documents? Who wrote them? What was their content? We have no information about them. What we do have is Elgin's letter to Lusieri of 8 October 1802, which contained some comforting words for the disdar followed by the statement: 'I have the means of watching over his interests. *So long as he is my friend* he will have solid proofs of my friendship.'[128] If one is inclined to be a little cynical, one might discern the implicit threat in these words. If a formal permission had been given, why would the disdar fear? That the Ottoman officials in Athens feared retribution from their superiors can only mean that they knew they did not

---

[120] Merryman (1985) 1899.

[121] Merryman (1985) 1899.

[122] Merryman (1985) 1899.

[123] St Clair (1998) 110, 135.

[124] Text to n 115.

[125] St Clair (1998) 135.

[126] St Clair (1998) 110-111.

[127] Rudenstine (2002) 463.

[128] Elgin to Lusieri (8 October 1802), cited in Smith (1916) 234 (emphasis added).

have the power to allow the removal of the Parthenon marbles, which had been authorised neither by prior nor by later permission.

As we have seen, in early 1804, operations had to stop, because the Ottoman officials were frightened again, this time by Fauvel, who told them that he had been instructed by the French ambassador to take down a list of all the marbles Elgin's men had removed and to send it to him.[129] If Elgin had a permission from the central Ottoman government, why would the local officials bow to Fauvel? Lusieri tried to take advantage of this lull in work on the Acropolis to excavate elsewhere and accumulate a collection of vases and coins, but the new voivode put an end to that too.[130] The new voivode had been accused of receiving a bribe and had been asked to account for the money, although the last of the marbles had already been removed before his arrival.[131] Had a firman been granted by the highest authority, why would he call a halt to the works? In any case, the 1805 stop-work order from the Porte settled the matter for good. The above contradicts, rather than supports, any claim of retroactive ratification.

3.3.3.2 The Ottomans allow the remainder of Elgin's collection to be shipped

The second claim of ex post facto ratification is based on an order from the kaymakam to the voivode of Athens allowing the marbles that remained in Athens in 1810 to be shipped.[132] When Adair tried to help Elgin obtain the relevant permission, he found that this was no easy task.[133] Adair explained that, since the initial steps for the embarkation of the marbles had not 'been taken under the sanction of a firman', he 'met with much difficulty in forwarding his Lordship's wishes, and even now it is very doubtful whether the object would be effected so certainly through a firman as through a private application to the [voivode] of Athens'.[134] But in February 1810, Adair was at last able to confirm that he had received 'an order' allowing the remainder of Elgin's collection to embark: 'I have at length succeeded in obtaining an order from the Caimakam to the Voivode of Athens, for the embarkation without further detention of the antiquities collected by Lord Elgin and now lying at Athens'.[135]

[129] Lusieri to Elgin (6 February 1804), cited in Smith (1916) 258. See also text to nn 60-65. According to St Clair, the French ambassador, Brune, probably intended to seize the part of Elgin's collection that was still in Athens and send it to France but logistical considerations prevented him from doing so, St Clair (2022) 672.

[130] Smith (1916) 262; St Clair (1998) 137-138.

[131] Smith (1916) 262; St Clair (1998) 138.

[132] Adair to Wellesley (27 February 1810), cited in Smith (1916) 279.

[133] Adair to Canning (25 September 1809), reproduced in Adair (1845) 272.

[134] Adair to Canning (25 September 1809), reproduced in Adair (1845) 272.

[135] Adair to Wellesley (27 February 1810), cited in Smith (1916) 279.

The scant information we have about this incident offers no support to the claim that the order ratified retroactively Elgin's actions.[136] The mere fact that the Ottomans allowed Elgin's collection to be shipped in no way suggests an official approval of the removals.[137] For a start, the Ottoman officials 'were faced with a fait accompli and had to make the best of a bad situation'.[138] To interpret this as 'an "act of ratification" gives their laissez-faire actions a legal dignity they perhaps do not merit'.[139]

A more critical question is what antiquities were subject to the order. Edhem Eldem has found a copy of the order and related correspondence in the Ottoman archives, and in 2011 he published a translation.[140] There is nothing in these documents to show that the central Ottoman authorities had accurate knowledge of the antiquities concerned by the shipment; on the contrary, it is likely that they were unaware of the details.[141] Both the correspondence and the order contain wording that remains eminently vague about the items in question and the manner in which they were obtained by Elgin. It is impossible to identify the antiquities that are the subject of the order as the Acropolis marbles. Certainly, the responsible officials in Athens had no reason to supply accurate information about the removals,[142] since only a handful of years earlier they had accepted bribes and feared for their lives for having permitted the removal of the marbles. Adair had even less reason to provide a detailed account, and it is probable that he did not have one.[143] What Adair had been told by the Foreign Office was that there were 'at Athens several very valuable Antiques which [Elgin] collected in the Levant, & which he has hitherto been prevented by the war with the Porte from transporting to this Country' and that he should do his best to prevail upon the Ottoman government to allow their shipment.[144]

The Ottoman ambassador in London too wrote to the Porte (probably to the reis efendi or foreign secretary) in relation to the transport of 'objects such as old marble stones and earthen pots decorated with figures ... which belonged to the former ambassador Lord Elgin' and requested that 'no impediment be made to the transport

---

136 Rudenstine (2002) 465.

137 Rudenstine (2002) 465.

138 Neils (2001) 241.

139 Neils (2001) 241.

140 Eldem (2011) 291-293. According to Edhem Eldem, these documents are chancery copies or drafts of outgoing orders and decrees, so they are not signed and they are undated. The order is probably from the office of the grand vizier for the voivode of Athens. There is no way of knowing whether it was issued by the grand vizier himself or his deputy, for we do not have a precise date. The archivists dated them to 1810/1811, but since Adair referred to an order he obtained from the kaymakam in 1810 and some marbles were shipped from the Piraeus in that year, we can probably conclude that this is the same order, and that it was issued in 1810 by the kaymakam. Contrast Korka and Shariat-Panahi (2019) 235-237.

141 Rudenstine (2002) 465.

142 Rudenstine (2002) 465.

143 cf Rudenstine (2002) 465.

144 Foreign Office to Adair (29 July 1809), as cited in St Clair (2022) 673.

and passage of the said *pottery*'.[145] A petition to the sultan probably submitted by either the grand vizier or the kaymakam also refers to 'a few pieces of image-bearing stones',[146] which Elgin 'had purchased in Athens during his embassy and had then placed and loaded into crates to be left there for safekeeping'.[147] Several aspects of this letter are noteworthy. The mention of 'a few pieces of image-bearing stones' appears to echo the term '*qualche pezzi di pietra*' of the 1801 document and, as a consequence, implies that the order did not go any further than that first document. It would allow the shipment of a few pieces of stone (found in the rubble)—not what exceeded the authority granted in 1801. The letter referred to 'image-bearing stones' that Elgin 'purchased' in Athens—well, Elgin did *not* purchase any stones in Athens. Nor did he leave them there for safekeeping—he left them there because Lusieri had been prevented from sending them away.

The order ultimately issued concerned 'the matter of the transport of some broken marble pieces and earthen pots decorated with figures' that Elgin 'had obtained in Athens and placed in crates in order to be transported to his country'.[148] The order added:

> as stones of this kind, decorated with figures, are not held in consideration among Muslims, but are appreciated by the Frankish states, there is no harm in granting permission for the transport and passage of the said stones, and this letter [is written so that] no impediment be offered to the transport and passage of the said stones that have been placed in the crates located there.[149]

Are these 'broken marble pieces and earthen pots decorated with figures' the Parthenon marbles? Or are they the objects identified by the 1801 document—pieces of stone found in the rubble but not parts of a standing building? If the central Ottoman government was deceived as to the magnitude and content of the items concerned, this would deal a blow to the argument that the order retroactively condoned the removals from the Parthenon and the other monuments on the Acropolis.[150] In any case, the order related to part of the collection only—that part which still remained in Athens in 1810. In addition, even this order, allowing the marbles to be shipped, was obtained through bribery. We have already seen that Adair found it necessary to give gifts both to the (presumably local) Ottoman officials and to the kaymakam.[151] It was by these means that, after long negotiations, he obtained the

---

[145] Eldem (2011) 293 (emphasis added).

[146] It appears that this could make reference to either or both pictures and statues, since the Ottoman language made no distinction between two-dimensional and three-dimensional images, see St Clair (2022) 664 n 2.

[147] Eldem (2011) 292.

[148] Eldem (2011) 293.

[149] Eldem (2011) 293.

[150] Rudenstine (2002) 465.

[151] See text to n 73.

order for the voivode of Athens to allow the shipment of the marbles.[152] The bribes contradict the lawfulness of yet another transaction.

But there are other reasons why the argument of the ex post facto approval falls flat on its face. On more than one occasion, the Ottomans condemned the activities of Elgin's agents in Athens and prevented them from continuing with the removals, despite the existence of the 'firman'. Their reaction to Elgin's loot was to issue 'a prohibition against taking down any marbles whatever',[153] yet again indirectly underlining that the removals were unauthorised. Last, and certainly not least, the 1810 order raises the question of how the earlier shiploads of marbles had been allowed to be transported. It appears that no permission had been sought for them. And how about the later shipments? Was permission obtained for them?

3.3.3.3 Evidence contradicting approval

In reality, not only is there no proof of an actual ratification of Elgin's actions, but there is overwhelming evidence of disapproval. It appears that it was only bribes and a malfunctioning system that allowed Elgin's men to engage in the massive removals from the Parthenon and the eventual shipment of the marbles. Had there been such ex post facto approval, why did the parliamentary select committee not try to confirm it? Why did the select committee not attempt to speak to the Ottoman authorities?

What we in fact have are a destruction on an unprecedented scale and several expressions of remorse on the part of the Ottomans who, every so often, stopped the work. If, as Merryman argued, the Ottoman government retroactively approved the removals from the Parthenon in 1810 and permitted Elgin to have the marbles shipped to England, why did Adair a year later told the world that the Ottomans absolutely denied that Elgin had any authorisation to do what he did? (See also Fig. 3.1.) The statement of the Ottoman authorities is loud and clear—it contradicts any claim of retroactive ratification. Adair's insistence on the word 'absolutely' is revealing.

Or, is there a further factor to be taken into account in any explanation? What we know of the truth suggests that the case could be even more twisted. As we shall see later (Sect. 4.5.3), one of the uncomfortable questions Elgin had to answer was whether he obtained the marbles as a private citizen or in his capacity as ambassador. If parliament considered that he had acquired the marbles as ambassador, then it might conclude that they had never belonged to Elgin but to the nation. Two researchers have cited 'letters discovered in the British Library', according to which Elgin, who was anxious to get paid for the marbles, would have concocted this letter together with Adair. According to their interpretation, through the

[152] Smith (1916) 279-280.

[153] Williams (1820) 212.

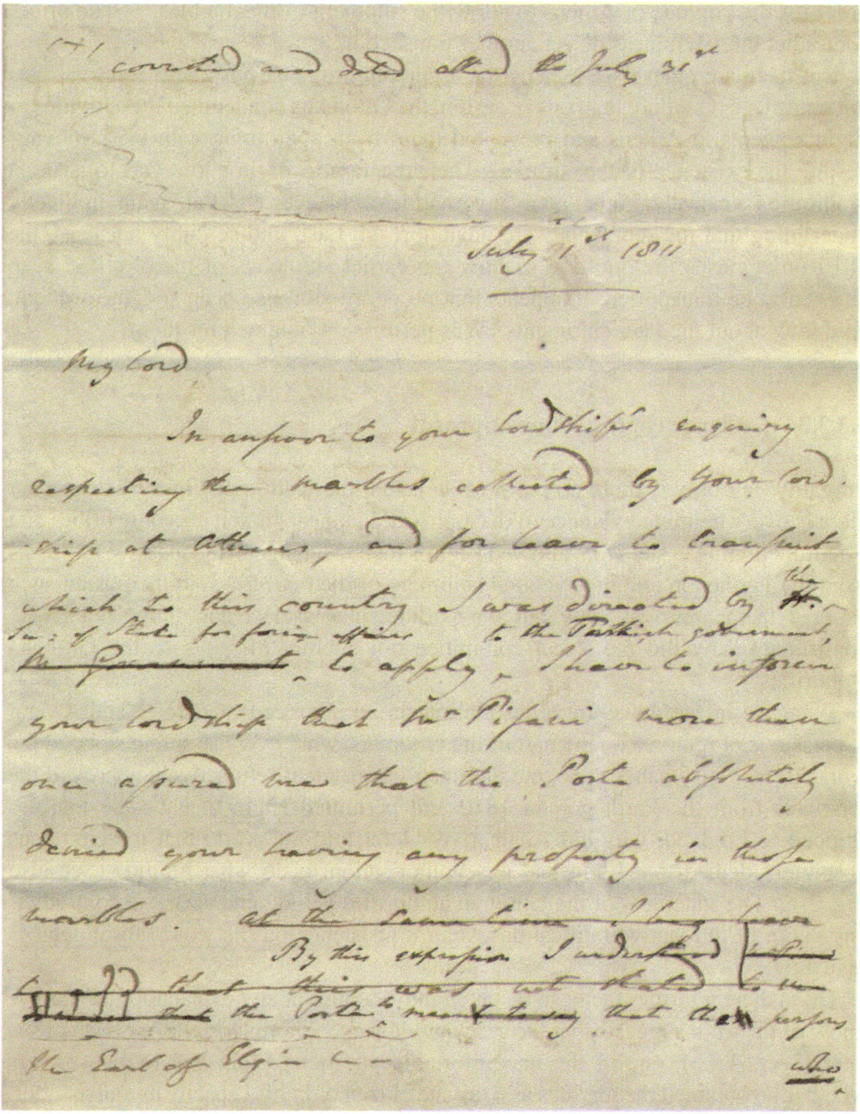
(+) corrected and dated altered the July 31st

July 31st 1811

My Lord

In answer to your Lordship's enquiry respecting the marbles collected by your Lordship at Athens, and for leave to transport which to this country I was directed by the Sec: of State for foreign affairs to the Turkish government, ~~the Government~~ to apply, I have to inform your Lordship that Mr Pisani more than once assured me that the Porte absolutely denied your having any property in those marbles. ~~At the same time I beg leave~~

By this expression I understood ~~that this was not stated to the~~ ~~that~~ the Porte to mean ~~to deny~~ that the persons ~~the Earl of Elgin [illegible]~~ who

Fig. 3.1 Robert Adair's draft letter to Elgin, dated 31 July 1811. Collection of T Theodorou. 'Mr Pisani more than once assured me that the Porte absolutely denied your having any property in those marbles. By this expression I understood the Porte to mean that the persons who had sold the marbles to your Lordship had no right so to dispose of them' (page 1, lines 7ff to page 2, line 2) For a full transcript, see http://www.adairtoelgin.com

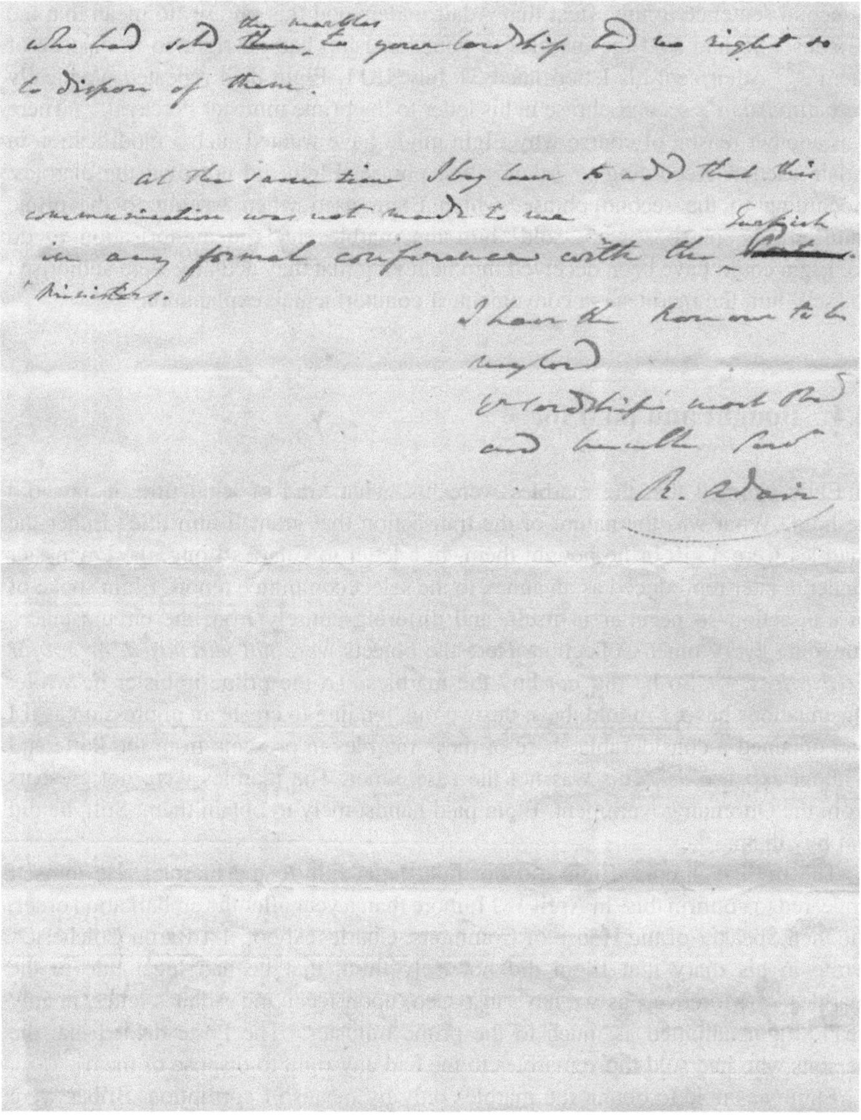

who had sold the marbles to your lordship had no right to dispose of them.

At the same time I beg leave to add that this communication was not made to me in any formal conference with the English ministers.

I have the honour to be
my Lord
Your Lordship's most obed
and humble serv
R. Adair

Fig. 3.1 (continued)

admission that the Ottoman government never authorised the removals, Elgin thought that he could prove that he obtained the marbles in his personal capacity.[154] It appears that after Adair wrote to Elgin informing him that the Porte had denied that he owned the marbles, Elgin requested changes to his letter leading to the addition of

[154] Korka and Shariat-Panahi (2019) 238-240.

a second sentence to the effect that Adair understood this phrase 'to mean that the persons who had sold the marbles to your Lordship had no right so to dispose of them'.[155] Adair sent his letter dated 31 July 1811. Elgin then repeated practically verbatim Adair's second phrase in his letter to the prime minister Perceval.[156] There was another reason of course why Elgin might have wanted such a modification in Adair's letter. According to Adair's first phrase, Elgin did not own the marbles. According to the second phrase, which Elgin used when writing to the prime minister, the persons who 'sold' him the marbles had no authorisation to do so. Elgin could have been deceived into believing that they actually were authorised to 'sell' him the marbles—a convenient, if counterfactual, explanation.

3.4 Bought and paid for

If Elgin claimed that the marbles were his, what kind of legal title, if any, did he hold? What was the nature of the transaction that granted him title? Either the marbles were a gift or he bought them. In a letter to Charles Long, the Paymaster General, later reproduced as an annex to the select committee report, Elgin spoke of 'a transaction so peculiar in itself, and differing entirely from the circumstances attending every other Collection. Here the objects *were not purchased, or got for fixed prices*.'[157] So he did *not* buy the marbles. To the prime minister he wrote: 'Insinuations have, I'm told, been thrown out, tending to create an impression as if I had obtained a considerable share of these marbles in presents from the Porte and without expense'.[158] This was not the case either. The marbles were not presents from the Ottoman government. Elgin paid handsomely to obtain them. Still, he did not buy them.

The truth is simple. Elgin did not hold legal title to the marbles. He himself appeared to confirm this. In April 1811, more than a year after the embarkation order, the then Speaker of the House of Commons, Charles Abbot, 1st Baron Colchester, wrote in his diary that Elgin did not truly think that he had legal title to the marbles.[159] Moreover, as we have just seen, upon receiving Adair's letter, in July 1811, Elgin admitted as much to the prime minister: 'The Porte denied that the persons who had sold those marbles to me had any right to dispose of them'.[160]

Elgin was able to obtain the marbles only by means of corruption. Bribes were tendered to the local Ottoman officials both to ensure they turned a blind eye to the removals and later in order to obtain the permission to ship the marbles. Hunt himself

[155] Korka and Shariat-Panahi (2019) 238-240.

[156] See text to n 160.

[157] Elgin to Long (1811; with a Postscript added February 1816) reproduced in Select Committee (1816) as Appendix No 5, x (emphasis added).

[158] Elgin to Perceval (31 July 1811), cited in Hitchens (2008) 43.

[159] Abbott (1861) (diary entry of 29 April 1811).

[160] Elgin to Perceval (31 July 1811), cited in Hitchens (2008) 44.

admitted as much to the parliamentary select committee. When asked whether the voivode's 'extensive' interpretation of the 'firman' had been encouraged by means of 'any sum of money', Hunt replied that he was not aware of any monetary transactions but that 'presents' were given to the voivode.[161] Then the committee asked him if he had any information about 'the expense incurred in the way of *bribes*'.[162] But Hunt refused to be drawn on the exact amount: Elgin's expenses did not pass through his hands, he only handed out the presents to the local officials.[163] He described the presents given to the voivode as consisting of 'brilliant cut glass lustres, fire-arms, and other articles of English manufacture'[164] and suggested that Elgin's weekly and monthly expenses 'must have been very considerable, owing to [...] the continued presents that were given to the Turkish officers at Athens'.[165]

Elgin himself made no secret of the bribes. As we have seen, when he produced his list of expenses for the government, not only did he document the bribes but he also included them in his asking selling price.[166] The select committee also had a copy of Elgin's letter to Long discussing firmans. Firmans, he said, allow 'secret negotiations' to be carried with 'persons in office or in power', upon whom 'no influence can possibly be efficient, from a Christian, excepting only *weight of gold*'.[167]

In light of the evidence, no doubt is permitted: the marbles were obtained through bribes. They were not a gift. Nor were they purchased. Merryman minimised the legal significance of the bribes. He wrote:

> The Ottomans who were bribed were the responsible officials. Whatever their motivation may have been, they had the legal authority to perform those actions. At a time and in a culture in which officials routinely had to be bribed to perform their legal duties (as is still true today in much of the world), the fact that bribes occurred was hardly a significant legal consideration.

However, this statement relies on two cumulative assumptions that are not borne out by the facts: first, that the Ottoman officials who allowed the removal of the marbles had the authority to do so (they did not—this authority evidently rested with the central government in Constantinople and not with the local officials in Athens, who, tellingly, had been afraid for their lives since they allowed Elgin's men to remove the marbles);[168] and, second, that corruption in such circumstances was legally insignificant. Merryman's selection of words is unfortunate. He indirectly claimed that the removal of the marbles entered into the scope of the Ottoman officials' 'legal

[161] Select Committee (1816) 142-143.

[162] Select Committee (1816) 143 (emphasis added).

[163] Select Committee (1816) 143.

[164] Select Committee (1816) 146.

[165] Select Committee (1816) 146-147.

[166] See Chap. 1, text to nn 63-65.

[167] Select Committee (1816) 36 and Elgin to Long (1811; with a Postscript added February 1816) reproduced in Select Committee (1816) as Appendix No 5, xii-xiii (emphasis in original).

[168] Rudenstine (2002) 459; St Clair (1998) 95.

duties'. It is unclear how under any circumstances denuding the Parthenon of its marbles could qualify as anyone's legal *duty*. Either way, the veracity of the statement, on its own terms, relies on the premise that the removal of the marbles was otherwise lawful, so that it was not a crime to bribe an official to do what was otherwise lawful to do.[169] In any event, whatever the status of bribery under Ottoman law,[170] Elgin was a British ambassador tendering a bribe. How would English law view a bribe coming from a British ambassador while performing his official duties abroad?[171]

3.5 A Spoiler Worse than Turk and Goth

3.5.1 Destruction

In September 1802, Lusieri described to Elgin the removal of the eighth metope, 'that one where there is the Centaur carrying off the woman'.[172] The metope, he wrote, had 'caused much trouble in all respects', and he had 'been obliged to be a little barbarous'.[173] In the account of his travels, Edward Daniel Clarke (also a collector)[174] gave an eyewitness account of what is almost certainly the same event:

> After a short time spent in examining the several parts of the temple, one of the workmen came to inform [Lusieri] that they were then going to lower one of the metopes. We saw this fine piece of sculpture raised from its station between the triglyphs: but the workmen endeavouring to give it a position adapted to the projected line of descent, a part of the adjoining masonry was loosened by the machinery; and down came the fine masses of Pentelican marble, scattering their white fragments with thundering noise among the ruins. The Disdar, seeing this, could no longer restrain his emotions; but actually took his pipe from his mouth, and, letting fall a tear, said, in a most emphatical tone of voice, '*Τέλος*!' positively declaring that nothing should induce him to consent to any further dilapidation of the building.[175]

Lusieri also described to Elgin how the central slab of the east frieze broke in two on its way to the Piraeus:

> Not being well sawn, for want of sufficiently fine saws, and being a little weak in the middle it parted in two in course of transport, in spite of all the precautions taken. Happily it broke in

[169] Rudenstine (2002) 467.

[170] But see text to n 131.

[171] This issue is addressed in Sect. 4.5.2.

[172] Lusieri to Elgin (16 September 1802), cited in Smith (1916) 232.

[173] Lusieri to Elgin (16 September 1802), cited in Smith (1916) 232.

[174] Clarke (1818) *passim*.

[175] Clarke (1818) 224.

> the middle, in a straight line, at a place where there was no work, so that the accident has helped us to transport it quickly and put it onboard.[176]

A silver lining if ever there was one! A fortnight later Lusieri reported that a Doric capital he was about to remove from the Parthenon would have to be sawn in two, because the Acropolis gates were not sufficiently wide to let it pass through.[177] The scale of the destruction caused by the exertions of Elgin's agents on the Acropolis was not lost on other contemporaries either. In his *Classical and Topographical Tour*, Edward Dodwell, described how in order to remove several metopes, 'the magnificent cornice by which they were covered' had to be thrown down and commented on the similar fate of the south-east angle of the pediment.[178] Elsewhere, he described the destruction of the Erechtheion by its 'dilapidators', when part of the building was simply thrown to the ground. He referred in particular to part of a column with its capital:

> to obtain this comparatively unornamental mass, which at present serves as the pedestal for a vase [in the British Museum], recourse was had to the most shameful and barbarous dilapidations. Every thing relative to this catastrophe was conducted with an eager spirit of insensate outrage, and an ardour of insatiate rapacity, in opposition, not only to every feeling of taste, but to every sentiment of justice and humanity.[179]

The architect Robert Smirke, who also left Athens with a few prize pieces of the Erechtheion,[180] was similarly distressed to witness the damage caused to the Parthenon:

> It particularly affected me when I saw the destruction made to get down the [frieze]. The men were labouring long ineffectually with iron crows to move the stones of these firm-built walls. Each stone as it fell shook the ground with its ponderous weight, with a deep hollow noise; it seemed like a convulsive groan of the injured spirit of the Temple.[181]

And Hugh W Williams regretted the 'unworkmanlike manner in which the deed was done' and that Elgin should have dared to make 'a quarry of a work of Phidias'.[182] Slowly, a legend started to be born that as Elgin's men wrenched the statues from the Parthenon, they screamed aloud—a vivid image, which was later captured in Byron's 'shrieking gods'.[183]

---

[176] Lusieri to Elgin (16 September 1802), cited in Smith (1916) 233.

[177] Lusieri to Elgin (4 October 1802), cited in Smith (1916) 233.

[178] Dodwell (1819) 322.

[179] Dodwell (1819) 348.

[180] St Clair (1998) 135.

[181] Robert Smirke, as cited in St Clair (1998) 134.

[182] Williams (1820) 322-323.

[183] Harold Nicolson, 'The Byron Curse Echoes Again', The New York Times (27 March 1949). See also George Gordon Byron, *Childe Harold's Pilgrimage*, Canto II, stanza XV.

3.5.2 Marbles at Sea and the Mentor *Shipwreck*

Elgin's collection was transported to Britain on various ships that followed different routes, sometimes taking long detours, usually through Alexandria or Smyrna.[184] Most of the collection would be unloaded at Malta and continue from there as opportunity arose.[185] The following are only some of the vessels and routes involved. The cargo of the Ragusan brig *Constanza*, containing among others two metopes and cases of reliefs, travelled by way of Egypt, where it was also unloaded for a time.[186] Hunt travelled on the *Constanza*, and when bad weather on the way to Egypt forced the crew to put in at Halicarnassus and Cnidus, Hunt carried off more loot: a votive altar, fragments of Ionic and Corinthian cornices, friezes, etc.[187] Hunt seems to have been able to remove other pieces too, but, finding them unwieldy to load, he was forced to abandon them and hoped that he might pick them up on his return.[188] HMS *Braakel*, a troopship,[189] carried a large cargo of marbles, which included the main sculptures of the east pediment, the Hermes and the Ilissos from the west pediment, two metopes and seventeen cases containing slabs of the Parthenon frieze, fragments of the cornice and architrave of the Erechtheion and architectural fragments of the Theseum, the Dionysos from the choragic monument of Thrasyllos (the memorial building erected inside the vertical slope of the Acropolis above the Theatre of Dionysos), numerous inscriptions, fragments probably from Mycenae, the sundial of Phaidros, some Egyptian antiquities, etc.[190]

The story of a small brig, the *Mentor*, this one belonging to Elgin, is worth recounting in more detail. The *Mentor* left the Piraeus for Alexandria with its first cargo of moulds, marble torsos, and a piece of the Parthenon frieze on 5 January 1802, before Elgin had set eyes on them.[191] In Alexandria, the *Mentor* unloaded its cargo and picked up Hamilton, who in the meantime had secured another famous and contested treasure, the Rosetta Stone.[192] Then the *Mentor* returned to the Piraeus for a second shipment of marbles, and Hamilton, who was onboard, arrived in Athens in time to meet Elgin just as his 'Greek tour' was drawing to a close, and he was about to return to Constantinople.[193] Elgin left instructions stressing his

[184] St Clair (1998) 113; Smith (1916) 206ff.

[185] St Clair (1998) 113; Smith (1916) 293-294.

[186] Smith (1916) 206.

[187] Hunt to Elgin (8 January 1802), cited in Smith (1916) 206.

[188] Hunt to Elgin (8 January 1802), cited in Smith (1916) 206. It appears that at least some of the items that Hunt left behind on that journey may have made their way to the British Museum, see Smith (1916) 206, n 87.

[189] St Clair (1998) 118.

[190] Smith (1916) 254.

[191] Smith (1916) 206.

[192] Smith (1916) 221.

[193] St Clair (1998) 115-116.

'urgent desire' for the *Mentor*'s departure with the second cargo.[194] The *Mentor* sailed again in September 1802 with a consignment of seventeen cases of marbles, including fourteen pieces of the Parthenon frieze and four pieces of the frieze of the temple of Athena Nike.[195] Then, 2 days out from the Piraeus, the *Mentor* ran into a storm and sank at the entrance to the harbour of Cythera.[196] Those onboard managed to reach the shore and save themselves. Not so for Elgin's collection, including some of the Parthenon's choicest pieces, which now lay on the seabed, buried under several fathoms of water.[197]

In the months following the *Mentor* shipwreck, Hamilton asked for help from passing ships offering money and recruited sponge divers in order to try to recover what could be salvaged.[198] Luckily, the ship had foundered in shallow waters, for had it sunk a little further out on its journey, it might have been impossible to recover.[199] Of the seventeen cases known to have been onboard, Hamilton managed to recover four, which he sent to Smyrna.[200] From Constantinople, HMS *La Victorieuse* was dispatched in November 1802 to offer help at the site of the wreck.[201] Before reaching Cythera, the ship stopped at the Piraeus, where Hunt, who had been onboard, took the opportunity to load more cases.[202] According to one account, once at Cythera, the *Victorieuse* tried to raise the *Mentor*.[203] It did so for two fathoms, before the cables broke and the wreck sank back to the bottom of the sea.[204] Hamilton assumed that if another vessel had been available to assist the *Victorieuse*, together they would have succeeded in raising the *Mentor*.[205] But this was not to be, and the *Victorieuse* left without salvaging the *Mentor* and its marbles. The divers, who had stopped because of the cold, returned to the site of the wreck the following February and worked there through the spring and the summer.[206] If the heavy pedimental figures had been onboard, as Elgin had instructed, they would probably have needed to be left on the bottom of the sea[207] and would have been

[194] Elgin to Lusieri (June 1802), cited in Smith (1916) 225.

[195] Smith (1916) 231; Lusieri to Elgin (16 September 1802), cited in Smith (1916) 232; St Clair (1998) 116.

[196] St Clair (1998) 116.

[197] St Clair (1998) 116; Galt (1813) 138.

[198] St Clair (1998) 132; Adolphus (1812) 587.

[199] The Calypso Deep, only a few nautical miles away from Cythera, is the Mediterranean Sea's deepest point, with a depth of 5267 m (17,280 ft), Barale (2008) 14. By comparison, the wreck of the Titanic appears to be located at a 'modest' depth of about 3800 m (12,500 ft).

[200] St Clair (1998) 132; Smith (1916) 244; Adolphus (1812) 587.

[201] St Clair (1998) 116.

[202] St Clair (1998) 116.

[203] St Clair (1998) 133.

[204] St Clair (1998) 133; contrast Hamilton to Elgin (9 December 1802), cited in Smith (1916) 248.

[205] Hamilton to Elgin (9 December 1802), cited in Smith (1916) 248.

[206] St Clair (1998) 133; Smith (1916) 258.

[207] St Clair (1998) 133.

salvaged by the Greek authorities only in more recent years. As it were, only five out of the remaining thirteen cases could be salvaged in the summer of 1803 and, by September, eight still remained under water.[208] Six additional cases were eventually recovered by the end of that year.[209] The divers returned the following April and worked again during the summer.[210] At last, in October 1804, over 2 years after the shipwreck, Lusieri was able to report that 'all the marbles' had been recovered.[211]

As the cases of marbles were salvaged, they were buried on the beach under seaweed and brushwood, and they were covered with large stones in an attempt to protect them against erosion.[212] Following Elgin's request, admiral Nelson ordered a government ship to call at Cythera in order to pick up the marbles.[213] So it was that the antiquities made their way to Malta and, ultimately, to Britain.

Archaeological salvage operations on the site of the *Mentor* wreck continue to yield objects at the time of writing. Besides more mundane passenger possessions and bric-a-brac, recent finds include ancient coins, fragments of ancient amphorae and of Egyptian antiquities. It is unclear whether these and other possibly lost or not yet found objects were part of Elgin's collection, since the record of what was on board seems incomplete,[214] or whether they were in the possession of others who took passage on the *Mentor*.

3.5.3 Reaction to the Looting

Looting was not uncommon at the time when Elgin's men stripped the Parthenon of its most beautiful marbles. (Some might say, looting is not uncommon today.) However, the first to condemn Elgin's actions were his contemporaries, including some who by our modern standards would qualify as looters. Even in his own time, what Elgin did was deemed unacceptable. Support for Elgin waned even while work on the removals was underway. No sooner was the first stone prised off the Parthenon than Elgin faced a barrage of criticism. Influential voices were raised in Britain and abroad to denounce his actions, and what started as the talk of the 'reckless behaviour' of his agents metamorphosed into severe criticism on his return to London.[215] No critic was so formidable as Byron, whose poems, accompanied by

---

[208] Smith (1916) 259.

[209] Smith (1916) 259; contrast St Clair (1998) 133.

[210] Smith (1916) 259.

[211] Lusieri to Hamilton [?] (24 October 1804), cited in Smith (1916) 259.

[212] Smith (1916) 260.

[213] Nelson to Schomberg (2 September 1804), cited Smith (1916) 259-260.

[214] See Smith (1916) 231.

[215] Michaelis (1882) 138-139; Vrdoljak (2006) 30.

commentaries in prose, have had a deep influence to this day on the way we think about the Parthenon marbles and about the protection of cultural property.

Elgin had written to Byron in the hope of seeing him, although there is no evidence that the two ever did meet.[216] In a letter to Hobhouse, shortly before the publication of *Childe Harold's Pilgrimage*, Byron wrote that he had replied to Elgin telling him 'all I knew about his *robberies*' and explaining his intention to publish on the matter, so that Elgin, who appeared keen on meeting him, could not later accuse him of 'double dealing'.[217] Byron's position was loud and clear: Elgin 'ruined Athens'.[218] 'I know no motive', he wrote, 'which can excuse, no name which can designate, the perpetrators of this dastardly devastation'.[219] He was shocked at the 'most unblushing impudence' that it was to 'affix the name of its plunderer to the walls of the Acropolis'.[220] And he insisted that he did 'not think the honour of England advanced by plunder, whether of India or Attica'.[221] In *Childe Harold's Pilgrimage*, he wrote:

But most the modern Pict's ignoble boast,
To rive what Goth, and Turk, and Time hath spar'd:
Cold as the crags upon his native coast,
His mind as barren and his heart as hard,
Is he whose head conceiv'd, whose hand prepar'd,
Aught to displace Athena's poor remains:
Her sons too weak the sacred shrine to guard,
Yet felt some portion of their mother's pains,
And never knew, till then, the weight of Despot's chains.

What! shall it e'er be said by British tongue,
Albion was happy in Athena's tears?
Though in thy name the slaves her bosom wrung,
Tell not the deed to blushing Europe's ears:
The ocean queen, the free Britannia, bears
The last poor plunder from a bleeding land:
Yes, she, whose gen'rous aid her name endears,
Tore down those remnants with a Harpy's hand
Which envious Eld forbore, and tyrants left to stand.

In *The Curse of Minerva*, it is Athena (Minerva) herself that addresses the poet:

'Mortal!' – 'twas thus she spake – 'that blush of shame
Proclaims thee Briton, once a noble name;
First of the mighty, foremost of the free,
Now honour'd *less* by all, and *least* by me:
Chief of thy foes shall Pallas still be found.
Seek'st thou the cause of loathing? – look around.

---

[216] Byron to Hobhouse (31 July 1811), reproduced in Byron (2011) 42-43.

[217] Byron to Hobhouse (31 July 1811), reproduced in Byron (2011) 42-43 (emphasis added).

[218] Byron (1832) Note 6 to Canto II, 67.

[219] Byron (1832) Note 6 to Canto II, 67.

[220] Byron (1832) Note 6 to Canto II, 67.

[221] Byron (1832) Note 6 to Canto II, 67.

Lo! here, despite of war and wasting fire,
I saw successive tyrannies expire.
'Scaped from the ravage of the Turk and Goth,
Thy country sends a spoiler worse than both.
...
What more I owe let gratitude attest –
Know, Alaric and Elgin did the rest.
That all may learn from whence the plunderer came,
The insulted wall sustains his hated name:
For Elgin's fame thus grateful Pallas pleads,
Below, his name – above behold his deeds!
Be ever hailed with equal honour here
The Gothic monarch and the Pictish peer:
Arms gave the first his right, the last had none,
But basely stole what less barbarians won.
So when the lion quits his fell repast,
Next prowls the wolf, the filthy jackal last ...[222]

Byron's eloquence certainly carried the day, but he was by no means Elgin's only critic. Clarke, who as we have seen gave a stirring contemporary account of the removals, deplored the wanton destruction caused by the lowering of metopes, 'which all the ambassadors of the earth, with all the sovereigns they represent, aided by every resource that wealth and talent can now bestow, will never again repair'.[223] He stressed that he would have gladly avoided the topic but, as an eyewitness, he had a duty to discuss it, so that his silence 'with regard to the spoliation of the Athenian temples' would not appear 'to indicate any thing like an approval of the measures which have tended so materially towards their destruction.'[224] Dodwell, whose description of the removals we have also noted, commented:

> It is painful to reflect that these trophies of human genius, which had resisted the silent decay of time, during a period of more than twenty-two centuries, which had escaped the destructive fury of the [iconoclasts], the inconsiderate rapacity of the Venetians, and the barbarous violence of the Mohamedans, should at last have been doomed to experience the devastating outrage which will never cease to be deplored.[225]

Other contemporary criticisms include that of Frederick Douglas, who regarded it 'a very flagrant piece of injustice to deprive a helpless and friendly nation of any possession of value to them ... I wonder at the boldness of the hand that could venture to remove what Phidias had placed under the inspection of Pericles'.[226] Another traveller, Thomas Hughes, declared that he was 'struck forcibly by the lamentable overthrow and ruin occasioned during [the] spoliation'.[227] He described

[222] Emphasis in original.
[223] Clarke (1818) 225-226.
[224] Clarke (1818) 227.
[225] Dodwell (1819) 322.
[226] Douglas (1813) 89.
[227] Hughes (1820) 261.

how architectural fragments (shafts, capitals, entablature) lay jumbled together in quantities that would have been 'capable of furnishing materials to build a palace of marble'.[228] He concluded that one

> cannot but grieve at the wanton devastation committed in their removal, at that avidity for plunder which in carrying off parts of little comparative value, but which helped to sustain the fabric, has exposed this venerable structure to premature ruin, and has removed from their ancient sites, whence most of them acquired their beauty and all their interest, numerous monuments.[229]

And John Cam Hobhouse recalled that 'singular speech of a learned Greek of Ioannina', who told him: 'You English are carrying off the works of the Greeks our forefathers—preserve them well—we Greeks will come and re-demand them.'[230]

3.6 Arrival in London

Sometime after their arrival in England, the marbles ended up in Elgin's London residence at the corner of Piccadilly and Old Park Lane. Elgin's idea of using them as home decoration in Broomhall had been abandoned,[231] as had his plan of turning his London residence into a private museum.[232] By now, he was in undeniable financial difficulties and could not afford to keep his London house.[233] He wanted to sell it and thought it best not to scare off prospective buyers by confronting them with perambulating visitors attempting to catch a glimpse of the marbles.[234] In any case, once the house was sold, the marbles would have to go.[235] It became urgent to find a new home for the marbles.[236] An earlier attempt to interest the British Institution in housing the marbles had fallen through,[237] as had, apparently, overtures to the

[228] Hughes (1820) 261.

[229] Hughes (1820) 261.

[230] Hobhouse (1813) 347-348. For other contemporary criticisms, see Canning (1888) 501-502 ('But when I learnt that one whole side of the reliefs was, and still is, buried under the ruins ... I could not help thinking that the Scottish Earl might have better employed his time and money in fishing these up, than in pulling down those reliefs which were still in their places'); Chateaubriand (1835) 33; Williams (1820) 322-323.

[231] St Clair (1998) 173.

[232] Chapter 1, text to n 72.

[233] St Clair (1998) 173.

[234] Smith (1916) 305.

[235] Smith (1916) 305-306.

[236] St Clair (1998) 178.

[237] Abbott (1861) 331 (diary entry of 17 May 1811).

British Museum, which claimed not to have room for them. At least this is what was stated in a parliamentary debate in 1815.[238]

In the summer of 1810, deep in debt, Elgin decided that the only way forward was for him to sell his collection.[239] Little progress was made in the months that followed and, by May 1811, his situation had become unsustainable.[240] Fortunately, a purchaser was at last found for his London house, as well as a temporary solution for storage of the marbles: the owner of Burlington House offered Elgin the walled enclosure at the rear and sides of the house as storage space for the marbles, warning him however that this may only be for a brief time.[241] So, in July 1811, the marbles began to be carted to what was to be their fourth makeshift home since their arrival in London.[242] Some of the marbles were placed in 'a half-timbered outhouse' in the back yard of Burlington House, but, since this was rather small, some of the larger pieces had to remain outside in the open air.[243] Contemporary drawings show marble fragments 'piled higgledy-piggledy on top of one another'.[244] At this point, Burlington House was sold and the new owner intended to do extensive building work.[245] By April 1815, the building work had commenced, and the marbles had to be rearranged within the courtyard.[246] The owner started to press Elgin to remove the marbles altogether.[247] There was no option but that the marbles should be moved again.

Accounts of the state of the marbles at Burlington House at around this time show that they were in a sorry state. Grass had begun to grow around the architectural fragments abandoned outside to the vagaries of the English weather.[248] Artist Benjamin Robert Haydon wrote in his diary in May 1815:

> I came home from the Elgin Marbles melancholy. I almost wish the French had them; we do not deserve such productions. There they lie, covered with dust & dripping with damp . . . I sat amidst the ruins of Athens this evening, piled on each other as if shaken by an earthquake.[249]

While the marbles lay aimlessly at Burlington House, being regularly moved around inside the courtyard to make room for the building work,[250] some fragments were

[238]Hansard (1815).

[239]St Clair (1998) 174.

[240]St Clair (1998) 178.

[241]Smith (1916) 313.

[242]St Clair (1998) 178-179.

[243]St Clair (1998) 179, 214; St Clair (1999) 401.

[244]St Clair (1998) 214 and plates 8 and 9.

[245]St Clair (1998) 218-219.

[246]St Clair (1998) 219-220.

[247]St Clair (1998) 220.

[248]St Clair (1998) 214.

[249]Haydon (1960) 439, 441.

[250]St Clair (1998) 225.

stolen, never to be seen again.[251] It was around that time that another consignment of marbles arrived in London.[252] These late arrivals would not be included in the collection but were instead shipped to Scotland and Broomhall, which was thus to have its share of sculptured marble.[253] These marbles and other antiquities remained in the possession of the Elgin family at Broomhall, where Adolf Michaelis saw and described them in 1884.[254] It appears that some of them have now been sold.[255]

3.7 Conclusion

This chapter has reviewed the circumstances of the removal of the Parthenon marbles and other antiquities from the Acropolis and the destruction that was thus caused. It asked the question whether Elgin had permission to remove the marbles from the walls of the Parthenon and argued that he never did have permission (whether prior or ex post), a fact that was confirmed by the British ambassador, Adair. The chapter further looked into how the marbles were obtained and found that they were neither a gift nor purchased but acquired through bribes. Once removed, the marbles were shipped on various vessels following different routes. Those included in the *Mentor*'s second cargo found themselves on the bottom of the sea, some of them lying there for 2 years before they were rescued. The destruction and the circumstances in which the collection was obtained did not fail to move Elgin's contemporaries, many of whom criticised him strongly. Ultimately, Elgin's collection reached London, where it changed home several times, some of it was placed in a temporary shed, some of it in the open air, some of it made its way to Broomhall, and some of it was stolen.

References

Charles Abbott, *Diary and Correspondence of Charles Abbott, Lord Colchester* (vol 2, John Murray 1861)
Robert Adair, *The Negotiations for the Peace of the Dardanelles in 1808-9* (vol 1, Longman 1845)
John Adolphus, *Voyages and Travels* (Jones 1812)
Vittorio Barale, 'The European Marginal and Enclosed Seas: An Overview' in Vittorio Barale and Martin Gade (eds), *Remote Sensing of the European Seas* (Springer 2008)
Jakob Ludwig Salomo Bartholdy, *Voyage en Grèce* (vol 1, Dentu 1807)

[251] British Museum (1833) 107.
[252] St Clair (1998) 226.
[253] St Clair (1998) 226.
[254] Michaelis (1884).
[255] St Clair (1998) 260.

Stanley Thomas Bindoff, Elizabeth Frances Malcolm-Smith, and Charles Kingsley Webster, *British Diplomatic Representatives, 1789-1852* (Royal Historical Society 1934)

British Museum, *Elgin and Phigaleian Marbles* (vol 2, Society for the Diffusion of Useful Knowledge 1833)

George Gordon Byron, *Lord Byron's Correspondence* (ed John Murray, vol 1, Cambridge University Press 1922, reprinted 2011)

George Gordon Byron, *The Complete Works of Lord Byron, including his Suppressed Poems* (vol 1, Baudry's Foreign Library 1832)

Stratford Canning, *The Life of the Right Honourable Stratford Canning* (Stanley Lane-Poole ed, vol 1, Longmans, Green, and Company 1888)

François-René de Chateaubriand, *Travels to Jerusalem and the Holy Land through Egypt* (3rd edn, vol 1, tr Frederic Shoberl, Henry Colburn 1835)

Edward Daniel Clarke, *Travels in Various Countries of Europe, Asia and Africa: Greece, Egypt, and the Holy Land* (pt 2, section II, 4th edn, T Cadell and W Davies 1818)

Edward Dodwell, *A Classical and Topographical Tour through Greece* (vol 1, Rodwell and Martin 1819)

Frederick SN Douglas, *An Essay on Certain Points of Resemblance between the Ancient and Modern Greeks* (John Murray 1813)

Edhem Eldem, 'From Blissful Indifference to Anguished Concern: Ottoman Perceptions of Antiquities, 1799–1869' in Zainab Bahrani, Zeynep Çelik, and Edhem Eldem (eds), *Scramble for the Past: A Story of Archaeology in the Ottoman Empire, 1753-1914* (SALT/Garanti Kültür 2011)

John Galt, *Voyages and Travels in the Years 1809, 1810, and 1811* (2nd edn, Cadell and Davies 1813)

Michael Greenhalgh, *Plundered Empire: Acquiring Antiquities from Ottoman Lands* (Brill 2019)

Hansard, *Parliamentary Debates 1815* ('Petition of the Earl of Elgin Respecting His Collection of Marbles', 15 June 1815) (vol 31, Hansard 1815)

Benjamin Robert Haydon, *The Diary of Benjamin Robert Haydon* (ed Willard Bissell Pope, vol 1, Harvard University Press 1960)

Christopher Hitchens, *The Parthenon Marbles* (first publication 1987, Verso 2008)

John Cam Hobhouse, *A Journey Through Albania: And Other Provinces of Turkey in Europe* (vol 1, James Cawthorn 1813)

Thomas S Hughes, *Travels in Sicily, Greece and Albania* (vol 1, J Mawman 1820)

George Keith Elphinstone, *The Keith Papers* (vol 2, Navy Records Society 1927)

Elena Korka and Seyyed Mohammad Taghi Shariat-Panahi, 'Early 19th-century Athens, the Great Powers, and the Parthenon Sculptures' in Maria Georgopoulou and Konstantinos Thanasakis (eds), *Ottoman Athens: Archaeology, Topography, History* (Gennadius Library of the American School of Classical Studies at Athens and Aikaterini Laskaridis Foundation 2019)

John Henry Merryman, 'Thinking about the Elgin Marbles' (1985) 83 (8) Michigan Law Review 1881

Adolf Michaelis, 'Ancient Marbles in Great Britain Supplement I' (1884) 5 Journal of Hellenic Studies 143

Adolf Michaelis, *Ancient Marbles in Great Britain* (tr Charles Augustus Maude Fennell, Cambridge University Press 1882)

Jenifer Neils, *The Parthenon Frieze* (Cambridge University Press 2001)

John Patrick Nisbet Hamilton Grant (ed), *The Letters of Mary Nisbet of Dirleton, Countess of Elgin* (J Murray 1928)

Geoffrey Robertson, *Who Owns History? Elgin's Loot and the Case for Returning Plundered Treasure* (Biteback Publishing 2019)

David Rudenstine, 'Lord Elgin and the Ottomans: The Question of Permission' (2002) 23 (2) Cardozo Law Review 449

David Rudenstine, 'A Tale of Three Documents: Lord Elgin and the Missing, Historic 1801 Ottoman Document' (2001) 22 Cardozo Law Review 1853

Select Committee of the House of Commons, *Report on the Earl of Elgin's Collection of Sculptured Marbles* (Bulmer 1816)
AH Smith, 'Lord Elgin and his Collection' (1916) 36 Journal of Hellenic Studies 163
William St Clair, *Who Saved the Parthenon?* (Open Book Publishers 2022)
William St Clair, *Lord Elgin and the Marbles* (Oxford University Press 1967, 1998, reprinted 2003)
William St Clair, 'The Elgin Marbles: Questions of Stewardship and Accountability' (1999) 8 International Journal of Cultural Property 391
Ana Filipa Vrdoljak, *International Law, Museums and the Return of Cultural Objects* (Cambridge University Press 2006)
Hugh W Williams, *Travels in Italy, Greece and the Ionian Islands* (vol 2, Constable 1820)

Chapter 4
The Acquisition of the Marbles by the UK Government

> These pieces have all been obtained with open eyes, knowing quite well how they were stolen, and what damage was done for this filthy lucre.
>
> WM Flinders Petrie, *Eastern Exploration* (Robert McBride and Co 1918) on the destruction of monuments in Egypt

> Elgin . . . acted with the full knowledge and permission of the legal authorities of the day in . . . London.
>
> British Museum, 'The Parthenon Sculptures: The Trustees' Statement'

4.1 Introduction

When Elgin resolved to sell his collection and first approached the government, the response he received could best be described as lukewarm. In 1811, the government was willing to meet him halfway with respect to the matter about which he must have cared the most, the purchase price: a tentative offer was made for less than half his expenses. Elgin declined. St Clair observed that surviving correspondence between Elgin and government ministers reveals that, if they did agree to purchase the marbles at that stage, they would do so 'grudgingly', and Elgin would be presented 'as someone who had brought misfortune on himself and his country'.[1] Within the space of four short years, priorities would change, even though the ultimate purchase price would not rise much from that first offer. If the initial scepticism did not transform into unconditional enthusiasm, in 1815, the UK government became decidedly interested in buying the collection, partly in order to pre-empt the possibility that the 'noble lord' should sell it abroad—a 'threat' that Elgin himself had made.

[1] St Clair (1998) 178.

C. Titi, *The Parthenon Marbles and International Law*,
https://doi.org/10.1007/978-3-031-26357-6_4

Circumstances now seemed propitious. In June 1815, the same month when Elgin's petition to sell the marbles was at last presented to parliament, Napoleon faced a humiliating defeat at Waterloo. His spoliations that had enriched the Louvre were now to be returned to the places from which they had been taken. Ironically, it was Hamilton, Elgin's private secretary and a future trustee of the British Museum,[2] who supervised the restitution of Napoleon's looted art.[3] Sixteen years earlier, in 1799, he had been deploring Napoleon's sack of Rome's treasures and gave thanks that the frescoes were immovable.[4] In October 1815, he recalled in a letter to Elgin the arguments he had employed to encourage the return of Napoleon's loot: 'these works are considered so sacred a property, that no direct or indirect means are to be allowed for their being conveyed elsewhere than where they came'.[5]

One might assume that the restitution of Napoleon's loot could discourage the UK government from buying the marbles, but it seems to have had the opposite effect. With Napoleon well and truly defeated, Britain emerged as the new uncontested imperial power. Purchasing Elgin's collection for the nation must have seemed as an opportunity to crown the perfect victory and boost the image of the empire.[6] From that point on, the purchase became virtually a foregone conclusion. In early 1816, a parliamentary select committee convened to decide on the merits of Elgin's petition that the government purchase his collection of marbles and other antiquities and determine its value. And in June 1816, the government approved the purchase and transferred the collection to the space and trusteeship of the British Museum.

This chapter examines the purchase negotiations and the debates that led first to the constitution of the parliamentary select committee and later to the purchase of the marbles. The chapter looks into the witness statements made to the select committee in relation to Elgin's 'permission' to remove the marbles and the alleged indifference of the local populations, and it considers the committee's report, which recommended the purchase. It points out the discrepancies between the witness testimonies and the committee's findings, and it questions the report's silence on the irregularities that emerged. The chapter then turns to the final parliamentary debate, which ended with a vote in favour of the purchase, and shows that the doubts we raise today about the purchase are not new but had already been voiced by MPs during that debate. Finally, the chapter reviews the question of title and ownership by addressing a number of distinct issues, from the protection of cultural property in occupied territories to the matter of good faith. It concludes that Elgin did not have legal title to the marbles and therefore he could not pass to the government title that he did not have.

[2] Smith (1916) 369.

[3] Smith (1916) 171.

[4] Hamilton to Elgin (14 November 1799), cited in Smith (1916) 171.

[5] Hamilton to Elgin (*c* 15 October 1815) Elgin, cited in Smith (1916) 332.

[6] Editorial, 'Opinion: The Guardian View on the Parthenon Marbles: Not Just a Brexit Sideshow', The Guardian (23 February 2020).

4.2 Negotiations and Debates

Once Elgin knew he would sell his collection, he decided to provide his version of the story. The anonymously published *Memorandum on the Subject of the Earl of Elgin's Pursuits in Greece* was a powerful piece of self-promotion and propaganda. It explained how, from the start, Elgin's intention had been to serve the arts, that the UK government had discouraged him but that he went on to obtain the collection anyway, and that, once he was aware of the destruction caused by the Ottomans and of French avarice, he resolved to do his best to save all the sculptures on which he could lay his hands.[7] With his version of the story now public, Elgin wrote to Long, the Paymaster General, citing the *Memorandum* and offering an account of the expenses he incurred in order to acquire the marbles: £62,440 in total (in today's money almost £7.2 million),[8] although a whopping 37% was for interest of 5% over 14 years.[9] He mentioned three additional items, to which he did not attach a price, perhaps hoping, as St Clair thought, that the government would round the amount up to £70,000.[10] On the same day, he wrote to the prime minister, Perceval, making an additional request in exchange for his collection: 'To a Scotch peer', he said, 'nothing could be so desirable as a British peerage'.[11] If he was accorded a peerage, he would be prepared to accept payment by instalments or, in part, by annuity.[12]

The prime minister ruled out the possibility of a peerage, and Long let Elgin know that he was willing to propose the sum of £30,000 to parliament for the purchase of the collection, an offer which Elgin found he was unable to accept.[13] He produced a list of his expenses ruefully contending that he had spent double that amount on the marbles.[14] Negotiations continued for a short while but the government did not budge.[15] Later, Elgin provided an updated account of his expenses, which raised significantly the total amount.[16] However, after it was pointed out to him that

[7] St Clair (1998) 175. See *Memorandum* (1811) and *Memorandum* (1815).

[8] CPI Inflation Calculator https://www.officialdata.org/uk/inflation/1816?amount=21902 (information correct as of November 2022). The price is inflation-adjusted using 1816, the purchase year, as reference.

[9] Elgin to Long (1811; with a Postscript added February 1816) reproduced in Select Committee (1816) as Appendix No 5.

[10] St Clair (1998) 177.

[11] Elgin to Perceval (6 May 1811), as cited in St Clair (1998) 177.

[12] St Clair (1998) 177-178.

[13] Select Committee (1816) 54.

[14] Select Committee (1816) 54.

[15] St Clair (1998) 178.

[16] Elgin to Long (1811; with a Postscript added February 1816) reproduced in Select Committee (1816) as Appendix No 5; Elgin to Bankes (13 March 1816), reproduced in Select Committee (1816) as Appendix No 6.

expenses such as the salaries of his agents could not be taken into account,[17] he lowered the amount to £74,240[18] (about £8 million today).

Elgin's petition to sell his collection to the government was brought to parliament in June 1815. In that debate, John Newport voiced his concern that Elgin 'had availed himself of most unwarrantable measures, and had committed the most flagrant acts of spoliation'.[19] If the government 'should consent to purchase the collection, they would evidently sanction acts of public robbery'.[20] He argued that 'a full inquiry ought to be made into the manner in which the collection had been acquired'.[21] The British Museum, which appeared to have previously refused the marbles for lack of space, was now determined to have them, if the government bought them.[22] A decision was postponed until early 1816, when the matter was brought again to parliament.

On 15 February 1816, the Chancellor of the Exchequer presented Elgin's petition to the House of Commons.[23] The narrative this petition offers is consistent with the image Elgin wished to project in the *Memorandum*: Elgin, lamenting the depredations to which the Turks exposed the marbles and wishing to rescue them from danger and preserve the archaeological record, first removed them and now wished to transfer them to the public.[24] Yet make no mistake, this was not an act of generosity. Elgin solicited parliament to look into 'the merits and value' of his collection and to consider 'how fair and upon what conditions it may be advisable that the property of the said collection should be transferred to the public'.[25] From the beginning, the primary task of the select committee was *not* to investigate the circumstances in which Elgin removed the marbles from the Acropolis nor to determine whether he had obtained them lawfully, but to examine whether and at what price he should be able to sell his collection to the UK government. This was reiterated a few days later, in the parliamentary debate that took place on 23 February 1816, when the Chancellor of the Exchequer, plainly favourable to Elgin, dismissed any doubt as to the 'circumstances under which the noble lord had become possessed of those matchless productions'.[26] These circumstances were 'so well-known', he said, that 'he would not trouble the House at any length on the subject'.[27] At this point, he repeated his earlier eulogy of Elgin's actions ('his object has been solely

---

[17] Smith (1916) 340.

[18] Elgin to Bankes (13 March 1816), reproduced in Select Committee (1816) as Appendix No 6, xxi; cf Select Committee (1816) 13.

[19] Hansard (1815).

[20] Hansard (1815).

[21] Hansard (1815).

[22] Hansard (1815).

[23] Hansard (1816a) c 577.

[24] Hansard (1816a) cc 577-578.

[25] Hansard (1816a) c 578.

[26] Hansard (1816a) c 823.

[27] Hansard (1816a) c 823.

directed to the advancement of the arts'; '[t]he desire of conferring honour on the arts as well as on the arms of this country was the object of his motion', etc.).[28]

The sceptical reader is likely to wonder why Elgin, so desirous of advancing the arts in his country, also warned the government that, 'if the present opportunity was neglected it might never occur again' and that, if the marbles were not bought by the UK government, he saw no prospect but that 'these exquisite works of art must be dispersed, or disposed of to foreign purchasers'.[29] So much for his love of arts and patria. But the possibility that the marbles might be sold outside the United Kingdom—let alone to the French!—was reason enough to encourage the purchase.

But others did not share the Chancellor of the Exchequer's enthusiasm. While some objected to the purchase on account of its expense and the nation's distressed finances,[30] others denounced the manner in which the collection had been acquired and advised that the select committee should look carefully into whether 'the whole transaction was consonant with national honour'.[31] If it were not, the government 'should have nothing to do' with the marbles.[32] But it appears that these doubts did not inform the mandate ultimately given to the select committee, which was appointed following this debate.[33] Elgin's case was back with a vengeance.

4.3 The Select Committee Inquiry

The select committee of the House of Commons was appointed in late February 1816 to consider the question whether Elgin's collection should be purchased by the UK government and if so at what price.[34] It was composed of eighteen MPs, including the Chancellor of the Exchequer and Long, who had been involved in the earlier purchase negotiations.[35] Although the select committee was not constituted in order to consider the lawfulness of Elgin's actions, nor for that matter whether Elgin had been able to acquire the marbles thanks to his ambassadorial position (a topic to which we will return), it is perhaps revealing that the select committee did ask both questions. Consequently, the inquiry addressed four matters: first, the authority by which the collection was obtained; second, the circumstances under which such authority was granted; third, the 'merit' of the marbles 'as works

[28] Hansard (1816a) cc 823-824.

[29] Hansard (1816a) cc 824, 827. See also Abbott (1861) 328. It was also reported that the Crown Prince of Bavaria had 'deposited a large sum of money in a London bank' and was eager to buy the marbles, if the British government did not, St Clair (1998) 225.

[30] Hansard (1816a) cc 826-827.

[31] Hansard (1816a) c 828.

[32] Hansard (1816a) c 828. See also Chap. 1, text to n 127.

[33] Hansard (1816a) c 828.

[34] Select Committee (1816) 1.

[35] St Clair (1998) 246.

of Sculpture, and the importance of making them Public Property, for the purpose of promoting the study of the Fine Arts in Great Britain'; and, fourth, the value of the marbles 'as objects of sale', including by taking into account Elgin's expenses in removing them and bringing them to the United Kingdom.[36] The bulk of the select committee's report was dedicated to the last two questions. We will focus instead on the first two questions, considering, first, the witness testimonies in relation to Elgin's 'permission' and the alleged indifference of the local populations to the removals; and, second, the report and findings of the select committee. Witness testimonies concerning whether Elgin obtained the marbles as a private citizen or as ambassador will be examined separately later in the chapter (Sect. 4.5.3).

4.3.1 Witness Testimonies

4.3.1.1 The question of permission (again)

Elgin was the first witness to appear before the select committee.[37] His testimony was evasive, muddled, and contradictory. He announced to the select committee that the July 1801 Ottoman document, the purported firman, was 'addressed by the Porte to the local authorities, *to whom I delivered it*; and I have retained none of them'.[38] Yet, as we have seen, it was Hunt who delivered the document to the authorities in Athens—during that time, Elgin was in Constantinople and he would not visit Greece until the following spring. It is also unclear why Elgin referring to the 'permission' used the plural pronoun 'them'. He seemed to either be mixing things up or to be thinking of more than one document—Hunt's 'letters' for the voivode perhaps? Since he had not kept any of the original documents, the select committee asked:

> [D]id not your Lordship keep any copy of any of the written permissions that were given to your Lordship? – I kept no copies whatever; every paper that could be of use at Athens, was left there as a matter of course, because Lusieri, continued there: the few papers I brought away with me, were burnt on my detention in France; my private papers I mean, and all my accounts, which I had brought away from Turkey.[39]

This is rather strange. Elgin did not have a copy of such an important document as the assumed permission that made the removal of the Parthenon marbles possible (and lawful) and he did claim that all his 'private papers' were burnt. But his claim is contradicted by his personal papers that *have* survived from his time in Athens: a *travel* firman for him and his family, currently in Broomhall;[40] or correspondence he

[36] Select Committee (1816) 1.

[37] Select Committee (1816) 31.

[38] Select Committee (1816) 35 (emphasis added).

[39] Select Committee (1816) 36.

[40] A photograph of this travel firman is published in Williams (2009) 58, fig 6.

received during the time he was ambassador, actually relied upon in this book. Then why would Elgin claim that all his papers were destroyed? No doubt, this was a convenient—if untrue—explanation as to why he did not have the purported firman. If one firman were kept religiously and should survive, why is that a mere travel firman?

> In point of fact, your Lordship has not in England any copy of any of those written permissions? – None.
>
> Did the Committee understand you to say, that it is possible Lusieri has such copies? – Certainly; they will be at Athens, either in his possession or in the possession of the authorities there.
>
> Has your Lordship any distinct recollection of having had such copies of the authorities, and of having left them in Lusieri's possession? – I cannot speak to the fact so precisely as the Committee may wish; the authority itself was given over to the proper officer and then Lusieri obtained from him any part of it that was necessary to be exhibited on any future occasion.
>
> Did your Lordship, for your own satisfaction, keep any copy of the terms of those permissions? – No, I never did.[41]

Elgin's claim that he had permission to remove the marbles from the Parthenon walls receives another blow from his own testimony. When asked by the select committee whether the Ottoman government knew that he was removing the marbles from the Parthenon, his answer was not a straightforward 'yes', as one might expect, but rather: 'No doubt was ever expressed to me of their knowledge of it.'[42] How would someone express a doubt about knowing a matter they didn't know? While the operations had been going on at Athens for a long time, the local officials had been kept sweet with bribes and, for that very reason, they were afraid for their lives. This is hardly an indication that the central Ottoman authorities knew. Elgin's conclusion that, since no doubt was expressed to him about them knowing, 'they must have been in the intimate knowledge of every thing that was doing'[43] seems entirely unfounded. The select committee pressed the matter: 'Did your Lordship ever apprise any of the Government of it in conversation?' To this Elgin replied: 'The chance is, that I have done it five hundred times, but I cannot answer specifically when or how'.[44] In short, Elgin could not identify one single occasion when he discussed the extent of the removals with the Ottoman government. It seems curious that, on the basis of this very testimony, St Clair would conclude that to 'every question' that was put to him, Elgin 'was able to give honest and convincing answers'![45]

---

[41] Select Committee (1816) 36-37.

[42] Select Committee (1816) 42.

[43] Select Committee (1816) 42.

[44] Select Committee (1816) 42.

[45] St Clair (1998) 246.

Later, when Hamilton was asked by the select committee whether he knew anything about the permission Elgin may have received from the Ottoman government, his answer was that he had no personal knowledge of the matter.[46] This should have surprised the select committee: Hamilton was, after all, Elgin's private secretary.

Elgin's first testimony before the parliamentary select committee took place on 29 February and 1 March 1816.[47] Hunt appeared before the select committee about a fortnight later, on 13 March 1816.[48] What happened during these 2 weeks is a matter of speculation. But when the select committee asked Hunt whether he had seen any of the written permissions granted to Elgin, he replied that he had.[49] He explained that he had advised Elgin to apply to the Ottoman government for a firman and, since he had been deceived on previous occasions as to the content of a firman, he asked that the document should be 'accompanied by a literal translation'. This translation he now possessed. It was the Italian translation, although in his statement Hunt failed to mention this. Did Hunt speak Italian? Why would the translation be in Italian? He was for the moment unable to show the translation to the select committee: 'It is left at Bedford, and I have no means of directing any person to obtain it'.[50] It is curious that Elgin knew nothing of Hunt's possession of a copy of the alleged firman. During his testimony, it became clear to him that the select committee was keen on seeing some proof of his permission to remove the marbles. Two weeks later, Hunt appeared like a deus ex machina and announced that he had an accurate translation of the firman.[51]

4.3.1.2 The locals' 'indifference' to the removals

The committee also made great play of the locals' presumed indifference to the removals, although this is contradicted by various statements made to it in the course of its inquiry, including that of John Bacon Sawrey Morritt, a British politician who had been on a tour of Greece and Asia Minor some years earlier. Morritt explained that it was plain knowledge that the Porte 'wished to prevent any thing from being removed' and so 'the local governors of Athens, who were assailable by bribery, endeavoured to conduct the business as secretly as they could, whenever any thing was to be removed, even of the Marbles which were down'.[52] The local Ottoman governors could be bribed and give away antiquities lying on the ground but were

[46] Select Committee (1816) 56.
[47] Select Committee (1816) 31.
[48] Select Committee (1816) 140.
[49] Select Committee (1816) 140.
[50] Select Committee (1816) 141.
[51] Rudenstine (2021) 415-416.
[52] Select Committee (1816) 129-130.

terrified of their superiors finding out.[53] This account strikes a fatal blow to Elgin's statement that the central government somehow must have known what was going on in Athens. Asked whether he thought the Greeks were anxious that the marbles should not be removed from Athens, Morritt replied: 'They were decidedly and strongly desirous that they should not be removed'.[54]

The assumption that the locals were indifferent to the removal of the marbles is also contradicted by the eyewitness account of Clarke, who, described an incident that took place when Elgin's agents were preparing to take down the metopes. The disdar, Clarke explained, came to see for himself the work that was being done, 'but with evident marks of dissatisfaction'; he added that Lusieri himself reported that 'it was with great difficulty he could accomplish this part of his undertaking, from the attachment the Turks entertained towards a building'.[55] Lusieri registered the resistance of the Greeks and Turks on another occasion too. Commenting on Hunt's suggestion that the Erechtheion should be removed, he noted that the 'Turks and the Greeks are extremely attached to it, and there were murmurs when Mr Hunt asked for it'.[56]

Answering questions in relation to marbles looted in 1811 from the island of Aegina near Athens, John Nicholas Fazakerley, a member of the select committee, gave a singular account of the locals' opposition to their removal from Greece. Asked whether the marbles' 'proprietors' 'experienced great difficulty in removing them out of Greece', Fazakerley replied: 'Certainly, very great'.[57] The marbles had been temporarily placed in 'a building almost under ground' and were understood to be there 'in some degree in secret':

> they were not generally shown, and it was understood that the [local Ottoman authorities] had opposed impediments to their removal; and Mr Cockerell called upon me to consult with the English Consul upon the means of enabling him to remove them from Athens to Zante. The English Consul, when we consulted him on the subject, told me that he felt great embarrassment on the subject, and that they must be removed either in secret or by bribery.[58]

This account is complemented by another which tells of how the disdar asked Cockerell to come with a cart to the foot of the Acropolis so that he would give him a slab of the frieze; it was specified that he must come at night, because 'it could not be done in the daytime for fear of giving offence to the Greeks'.[59]

---

[53] Select Committee (1816) 129-130.

[54] Select Committee (1816) 131.

[55] Clarke (1818) 223; also Chap. 3, text to n 175.

[56] Lusieri to Elgin (11 January 1802), cited in Smith (1916) 209. See also Hunt to Elgin (31 July 1801), cited in Smith (1916) 196.

[57] Select Committee (1816) 135.

[58] Select Committee (1816) 135.

[59] Cockerell (1903) 262.

4.3.2 The Report

After the witness testimonies, the select committee issued its report addressing the four questions it set itself to answer but without necessarily providing all the answers. The matter of Elgin's alleged permission to remove the marbles was dealt with summarily in less than two pages[60] and was followed by statements about the purported indifference of the Greeks and Ottomans, as if such indifference, if substantiated, would render Elgin's actions lawful.

The select committee rehearsed Elgin's statements: he obtained 'permission to draw, model, and remove; to which was added, a special, licence to excavate in a particular place'.[61] The bribes were not directly discussed. It was stated only that, according to Elgin, 'all permissions issuing from the Porte to any distant provinces, are little better than authorities to make the best *bargain* that can be made with the local magistracies'.[62] The report observed that the permissions were addressed to the Ottoman authorities in Athens and the committee had no opportunity of learning about 'their exact tenor' from Elgin himself.[63] But it did cite Hunt, who 'has preserved, and has now in his possession, a translation' of the firman, but since he did not have it with him in London 'he stated the substance, according to his recollection'.[64] This 'substance', according to Hunt's recollection, was that, 'in order to show their particular respect to the Ambassador of Great Britain, the august ally of the Porte', the Ottomans gave Elgin and his agents 'the most extensive permission to view, draw, and model the ancient Temples of the Idols, and the sculptures upon them, and to make excavations, and to take away any stones that might appear interesting to them'.[65] It appears that the select committee received the actual translation later and added a postscript: 'A translation of the [firman] itself has since been forwarded by Dr Hunt, which is printed in the Appendix.'[66] Notice: a translation of the firman *itself*, although the committee never had any certain knowledge of the firman's existence.

The select committee printed an English translation in an annex to its report. This translation is not faithful to the Italian translation, so that, in the absence of an original Ottoman document, the story begins to resemble a game of Chinese whispers. The matter of the translation of '*qualche pezzi di pietra*' as 'any', instead of 'some', pieces of stone has already been discussed.[67] More troubling still are the discrepancies that may affect our appreciation of the authenticity of the Italian document. The English translation ends with the words: '(Signed with a signet.)

[60] Select Committee (1816) 3-4.

[61] Select Committee (1816) 3.

[62] Select Committee (1816) 3 (emphasis added).

[63] Select Committee (1816) 3.

[64] Select Committee (1816) 4.

[65] Select Committee (1816) 4.

[66] Select Committee (1816) 5.

[67] See Sect. 3.3.2.

Seged Abdullah Kaimacan',[68] the suggestion being that the document that the select committee inspected bore a signet impression and the signature of the acting grand vizier (or kaymakam).[69] However, the Italian letter has no signet impression nor is it signed, nor for that matter does it claim to have been the translation of a document that had been signed 'with a signet'![70] The Italian document simply reads: *Sotto^{tto}* (for *sottoscritto*, meaning undersigned). The English translation further includes the words: 'We therefore have written this Letter to you, and expedited it by Mr Philip Hunt, an English Gentleman, Secretary of the aforesaid Ambassador, in order that . . .'. Yet the Italian text does not include Hunt's name. It says: '*vi s'è scritta e spedita col NN la presente lettera, afin che . . .*', where NN (perhaps from either *non nullus*, *nomen nescio*, or *nomen nominandum*) indicates that the person whose name is thus omitted is unknown or has not yet been identified. The abbreviation appears to have been in common use 'in formal documents of the time when the name of the beneficiary [was] not yet known'.[71] Was the Italian translation a preparatory document, intended to function as a template?[72] Inconsistencies such as these led Rudenstine to suggest that the select committee 'actually misled' public opinion 'about the evidence it had concerning the authenticity of the document'.[73]

The report of the select committee repeated the statements made by Elgin and Hunt as if they were confirmed facts. It often did not provide its own conclusion, and nowhere did it find that the Ottoman authorities gave Elgin permission to remove any marbles from the Parthenon walls.[74] But it played on ambivalence and created a false impression, even if not saying the actual words. As to the 'crucial' questions, it recommended the purchase and considered that £35,000 would be 'a reasonable and sufficient price' for Elgin's collection.[75]

---

[68] Select Committee (1816), Appendix No 10, Translation from the Italian of a [Firman] or Official Letter xxiv, xxvi.

[69] Rudenstine (2021) 441. At the time in question, the kaymacam, Seyyid Abdullah Pasha, was indeed acting as the deputy of the grand vizier who was in Egypt for military operations. He has been identified as Ömer Paşazade Elhac Abdullah Pasha. The term 'Seyyid' preceding his name was in fact a title, Eldem (2011) 284. See also St Clair (1998) 88.

[70] For a facsimile of the letter, see St Clair (2022) 663-669.

[71] St Clair (2022) 665; David Rudenstine, 'Did Elgin Cheat at Marbles?', The Nation (29 May 2000).

[72] Rudenstine (2001) 1880.

[73] David Rudenstine, 'Did Elgin Cheat at Marbles?', The Nation (29 May 2000).

[74] Rudenstine (2021) 422.

[75] Select Committee (1816) 16.

4.4 The Purchase

Following the report of the select committee, the matter returned to parliament. The crucial debate took place in the House of Commons on 7 June 1816.[76] Those who supported the motion insisted that the marbles would 'promote public taste'.[77] It was suggested that 'the possession of these precious remains of ancient genius and taste would conduce not only to the perfection of the arts, but to the elevation of our national character, to our opulence, to our substantial greatness'.[78] One year after Waterloo, these were weighty arguments. Although it was admitted during the debate that Elgin would not have been able to obtain the marbles had he not been a British ambassador, it was also cryptically added that 'it was not solely as a British ambassador that he obtained them'.[79] No objection was made, they argued, by the government and the local Turks and Greeks, some of whom were employed as labourers.[80] One of the advocates of the purchase noted that 'some gentlemen' appeared to entertain the idea that 'these treasures ... should be restored to their original owners' and asked with apparent contempt: Did they mean that they should be returned to those who placed no value on them?[81] Much was made of the Parthenon's apparent 'state of constant dilapidation and danger' by the supporters of the purchase, who claimed that Elgin 'interfered with nothing that was not already in ruins, or that was threatened with immediate destruction'.[82] They could not 'hear such terms as dishonesty, plunder, spoliation, bribery, and others of the same kind, applied to the conduct of a British nobleman', who instead 'merited the greatest praise'.[83] In any case, anyone familiar with 'the Turkish character must be sensible that when they gave any thing away it was with the view of receiving an equivalent'.[84] A final argument in the pro-purchase camp was that the opportunity might in fact never arise again.[85]

Those who opposed the motion took the view that 'the vague words' of the firman did not allow Elgin to remove the marbles from the walls of the Parthenon.[86] This was plunder, and the marbles were brought to this country in bad faith.[87] They pointed out that the evidence before the select committee 'disproved the assertion

[76] Hansard (1816b) cc 1027-1040.

[77] Hansard (1816b) c 1028.

[78] Hansard (1816b) c 1034.

[79] Hansard (1816b) c 1028, cf 1036.

[80] Hansard (1816b) c 1028. See Chap. 3, text to n 37.

[81] Hansard (1816b) c 1028.

[82] Hansard (1816b) cc 1029, 1031, 1035-1037.

[83] Hansard (1816b) cc 1029, 1036.

[84] Hansard (1816b) c 1039.

[85] Hansard (1816b) cc 1029, 1030, 1039, 1040.

[86] Hansard (1816b) c 1031.

[87] Hansard (1816b) cc 1032, 1037.

that the Turkish government attached no value to these statues'.[88] Elgin had taken advantage of his ambassadorial position and of the British victory over the French to plunder Athens.[89] Bribery had been used.[90] Elgin's acquisition of the marbles itself was viewed as a bribe 'which our ambassador had received, to his dishonour and that of the country'.[91]

Hugh Hammersley's plea that a resolution be passed to the effect that the marbles should be held in trust until Greece should ask for them has already been mentioned.[92] Hammersley also lamented that the ambassador's actions were not in accordance with 'the high and dignified station' of his position and regretted 'that the government had not restrained this act of spoliation'.[93] He added: 'we should exert ourselves to wipe off the stain, and not place in our museum a monument of our disgrace' but restore it where it was taken away from.[94]

Serjeant Best, an MP and elite lawyer,[95] considered that Elgin had behaved unconscionably, whatever might be said in favour of the works of art he brought to Great Britain.[96] While he 'regarded the improvement of national taste much, … he valued the preservation of national honour still more', and he 'could not approve of a representative of his majesty laying himself under obligations to a foreign court, to which he was sent to watch the interests and maintain the honour of the country'.[97] Elgin had abused his ambassadorial rank; the firman had been granted to him as a favour, and he 'had used it contrary to the intention with which it was granted. What would be thought of an ambassador at [a] European court, who should lay himself under obligations by receiving a sum to the amount of 35,000£?'[98] Here again we have an understanding of not only the firman but also the acquisition of the marbles as a bribe to Elgin and indirectly as unjust enrichment. Best continued:

> But even the [firman] lord Elgin had obtained did not warrant him to do as he had done. The [firman] could do nothing without bribery. Could the words in which it was written admit the construction that was put upon them? It merely gave a power to view, to contemplate and design them. Did this mean that these works were to be viewed and contemplated with the design of being pulled down and removed? Lord Elgin himself did not say that he had authority to carry off any thing by means of the [firman]. His lordship was himself the best

88 Hansard (1816b) c 1031.

89 Hansard (1816b) c 1032.

90 Hansard (1816b) c 1032.

91 Hansard (1816b) c 1032.

92 See Chap. 1, text to nn 128-130.

93 Hansard (1816b) c 1032.

94 Hansard (1816b) c 1032.

95 Robertson (2019) Chap. 3 (unnumbered page), discussing the title of 'serjeant', a rank of barristers that no longer exists.

96 Hansard (1816b) c 1037.

97 Hansard (1816b) c 1037.

98 Hansard (1816b) c 1037.

> interpreter of the instrument by which he acted, and he was here an interpreter against himself.[99]

Best next took note of the bribes that had been tendered:

> Dr Hunt's evidence had been quoted, to show that his lordship had authority from the [voivode] of Athens for what he had done, but his words would not bear such an interpretation. Dr Hunt said only that the [voivode] was induced to allow the construction put upon the instrument by lord Elgin. The powerful argument by which the [voivode] was induced to allow the construction alluded to, consisted in a present of a brilliant lustre, fire-arms, and other articles of English manufacture. But these were the arguments that ought to have been used by a British ambassador?[100]

Best added that in any case, works of art such as those that Elgin had brought to Great Britain 'always appeared best in the places to which they were originally fitted'.[101] Finally, some resisted the purchase on account of the country's financial situation.[102]

Although the members who took the floor spoke in almost even numbers in favour of and against the purchase of Elgin's collection, the majority of MPs voted in favour.[103] The deal was struck. Elgin would be offered £35,000 and an act of parliament would ratify the purchase and vest the curation of the marbles in the trustees of the British Museum.[104] Fortunately, the collection would not be dispersed, nor would it be sold abroad, and the British Museum, now secure in its possession of these works of incomparable beauty and symbolism, would outshine the Louvre.

4.5 The Question of Ownership: Whose Marbles?

The purchase was completed in due order and form. But did Elgin have legal title to the marbles? And, if he did not, could he transfer title to the UK government? The remainder of this chapter will lay out a number of distinct matters that can help us answer these questions. This discussion is complementary to the question of permission, as this was addressed in Chap. 3 and earlier in this chapter.

[99] Hansard (1816b) cc 1037-1038.

[100] Hansard (1816b) c 1038.

[101] Hansard (1816b) c 1038.

[102] E.g. Hansard (1816b) c 1040.

[103] Hansard (1816b) cc 1028-1040.

[104] British Museum Act 1816.

4.5.1 Cultural Heritage and Occupied Territories

One issue that was not discussed in the June 1816 debate was whether the Ottoman authorities, as the occupying power, had the legal capacity to agree to the marbles' removal. In other words, even if the central Ottoman government had wished to allow Elgin to engage in the removals, could it validly give a firman to that effect and allow the transportation of the marbles? The Greeks never recognised the Ottoman government as legal and have argued that it did not have the authority to dispose of Greece's cultural heritage.[105] This is in line with modern international law, which in any event imposes on the occupier a duty to protect the cultural heritage of the occupied people.[106] Such protection is incompatible with disposing of their cultural heritage.

By the 1800s, most of what is today Greece was under Ottoman rule and had been part of the Ottoman empire for some centuries. Had then somehow the Greek antiquities become Ottoman property, and could the Ottomans, by exercising sovereignty over the territory, allow these antiquities to be removed? International law did not recognise the transfer of sovereignty to the occupier except in a very rare circumstance known as *debellatio*, a situation where the vanquished nation was completely subjugated to the occupying force.[107] In a case of *debellatio*, but not in a case of occupation, the Ottomans may have had the legal capacity to dispose of Greece's cultural heritage. Was then the Greek world under the Ottoman empire in a state of *debellatio* or was it an occupied territory? This is a vexed question, and not only because at the time of the fall of Constantinople to the Ottomans in 1453 Greece was part of the Byzantine empire and international law was still very much an inchoate system. *Debellatio* occurs when a number of cumulative conditions are met. These include the requirement that the entire territory should be occupied, that the occupied people's 'governing institutions' should cease to function, and that there should be no organised resistance and no third states still fighting on behalf of the occupied territory.[108] It is unclear that these requirements were satisfied in the case of the Greek world under the Ottoman empire, especially at the turn of the nineteenth century. Some regions, including those of the Stato da Màr, Venice's overseas' possessions, had either remained outside Ottoman rule (e.g. several Ionian islands, although they were not independent), or they changed occupier, and wars would be fought for them between Venice and the Ottoman empire (e.g. parts of the Peloponnese, Crete). Certain cities enjoyed a rudimentary form of self-governance, and the local rulers often were, or at least included, Greek magnates. The Orthodox Church continued to operate throughout Ottoman rule at a time when the church was

[105] 'Q&A Melina Mercouri: Greece's Claim to the Elgin Marbles', The New York Times (4 March 1984).

[106] For a discussion, see Sect. 9.2.1 and Chap. 10, *passim*.

[107] Dinstein (2017) 52; Benvenisti (2012) 8, 20, 27, 56; Schmitt (2009), para 1; Crawford (2006) 73; Verzijl (1970) 361; Fitzmaurice (1957) 132.

[108] Dinstein (2017) 53; Schmitt (2009), paras 2-4, 8.

distinctly a state institution. It was in effect incorporated in the Ottoman state machine, but it could hardly have been described as an 'Ottoman' institution.[109] It also appears that some pockets of resistance stubbornly persisted throughout the occupation, and rebellions took place with a certain regularity, often assisted by foreign powers.[110] More significant is that, at the turn of the nineteenth century, a philhellenic movement was already in operation, encouraging and supporting what, with the help of friendly nations, would become the Greek war of independence in a matter of a few years. These elements raise serious doubts about whether this was *debellatio*, as does the later achievement of independence, which reveals in hindsight this period as a *temporary*, if very long, transfer of control over the territory—an occupation, rather than *debellatio*. The notion of *debellatio* does not survive in contemporary international law.[111]

It is sometimes suggested that even the law of occupation was less favourable to Greece's claim to the marbles than the law of war would have been. If Elgin had removed the marbles during wartime, the international law of the time would have been much stricter on Elgin, and his actions would have been scrutinised more closely.[112] Contemporary international law tends to 'doubly' safeguard cultural heritage in occupied territories; the conventions that protect cultural heritage in *wartime* also cover occupations—as do the conventions that protect cultural heritage in *peacetime*.[113] But in the early nineteenth century, it was probably clearer that at least the law of war protected against the destruction of cultural property: plunder during war and an obligation to restore what had been removed had already become part of customary international law.[114] The negotiations in relation to the return of Napoleon's loot turned precisely on the legality of plunder in wartime. In 1815, Castlereagh proclaimed that the French war booty was 'contrary to every principle of justice, and to *the usages of modern warfare*'.[115]

However, let us assume that the principles articulated in 1815 did not concern an occupied territory, and let us even assume that Greece under the Ottoman empire

---

[109] Zachariadou (2006); Georgiades Arnakis (1952).

[110] Philip Chrysopoulos, 'Greeks Revolted More than 100 Times Before the War of Independence', The Greek Reporter (14 March 2022).

[111] Schmitt (2009), paras 11, 17. See also Benvenisti (2012) 95.

[112] Fincham (2013) 972.

[113] See Sect. 9.2.1.

[114] In an 1836 legal treatise, the jurist Henry Wheaton expressed the view that 'by the modern usage of nations, which has now acquired the force of law, temples of religion, public edifices devoted to civil purposes only, monuments of art, and repositories of science, are exempted from the general operations of war', Wheaton (1836) 252. See further Kowalski (2001) 61, arguing that from 1815, 'a ban on plunder and the corresponding obligation of restitution became commonly accepted international customs'; Séfériadès (1932) 64-81, arguing that such customary international law existed, drawing arguments principally from peace treaties. Contrast Francioni (2012) 8-12. See also Chap. 9, n 23.

[115] Note delivered by Viscount Castlereagh to the Allied Ministers, and placed upon their Protocol, Paris, 11 September 1815, reprinted in von Martens (1818) 606 (emphasis added).

was not an occupied territory but had been extinguished by *debellatio*. In 'allowing' the marbles to leave Greece, could the Ottoman authorities in fact transfer title to them? Public property of the state, including 'all public buildings and their contents', belongs to the sovereign state and, as such, 'can be claimed by the State at any time exercising sovereignty over the territory'.[116] This kind of property is inalienable, as the International Court of Justice held in the *Temple of Preah Vihear* case.[117] That state authorities do not divest themselves of title to such public and religious monuments is a principle now 'embodied in all the international conventions dealing with the protection of such buildings in war and peace'.[118] So, whatever use the Ottomans made of the Parthenon and its marbles, Greece could claim them back, once it became an independent sovereign state. This principle was eloquently articulated by Greenfield, who explained that 'title to "immovable property" never passes, regardless of how acquired'.[119] The Parthenon marbles are part of a building and a public monument, therefore 'they are legally "immovable"'.[120] Accordingly, she suggested that 'the continued retention of the marbles, however they were initially acquired, is contrary to such a principle of international law'.[121] We will briefly return to this principle when considering the *Temple of Preah Vihear* case in Chap. 7.

4.5.2 Corruption

The fact of corruption too contradicts the validity of Elgin's and the government's title to the marbles. Knowledge about the bribes that had been tendered for the acquisition of the marbles was public at the time of the purchase: the select committee had the information before it and so did the government.[122] The prominence given to the discussion of the bribes in the June 1816 debate in the House of Commons reveals how serious this issue was. During that debate, objections were made to the purchase of the marbles on account of the bribery that had been involved,[123] while those who defended Elgin refuted the claims of bribery.[124] As we have seen, these objections related to both Elgin tendering bribes and Elgin receiving the marbles as a bribe.

---

[116] O'Connell (1956) 226.

[117] *Case concerning the Temple of Preah Vihear (Cambodia v Thailand)* (Merits Judgment) [1962] ICJ Rep 6. This is discussed in Chap. 7, text to nn 107-112.

[118] Greenfield (2007) 81.

[119] Greenfield (2007) 82.

[120] Greenfield (2007) 82.

[121] Greenfield (2007) 82.

[122] E.g. see Chap. 3, text to n 162.

[123] E.g. Hansard (1816b) cc 1032, 1037-1038.

[124] Hansard (1816b) cc 1029, 1036, 1039.

Corruption was not only contrary to English law at the time of the events, it had been illegal already since the Magna Carta of 1215,[125] and over the years the country cultivated an image of proud opposition to corruption.[126] Concerns about corruption dominated early Stuart England (from 1603 onwards), and during this time the legal process of impeachment, a kind of trial by parliament, was revived in order to sanction corrupt officials.[127] It was so that at the turn of the 1620s the Lord Chancellor, Francis Bacon, was impeached for accepting bribes from litigants appearing before him in court.[128] He was found guilty, stripped of his office, declared to be forever 'uncapable' of holding 'any office, place, or employment, in the state or commonwealth', fined, and imprisoned in the Tower of London.[129] In 1725, Thomas Parker, Earl of Macclesfield, the Lord Chancellor until that year, was impeached.[130] Convicted of corruption for selling offices, he was fined and imprisoned in the Tower of London until payment of the fine.[131] In the sphere of electoral law, a candidate who bribed voters would have committed an offence already since the 1690s, and later, starting with the Bribery Act of 1729, electoral bribery was actionable in the courts rather than in parliament.[132]

In 1762, bribery at parliamentary elections was described as 'undoubtedly [having] always been a crime at common law, and consequently punishable'.[133] In another case, in 1778, John Whitaker, a public official, was found guilty of corruption, fined and imprisoned, for accepting bribes to relieve persons of jury duty.[134]

It was at about the same time, in the *Holman v Johnson* case, that William Murray, 1st Earl of Mansfield (more commonly known as Lord Mansfield), articulated his famous dictum, according to which, '[n]o court will lend its aid to a man who founds his cause of action upon an immoral or an illegal act'.[135] And later, in the nineteenth century, in *Barclay v Pearson*, the Court of Chancery shed light on the treatment of bribery in English law: 'if a man pays a sum of money by way of a bribe, he can never recover it in an action; because both plaintiff and defendant are equally criminal'.[136] Was it acceptable for an ambassador to tender (or receive) a bribe? Corruption is of course today unambiguously condemned in international law.[137]

---

[125] Magna Carta, para 40. See also Law Commission (2008) xiii.

[126] Knights (2017) 194.

[127] Tite (1974); Peck (2003); Knights (2017) 183.

[128] Howell (1816) 1087-1120.

[129] Howell (1816) 1113. See also Powell (1996).

[130] House of Peers (1725).

[131] House of Peers (1725) 282-284.

[132] Knights (2021) 100.

[133] Eardley-Wilmot (1853) 10.

[134] Oldham (2004) 20.

[135] *Holman v Johnson* (1775) 1 Cowp 341.

[136] *Barclay v Pearson* [1893] 2 Ch 154, 167, as cited in Fincham (2013) 1000.

[137] E.g. UNGA Res 58/4 (31 October 2003) UN Doc A/RES/58/4; GA Res. 25/26, UN GAOR, 25th session, Supp No 28, UN Doc A/8028 (24 October 1970).

4.5.3 Did Elgin Obtain the Marbles as a Private Citizen or as Ambassador?

Elgin may have originally intended the marbles to decorate his grand house in Scotland but did he obtain them as a private citizen? He knew that MPs had challenged his ownership of the marbles with the argument that these already belonged to the government. In the June 1815 parliamentary debate, many took the view that the marbles were 'more than half public property'; if Elgin had used the influence of his public position in order to acquire the marbles, the state already had a claim on his collection, which would impact the amount of any compensation to be paid to him.[138] Such arguments were also raised in the February 1816 debate in the House of Commons. Ossulston asked 'whether an ambassador, residing in the territories of a foreign power, should have the right of appropriating to himself, and deriving benefits from objects belonging to that power'.[139] The implicit answer to this rhetorical question was 'no'. Therefore, Ossulston thought that 'the House should go no farther than to remunerate the noble lord for the trouble and expense at which he had been in bringing over these marbles'.[140] Bankes took the view that the public already possessed a 'vested right' in the marbles and that Elgin had certainly not obtained them as a common traveller but 'had availed himself of his character as an English ambassador to facilitate the acquisition'.[141] Tierney noted that some of the marbles had been transferred to the United Kingdom in warships and therefore 'at the public expense'.[142] Preston suggested that Elgin should have offered the marbles as 'a present to the country' and that if ambassadors were encouraged to do what he had done, many would come back home as 'merchants'.[143] (One cannot help but be reminded of Roman provincial governors and that paragon of virtue among them, Verres, who used their governorships to feather their nest.[144]) For this reason, Preston considered that the government should defray only the expenses Elgin had incurred to obtain the marbles.[145]

Elgin needed the money desperately, so when he appeared before the select committee, he tried to convince it that he had not obtained the marbles because he was British ambassador.[146] He said that an architect had told him that there was little exposure of British art students to ancient Greek art and it might be beneficial for the

---

[138] Hansard (1815).

[139] Hansard (1816a) cc 824-825.

[140] Hansard (1816a) cc 824-825.

[141] Hansard (1816a) c 825.

[142] Hansard (1816a) c 826.

[143] Hansard (1816a) c 827.

[144] See Sect. 1.1.1.

[145] Hansard (1816a) c 827.

[146] See also Chap. 3, text to nn 154-155.

public to have access to cast models.[147] Elgin took soundings among government members about the possibility of receiving help, for creating such casts would be of great 'national importance'; but the response he received on that occasion was 'entirely negative'.[148] Having failed to secure government support, he then tried to disassociate his actions from the government; it was he who obtained the collection not the government, a government that had been unwilling to help him from the start.

In fact, the claim was not so much that he had obtained the antiquities for the government but rather that his 'assault on the Parthenon' was made possible by the fact that the Ottomans treated his 'request as a formal request by the British ambassador on behalf of the British government'.[149] Not only was Elgin British ambassador at Constantinople but at the crucial point in time he became the most powerful ambassador. In the aftermath of the British victory over the French military forces in Egypt, the Ottomans looked to the British to return the province to them—and what better way to convince them than by trying to curry favour with the British ambassador?[150] Elgin himself recognised the impact of this turn of events, but still he denied that he had acquired the marbles thanks to his official capacity.[151]

When interviewed by the parliamentary select committee, Elgin tried to buttress his claim by repeatedly declaring that the Ottomans did not treat him any differently than they did other travellers.[152] When the select committee asked him whether 'the same permission to erect scaffolding and make excavations' was given to others in Athens at that time, Elgin first responded that he was not aware of 'any such instance' and then added that the 'permission' he received 'was the same in substance and in purport as to any other person'.[153] Why he would think that, since he was not aware of any such other permission to have been given to anyone else, must have been as baffling to the parliamentary select committee in 1816 as it is to us today. The select committee did not allow the matter to rest there. Did Elgin suppose the 'permission' to have been the same as that given to others but that he used it to a greater extent? To this Elgin replied that 'no other person had applied for permission to remove or model'.[154] Yet Elgin could hardly have known what permissions others may have requested.[155] The select committee repeated the question: Did Elgin know whether any similar permission had been given to other people? This time, Elgin changed his tune: Choiseul-Gouffier, the former French ambassador to the Porte, who left Constantinople about 7 years before Elgin

[147] Select Committee (1816) 31-32.
[148] Select Committee (1816) 32.
[149] Rudenstine (2021) 404-405.
[150] Select Committee (1816) 3. See also Eldem (2011) 292.
[151] Select Committee (1816) 40, 47-50.
[152] Select Committee (1816) 33, 37.
[153] Select Committee (1816) 34.
[154] Select Committee (1816) 35.
[155] Rudenstine (2021) 407.

arrived,[156] actually 'had the same permission', Elgin said.[157] Patiently, the select committee pressed on: Did he mean that 'permissions to remove Marbles and carry them away had been granted to other individuals?' 'No', Elgin said, and added for good measure (somewhat contradictorily) that he had not obtained more as ambassador than others obtained as travellers.[158] If he did get away with more, it is because no one else sought such an extensive permission.[159] Elgin stated that no one had applied for permission to remove.[160] But the stubborn truth remains that Elgin could not have known if other travellers had sought a similar permission, nor could he have known how the Ottomans would have responded to such requests.[161]

Faced with these contradictions, the select committee probed further Elgin's last claim that no one else had received the same permission: 'Of course your Lordship means to except the permission that you stated before had been long antecedently given to Monsieur Comte de Choiseul?' to which Elgin responded 'Yes', before immediately afterwards admitting that he did not in fact know whether Choiseul-Gouffier had the same permission,[162] despite twice earlier having told the select committee that Choiseul-Gouffier had the same permission.

> Then within your Lordship's knowledge there is no instance of a private individual having obtained such permission? – I have no knowledge of any individual having applied for it, and I do not know whether it has been granted or not.[163]

Elgin's testimony is so contradictory and incoherent as to be unreliable.[164] He stated both that he received the same permissions as every other traveller and that he was not aware of anyone receiving the same permission; he claimed both that no other individual had obtained the same permission and that he did not know if any other person had obtained the same permission; he said that Choiseul-Gouffier had the same permission and that he did not know if Choiseul-Gouffier had the same permission. In fact, Choiseul-Gouffier was not even a good example to make the point that Elgin received no more than other travellers. Choiseul-Gouffier was not just any traveller; like Elgin, he was an ambassador.

Elgin's claims that his ambassadorial position was irrelevant to the 'permission' he obtained also flew in the face of evidence given by other witnesses appearing before the select committee. Hunt himself affirmed repeatedly that a person not in the position of ambassador would *certainly* not have been able to obtain such an

---

[156] Grell (1995).

[157] Select Committee (1816) 35.

[158] Select Committee (1816) 37.

[159] Select Committee (1816) 6, 38.

[160] Select Committee (1816) 38.

[161] Rudenstine (2021) 411.

[162] Select Committee (1816) 38.

[163] Select Committee (1816) 38.

[164] For a similar argument, see Rudenstine (2021) 414.

extensive 'permission' as Elgin did.[165] A similar statement was made by George Hamilton-Gordon, 4th Earl of Aberdeen, another 'collector' derided by Byron and a future prime minister of the United Kingdom.[166] Aberdeen stated unambiguously that a private citizen could not have obtained what Elgin did; it would have been necessary to take advantage of the authority of his position.[167]

Even more damning than Hunt's and Aberdeen's testimony is the purported firman itself, which repeatedly refers to Elgin as an ambassador and expressly suggests that the favour shown to him is 'in conformity with what is due to friendship, sincerity, alliance and good will subsisting ab antiquo between the Sublime and ever durable Ottoman Court and that of England'.[168] The same importance granted to Elgin's ambassadorial rank is evident in the surviving documents relating to the 1810 order that allowed the remainder of Elgin's collection to be shipped. One of these documents expressly stated that the shipment order would be issued as 'a sign of deference to the ambassador'.[169] Elgin's communications with the Ottoman authorities were carried out through the British dragoman, the interpreter of the embassy,[170] thus creating the impression that Elgin's requests in relation to the Acropolis were made on behalf of the UK government.[171] Elgin's later plea to be allowed to ship the remainder of his collection in Athens was also submitted by the British ambassador.[172]

Moreover, as it was rightly pointed out by Tierney in parliament, Elgin used warships and other vessels of the UK government to transport the marbles to England.[173] Everything other than Elgin's own impression points to the fact that he obtained the marbles crucially thanks to his ambassadorial position, even if he accumulated these treasures with a view to enhancing his personal collection. Yet the select committee report stopped short of drawing this conclusion, although it referred to both Aberdeen's and Hunt's accounts to the effect that only an ambassador could obtain what Elgin did.[174] Despite not arriving at an express conclusion, the report appeared to condone Elgin's position that he was not treated differently than other travellers. It stated:

---

[165] Select Committee (1816) 144-145.

[166] St Clair (1998) 137.

[167] Select Committee (1816) 122.

[168] Select Committee (1816), Appendix No 10, Translation from the Italian of a [Firman] or Official Letter, xxiv-xxvi.

[169] Eldem (2011) 292.

[170] Select Committee (1816) 56.

[171] Rudenstine (2021) 415.

[172] See Sect. 3.3.2.

[173] For a list of the ships that Elgin used, see Smith (1916) 292-294.

[174] Select Committee (1816) 7.

> [Elgin] looked upon himself in this respect as acting in a character entirely distinct from his official situation. But whether the Government from whom he obtained permission did, or could so consider him, is a question which can be solved only by conjecture and reasoning, in the absence and deficiency of all positive testimony.[175]

This absence of direct evidence was explained by the fact that the select committee did nothing to try to obtain the relevant information. The report continued by acknowledging that Elgin benefited from a particular geopolitical situation and pressed home his advantage to obtain the marbles.[176] The fact of the matter is that no other individual—or even ambassador for that matter—obtained what Elgin did. There was certainly something very irregular at work. The effect of the above statements in the report of the select committee was to endorse the understanding that Elgin acquired the marbles as a private citizen, and therefore the purchase could go ahead.[177]

This decision to allow the purchase, rather than consider that the marbles already belonged to the nation because Elgin had acquired them as ambassador, may have had an impact on the important issue at hand: how much to pay Elgin for the collection. As we saw at the beginning of this section, the MPs who argued that the marbles were already public property considered that the government should pay Elgin only for his expenses. However, Elgin had calculated his expenses at over double the sum the government ultimately offered him for the purchase. In other words, it may have been cheaper for the government to buy the marbles than to consider that it already owned them and pay Elgin for his expenses. But there is yet a subtler reason why it may have been preferable for the government to let well alone. It is possible that by disassociating itself from Elgin's actions, the government was hoping to also disassociate itself from eventual responsibility for his conduct: if Elgin had not acted as ambassador but in his personal capacity, the implicit suggestion was that in obtaining the marbles he did not act as an organ of state. However, eventual responsibility of the sending state for the conduct of its ambassador can be established independently of how the government characterises this conduct.

4.5.4 Did the UK Government Acquire Rights in the Marbles? (and the Question of Good Faith)

According to the legal rule (or principle) going by the maxim *nemo dat quod non habet* (no one gives what one does not have), Elgin could not transfer to the United

[175] Select Committee (1816) 6.
[176] Select Committee (1816) 6.
[177] E.g. see Merryman (1985) 1902.

Kingdom legal title that he did not hold.[178] The effect of the *nemo dat* rule is that one who does not have good title cannot convey good title.[179]

We have already established that Elgin did not hold a valid legal title to the marbles. Despite his defective title, could the UK government acquire rights, if it were a good faith purchaser? Civil law systems tend to protect the rights of good faith purchasers, although common law systems generally do not.[180] Modern international conventions that safeguard cultural heritage and provide a framework for its return when it has been stolen or illegally exported provide some protection for good faith purchasers. The 1970 UNESCO Convention establishes that 'just compensation' shall be paid to an 'innocent purchaser'.[181] The UNIDROIT Convention provides for 'fair and reasonable compensation' for a good faith possessor, that is, a possessor who 'neither knew nor ought reasonably to have known' that the object was stolen or illegally exported and can prove that he or she 'exercised due diligence' at the time of the acquisition of a stolen object.[182] While neither convention is directly applicable to the Parthenon marbles case, it must be observed that under these conventions good faith purchase would not allow title to pass nor would it prevent the return of the marbles, but an amount of compensation might have been required. It is then suggested that title to the marbles did not pass.[183]

In any event, the question of the protection of good faith purchasers is moot, because there was no good faith. As the British Museum trustees helpfully remind us, Elgin acted 'with the full knowledge' of the authorities in London.[184] If we were in any doubt, we would only need to look at the select committee investigation to know that at the time of the parliamentary debate on the purchase, the crucial information was out in the open and the government was in possession of the facts.

The select committee, whose report allowed parliament to rubber stamp the purchase, had done nothing to look for genuine testimonies but was content with calling in Elgin and his agents and taking their word. It always adopted the most convenient approach, sometimes against overwhelming evidence to the contrary. Its report did not actually state that Elgin's removal of the marbles was lawful. Although the committee set itself the task of examining this question and presumably coming to a conclusion, the report remained silent on the matter of the lawfulness of the removal but, by failing to condemn the removal, endorsed it. The select committee

[178] The rule is now reflected in the Sale of Goods Act 1979 s 21(1), according to which:

> Subject to this Act, where goods are sold by a person who is not their owner, and who does not sell them under the authority or with the consent of the owner, the buyer acquires no better title to the goods than the seller had, unless the owner of the goods is by his conduct precluded from denying the seller's authority to sell.

[179] Youngblood Reyhan (2001) 978; Merryman (2008).

[180] Merryman (2008); Renold (2009) 309. E.g. see Sale of Goods Act 1979, c 54, s 23.

[181] 1970 UNESCO Convention art 7.

[182] UNIDROIT Convention arts 4(1), 6(1).

[183] See also Greenfield (2007) 83.

[184] See annex, 'The Parthenon Sculptures: The Trustees' Statement' (British Museum).

had before it enough evidence to come to the only obvious conclusion: the removal was unlawful.

In particular, the select committee failed to corroborate Elgin's claim that he had permission to remove the marbles, and it also failed to address the issue of corruption, which, as we have seen, was regarded as a crime by English law. As for the alleged official Ottoman permission, it was not long after Elgin started to give evidence that it became clear that he had absolutely no proof of such permission. We saw that Elgin declared noncommittally that, 'certainly', Lusieri in Athens must have had a copy of the proof in his possession or the local Ottoman officials there must have had this.[185] Then why not send to Athens for Lusieri, surely a key witness, and for some proof of the permission? There was no 'absence and deficiency of all positive testimony' but rather a decision not to seek the testimony of those parties who could confirm or, most certainly, disprove Elgin's claims. The report stated:

> The Turkish ministers of that day are, in fact, the only persons in the world capable (if they are still alive) of deciding the doubt; and it is probable that even they, if it were possible to consult them, might be unable to form any very distinct discrimination as to the character in consideration of which they acceded to Lord Elgin's request.[186]

This was the easy way out. Why, one wonders, not talk to the Turkish officials? The phrase 'if they are still alive' borders on the ridiculous—such lack of interest in obtaining evidence! The sultan was still alive. Lusieri was still in Athens.[187] The British government had an ambassador, Liston—why not ask him? And why choose to ignore the testimony of another ambassador, the one who intervened for the shipment of the marbles, who stated explicitly that the Ottomans confirmed in no uncertain terms that Elgin never had permission? The former prime minister, Perceval, who had been assassinated a few years earlier, had held Elgin's written admission that the Ottomans did not take the view that he had acted lawfully.[188] Had Perceval kept this information to himself? This indifference that appears to belong to a solipsistic universe, where it is possible to ignore the existence of other witnesses and contrary evidence, must have been as shocking at the time as it is to us today—at least, this is what the reactions of some MPs participating in the June 1816 debate reveal. All the damning evidence pointed to the fact that Elgin had no permission to act as he did. The committee failed to exercise due diligence, and its report and the purchase that followed were tainted by a lack of good faith.

Following the purchase, parliament passed an act to vest the marbles in the trustees of the British Museum. It has been suggested that, since the select committee had made no finding that Elgin's title to the marbles was good, 'it was necessary to impair any defect by transmitting to the trustees a title by statute which could not in consequence be challenged'.[189] This has been described as 'a laundering device –

[185] See text to n 41.

[186] Select Committee (1816) 6.

[187] Select Committee (1816) 2.

[188] See Chap. 3, text to n 160.

[189] Robertson (2019) Chap. 5 (unnumbered page).

the first "whitewashing" of the Parthenon sculptures'.[190] The same legal device had been employed only a few years earlier to vest the Townley collection of (especially Roman) sculptures in the British Museum.[191]

As a consequence, under domestic law the trustees 'own' the marbles. An English court applying English law would have to respect the act and recognise the trustees as the 'owners' of the marbles. This legal construct then allows the British Museum today to invoke domestic law to argue that it owns lawfully the marbles—the marbles were transferred to the museum by act of parliament. But lawfulness under domestic law is not the same as lawfulness under international law, and an act of parliament can decree that a situation is legal in domestic law but cannot do any such thing for international law.

4.6 Conclusion

The chapter considered the negotiations and parliamentary debates on the purchase of Elgin's collection by the government. It looked into the inquiry of the parliamentary select committee, focusing on the question of Elgin's permission to remove the marbles and the local populations' alleged indifference to the despoliation. Next, the chapter turned to the debate on the purchase and showed that the concerns about Elgin's actions and the 'dishonour' they brought to the country are not new but had already been raised by MPs at the time. The chapter then addressed the crucial issue of whether Elgin was able to pass property title to the marbles to the UK government. It asked the question of whether the Ottomans, as the occupying force, had the legal capacity to dispose of the Parthenon marbles and argued that in international law public buildings are legally immoveable and belong to the sovereign state in perpetuity. It appraised the legal significance of the corruption involved in Elgin's acquisition of the marbles at a time when corruption was punishable under English law but observed that this did not prevent the select committee from recommending the purchase. The chapter further asked whether Elgin had obtained the marbles as a private citizen or as ambassador and determined that by purchasing the marbles from Elgin, instead of declaring them to have been public property, the UK government may have hoped to disassociate itself from his actions. The chapter concluded that the purchase was made without good faith and argued that ownership of the marbles did not pass. Yet, after the purchase, an act of parliament vested the marbles in the trustees of the British Museum, making the museum the 'owner' of the marbles under English law.

[190] Robertson (2019) Chap. 5 (unnumbered page).

[191] An Act to vest the Townleian Collection of antient Sculpture in the Trustees of the British Museum for the Use of the Public, 45 George III (1805) c 127.

References

Charles Abbott, *Diary and Correspondence of Charles Abbott, Lord Colchester* (vol 2, John Murray 1861)

Eyal Benvenisti, *The International Law of Occupation* (2nd edn, Oxford University Press 2012)

Edward Daniel Clarke, *Travels in Various Countries of Europe, Asia and Africa: Greece, Egypt, and the Holy Land* (pt 2, section II, 4th edn, T Cadell and W Davies 1818)

Charles Robert Cockerell, *Travels in Southern Europe and the Levant, 1810-1817* (Longmans, Green, and Company 1903)

James Crawford, *The Creation of States in International Law* (2nd edn, Clarendon Press 2006)

Yoram Dinstein, *War, Aggression and Self-Defence* (6th end, Cambridge University Press 2017)

John Eardley-Wilmot, *Is Bribery Without a Remedy? A Letter to the Right Honorable Lord John Russell* (James Ridgway 1853)

Edhem Eldem, 'From Blissful Indifference to Anguished Concern: Ottoman Perceptions of Antiquities, 1799–1869' in Zainab Bahrani, Zeynep Çelik, and Edhem Eldem (eds), *Scramble for the Past: A Story of Archaeology in the Ottoman Empire, 1753-1914* (SALT/Garanti Kültür 2011)

Derek Fincham, 'The Parthenon Sculptures and Cultural Justice' (2013) 23 Fordham Intellectual Property, Media and Entertainment Law Journal 943

Gerald Fitzmaurice, 'The General Principles of International Law Considered from the Standpoint of the Rule of Law' (1957) 92 Recueil des cours 1

Francesco Francioni, 'The Evolving Framework for the Protection of Cultural Heritage in International Law' in Silvia Borelli and Federico Lenzerini (eds), *Cultural Heritage, Cultural Rights, Cultural Diversity* (Martinus Nijhoff 2012)

G Georgiades Arnakis, 'The Greek Church of Constantinople and the Ottoman Empire' (1952) 24 (3) Journal of Modern History 235

Jeanette Greenfield, *The Return of Cultural Treasures* (3rd edn, Cambridge University Press 2007)

Chantal Grell, 'Les ambigüités du philhellénisme. L'ambassade du comte de Choiseul-Gouffier auprès de la Sublime Porte (1784-1792)' (1995) 27 Dix-huitième siècle 223

Hansard, *Parliamentary Debates 1816* (vol 32, Hansard 1816a)

Hansard, *Parliamentary Debates 1816* (vol 34, Hansard 1816b)

Hansard, *Parliamentary Debates 1815* ('Petition of the Earl of Elgin Respecting His Collection of Marbles', 15 June 1815) (vol 31, Hansard 1815)

House of Peers, *The Tryal of Thomas, Earl of Macclesfield in the House of Peers* (Samuel Buckley 1725)

Thomas Bayly Howell, A Complete Collection of State Trials and Proceedings for High Treason and Other Crimes and Misdemeanors (vol 2, Hansard 1816)

Mark Knights, *Trust and Distrust: Corruption in Office in Britain and Its Empire, 1600-1850* (Oxford University Press 2021)

Mark Knights, 'Anticorruption in Seventeenth- and Eighteenth-Century Britain' in Ronald Kroeze, André Vitória, and Guy Geltner (eds), *Anti-corruption in History: From Antiquity to the Modern Era* (Oxford University Press 2017)

Wojciech W Kowalski, 'Restitution of Works of Art pursuant to Private and Public International Law' (2001) 288 Recueil des cours 11

Law Commission, *Reforming Bribery* (Law Com No 313, House of Commons 2008)

Georg Friedrich von Martens, *Nouveau recueil de traités d'alliance, de paix, de trêve, de neutralité, de commerce, de limites, d'échange etc. et de plusieurs autres actes: 1814-1815* (vol 2, Librairie de Dieterich 1818)

Memorandum on the Subject of the Earl of Elgin's Pursuits in Greece (2nd edn, corrected, John Murray 1815)

Memorandum on the Subject of the Earl of Elgin's Pursuits in Greece (William Miller 1811)

John Henry Merryman, 'The Good Faith Acquisition of Stolen Art' in John D Jackson, Maximo Langer, and Peter Tillers (eds), *Crime, Procedure and Evidence in a Comparative and International Context* (Bloomsbury Publishing 2008)

John Henry Merryman, 'Thinking about the Elgin Marbles' (1985) 83 (8) Michigan Law Review 1881

DP O'Connell, *The Law of State Succession* (Cambridge University Press 1956)

James Oldham, *English Common Law in the Age of Mansfield* (University of North Carolina Press 2004)

Linda Levy Peck, *Court Patronage and Corruption in Early Stuart England* (Routledge 2003)

Damien X Powell, 'Why Was Sir Francis Bacon Impeached? The Common Lawyers and the Chancery Revisited: 1621' (1996) 81 History 511

Marc-André Renold, 'Stolen Art: The Ubiquitous Question of Good Faith' in Lyndel V Prott (ed), *Witnesses to History: A Compendium of Documents and Writings* (UNESCO 2009)

Geoffrey Robertson, *Who Owns History? Elgin's Loot and the Case for Returning Plundered Treasure* (Biteback Publishing 2019)

David Rudenstine, 'Trophies for the Empire: The Epic Dispute Between Greece and England Over the Parthenon Sculptures in the British Museum' (2021) 39 Cardozo Arts and Entertainment Law Journal 377

David Rudenstine, 'A Tale of Three Documents: Lord Elgin and the Missing, Historic 1801 Ottoman Document' (2001) 22 Cardozo Law Review 1853

Michael N Schmitt, 'Debellatio' (2009) Max Planck Encyclopedia of Public International Law

S Séfériadès, 'La question du rapatriement des « Marbres d'Elgin » considérée plus spécialement au point de vue du droit des gens' (1932) 10 Revue de droit international 52

Select Committee of the House of Commons, *Report on the Earl of Elgin's Collection of Sculptured Marbles* (Bulmer 1816)

AH Smith, 'Lord Elgin and his Collection' (1916) 36 Journal of Hellenic Studies 163

William St Clair, *Who Saved the Parthenon?* (Open Book Publishers 2022)

William St Clair, *Lord Elgin and the Marbles* (Oxford University Press 1967, 1998, reprinted 2003)

Colin GC Tite, *Impeachment and Parliamentary Judicature in Early Stuart England* (University of London Historical Studies 1974)

JHW Verzijl, *International Law in Historical Perspective* (vol 3, AW Sijthoff-Leyden 1970)

Henry Wheaton, *Elements of International Law* (Lea and Blanchard 1836)

Dyfri Williams, 'Lord Elgin's Firman' (2009) 21 (1) Journal of the History of Collections 49

Patricia Youngblood Reyhan, 'A Chaotic Palette: Conflict of Laws in Litigation between Original Owners and Good-Faith Purchasers of Stolen Art' (2001) 50 Duke Law Journal 955

Elizabeth Zachariadou, 'The Great Church in Captivity 1453-1586' in Michael Angold (ed), *The Cambridge History of Christianity: Eastern Christianity* (Cambridge University Press 2006)

Chapter 5
Greek Demands for Return

They are our soul.

Melina Mercouri, on the marbles

5.1 Introduction

In the wake of the Greek government's 1983 demand for the Parthenon marbles, much-publicised thanks to Melina Mercouri's international campaign, Merryman argued that Greece was time-barred from asking for the marbles, on the ground that this was 'the first official request' for their return.[1] Merryman was mistaken. The Greek state's first official demand for Elgin's loot dates at least as far back as 1836, a time when much of modern Greece was still under Ottoman occupation and the newly-minted state depended on its powerful protectors, including the United Kingdom, for its future survival.

Greece has been asking for the marbles since then with insistence and resolve that have never wavered, but its requests have fallen on deaf ears; they have been ignored or turned down flat. Yet Greece has stood its ground on the issue of ownership and keeps hammering away at its call to have the marbles returned. More recently, as attitudes towards the retention of unlawfully or unethically acquired cultural heritage have been changing, it seems that Greece stands a better chance of negotiating the marbles' return. While this is certainly not the first time its hopes are raised, this time things are probably different.

The formal Greek requests for return matter from the viewpoint of international law, because they refute the argument that the claim for the marbles' repatriation is time-barred. Their legal significance will be fully appreciated in Chap. 8, when that chapter reviews the effects of the passage of time on claims. In the meantime, this

[1] Merryman (1985) 1900-1901.

C. Titi, *The Parthenon Marbles and International Law*,
https://doi.org/10.1007/978-3-031-26357-6_5

chapter discusses some demands of the Greek state as a legally meaningful fact. A caveat is necessary: to focus on the formal Greek demands is not to forget that numerous British citizens, from Elgin's time to this day, have supported and in many cases actively advocated the repatriation of the marbles. As Hitchens aptly put it some years ago, 'I have been very impressed ... by the number of British people who, all down the generations since the marbles were removed, have looked at the matter in a sober and phlegmatic way and concluded that a wrong has been done.'[2] 'In a mostly dispassionate manner', he added, 'they have sought for nearly two centuries to put it right'.[3] These efforts continue. That this chapter does not discuss them other than in passing is certainly *not* a reflection on their importance, but only a matter of focus, in light of the legal argument presented in this book.

This chapter starts by discussing selective Greek requests for the return of the marbles spanning a period of almost 150 years. Then, it turns to more recent requests and developments. Finally, the chapter queries whether Greece should have resorted to an English court.

5.2 From Independence to EU Membership

According to the UK parliament, Greek demands for the return of the Parthenon marbles started as early as 1833.[4] That was the year when the Acropolis was surrendered by the Ottomans, after the recent formal recognition of Greece as an independent state.[5] Even during the Greek war of independence, the Greek temporary executive and so-called 'national assemblies' had been adopting legislation with a view to protecting antiquities.[6] After independence, in 1834, a law came into effect stipulating that all Greek antiquities on the national territory belong to all Greeks.[7] Ian Jenkins reported an 1835 request from the Archaeological Society at Athens addressed to the trustees of the British Museum for the return of the Acropolis marbles.[8]

---

[2]Hitchens (2008) xxvi.

[3]Hitchens (2008) xxvi.

[4]House of Commons (2000) annex IV, para 7.1.

[5]Neils (2001) 241; Stathi (2015) 176.

[6]Voudouri (2010) 548. See also Chap. 6, text to nn 205-206.

[7]Act of 10/22 May 1834 on scientific and technological collections, on the discovery and conservation of antiquities and the use thereof, OJ 22 of 16/28 June 1834, art 61. See also Chap. 2, text to n 183.

[8]Jenkins (1990) 106. However, it appears that the Archaeological Society at Athens was founded in 1837, see the Society's official website https://www.archetai.gr/index.php?lang=en. Without access to the official papers accompanying the minutes of the trustees of the British Museum that Jenkins consulted, it is impossible to establish exactly where the 1835 request originated, but we know that it was submitted by a certain Charles Holte Bracebridge, described by Jenkins as 'a philhellene of private means'.

Then in 1836, the Greek government made the first formal claim for the return of Elgin's loot, on the occasion of restoration work on the Temple of Athena Nike.[9] A delegation was constituted to initiate talks with the Cabinet of the United Kingdom and ask specifically for the repatriation of four reliefs removed by Elgin from the temple.[10] Copies of newly-discovered reliefs were to be offered in return. The Greek delegation was advised to 'make it clear that the legality of Lord Elgin's acts was abundantly doubtful', irrespective of whether he had a firman or not.[11] Elgin's actions were described as 'looting committed in the name of Britain'.[12]

But the overture to the UK government failed abjectly and the attempt to negotiate was shot down in flames. The UK foreign secretary, Henry John Temple (aka Lord Palmerston) delivered a stinging rebuff to the delegation making the Greek government decide to discontinue the negotiations for fear of 'compromising any future negotiation'.[13] The Greek envoy in London was advised to 'limit himself to investigating the availability of such persons as could contribute to initiating new negotiations only when some possibility of success can be foreseen'.[14] The UK government made it clear that, if ever there was going to be a good moment to negotiate the return of Elgin's loot, that was not it.

In 1844, a new request was made, this time directly to the trustees of the British Museum.[15] The request came from the Greek Conservator of Antiquities, Kyriakos Pittakis, and the Archaeological Society at Athens, which the trustees were reminded 'acts in connection with the [Greek] government'.[16] The trustees did not send the marbles back. However, after imposing a set of conditions, they did send cement casts to Greece.[17] These included a complete set of casts of the Parthenon marbles in the British Museum. While the trustees prided themselves on preparing copies 'as a

[9]Facsimiles of the official documents with transcripts and translations have been published in General State Archives (Greece) (2012). One of the documents discussing the fragments concerned and the exchange to be offered by Greece for their return is published on the website of the Archives Portal Europe, here https://bit.ly/3xoSdSh.

[10]Royal decree no 12546 (24 June/6 July 1836) and Letter from the Secretary for Ecclesiastical Affairs and Public Education to the Secretariat of State for the King's Household and the Secretariat for Foreign Affairs (6/18 July 1836), facsimiles and translation in General State Archives (Greece) (2012) 138-153.

[11]Letter from the Secretary for Ecclesiastical Affairs and Public Education to the Secretariat of State for the King's Household and the Secretariat for Foreign Affairs (6/18 July 1836), facsimiles and translation in General State Archives (Greece) (2012) 138-153.

[12]Letter from the Secretary for Ecclesiastical Affairs and Public Education to the Secretariat of State for the King's Household and the Secretariat for Foreign Affairs (6/18 July 1836), facsimiles and translation in General State Archives (Greece) (2012) 138-153.

[13]Letter to the Secretariat of State (27 November/9 December 1836), facsimile and translation in General State Archives (Greece) (2012) 120-123.

[14]Letter to the Secretariat of State (27 November/9 December 1836), facsimile and translation in General State Archives (Greece) (2012) 120-123.

[15]Jenkins (1990) 106.

[16]Jenkins (1990) 106.

[17]Jenkins (1990) 106-107. See also Sect. 6.3.1.4.

present to the Greek nation ... free of all expense',[18] the originals remained in Britain.

In 1890, John Gennadius, a senior Greek diplomat in London, suggested that at least the architectural fragments should be returned.[19] It was at about this time that the municipality of Athens submitted a request for the return of the 'Parthenon friezes' to the UK government and parliament.[20] Despite never being taken seriously, Greece regularly and consistently called for the return of the marbles over the years, so that, by 1939 it was common knowledge in Britain that '[s]uccessive Greek Governments have been anxious to see [the marbles] restored to their places on the Parthenon'.[21] Correspondence in The Times at around that time showed that the great majority of the British public was favourable to the return of the marbles to Greece.[22] So it appears was the Foreign Office.[23]

There was a time, early in World War II, when Greece and the United Kingdom were the only two states 'actively fighting' Nazi Germany,[24] and this certainly contributed to British good will towards Greece. In 1941, a parliamentary question was put to the government by MP Thelma Cazalet: would the prime minister 'introduce legislation to enable the Elgin Marbles to be restored to Greece at the end of hostilities, as some recognition of the Greeks' magnificent stand for civilisation?'[25] No, came the answer from Clement Atlee, then Lord Privy Seal; the government was 'not prepared to introduce legislation for this purpose'.[26] It is significant that this debate recognised what the UK government has denied since then, that is, that the return of the marbles is very much a government matter.

Although the end of the war put a temporary stop to the debate, the question of the fate of the Parthenon marbles continued to come up in the UK parliament. The possible return of the marbles has sometimes been dangled much like a carrot for political purposes.[27] In 1961, the Foreign Office recognised the merits of the Greek claim,[28] but when the prime minister, Harold Macmillan, addressed the matter, he remained non-committal. That was a 'complicated question', he said, and added: 'I will not dismiss it from my mind'.[29] But we must assume that he did, and that even before the Profumo affair, which would soon cost him his seat, broke out. Later in

[18] Robertson (2019) Chap. 5 (unnumbered page).

[19] St Clair (1998) 333.

[20] Robertson, Palmer, and Clooney (2015) 68.

[21] Jenkins (2001) 57. In another 1939 press cutting, we read that 'Greece has never relinquished her claim to the marbles' return', ibid 60.

[22] Stewart (2001) 45. See also Jenkins (2001) appendix 11.

[23] Stewart (2001) 45-46; Greenfield (2007) 62-63.

[24] Stewart (2001) 45.

[25] Hansard (1941) c 319W.

[26] Hansard (1941) c 319W.

[27] St Clair (1998) c 334.

[28] Robertson (2019) Chap. 5 (unnumbered page).

[29] Stewart (2001) 46.

1961, the Mayor of Athens sent telegrams to Macmillan, the Lord Chancellor, and the Speaker of the House of Commons asking for the return of the marbles.[30] Although the Foreign Office was sympathetic to the request, the British Museum would not hear of it and, 'in a single paragraph letter', informed the Foreign Office that the museum trustees were 'not prepared to enter into discussions on the subject'.[31] Between the years 1967 and 1974, a military junta took over Greece, and an 'unspoken moratorium' was imposed on the question of the marbles' return.[32] The matter was revived again with the restoration of democracy, and, a few years later, the accession of Greece to the European Union (then European Communities) paved the way for the next formal Greek claim.

5.3 UNESCO

5.3.1 Sorry, Melina:[33] Never on Sunday *or Any Other Day*

In 1982, at a conference of the United Nations Educational, Scientific and Cultural Organization (UNESCO) held in Mexico City, the Greek culture minister, Mercouri, announced that Greece would make use of the good offices of UNESCO's Intergovernmental Committee for Promoting the Return of Cultural Property to its Countries of Origin or its Restitution in case of Illicit Appropriation (ICPRCP or Intergovernmental Committee) and present a formal claim to the United Kingdom for the return of the 'Acropolis marbles'.[34] She explained that 'museums cannot be emptied' but that, in the case of the Parthenon, what Greece is asking for is not 'the return of a painting or a statue', but 'the return of a portion of a unique monument'.[35] Mercouri's speech made it clear that Greece is not asking for all Greek treasures in British museums or in other museums around the world;[36] the request is rather specific, even though it has not always been clear whether it is limited to the Parthenon marbles or to the Acropolis marbles. The reaction of Paul Channon, the UK arts minister, started the famous buck-passing between the UK government and the British Museum. He was reported as telling the UNESCO conference that 'his Government could not interfere in the affairs of a private establishment like the

[30] Stewart (2001) 46.

[31] Stewart (2001) 46.

[32] Hitchens (2008) 81.

[33] 'Sorry, Melina', The Economist (28 May 1983).

[34] Melina Mercouri's speech is available on the website of the Melina Mercouri Foundation https://melinamercourifoundation.com/speeches1/.

[35] See https://melinamercourifoundation.com/speeches1/.

[36] See also 'Greece Is Pressing Britain for Return of Antiquities', The New York Times (21 November 1982).

British Museum'.[37] These were possibly not Channon's exact words, for, as we shall see in Chap. 8, the British Museum is anything but a 'private' institution. Channon was expressing the official view of the UK government: the marbles should stay in the British Museum.[38] But it was Mercouri's plea that carried the day. The UNESCO conference adopted a recommendation, according to which the removal of the marbles 'has disfigured a unique monument' and it is 'right and just that those marbles should be returned to Greece'.[39] In this light, the conference recommended 'that Member States view the return of the Parthenon marbles as an instance of the application of the principle that elements abstracted from national monuments should be returned to those monuments'.[40]

Sometime later, in October 1983, the Greek government formally requested the return of the marbles.[41] Mercouri, who by now had been campaigning for over a year, had been 'fully authorized to undertake all necessary procedures'.[42] But almost a year went by, and Greece received no formal response. So, in September 1984, the Greek government submitted a new claim, this time through UNESCO.[43] Another year went by, and, eventually, in October 1985 the UK government rejected the Greek request.[44] While, after 2 years of silence, conventional wisdom must have prepared the Greek side for a rejection, the ground on which this rejection was based must have come as a surprise nonetheless. It was that 'the trustees of the British Museum were prohibited by law from disposing of these sculptures' and returning them to Greece.[45] The UK government invoked domestic law as an excuse before an international organisation.

Although the Greek call for the return of the marbles was rejected, Mercouri continued to wage an international campaign garnering sympathy for the marbles' return. It was during this campaign that former British prime minister Johnson, then president of the Oxford Union, wrote to Mercouri deploring the British retention of the marbles as 'unacceptable to cultured people' and declared that 'there is absolutely no reason' why the marbles 'should not be returned immediately from the

[37] 'Greece Is Pressing Britain for Return of Antiquities', The New York Times (21 November 1982).

[38] Hansard (1983a).

[39] Recommendation 55, in UNESCO 'Final Report of the World Conference on Cultural Policies' (Mexico City, 26 July-6 August 1982).

[40] Recommendation 55, in UNESCO 'Final Report of the World Conference on Cultural Policies' (Mexico City, 26 July-6 August 1982).

[41] Hansard (1983b) cc 16-18.

[42] 'Greece to Ask Britain for the Elgin Marbles', The New York Times (15 May 1983).

[43] ICPRCP, 'Report by the UNESCO Secretariat on measures taken to implement the recommendations of the 3rd session of the ICPRCP (9-12 May 1983)' (adopted during its 4th session) UN Doc CLT-85/CONF.202/2 (15 February 1985), para 4.

[44] ICPRCP, Twenty-fourth session of the General Conference, 'Report', UN Doc 24 C/94 (29 June 1987), para 7.

[45] ICPRCP, 'Report', 24th session of the General Conference, UN Doc 24 C/94 (29 June 1987), para 7.

British Museum to their rightful home in Athens'.[46] More than 20 years later, as prime minister, he would change his tune.

5.3.2 UNESCO Mediation

The Parthenon marbles case has remained as a pending item in the agenda of UNESCO's Intergovernmental Committee since its submission in 1984.[47] The committee has examined it in successive sessions and adopted numerous recommendations that express concern for a 'mutually-acceptable solution' to be found and reiterate 'its readiness to act as facilitator between Greece and the United Kingdom' in this matter.[48] In a meeting that took place in July 2013 between UNESCO's director-general and the then Greek culture minister, Panos Panagiotopoulos, the latter expressed the hope 'that UNESCO could use its good offices with the authorities of the United Kingdom as a facilitator' in the Parthenon marbles case.[49] He referred in particular to the Intergovernmental Committee's mediation and conciliation rules that had been adopted in 2010.[50] Soon after that meeting, in August 2013, UNESCO sent an official letter to the UK government and the British Museum informing them that the Greek government had 'approached UNESCO with a request that the Organization deploy its good offices to explore the possibility' of mediation or conciliation under the aegis of the ICPRCP, according to the 2010 Rules of Procedure for Mediation and Conciliation.[51] More than a year later, in October 2014, the official letter remained unanswered and the Intergovernmental Committee took note of the fact that the United Kingdom had not yet responded, despite having earlier acknowledged UNESCO's readiness to assist with mediation.[52] The Intergovernmental Committee called on the two parties to 'consider making use of the mediation process'.[53] Eventually, a year and a half after

---

[46] Helena Smith, 'Letters Show How Boris Johnson Backed Return of Parthenon Marbles', The Guardian (3 July 2022).

[47] ICPRCP, 22nd session, 27-29 September 2021, ICPRCP/21/22.COM/Decisions, Decision 22. COM 6, para 2.

[48] ICPRCP, 'Report of the Secretariat on the follow-up to the recommendations and decisions adopted during the 19th session' UN Doc ICPRCP/16/20.COM/5 (August 2016), para 28.

[49] ICPRCP, 'Report of the Secretariat on the follow-up to the recommendations and decisions adopted during the 19th session' UN Doc ICPRCP/16/20.COM/5 (August 2016), para 29.

[50] These are the ICPRCP's Rules of Procedure for Mediation and Conciliation, see ICPRCP, 'Report of the Secretariat on the follow-up to the recommendations and decisions adopted during the 19th session' UN Doc ICPRCP/16/20.COM/5 (August 2016), para 29.

[51] ICPRCP, 'Report of the Secretariat on the follow-up to the recommendations and decisions adopted during the 19th session' UN Doc ICPRCP/16/20.COM/5 (August 2016), para 30; ICPRCP, Recommendation 19.COM 8 UN Doc ICPRCP/14/19.COM/8 (October 2014).

[52] ICPRCP, Recommendation 19.COM 8 UN Doc ICPRCP/14/19.COM/8 (October 2014).

[53] ICPRCP, Recommendation 19.COM 8 UN Doc ICPRCP/14/19.COM/8 (October 2014).

the UNESCO letter, in late March 2015, the UK government and the British Museum informed UNESCO in separate letters that 'they did not believe that the application of the mediation procedure would substantially carry forward the debate and that they had decided respectfully to decline the request'.[54] A letter signed by the then culture minister, Ed Vaizey, and the minister for Europe, David Lidington, for the UK government stated the following:

> While we remain keen to cooperate with UNESCO in its work, the fact remains that the Parthenon sculptures in the British Museum were legally acquired by Lord Elgin under the laws pertaining at the time and the Trustees of the British Museum have had clear legal title to the sculptures since 1816. Neither the British Government nor the British Museum are aware of any new arguments to the contrary since 1985, when a formal Greek request for the return of the sculptures was turned down by the British Government. We have seen nothing to suggest that Greece's purpose in seeking mediation on this issue is anything other than to achieve the permanent transfer of the Parthenon sculptures now in the British Museum to Greece and on terms that would deny the British Museum's right of ownership, either in law or as a practical reality. Given our equally clear position, this leads us to conclude that mediation would not carry this debate substantially forward.
>
> . . . [A] further relevant factor is that the Trustees of the British Museum are prevented by law from de-accessioning objects in the Museum's collections unless they are duplicates or unfit for retention. Successive governments have indicated their support for this important legal principle . . .[55]

This letter is noteworthy for a number of reasons beyond the rejection itself. The United Kingdom declined UNESCO's mediation offer on the grounds, inter alia, that Greece only wishes to mediate to seek the return of the marbles and that the respective positions of the parties are antithetical, that is, irreconcilable. Mediation is assumed to require a compromise of some kind and it is possible that Greece might propose a long-term loan of some other antiquity or it could offer exclusive 3D marble copies of the Parthenon sculptures. A proposal for a long-term loan of other antiquities was made by the Greek prime minister, Kyriakos Mitsotakis, when discussing the return of the Parthenon marbles.[56]

But more significant are some further elements that emerge from the letter. First, the UK government insisted on the legality of the acquisition of the marbles. Second, it invoked domestic deaccession legislation, which the government itself can make and unmake, as an excuse at the international level.[57] Finally, the UK government stated clearly that it does not see the case as a dispute but as a '*debate*' ('mediation would not carry this *debate* substantially forward').[58] It saw no reason to mediate a

[54] ICPRCP, Decision 20.COM/5 and Recommendation on the Parthenon Sculptures, UN Doc ICPRCP/16/20.COM/Decisions (October 2016).

[55] Letter of the UK government of 26 March 2015 to UNESCO. The letter is published here: https://www.iefimerida.gr/sites/default/files/archive-files/ministers.pdf.

[56] Nick Squires, 'Italian Handover of Elgin Marbles Fragment Puts Pressure on UK to Follow Suit', The Telegraph (2 January 2022).

[57] See Sect. 6.4.

[58] Emphasis added.

debate. This is consistent with the fact that for two centuries, successive UK governments have downplayed the importance of the retention of the marbles.

The British Museum letter, signed by the then chair of the museum, Richard Lambert, declined the Greek request for mediation, invoking the trustees' conviction 'that the more constructive way forward ... is to collaborate directly with other museums and cultural institutions, not just in Greece but across the world'.[59] There are all kinds of irony to this statement but, especially, it appears to be unrelated to the Greek request for mediation. Rather it seems to only be acknowledging UNESCO. The letter makes polite noises about UNESCO, stating how the museum 'admires and supports' its work, although apparently not enough to accept its offer of mediation. Then the letter invokes the legal duty the trustees have to preserve the museum collections and states that 'the Trustees would want to develop existing good relations with colleagues and institutions in Greece, and to explore collaborative ventures, not on a government-to-government basis but directly between institutions. This is why we believe that UNESCO involvement is not the best way forward.' The letter goes on about collaboration between museums, British Museum exhibitions, its sense of pride (albeit not in so many words) in the controversial lending of the pedimental statue of the river god Ilissos to Russia, there is more about collaboration and, finally, information about British Museum loans to Greece. The letter concludes with an invitation to 'our colleagues in Greek museums to continue to work with us and to explore new ways of enabling the whole world to see, study and enjoy the sculptures of the Parthenon'. Since some of the arguments presented in the letter are now part of the trustees' statement, which is discussed in Chap. 6,[60] these arguments are not considered here further. Suffice it to note that the letter barely relates to the issue at hand (Greece's request for mediation of the Parthenon marbles case) and does little except in the nature of self-praise.

Since then, UNESCO has continued to adopt recommendations in relation to the Parthenon marbles. It has expressed its concern that a solution should be found and its wish that Greece and the United Kingdom should continue to cooperate 'with a view to concluding the ongoing discussions in respect of the reunification of the Parthenon Sculptures'.[61] With time, the language became stronger until, in 2021, the Intergovernmental Committee adopted—no longer just a recommendation but also—a decision, expressly referring to 'the obligation' of the United Kingdom to return the marbles.[62]

[59] The letter is reproduced here: http://www.elginism.com/elgin-marbles/uk-government-rejects-parthenon-marbles-unesco-mediation/20150327/7859/.

[60] See Sect. 6.3.3.

[61] E.g. ICPRCP, Recommendation on the Parthenon Sculptures, UN Doc ICPRCP/16/20.COM/Decisions (October 2016).

[62] ICPRCP, 22nd session, 27-29 September 2021, ICPRCP/21/22.COM/Decisions, Decision 22.COM 6, para 7.

5.4 Recent Developments

Greece continues to formally and informally lobby for the marbles' repatriation, and the matter is debated as vigorously as ever. In November 2021, during an official state visit to the United Kingdom, the Greek prime minister, Mitsotakis, raised the issue of the Parthenon marbles with his UK counterpart, Johnson. Johnson, no longer the exuberant apologist for the marbles' return that he had been in his younger days, immediately turned down the request.[63] His successor, Liz Truss, had the occasion during her short-lived premiership to declare that she did not support the marbles' repatriation, as did Rishi Sunak,[64] and the official Tory government line is opposed to the return.[65]

Recently, much has been made of statements made by British Museum chair, Osborne, and deputy director, Jonathan Williams. Answering a question about the Parthenon marbles on the LBC show, Osborne announced that there is 'a deal to be done, but' (it is significant that he immediately qualified this statement with a 'but') 'I think there's a deal to be done where we can tell both stories in Athens and in London'.[66] Shortly thereafter, on a different occasion, he made it clear that he did not believe in 'dismantling' the museum's collections.[67] British Museum deputy director, Williams, was also quoted as 'calling for . . . an active "Parthenon partnership" with our friends and colleagues in Greece'—another statement he qualified by recalling that the marbles are 'an absolutely integral part of the British Museum' and that '[t]here are many wonderful things we'd be delighted to borrow and lend'.[68] 'It is', as Williams helpfully added, 'what we do'.[69] The British Museum borrows and lends. It does not return.

Yet the climate seems to be changing and even the British Museum cannot be as dismissive as it would have been in the past. Latterly, several public figures have come out in favour of returning the missing Parthenon marbles to Greece. They include Vaizey, former British culture minister, who, only a handful of years after turning down flat the Greek request for mediation, found it 'so obvious' that the

---

[63] UK Government, 'PM meeting with PM Mitsotakis of Greece: 16 November 2021' (Press release, 16 November 2021).

[64] Katie Razzall, 'Elgin Marbles: New Body Aims to Return Sculptures to Greece', BBC News (13 October 2022); Aubrey Allegretti, 'No Plans to Return Parthenon Marbles to Greece, Says Rishi Sunak', The Guardian (13 March 2023).

[65] Hansard (2022).

[66] EJ Ward, 'Britain and Greece Could Strike 'Deal' to Share Elgin Marbles, George Osborne Tells LBC', LBC News (15 June 2022).

[67] Cristina Ruiz, 'As Infrastructure Crumbles, British Museum Plans to Fix Parthenon Marbles Gallery Next', The Art Newspaper (3 November 2022); Tessa Solomon, 'British Museum Chair Rebukes Calls to "Dismantle" Parthenon Marbles Collection', ARTnews (9 November 2022).

[68] Sarah Baxter, 'Why the Elgin Marbles May Finally Return to Greece', The Times (30 July 2022).

[69] Sarah Baxter, 'Why the Elgin Marbles May Finally Return to Greece', The Times (30 July 2022).

marbles 'are so woven into Greek identity' that it 'would be a wonderful thing if they could be returned'.[70] As of October 2022, Vaizey heads the Parthenon Project,[71] which makes the case for 'a cultural partnership' between Greece and the United Kingdom 'that would include rotating exhibits of significant artefacts yet unseen in London'.[72] Vaizey is also backing the amendment of strict deaccessioning laws to give major national museums more autonomy from parliament when deaccessioning items in their collections.[73]

Another U-turn came in January 2022, when The Times, traditionally favouring the marbles' retention in the British Museum (in contrast with other major newspapers, such as The Guardian),[74] argued in a leader that the case for returning the marbles had become 'compelling':

> For more than 50 years, artists and politicians have argued that artefacts so fundamental to a nation's cultural identity should return to Greece. The museum and the British government, supported by The Times, have resisted the pressure. But times and circumstances change. The sculptures belong in Athens. They should now return.[75]

This article was complemented by others that followed, such as an article published soon afterwards, which suggested that 3D printing technology could be pressed into service to replicate the marbles currently in the British Museum,[76] that the marbles should return to Greece, and that '[t]he British Museum should agree to display a 3D replica'.[77] No wonder a later article in The Times reported the British Museum 'to be wary that the creation of precise replicas could make it impossible to argue that the originals should be retained in London'.[78] A poll held by The Times in the summer

---

[70] Sarah Cascone, 'Former UK Culture Minister Says the Parthenon Marbles Should Be Returned to Greece: "It Would Be a Wonderful Thing"', Artnet News (22 December 2021).

[71] Hansard (2022).

[72] See https://parthenonproject.co.uk. It is unclear whether this would achieve the repatriation of the marbles or a loan in exchange for loans of other Greek treasures to be held as collateral in the British Museum. It appears that the British Museum may have entertained this idea. For a critical account, see Catharine Titi, 'Sorry, British Museum, a Loan of the Parthenon Marbles Is Not a Repatriation', The Conversation (15 February 2023).

[73] Hansard (2022); Ed Vaizey, 'It's Time to Discuss the Repatriation of Our Looted Artefacts', The Times (13 October 2022).

[74] Newspapers abroad too have formally supported the marbles' return to Athens, e.g. this is the case of The New York Times, see 'Opinion: Return the Parthenon Marbles', The New York Times (2 February 2002).

[75] 'Comment, Leading Article: The Times View on the Elgin Marbles: Uniting Greece's Heritage', The Times (11 January 2022).

[76] Simon de Bruxelles, 'Greece Renews Calls for Return of Elgin Marbles Now Perfect Replicas Possible', The Telegraph (29 January 2022); cf Valentine Low, 'Create Virtual Elgin Marbles and Return Real Thing, Urges Stephen Fry', The Times (13 December 2021).

[77] 'Leading Article: The Times View on Replicating the Elgin Marbles: Greek Gifts', The Times (14 February 2022).

[78] Billy Kenber, 'British Museum Accused of "Gross Distortion" by Elgin Marbles Scanner', The Times (28 March 2022). As of November 2022, the Oxford-based Institute of Digital Archaeology has unveiled a 3D copy in Pentelic marble of Selene's horse, a Parthenon sculpture in the British

of 2022 revealed that 78% of its readers now think that the marbles should be returned to Athens.[79]

5.5 Should Greece Have Applied to an English Court?

In his famous polemical article about the Parthenon marbles, Merryman argued that 'the Greeks' could have applied to an English court[80] and the fact that they did not means that Greece has lost its right to ask for the marbles,[81] thus offering yet another legally dubious argument aimed at disarming those who favour the marbles' return. He justified this as follows: 'If X steals my painting and takes it to Mexico, I can sue in a Mexican court for its recovery. Thus, to refer to the case of the Marbles, if Greece believes that they were stolen, it can sue the British Museum in a British (*sic*) court for their return'.[82] This argument is untenable for several reasons. Let us consider it more closely. For a start, Merryman appeared to misunderstand the public international law nature of the case and the questions it raises. Greece cannot be equated with an individual whose painting was stolen. *Pace* Merryman, the dispute is not one between Greece and the British Museum. Merryman considered that Greece has been in a position 'to sue for the Marbles' in English courts 'since 1828' (it is arguable whether the right date is 1828, 1830, or 1832) and, since it did not do so, 'the Greeks have lost any right of action they might have had for the recovery of the Marbles before an English court, where the applicable statute of limitations is six years'.[83] First, at the time when the removals took place, Greece

Museum. The replica went briefly on display at the Freud Museum in London, see David Sanderson, 'Elgin Marbles Perfect Replica Unveiled with British Museum in Talks', The Times (31 October 2022).

[79] 'Readers' Poll: Should the Elgin Marbles be Given Back to Greece?', The Times (31 July 2022). See also Maria Paravantes, 'London Times' Readers: Give the Parthenon Marbles Back to Greece', GTP Headlines (8 August 2022). This is not the first poll that suggests British support for the marbles' return to Greece. An earlier, November 2021 YouGov poll revealed that 59% of the British public supported the return of the marbles to Greece – only 18% thought that the marbles should stay in the United Kingdom, while 22% said they did not know, see https://yougov.co.uk/topics/travel/survey-results/daily/2021/11/23/9b053/2. In 2012, after an IQ^2 debate, 72% of participants voted in favour of the marbles' return, see https://www.intelligencesquared.com/events/parthenon-marbles/. In 1996, following a television programme by William G Stewart for the Channel 4 Without Walls series, 'a phone-in vote, conducted by the independent BBC Audio-call registered 99,340 calls of which 91,822 (92.5 per cent) were in favour of return', see Memorandum submitted by William G Stewart House of Commons, published as Appendix 15 of the Appendices to the Minutes of Evidence, House of Commons, Culture, Media and Sport—Seventh Report (vol 3, HC 371-III 2000).

[80] Merryman (1985) 1900-1901.

[81] Merryman (1985) 1900-1901.

[82] Merryman (1985) 1889.

[83] Merryman (1985) 1901.

was not an independent state but under Ottoman occupation. The Greeks were essentially bystanders in their own history and would have no means of action within the '6 years' of the statute of limitations. Even when Greece was in a position to start a dispute, it would hardly have been able to do so against a powerful ally. But more crucially, the dispute would be between sovereign states—the marbles were taken by a British ambassador and they were bought and entrusted to the trustees of the British Museum by act of parliament. It would not be for Greece to turn to English courts. But let us consider for a moment that, all other objections aside, Greece would sue for the marbles in an English court. Such a claim would be doomed to fail. An English court would have to apply English law, and it is English law that entrusted the marbles to the British Museum. In other words, Greece would not be able to obtain the marbles by applying to an English court. Even assuming that recourse to an English court were an option, such recourse would be futile. As we shall see in Chap. 7, international law recognises that there is no need to resort to domestic courts, when such recourse is futile.[84]

Ironically, in support of his argument, Merryman cited the Limitation Act 1939, which was in force neither at the time of the marbles' removal, nor, interestingly, at the time when he wrote his article. The Limitation Act 1939 had been repealed some years earlier and was replaced by the Limitation Act 1980, in force as of 1 May 1981.

Arguments such as the above have led to the assumption that the claim for the return of the marbles is time-barred. Yet, this is not certain. At the international level, there is no prescription. Greece's insistent demands for the marbles' return are incontrovertible evidence of the fact that it has never abandoned its claim, even if it has not applied to an English court. The significance of this will become obvious in Chap. 8, which will examine the objections of waiver, estoppel, acquiescence, and extinctive prescription.

5.6 Conclusion

This chapter has reviewed Greece's repeated demands for the return of the marbles in the course of the last 200 years. It has shown that Greece has been unwavering in its insistence that the marbles belong to Athens. The chapter also explained why Greece should not have turned to an English court and it touched upon the issue of prescription, which is considered in depth in Chap. 8. Although the UK government and the British Museum have so far refused the marbles' return, as attitudes towards the retention of unlawfully or unethically removed cultural heritage are changing, and international law is changing with them, the resolution of the Parthenon marbles conundrum by negotiations becomes more likely than it has ever been.

[84] See Sect. 7.5.1.

References

General State Archives (Greece), *Akropolis von Athen* (Alitheia 2012)

Jeanette Greenfield, *The Return of Cultural Treasures* (3rd edn, Cambridge University Press 2007)

Hansard, 'House of Lords National Heritage Act 1983 Debate' (13 October 2022) (vol 824, Hansard 2022)

Hansard, 'House of Commons Elgin Marbles Debate' (7 March 1983) (vol 38, Hansard 1983a)

Hansard, 'House of Commons Debate (21 November 1983) (vol 49, Hansard 1983b)

Hansard, 'Greece (Elgin Marbles) House of Commons Debate' (23 January 1941) (vol 368, Hansard 1941)

Christopher Hitchens, *The Parthenon Marbles* (first publication 1987, Verso 2008)

House of Commons, 'Culture, Media and Sport – Minutes of Evidence' (Culture, Media and Sport Committee Publications 8 June 2000)

Ian Jenkins, 'Cleaning and Controversy: The Parthenon Sculptures 1811-1939' (2001) The British Museum Occasional Paper No 146

Ian Jenkins, 'Acquisition and Supply of Casts of the Parthenon Sculptures by the British Museum, 1835–1939' (1990) 85 The Annual of the British School at Athens 89

John Henry Merryman, 'Thinking about the Elgin Marbles' (1985) 83 (8) Michigan Law Review 1881

Jenifer Neils, *The Parthenon Frieze* (Cambridge University Press 2001)

Geoffrey Robertson, *Who Owns History? Elgin's Loot and the Case for Returning Plundered Treasure* (Biteback Publishing 2019)

Geoffrey Robertson, Norman Palmer, and Amal Clooney, 'The Case for Return of the Parthenon Sculptures' (31 July 2015) (unpublished report, leaked on The Guardian website)

William St Clair, *Lord Elgin and the Marbles* (Oxford University Press 1967, 1998, reprinted 2003)

Katerina Stathi, 'The Carta Incognita of Ottoman Athens in Marios Hadjianastasis (ed), *Frontiers of the Ottoman Imagination* (Brill 2015)

William G Stewart, 'The Marbles: Elgin or Parthenon?' (2001) 6 Art Antiquity and Law 37

Daphne Voudouri, 'Law and the Politics of the Past: Legal Protection of Cultural Heritage in Greece' (2010) 17 International Journal of Cultural Property 547

Chapter 6
The British Museum and the Marbles

> In her sooty vitals, London stores these marble monuments of the gods, just as some unsmiling Puritan might store in the depths of his memory some past erotic moment, blissful and ecstatic sin.
>
> Nikos Kazantzakis, *England* (Simon and Schuster 1965)

6.1 Introduction

The main collection of sculptured marbles that Elgin sold to the government was entrusted to the British Museum on 8 August 1816. In February 1817, the marbles finally arrived at the museum.[1] But their perilous journey did not end there. First placed in a pre-fabricated room,[2] they were later removed to a temporary gallery in Robert Smirke's Greek Revival building.[3] In the late 1930s, the purpose-built Duveen Gallery was ready to house them but, as we shall see, a cleaning scandal, followed by World War II, kept the marbles out of public view for decades. Ultimately, the marbles were put on display in 1949, but it was not until the 1960s that the gallery was regularly open to the public.[4]

From the beginning, the museum experimented with the arrangement of the marbles almost constantly, and their layout changed several times.[5] On the actual Parthenon, the marbles were facing out. However, in the British Museum, they are displayed looking inwards. The east (front elevation) frieze, culmination of the

[1] Jenkins (2001) 3.

[2] Smith (1916) 350; House of Commons (2000), annex IV, para 4.1; Jenkins (2001) 3.

[3] Jenkins (2001) 3.

[4] St Clair (1998) 303; Beard (2010) 162.

[5] Jenkins (2001) 3; Beard (2010) 162-168.

C. Titi, *The Parthenon Marbles and International Law*,
https://doi.org/10.1007/978-3-031-26357-6_6

decorative narrative of the Panathenaic procession,[6] which on the Parthenon was placed above the entrance on one of the temple's short sides, has been put instead on one of the gallery's long sides.[7] The metopes, which on the Parthenon ran around all four sides of the building, are placed in the alcoves to the left and right of the pediments. The marbles were also meant to be viewed from below but the museum prides itself on presenting them at eye level.[8] Moreover, plaster casts of the original marbles remaining in Athens, which were formerly included in the display, have long since been removed.[9] The intention of the current display is to present the marbles in the British Museum as if they are complete, effacing what remains in Athens.[10] The marbles in the British Museum thus become the Parthenon itself.[11] The Duveen Gallery's dimensions are intended to echo those of the original building. However, seeing the marbles around the inside walls of the gallery and gaining unrestricted views of standalone statues, metopes and frieze slabs, in apparent completeness, twist our understanding of the monument.[12] We are looking at isolated 'sculptures', the monument well and truly disappears.

This chapter will engage in the debate about where the marbles should be located, and it will start by considering the museum's claim to their custodianship. The chapter will show that the British Museum has cared for the marbles it houses for over 200 years. In World War II, the museum removed the marbles to a disused London tube station, so that when the Duveen Gallery was bombed during the Blitz, they were already ensconced in safety. But the museum has also taken controversial decisions and one of them in particular has had an impact on the conservation of the marbles; this is the case of the Duveen cleaning, which was kept a secret for nearly 60 years. Next, the chapter will turn to the debate proper, using as its starting point the arguments that have been deployed against the marbles' return. Over the years, the British Museum has held on to the marbles and has ruled out the possibility of returning them to Athens other than as a loan, relying on reasoning that has changed over time. The chapter will argue that the arguments used to resist the marbles' return are weak at best. Finally, the chapter will turn to the British Museum Act 1963, which prohibits the trustees from deaccessioning items in the museum's collections, effectively preventing them from returning the Parthenon marbles. This ban on deaccession is the only impediment the chapter recognises to the marbles' return. This legal technicality matters under English law, but not under international law, and we will return to it in Chap. 8.

[6]For the debate about the iconography of the frieze, see Sect. 2.2.2.

[7]St Clair (1998) 304.

[8]Jenkins (2002) 19.

[9]Beard (2010) 163-168.

[10]Beard (2010) 167-168.

[11]Beard (2010) 167.

[12]Osborne (1987) 105. See also Neils (2001) 247.

6.2 In the Care of the British Museum

One day in the early 1960s, two unruly schoolboys started fighting in the British Museum in front of a Parthenon sculpture. Some moments later, one of them fell on the sculpture breaking off a centaur's leg. The museum was unable to make the broken sculpture entirely whole again.[13] In 1981, a work accident caused a pedimental sculpture to suffer 'slight chips and scratches'.[14] Mishaps in museums do occur from time to time, since accidents cannot always be avoided. However, more often it is museums' stewardship choices that impact the state of preservation of their exhibits. This section will look into the marbles in the care of the British Museum, focusing on questions of stewardship and the Duveen cleaning in particular, which permanently damaged the marbles and was concealed for more than half a century. Some more recent events and management decisions will also be considered.

6.2.1 Whitening the Marbles: The Duveen Scouring Scandal

When Elgin stopped in Rome on his way back home and appealed to Antonio Canova, famous for his neoclassical sculptures, with the idea of having the marbles restored by him,[15] Canova's reaction was unequivocal. It 'would be sacrilege in him, or any man', he said, 'to presume to touch them with a chisel'.[16] After Canova's refusal, Elgin turned to John Flaxman, a British neoclassical sculptor, but he too appeared to hesitate and explained that the restoration on the whole 'would lower rather than raise the intrinsic value of the collection'.[17] Elgin remained unconvinced, but the plan was ultimately abandoned, and the marbles escaped the restorer's chisel by the skin of their teeth.[18] It was not to be so forever. In the late 1930s, the British Museum appeared to know better. What followed may have been as much the result of bad faith as ignorance. In order to understand what happened, it is necessary to consider first the marbles' original decoration and surfaces, and how these fared in the nineteenth and early twentieth centuries, before turning to the Duveen cleaning.

[13] Chris Hastings, 'Revealed: How Rowdy Schoolboys Knocked a Leg off one of the Elgin Marbles', The Telegraph (15 May 2005).

[14] Chris Hastings, 'Revealed: How Rowdy Schoolboys Knocked a Leg off one of the Elgin Marbles', The Telegraph (15 May 2005).

[15] *Memorandum* (1811) 39.

[16] *Memorandum* (1811) 40.

[17] Hamilton to Elgin (23 June 1807), cited in Smith (1916) 297-298.

[18] St Clair (1998) 150.

6.2.1.1 Polychrome decoration and the historic patina

The polychromy of ancient Greek temples would have been known to those familiar with Greek art. True, the colourful decoration has especially survived in artefacts made in media other than marble; porous limestone has preserved the ancient colour better than close-grained marble.[19] The temple on the Athenian Acropolis known as the Hekatompedon, a forerunner of the Parthenon, is an excellent example of how the colourful decoration has survived on limestone pedimental statuary. It is also very probable that long exposure to the open air has affected the colours of the Parthenon.[20] Stuart and Revett were possibly the first to remark upon the polychromy of ancient Greek temples in the first volume of *The Antiquities of Athens* in 1762.[21] The 'discovery' took by surprise many in the art world, who had assumed that classical Greek sculptures were uniformly white and that the eyes were left blank, although this seemed to fly in the face of a good deal of evidence.[22]

It is now believed that the pediments and the metopes had a red background.[23] The background of the frieze is often assumed to have been painted blue, similar to the background of other fifth-century BC relief sculptures, including grave stelae and temples, echoing the sky.[24] It is probable that the background to the Parthenon frieze was very much as Lawrence Alma-Tadema presented it in his famous painting *Pheidias and the Frieze of the Parthenon* (Fig. 6.1).[25] Red was probably used for the drapery of some of the frieze figures.[26] Egyptian blue was certainly used on others. Laser cleaning of sculptures at the Acropolis Museum has very recently revealed previously hidden traces of colour, such as blue in the folds of the chlamys (or cloak) of the wonderfully beautiful horseman on slab IX of the west frieze[27] or on the Kekrops and Pandrosos group from the west pediment.[28] Blue appears to have been also used for the cloaks of other riders on the west frieze. It is not yet entirely understood how the blue cloaks would stand out against the (presumed) blue background.

[19] Richter and Hall (1944) 236.

[20] British Museum (1830) 26, see also 10-11.

[21] St Clair (1998) 51.

[22] St Clair (1998) 51.

[23] Vlassopoulou (2010) 219.

[24] Neils (2001) 88; Ridgway (1999) 117-118; Harrison (1988) 339.

[25] Neils (2001) 88.

[26] Neils (2001) 89.

[27] This is horseman 17. The chlamys was a short cloak-like garment sometimes worn by soldiers and horsemen. Typically secured on the right shoulder with a brooch, it left the right arm free to move easily. See https://www.theacropolismuseum.gr/en/parthenon-west-frieze-block-9-ix.

[28] For a discussion, see Vlassopoulou (2010) 220, 222, and figs 165-167. That author describes the colour on horseman 17 as 'light green'. The chemical composition of the pigment is not provided.

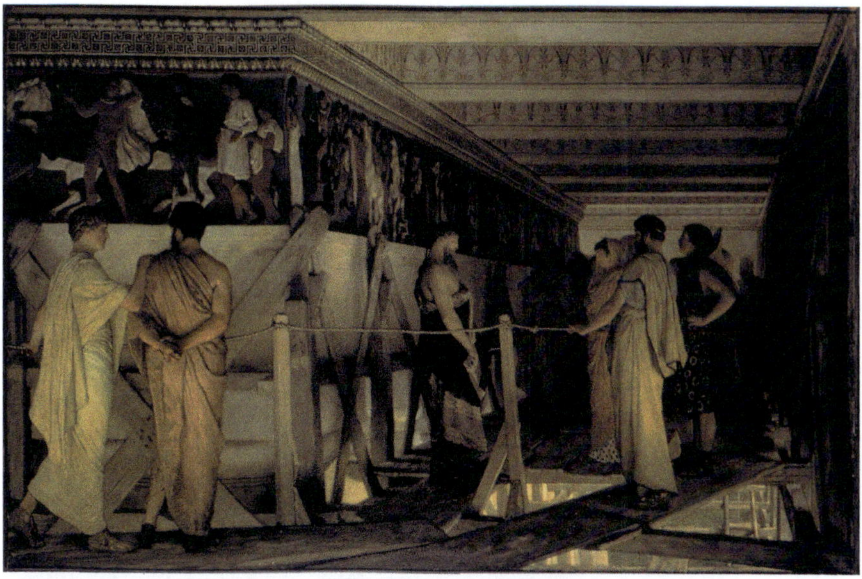

Fig. 6.1 Lawrence Alma Tadema, *Pheidias and the Frieze of the Parthenon*, 1868–1869. Photo by Birmingham Museums Trust

Reddish-brown pigments may have been used to paint the torsos of male figures to distinguish them from women, whose skin could have been painted white,[29] by analogy with the colours used to depict men and women in earlier Greek art.[30] By the same token, overlapping horses that are now notoriously difficult to distinguish in their 'colorless jumble of legs and head profiles', would have been made more legible by applying contrasting colours to them (e.g. brown, white, black).[31] Even so, it is also possible that such assumptions reflect our own expectations and until confirmed by chemical analysis or a fifth-century text, they remain just that: assumptions. Colour would have also been used to depict details that would have been impractical or difficult to carve or add in metal.[32] Examples include the painted irises of Poseidon's and Apollo's eyes (Acropolis Museum, east frieze), still visible, and where figures appear to be clutching invisible objects and there are no drill holes to indicate metal attachments, as in the case of the attributes of gods (e.g. Poseidon's trident, east frieze) (Fig. 6.2).[33]

The honey-brown surface patina (or epidermis), in part the result of ancient coating applied to the building either as a primer for paint and/or as a protective

---

[29] Neils (2001) 89; Connelly (2014) Chap. 5 (unnumbered page).

[30] E.g. see Richter and Hall (1944) 237-238 Eaverly (2013).

[31] Ridgway (1999) 117-118; Neils (2001) 89; Vlassopoulou (2010) 219. See also Chap. 2, text to n 62.

[32] Neils (2001) 90; Vlassopoulou (2010) 219.

[33] Neils (2001) 90-91.

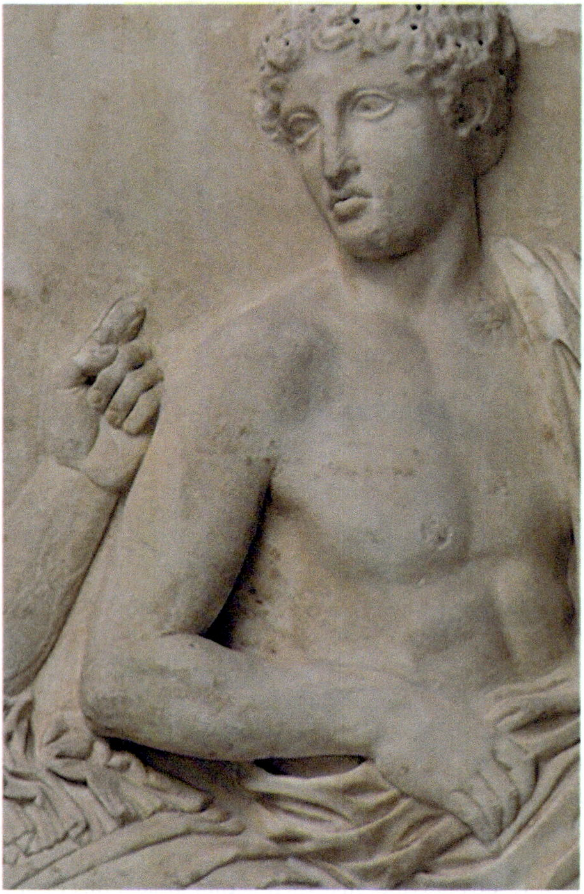

Fig. 6.2 Parthenon, East frieze, slab VI, detail, Acr. 856 © Acropolis Museum, 2013. Photo by Socratis Mavrommatis

coating, seals within it any remaining traces of colour.[34] The texture of the original marble surface as worked by the fifth-century BC artists, to the extent it survives, is also enclosed within the patina—for example, chisel marks are visible.[35] A recent study of the Parthenon's west cornice blocks revealed the presence of a miscellany of pigments (Egyptian blue, azurite, red ochre, red lead, conichalcite, which is a vivid green), as well as information about the technique employed by the artists (e.g. beeswax was used to bind the pigments).[36] Its findings allow us to visualise the cornice's colourful combination of geometric and meander patterns. This is what makes the historic patina so valuable. It can yield important information about the

[34] Jenkins and Middleton (1988) 198; St Clair (1998) 287.

[35] St Clair (1998) 287-288.

[36] Aggelakopoulou and Bakolas (2022).

ancient working methods (pigments, traces of tool marks),[37] the monument and its decorative scheme, and it can inform its conservation.[38]

6.2.1.2 The historic patina in the nineteenth century and in the early twentieth century

Even before the marbles were hacked off and out of the Parthenon, the *formatori* (or makers of casts) employed by Elgin made mouldings by applying wet plaster to the frieze and metopes on the Parthenon.[39] Additional mouldings were made at the British Museum, after the latter acquired the marbles.[40] A committee appointed in 1836 to examine the marbles in the British Museum for traces of paint could not find any,[41] although as recently as 6 years earlier an official publication of the museum had identified colour in various parts.[42] The *formatore* who had been employed by the museum for many years to make moulds from the marbles reported that the entire 'surface of the marbles had been twice washed over with soap lyes as that, or some other strong acid, is necessary for the purpose of removing the soap which is originally put on the surface in order to detach the plaster of the mould'.[43] This, as the famous physicist and chemist Michael Faraday, a member of that committee, observed, would have been enough to remove 'every vestige of colour, which might have existed originally on the surface of the marble'.[44]

The destruction thus caused was therefore certain, but mould-making from the originals continued regardless.[45] By the 1900s, the moulds had deteriorated, and the museum, mindful of the need to keep its customers happy, ordered new moulds to be made from the original sculptures, and this work went on until about 1912.[46] Older moulds that were regarded as 'unserviceable' were destroyed.[47] It appears that these included the original moulds created from the Parthenon itself by Elgin's *formatori*.[48]

Periodic cleaning too was certainly to blame for destruction and, as early as 1858, a flurry of letters published in The Times expressed anger at the scrubbing of the

37 Galanos and Doganis (2003) 3; del Monte and Sabbioni (1987) 114-116; St Clair (1998) 285.
38 St Clair (1998) 285.
39 St Clair (1998) 286.
40 Jenkins (1990) 102.
41 Jenkins and Middleton (1988) 185.
42 British Museum (1830) 26, see also 10-11.
43 Jenkins and Middleton (1988) 185-186. See also Jenkins (2001) 4.
44 Jenkins and Middleton (1988) 185-186.
45 See in general Jenkins (1990).
46 St Clair (1998) 286.
47 Jenkins (1990) 109; St Clair (1998) 287.
48 Jenkins (1990) 109; St Clair (1998) 287.

marbles and accused the museum of 'vandalism',[49] foreshadowing the Duveen cleaning scandal and poignantly showing that it could have been avoided.

Moulding and cleaning aside, the marbles' original surfaces had certainly already been partly destroyed during their transport, having been exposed for a lengthy period to sea water (the marbles in the second cargo of the *Mentor*), long storage in ports while waiting for the next available ship to take them to Britain, and constant moves, including during their time in the back yard of Burlington House.[50] Writing in 1819, Dodwell, who had seen the Parthenon in Greece, observed that the marbles' 'ochreous patina' that gave them 'the warm and mellow tint of an autumnal sun-set' had been 'much diminished since their removal from Athens'.[51] Still, from oil-paintings and watercolours made in the years following the acquisition of the marbles for the British Museum, it appears that the historic patina survived to a large extent.[52]

6.2.1.3 Quis custodiet ipsos custodes?

From the start, some were uneasy about the honey-brown patina they saw.[53] It did not match their idealised image of classical Greek sculpture. Ancient sculptures were meant to be white. The Pentelic marble used for the Parthenon and its sculptures is a

[49] These are reproduced in Jenkins (2001) 5. We read, for instance:

> Sir – I have seen with amazement and indignation the Colosseum . . . "restored" in part . . ., its crevices plastered up and the rich, varied, golden hue, the result of nearly 2,000 Italian summers, obliterated by a monotonous coating of filthy colour. . . . [O]n walking through the Elgin room at the British Museum to-day I witnessed proceedings which in absurdity and atrocity may vie with [this].
>
> Sir, they are scrubbing the Elgin Marbles!

The criticism did not only concern the cleaning of the Parthenon marbles. The following letter refers to a marble portrait bust from the Townley collection:

> The vandalism complained of [in the letter cited above] has been of some duration and first attracted my attention on the opening of the new Graeco-Roman Saloons. Last Christmas I saw a man scrubbing away with some vile compound. The celebrated bust of "Clytie", one of the most beautiful antiques existing, has had its face mauled in this manner, and I am positive that anything beyond the simplest application of water, and that by persons acquainted with the exquisite finesse of sculptured flesh, must prove prejudicial to such a work. I am told this bust was cleaned about ten years ago, and if the scrubbing process is to be renewed every now and then we may bid adieu to the antique beauty of these marbles. Blurred edging and modelling . . . will be the inevitable result with the loss of all those delicate touches which give life and individuality, and over which the sculptor lingered lovingly at the completion of his work. Time needs no human assistance to destroy.

[50] St Clair (1998) 289.

[51] Dodwell (1819) 344.

[52] St Clair (1998) 289; *contra* Jenkins (2001) 1.

[53] St Clair (1998) 289.

bright white when freshly cut.[54] Faraday himself, testing different cleaning methods on the marbles (water, rubbing, powder, alkalis, acid), seemed to search for the colour of freshly cut marble and was concerned that it would not be possible to present the marbles 'in that state of whiteness which they originally possessed'.[55] Yet one need only think of the brilliance of the painted front of the basilica of San Marco in Venice to know that the polychromy of ancient temples need not be an assault on the visual senses in the manner the sceptical connoisseurs of the time assumed.[56] So it was that others opposed the monochromatic ideal and were prepared to recognise beauty and splendour in a richly decorated temple.[57]

Still, to many the marbles looked dingy.[58] London air in the 1800s and until the mid-1950s was very polluted, as a result especially of home coal-burning stoves.[59] (As we shall see, the marbles have not escaped pollution in either London or Athens.) This pollution, combined with fog, could at times reduce visibility so much that not only was it impossible to see across the street but people were reported to drown in the Thames, having inadvertently fallen into the water that they could not see.[60] The marbles, whose patina in the strong Attic sun absorbed the light and reduced glare, in London were a patchwork of white, brown, and occasionally black (especially in the folds and crevices of drapery).[61] By contrast, their plaster casts—plain white and seemingly translucent thanks to varnish—may have seemed to some viewers even better than the real thing.[62] Slowly, the unthinkable came to pass, and, in a misguided attempt to remove what looked like dirt,[63] the ancient patina and the originally polychrome decoration were removed.

In a 1921 letter to The Times, the sculptor Jacob Epstein voiced his dismay and alarm at the cleaning and restoration of Greek antiquities in the British Museum.[64] He protested abundantly in particular against the 'incredible crime' and 'atrocity' endured by the Demeter of Cnidus, whose head not only was equipped with a new plaster nose, but was then 'scraped and cleaned' in order to fit in with the plaster

---

[54] St Clair (1998) 283-284.

[55] Jenkins (2001) 4.

[56] Mahaffy (1878) 39.

[57] Mahaffy (1878) 35-42; cf Hervé (1837) 126.

[58] St Clair (1998) 290-291.

[59] Vanessa Heggie, 'Over 200 Years of Deadly London Air: Smogs, Fogs, and Pea soupers', The Guardian (9 December 2016).

[60] Geoffrey Lean, 'The Great Smog of London: The Air Was Thick with Apathy', The Telegraph (6 December 2012); Vanessa Heggie, 'Over 200 Years of Deadly London Air: Smogs, Fogs, and Pea soupers', The Guardian (9 December 2016).

[61] St Clair (1998) 290-291.

[62] St Clair (1998) 290-291.

[63] AG Thornton, "'Patina' Was Just Dirt to this Cleaner', The Star (21 March 1939), as cited in Jenkins (2001) appendix 11 ('Passing over the hopeless ones who think that the Elgin Marbles are a Scottish ground game, we come to the larger artistic minority who do not know a patina when they see it').

[64] Epstein (1940) 167-168.

nose, destroying its 'mellow golden' patina.[65] Epstein did not mince his words. He described the museum authorities as 'vandals' who should have left the treasures 'in their "care"' 'untouched'.[66] Then, in 1939, Epstein wrote again to The Times.[67] This time he did not only talk of the 'scraping of the surfaces', but he also declared himself 'horrified by the methods employed' and alerted readers to the risk that the marbles were 'being permanently ruined' by the museum.[68] Something had occurred that even the staunchest supporter of the British Museum would have trouble justifying. The narrative requires a small detour to shed light on how we got there.

In 1928, the UK government accepted Duveen's offer to finance the construction of a new gallery at the British Museum.[69] Duveen was a millionaire art dealer with a reputation for unscrupulousness, deceit, and destruction.[70] He was known to retouch the old masters that passed through his hands in order to make a handsome sale.[71] Duveen shared his views about cleaning with the trustees of the museum and 'bombarded the authorities with proposals for making the Marbles look more attractive to the public'.[72] One of the museum trustees described this in the following terms:

> Duveen lectured and harangued us, and talked the most hopeless nonsense about cleaning old works of art. I suppose he has destroyed more old masters by overcleaning than anybody else in the world, and now he told us that all old marbles should be thoroughly cleaned – so thoroughly that he would dip them into acid. Fancy – we listened patiently to these boastful follies . . .[73]

Experiments were conducted with the frieze by one of Duveen's agents without curatorial supervision in an attempt to fill in gaps and achieve greater uniformity of colour.[74] Against best practices and curatorial ethics, Duveen's men were allowed their own keys giving them access to the museum anytime they pleased.[75] They were also permitted to give orders to museum staff, including the museum's foreman mason, Arthur Holcombe.[76] The marbles were cleaned in 1932–1933 and then again in 1937.[77]

---

[65] Epstein (1940) 167-168.

[66] Epstein (1940) 168.

[67] Epstein (1940) 170-173.

[68] Epstein (1940) 173.

[69] St Clair (1998) 293.

[70] St Clair (1998) 293; Simpson (1987).

[71] St Clair (1998) 293.

[72] St Clair (1998) 295.

[73] Lindsay (1984) 537 (diary entry of 8 May 1931).

[74] St Clair (1998) 295.

[75] St Clair (1998) 295.

[76] St Clair (1998) 295.

[77] Jenkins (2001) 6.

In late September 1938, John Forsdyke, the British Museum director, apparently happened to pass through the basement of the Greek and Roman department, where the Helios group was being cleaned.[78] He noticed several copper tools and a piece of coarse carborundum lying about, and it was immediately obvious to him that these had been used on the sculpture.[79] There is little doubt that marble tools were improper for cleaning ancient marbles. As for carborundum, it is next to diamond one of the hardest minerals, and it would normally serve to grind steel and polish granite.[80] On the following day, Roger Hinks, the assistant keeper, found the statue of Iris, another pedimental sculpture, to be undergoing a similar cleaning process, while the head of the horse from the chariot of the moon goddess Selene was in the workshop of the foreman mason.[81] The Helios group and the statue of Iris were now a mismatched jigsaw puzzle of cleaned and uncleaned surfaces.[82] The head of Selene's horse, one of the choicest pieces in Elgin's collection (and indeed an attraction today in the British Museum) had turned from brownish to white.[83] The director called a halt to the cleaning and reported that 'through unauthorised and improper efforts to improve the colour of the Parthenon sculpture for Lord Duveen's new gallery, some important pieces had been greatly damaged'.[84] An internal board of enquiry was constituted 'to consider the nature of the damage and the policy of the Trustees in regard to publication of the facts, to determine responsibility for the damage, and to advise upon the necessary disciplinary action'.[85] The board of enquiry was tasked with investigating the three pedimental sculptures that were being cleaned at the time when the director ordered the cleaning to stop.[86] The board's mandate was restrictive: it did not cover eventual damage caused to other pedimental sculptures, the metopes, or the frieze.[87] According to St Clair, a broader mandate would have ended up with the board of enquiry pointing the finger at the

[78] Extracts from the Report of the Board of Enquiry (December 1938), reproduced in St Clair (1998) 342-344.

[79] Extracts from the Report of the Board of Enquiry (December 1938), reproduced in St Clair (1998) 342-344.

[80] St Clair (1998) 296. On the Mohs Hardness Scale, carborundum scores 9 out of 10.

[81] Extracts from the Report of the Board of Enquiry (December 1938), reproduced in St Clair (1998) 342-344. This is not the only head of a horse from Selene's chariot. Other two heads are in the Acropolis Museum, while a fourth, possibly a victim of the 1687 Venetian bomb, has been lost, see Acropolis Museum, 'Parthenon. East Pediment. Heads of Horses' https://theacropolismuseum.gr/en/parthenon-east-pediment-heads-horses.

[82] St Clair (1998) 296.

[83] St Clair (1998) 296.

[84] Extracts from the Report of the Board of Enquiry (December 1938), reproduced in St Clair (1998) 342-344; Minutes of British Museum Standing Committee, meeting on 8 October 1938, reproduced in St Clair (1998) 342.

[85] Minutes of British Museum Standing Committee, meeting on 8 October 1938, reproduced in St Clair (1998) 342.

[86] St Clair (1998) 296-297.

[87] St Clair (1998) 297.

director himself.[88] So it was that, from the start, the damage to the marbles was kept a secret.[89]

It soon became clear that the scrubbing of the Helios group, Iris, and the head of Selene's horse was not an isolated initiative but part of a broader cleaning programme that had started about a year and a half earlier.[90] The board concluded that copper tools had been used to clean the three sculptures.[91] In a public interview, in May 1939, Holcombe admitted that they were using 'blunt copper tools' to rub the marbles but declared confidently that he 'knew it would not do them any harm, because the copper is softer than the stone'.[92] He added: 'One or two of the slabs of the frieze came up rather white, and I am afraid they caused the trouble.'[93] He revealed that he had been using the same copper tools since 1937, under four museum directors.[94] During all this time, museum officials would pass through the room—a whole 15 months went by before there was a complaint.[95] Epstein commented on the absurdity of the 'softer than marble' argument, recalling 'the bronze toe of the statue of St Peter in Rome kissed away by the worshipers' soft lips' and inveighed against the museum for not taking responsibility.[96]

Privately, the board of enquiry declared that it was 'impressed' that it had been possible for 'such improper methods of cleaning' to be used for so long.[97] It appears that Duveen had imparted his wish that the marbles should be made 'as clean and white as possible' and money had been given to the workmen to motivate them.[98] On one occasion, one of Duveen's agents found that a slab 'was not white enough', and it 'was in consequence recleaned'.[99] The cleaning had the effect of removing the original surface of the marble and of making it 'smooth and white'.[100] The board found that the head of Selene's horse looked as if it had been 'skinned'.[101] It

[88] St Clair (1998) 297.

[89] St Clair (1998) 296.

[90] St Clair (1998) 297.

[91] Extracts from the Report of the Board of Enquiry (December 1938), reproduced in St Clair (1998) 343.

[92] Epstein (1940) 169.

[93] Epstein (1940) 169.

[94] Epstein (1940) 169.

[95] Epstein (1940) 169.

[96] Epstein (1940) 172-173.

[97] Extracts from the Report of the Board of Enquiry (December 1938), reproduced in St Clair (1998) 343.

[98] Extracts from the Report of the Board of Enquiry (December 1938) and Extracts from the Second Report of the Board of Enquiry (December 1938), reproduced in St Clair (1998) 344-345.

[99] Extracts from the Second Report of the Board of Enquiry (December 1938), reproduced in St Clair (1998) 345.

[100] Extracts from the Report of the Board of Enquiry (December 1938), reproduced in St Clair (1998) 344.

[101] Extracts from the Report of the Board of Enquiry (December 1938), reproduced in St Clair (1998) 344.

acknowledged that the original surface of the marbles 'was a document of the utmost importance' and concluded: 'The damage which has been caused is obvious and cannot be exaggerated.'[102]

However, it was imperative to avoid 'a serious blow' to the museum's reputation.[103] Forsdyke had warned that the museum would find no 'kind of condonation among the experts, least of all from the Greeks', since there was 'no excuse for what happened'.[104] So, publicly, the museum kept quiet and denied that any wrongdoing had taken place.[105] The board of enquiry had already resolved that silence was the best approach: 'As regards the question of apprising the public of what has occurred the Board are of opinion that a public statement need not be made.'[106] The board took the view that only experts would spot the damage, but the general public would not know better.[107] As a consequence, it was confirmed that no communication should be made to the press.[108] The marbles, it seems, were covered up with some coating (since 'brown had been taken off, brown could be put back on', as St Clair caustically remarked).[109] No formal disciplinary action was taken.[110]

Information about the scandal started to trickle down in the spring of 1939, and it was about this time that Epstein wrote to The Times to protest about the damage to the marbles.[111] The trustees responded with a statement in The Times, in which they recognised that some unauthorised cleaning methods had been used but explained that they immediately took the necessary measures to prevent such 'innovations' from happening in the future.[112] Instead of taking responsibility, the trustees, in self-congratulatory mode, now tried to show how swift and firm they had been in their

---

[102]Extracts from the Report of the Board of Enquiry (December 1938), reproduced in St Clair (1998) 344.

[103]Peers to Forsdyke (3 December 1938), cited in Jenkins (2001) 9.

[104]Forsdyke's letter of 15 December 1938, cited in Jenkins (2001) 9.

[105]E.g. see George Hill's letter to the Times, cited in Epstein (1940) 171, denying the use of copper tools to clean the marbles ('no "cleaning" other than simple washing with neutral soap and distilled water is authorised in the Museum').

[106]Extracts from the Second Report of the Board of Enquiry (December 1938), reproduced in St Clair (1998) 345.

[107]Extracts from the Second Report of the Board of Enquiry (December 1938), reproduced in St Clair (1998) 345.

[108]Extracts from the Second Report of the Board of Enquiry (December 1938), reproduced in St Clair (1998) 345. It is surprising that in a memorandum submitted to parliament by the British Museum as recently as 2000 we read that the trustees had 'resolved to publish a full report on the effects of the cleaning, but the outbreak of war intervened', House of Commons (2000), annex IV, para 5.2.

[109]St Clair (1998) 299; contrast Jenkins (2001) 18, who whoever does not rule out the possibility that a colour coating was applied.

[110]St Clair (1998) 300.

[111]Jenkins (2001) 9-10 and appendix 11; Epstein (1940) 169-170; Harold Nicolson, 'The Byron Curse Echoes Again', The New York Times (27 March 1949).

[112]St Clair (1998) 301; Jenkins (2001) 10.

response to the situation.[113] Any failing in the custodianship of the marbles was brushed aside; this was just an unfortunate oversight, a lapse in the supervision of staff.[114]

After the war, the trustees appeared to be in no rush to go back to the unfinished matter of the cleaning, which would have been forgotten while the nation was dealing with more important matters.[115] As of late 1948, the marbles had not reappeared, and many started to wonder for how long they would remain hidden from public view.[116] Finally, in September 1949, almost four and a half years after the war, the marbles went on display again.[117] The papers relating to the Duveen cleaning had become, to all intents and purposes, classified.[118] The matter was a source of embarrassment and shame for many of those in the know, and some may have been willing to blow the whistle.[119] However, there was not much to go on, and there the matter rested for almost 60 years.

There the matter rested, that is, until St Clair looked into it. Between 1949, when the marbles were placed again on public view, and 1998, when St Clair exposed the cleaning, guides and books published by the British Museum about the Parthenon and its marbles kept discreetly quiet both about the cleaning and about the damage to the marbles.[120] And in 1983, in a debate in the House of Lords, Richard Nugent, a member of that house, was able to declare that the British Museum has looked after the marbles 'with expert care for nearly two centuries'.[121]

After St Clair revealed the damage caused by the cleaning, a response of sorts became necessary. This was published by Ian Jenkins 3 years later, and it sought to defend as best it could the British Museum.[122] In the British Museum publication *Cleaning and Controversy*, Jenkins conceded that the cleaning should not have happened. Still, 60 years on, he could not refrain from mentioning those who thought that, 'with their disfiguring coatings removed, the sculptures look better than ever';[123] and that photographs show that the marbles 'look better now after their 1930s cleaning and the further cleaning of 1969-70'.[124] The cleaning does not seem to be mentioned on the British Museum website, and it is certainly not mentioned on the museum's webpage on the Parthenon marbles nor in the trustees' statement as it

[113] St Clair (1998) 301. A similar statement was made sometime later by a minister in the House of Commons, ibid 302.

[114] St Clair (1998) 299.

[115] St Clair (1998) 303.

[116] St Clair (1998) 303.

[117] St Clair (1998) 303.

[118] St Clair (1998) 303.

[119] St Clair (1998) 303.

[120] St Clair (1998) 305.

[121] Hansard (1983).

[122] Jenkins (2001).

[123] Jenkins (2001) 30.

[124] Jenkins (2001) 30.

stands at the moment of writing.[125] The museum has a dedicated page on Duveen, where he is described as a 'dealer' and 'benefactor' and a short biography is provided; there is no mention of the cleaning, nor of his dubious professional ethics.[126]

At this point, let us take a step back and consider how St Clair came to expose the cleaning. The Public Records Act 1967 established the so-called '30-year rule', according to which public records would enter the public domain 30 years after they were created.[127] For 60 years, all record requests concerning the cleaning of the Parthenon marbles were turned down flat by the British Museum.[128] In 1984, David Wilson, then director of the museum, invoked 'security implications' to deny access, even though departures from the 30-year rule required the authorisation of the Lord Chancellor.[129] In 1995, after St Clair's insistent complaints that he was being denied his statutory rights to access the records, he was approached by one of the museum's trustees who appeared to be offering to negotiate.[130] At last, the prevarications ended. In 1996, St Clair was given access to the records, and in the revised 1998 version of his 1967 book *Lord Elgin and the Marbles*, he exposed the damage that had been caused.[131] He estimated that the destruction concerned 80% or 90% of the frieze, while the metopes were affected to an even greater extent.[132] The pedimental sculptures had fared better, since some of them had escaped the cleaning,[133] and so it is that, exceptionally, traces of Egyptian blue and tool marks have been found in areas that were spared and retain the golden patina.[134]

Except for the few such pieces that were either not cleaned or whose cleaning was never completed, the Parthenon marbles in the British Museum are now a drab grey-white.[135] By contrast, the marbles that remained in Athens retain their golden-brown patina and textural details that formerly would also have been observable in the

[125] See respectively 'The Parthenon Sculptures' https://www.britishmuseum.org/about-us/british-museum-story/contested-objects-collection/parthenon-sculptures and annex, 'The Parthenon Sculptures: The Trustees' Statement' (British Museum).

[126] British Museum, 'Joseph Duveen, Baron Duveen of Millbank' https://www.britishmuseum.org/collection/term/BIOG26037 (information correct as of November 2022).

[127] Public Records Act (1967) c 44, amending Public Records Act 1958. The 30-year timeframe has more recently been reduced to 20 years, see Constitutional Reform and Governance Act (2010) c 25; The National Archives, 'History of the Public Records Acts' https://www.nationalarchives.gov.uk/information-management/legislation/public-records-act/history-of-pra/.

[128] St Clair (1998) 306-307.

[129] St Clair (1998) 307.

[130] St Clair (1998) 308.

[131] St Clair (1998) Chap. 24.

[132] St Clair (1998) 308-310; cf Jenkins (2001) 28-30.

[133] St Clair (1998) 308-309; Jenkins (2001) 13.

[134] Jenkins and Middleton (1988) 188 and *passim*; Kasia Weglowska, 'Paint and the Parthenon: Conservation of Ancient Greek Sculpture', British Museum Blog (23 May 2018). See also Payne (2021) 147.

[135] St Clair (1998) 309.

marbles at the British Museum.[136] The archaeological damage is obvious.[137] Plaster casts that come, directly or indirectly, from moulds made from the original sculptures show impressions of tool marks that are no longer visible in the marbles that were cleaned in the British Museum.[138] Although the use of casts as evidence of the past condition of a surface is problematic,[139] it is clear that the Duveen scrubbing caused a layer of the original marble surface to be lost forever, along with the pigments and tool marks it enclosed.[140] It has also been suggested that the subsequent suppression of what had happened had the effect of distorting our appreciation of Greek art, since researchers studied *altered* primary sources unawares.[141] But the damage is also aesthetic.[142] As was pointed out in a letter by distinguished Byzantinist art historian Robert Byron to The Times in 1939, it is immediately obvious to the viewer that 'the marbles in Lord Duveen's new gallery have lost [their] patina. The lustre and the gentleness have vanished. The lumps of stone remain, robbed of life, dead as casts.'[143]

St Clair, who had previously favoured the retention of the marbles in the British Museum (and indeed in many respects St Clair has been sympathetic to Elgin), now did an about-face and argued that the marbles should return to Athens. He described what caused this about-turn: it was the fact that the museum's custodianship of the marbles now appeared to have been 'a cynical sham for more than half a century'; for St Clair this meant that the museum's 'claim to a trusteeship has been forfeited'.[144] This failing in stewardship contrasts markedly with one of the museum's favourite arguments: that of how Elgin 'saved' the marbles.

6.2.2 A Near Miss: Bombing of the British Museum during the Blitz

As World War II drew near, precautions were taken to preserve the museum's collections. Initially, the marbles were protected with corrugated metal, timber, and sandbags.[145] We now know that these measures would not have been enough.

---

136 St Clair (1998) 309.

137 St Clair (1998) 309.

138 St Clair (1998) 311-312; contra Jenkins (2001) 22.

139 Jenkins (2001) 22; Jenkins (1990) 112.

140 St Clair (1998) 311.

141 St Clair (1998) 312.

142 St Clair (1998) 309.

143 Robert Byron's letter to The Times (14 May 1939), cited in Jenkins (2001) 10.

144 St Clair (1998) 336. See also US Congress, Senate, S Con Res 134 'Expressing the sense of the Congress that the Parthenon Marbles should be returned to Greece', 108th Congress, 2nd session (22 July 2004).

145 St Clair (1998) 302.

Providentially, the decision was soon taken to move the frieze slabs from the museum to a disused section of the Aldwych tube station, while the metopes and pedimental sculptures were placed in the museum vaults.[146] In 1940, the Duveen Gallery was badly damaged by bombing, but the marbles had already been removed to safety.[147] It has been suggested that the marbles may have been 'safer in England during the nineteenth century, but they were not so secure in the London of 1940 and 1941'.[148] Repairs to the gallery were put off for more than 20 years as was the gallery's reopening.[149] Eventually, procrastination came to an end, and the Duveen Gallery with the marbles now lining its walls reopened in 1962.[150]

6.2.3 Receptions, Dinners, and Fundraisers

An academic symposium held at the British Museum in 1999 that aimed precisely to discuss the cleaning of the Parthenon marbles fanned the flames, when drinks and sandwiches were laid out in the Duveen Gallery, a tactless reminder of the fact that the British Museum regularly rents out its galleries for private events.[151] What made things worse on that occasion was that delegates had been encouraged to actually touch the marbles.[152] Several delegates (including St Clair) regarded the gesture as so disrespectful that they refused to eat.[153] The incident led a New York Times journalist to comment, wordplaying with Keats's famous poem: *On Seeing the Elgin Marbles, With Sandwiches*.[154]

[146] St Clair (1998) 302.

[147] St Clair (1998) 303; Jenkins (2001) 12.

[148] Harold Nicolson, 'The Byron Curse Echoes Again', The New York Times (27 March 1949).

[149] St Clair (1998) 304.

[150] Mary Beard (2010) 162; cf St Clair (1998) 304, who refers to a 1961 reopening. The author has on file the copy of a British Museum document that confirms that the transfer of the marbles to the Duveen Gallery was completed in 1962. However, on the website of the British Museum, we read that the Parthenon marbles 'have been on permanent display since 1817', although we know this to be inaccurate, see https://www.britishmuseum.org/collection/galleries/greece-parthenon (information correct as of November 2022).

[151] Maev Kennedy, 'Mutual Attacks Mar Elgin Marbles Debate', The Guardian (1 December 1999); Warren Hoge, 'London Journal; On Seeing the Elgin Marbles, With Sandwiches', The New York Times (2 December 1999).

[152] Maev Kennedy, 'Mutual Attacks Mar Elgin Marbles Debate', The Guardian (1 December 1999).

[153] Warren Hoge, 'London Journal; On Seeing the Elgin Marbles, With Sandwiches', The New York Times (2 December 1999); Maev Kennedy, 'Mutual Attacks Mar Elgin Marbles Debate', The Guardian (1 December 1999).

[154] Warren Hoge, 'London Journal; On Seeing the Elgin Marbles, With Sandwiches', The New York Times (2 December 1999).

6.2.4 *On Loan to Russia*

Controversy began again when in 2014 the British Museum loaned the headless pedimental statue of the river god Ilissos to the State Hermitage Museum in St Petersburg, Russia, to be included in an exhibition celebrating the 250th anniversary of that museum's foundation.[155] The move, which was cloaked in secrecy and was only announced post eventum, elicited a strong reaction from the Greek government, not least because the British Museum had previously insisted that the marbles could not be moved.[156] The secrecy and the fact that Europe was at the time imposing sanctions on Russia for the annexation of Crimea only added insult to injury.

6.2.5 *Water Leaking in the Marbles Gallery*

The most recent event to stoke the debate was the continued closure of the Duveen Gallery owing to a stubbornly leaky roof following heavy rainfall in 2021.[157] Leaking appears to be a recurrent issue, and Greek officials have expressed their concern 'that wet and damp will damage the ancient artworks'.[158] A few years earlier, in 2018, images of water dripping into the Duveen Gallery were broadcast on Greek television.[159] The museum explained that the marbles had not been damaged and that 'the issue ha[d] been addressed', but the Greek government regarded this as proof of the museum's failure to look after the Parthenon marbles.[160] The leaking has elicited a humorous comment: 'When the British Museum resorts to the

---

[155] See annex, 'The Parthenon Sculptures: The Trustees' Statement' (British Museum); Steven Erlanger, 'Greek Statue Travels Again, but Not to Greece' The New York Times (5 December 2014).

[156] Ben Hoyle and Jack Malvern, 'Elgin Marbles Moved out of Britain for First Time', The Times (5 December 2014); Ben Hoyle, Jack Malvern, and Philippe Naughton, 'Greek PM Furious after Britain Loans Elgin Marble to Russia', The Times (5 December 2014); Steven Erlanger, 'Greek Statue Travels Again, but Not to Greece', The New York Times (5 December 2014).

[157] Dan Hicks, 'The UK Has Held onto the Parthenon Marbles for Centuries – But the Tide Is Turning. Here's Why I Expect Them to Be Returned by 2030', Artnet News (15 December 2021); Craig Simpson, 'British Museum's Leaking Roof Proves Elgin Marbles Should Be Returned to Greece, Say Officials', The Telegraph (14 August 2021). See further 'As Infrastructure Crumbles, British Museum Plans to Fix Parthenon Marbles Gallery Next', The Art Newspaper (3 November 2022).

[158] Cristina Ruiz, 'Is it Raining Again in the British Museum's Parthenon Gallery?', The Art Newspaper (11 August 2021); Craig Simpson, 'British Museum's Leaking Roof Proves Elgin Marbles Should Be Returned to Greece, Say Officials', The Telegraph (14 August 2021).

[159] Cristina Ruiz, 'Is it Raining Again in the British Museum's Parthenon Gallery?', The Art Newspaper (11 August 2021).

[160] Cristina Ruiz, 'Is it Raining Again in the British Museum's Parthenon Gallery?', The Art Newspaper (11 August 2021).

"floodgates" argument in opposing the reunification of the Parthenon Sculptures, little did I realise that the flooding would be from within.'[161]

6.3 The Positions of the British Museum: Engaging with the Debate

Over the years, the UK government and the British Museum have resisted the restitution and reunification of the Parthenon marbles on the basis of arguments that evolved and continue to evolve over time. They range from the debatable to the non sequitur. The latter include claims such as that modern Greeks are not descended from ancient Greeks,[162] that those who call for the return of the marbles are like Hitler and Mussolini, cultural fascists,[163] and that 'much of the frieze' was retrieved 'in the rubble' rather than hacked from the Parthenon.[164] This section will start by considering the traditional positions favouring the marbles' retention in the British Museum, before turning to the theory of cultural 'internationalism' and, ultimately, the arguments currently employed by the museum trustees.

6.3.1 Traditional Positions

6.3.1.1 The removal of the marbles was a boost to the fine arts and interest in the classics

That the removal of the marbles was a boost to the fine arts in Britain and helped promote an interest in the classics is undeniable. But how does boosting the fine arts in one country justify looting another's cultural heritage? Byron had an apt response: 'I opposed, and will ever oppose, the robbery of ruins from Athens, to instruct the English in sculpture'.[165] And, if the removal of the marbles was a boost to the fine arts in Britain in the nineteenth century, would this justify their continued retention in the British Museum today?[166]

---

[161] George Vardas, as cited in Craig Simpson, 'British Museum's Leaking Roof Proves Elgin Marbles Should Be Returned to Greece, Say Officials', The Telegraph (14 August 2021).

[162] For a discussion and refutation, see Hitchens (2008) 101-104.

[163] Chapter 1, text to n 181.

[164] Jonathan Williams (British Museum deputy director), as cited in Helena Smith, 'Greece Rebuts British Museum Claim Parthenon Marbles Were "Removed from Rubble"', The Guardian (23 May 2022).

[165] George Gordon Byron, 'Letter on the Rev WL Bowles' Strictures on the Life and Writings of Pope' (7 February 1821).

[166] Harold Nicolson, 'The Byron Curse Echoes Again', The New York Times (27 March 1949).

6.3.1.2 The marbles were saved by their removal

'We are indebted to Elgin', declared Robert Anderson, former director of the British Museum, 'for having rescued the Parthenon sculptures and others from the Acropolis from the destruction they were suffering'.[167] This image of Elgin as the saviour of the marbles is that of an invented story that has been repeated so often and with such apparent conviction that it came to be considered as true.[168] The myth (for myth it is) relies on a combination of arguments, including that altruism motivated Elgin's actions, that other foreign travellers had been removing what antiquities they could get their hands on, and that, if Elgin had not removed the marbles, they would have been destroyed by someone else.

Elgin's motives in removing the marbles have already been examined. Elgin intended the marbles as home decoration, he was not personally familiar with the state of the marbles, indeed he did not see some of them until they reached England, his correspondence reveals glee at what he might accomplish and fails to show concern for the safety of the marbles. Had he ever become concerned for their safety, he was in a position to take steps to protect them without removing them from the Parthenon.[169] His leverage with the Ottomans would have allowed him to bring pressure to bear on the Porte to take the necessary actions to protect the Parthenon from destruction, thus avoiding the irreparable damage he instead caused to it.[170] The fact that Elgin did not care about any 'destruction' the antiquities may have been suffering is also evident in another piece of correspondence, concerning Olympia this time. On 23 December 1801, Elgin wrote to Lusieri:

> In particular you have, I fancy, to excavate at Olympia. It is one of the most interesting and curious pieces of work – *a place that has never been touched.* ... At Olympia, assuredly excavation is of the greatest consequence. *You would be the first*, and history assures us that there are statues, riches, monuments of all sorts in such abundance, that this dig is deserving of any effort that can be made there.[171]

Did Elgin wish to save Olympia from destruction too? Apparently not. Olympia was 'untouched'. But what justified the endeavour, in Elgin's own words, was its abundance of 'statues', 'riches', and 'monuments of all sorts'. All we see in Elgin's correspondence is his obsession, like that of Verres, with hoarding the finest Greek art. At no stage did Elgin show an interest in the archaeological record nor did he seem to care about the protection of the monuments and antiquities that caught his fancy.

Today, the British Museum stresses the ruined state of the temple when Elgin arrived on the scene. We read on its website that the 1687 explosion 'left the

---

[167] Robert Anderson, then director of the British Museum, as cited in Imogen Tilden, 'Elgin Marbles Will Never Leave UK, Says Museum Chief', The Guardian (15 January 2002).

[168] St Clair (2022) 433.

[169] Rudenstine (2021) 413.

[170] Rudenstine (2021) 413.

[171] Elgin to Lusieri (23 December 1801), cited in Smith (1916) 207 (emphasis added).

Parthenon as a ruin'.[172] No doubt. But how did Elgin leave the Parthenon *he* found? He removed half the frieze, a series of metopes, about half of its sculpture—his men selected the most beautiful and best-preserved parts of the Parthenon. In the process the fabric of the building was attacked, a cornice was removed, and the entablature that held the metopes was broken, large marble blocks were removed, and so on. A drawing by William Gell, now in the British Museum, offers a view of the south-east corner of the Parthenon just as scaffolding is prepared to lower the first metope on 31 July 1801,[173] and it contrasts heavily with drawings and watercolours of the same south-east corner after the removals, making it evident how greatly the Parthenon was denuded.[174] The removals caused grave damage to the Parthenon's structure, much of which subsequently collapsed as a result.[175] International experts who studied the Parthenon at the turn of the twentieth century to understand what conservation works were needed concluded that the damage done by Elgin's men had affected the stability of the part of the building still standing and that there was, as a consequence, a risk of impending collapse.[176] This led St Clair to comment that, if Elgin was the 'saviour' of the marbles, his actions 'had come within a whisker of causing the collapse of the last substantial part of the Parthenon itself'.[177] If the Parthenon was a ruin when Elgin's men arrived on the scene, it was certainly less of a ruin than when Elgin was done with it.

Another argument used to support the 'saving' claim is that other travellers were anyway destroying the Parthenon. Choiseul-Gouffier, French ambassador to the Ottoman Porte only a few years before Elgin, had established a collection of antiquities, including a Parthenon metope and a slab from the frieze that had been discovered in the rubble and which his agent at Athens, Fauvel, obtained from the disdar with bribes.[178] Fauvel also bought another metope that had fallen to the ground after a storm.[179] The frieze slab is now in the Louvre, as is one of the metopes,[180] while the metope that had fallen to the ground in the storm ended up in the British Museum, after it was bought for Elgin at the London Custom House in the mistaken belief that the box that contained it belonged to him.[181] Like Elgin,

[172]British Museum, 'The Parthenon Sculptures' https://www.britishmuseum.org/about-us/british-museum-story/contested-objects-collection/parthenon-sculptures.

[173]The drawing is available on the British Museum website here: https://www.britishmuseum.org/collection/object/G_1853-0307-109.

[174]E.g. contrast the watercolour by Lusieri painted in the same year after the removal of some metopes, available on the website of National Galleries Scotland: https://www.nationalgalleries.org/art-and-artists/20528/south-east-corner-parthenon-athens. Contrast further especially the 1813 depiction of the same corner in Hobhouse (1813) (plate appearing between 342-343).

[175]Michaelis (1882) 135; Merryman (1985) 1899; Rudenstine (2021) 461.

[176]Magne (1895) 28 and *passim*; Magne (1905); St Clair (2022) 463.

[177]St Clair (2022) 464.

[178]St Clair (1998) 64, 123.

[179]St Clair (1998) 64.

[180]Smith (1916) 357.

[181]Smith (1916) 357-365.

Choiseul-Gouffier had left unambiguous instructions to his agent: 'Remove everything you can. Do not neglect any opportunity to plunder in Athens and in its territory all that can be plundered. Spare neither the dead nor the living.'[182] Choiseul-Gouffier also wished to remove choice pieces from the building of the Parthenon, but the Ottomans put their foot down and adamantly refused him permission to take anything from the temple.[183]

These removals in particular made those who champion Elgin's cause assume that, had Elgin not made massive removals from the Parthenon, someone else, probably the French, would have done.[184] Certainly, there is an irony in arguing today that the British Museum is justified in retaining the marbles on the ground that they are part of world heritage (below Sect. 6.3.3.3) *and* because otherwise the French might have them! Since they are part of world heritage, the French might as well have them! And there is something disturbing in suggesting that the 'rape of the Parthenon' had become historically inevitable at the turn of the nineteenth century and Elgin was merely doing what fate had destined for the building;[185] or that he removed the marbles to save them from the destruction they would have suffered if *other* travellers removed them.[186] Consider the facts. No one else made a massive removal from the Parthenon. Only Elgin did. No one else caused destruction of such magnitude. It is no wonder that no other cultural heritage law dispute has captured the public debate so vividly and for so long.

A further argument used to support the 'saving' claim is the damage caused to the marbles by the Ottomans. We know that, since the explosion of 1687, the Ottomans had been using the marble lying in heaps around the Parthenon as building material; some was said to be used to make lime.[187] The Ottomans were even '*said* to have preferred for that purpose a sculptured block to a plain one, though the material was the same'.[188] Such destruction would of course be inexcusable. But to seek to justify Elgin for the destruction *he* caused, on the ground that during this period 'there was an open season on the Parthenon's fabric and remaining sculpture',[189] is to forget that even the Ottomans 'did not ruin the buildings which were still standing'[190]—but Elgin did.

Some of the arguments about the Ottomans' wanton destructiveness were put about by Elgin and his entourage and have since been discredited, including by some

---

[182] Auguste de Choiseul-Gouffier, cited in St Clair (1998) 63 (author's translation).

[183] St Clair (1998) 63-64.

[184] Select Committee (1816) 7. However, see Chap. 3, text to nn 62-64.

[185] Merryman (1985) 1905-1906. Contrast de Visscher (1949) 828.

[186] See also Baynes (1843) 219.

[187] See Chap. 2, text to nn 159-163.

[188] Dodwell (1819) 324-325 (emphasis in original). Notice the emphasis, which shows that Dodwell doubted the truthfulness of this statement. Hugh W Williams too was sceptical about this story, see Williams (1820) 317-320.

[189] Beard (2010) 85.

[190] Dodwell (1819) 325.

who are not necessarily unsympathetic to Elgin.[191] It was Elgin himself who spread the word about the Ottomans 'continually defacing the heads' and pounding the sculptures to make lime and recounted the singular story of a Turk who 'laughingly' told him that the marble had been converted into the mortar that he used to build his house.[192] It was after such acknowledgements were made to him, Elgin told the parliamentary select committee that inquired into the possibility of purchase that he decided to remove as many of the sculptures as circumstances permitted.[193] However, this account is not borne out by the facts: it was not Elgin but his men who took the decision to detach the marbles from the Parthenon, and that before Elgin had ever set foot in Athens. Hamilton too reported to the select committee 'the wantonness of the Turks, who amused themselves with firing upon the objects',[194] a statement that was later adopted almost verbatim in the committee's report.[195]

Dodwell had a different opinion. Stressing that the Ottomans did not destroy the building of the Parthenon and that certainly the metopes were 'out of their reach', he stressed that he 'never heard an instance of their firing at them, which it *is said* they did as an amusement'.[196] Dodwell was confident in this statement because, he explained, the Parthenon had been converted into a mosque when Greece came under Ottoman occupation,[197] the implication being that the Ottomans would respect the Parthenon because it had served as a mosque.[198] Dodwell further refuted another false accusation: the head of a sculpture that was '*said* to have been knocked off by a Turk' had, in fact, been 'detached by a sailor, who was however neither a Greek nor a Turk'.[199]

And what happened to the Parthenon after Elgin? Did the French or the Germans or the Ottomans or the Greek war of independence[200] claim the half of the Parthenon that Elgin left behind? Merryman, one of the scholars who advocated the 'saving' claim and even envisaged the possibility of portraying Elgin as 'a nobly tragic figure: a man so dedicated to the cause of classic Greek art and to the acquisition and

[191]Dodwell (1819) 324-325; Williams (1820) 316-323; Greenhalgh (2019) 403-404.

[192]Select Committee (1816) 41-42.

[193]Select Committee (1816) 41. A similar tale had already been concocted in *Memorandum* (1815) 15-16.

[194]Select Committee (1816) 57.

[195]Select Committee (1816) 5.

[196]Dodwell (1819) 325 (emphasis added).

[197]Dodwell (1819) 325.

[198]The high regard in which the Parthenon was held by the Ottomans, including by the seventeenth-century Ottoman traveller Evliya Çelebi, is documented in the work of Elizabeth Key Fowden, e.g. see Fowden (2019) and Fowden (2018).

[199]Dodwell (1819) 325 (emphasis added).

[200]There are contradictory accounts about how much was destroyed during the Greek war of independence, with some authors expressing the opinion that the damage to the buildings was minimal, e.g. Wines (1833) 298; Delaroière (1836) 33-34; Browning (2008) 12; St Clair (2022) 360, 369-370, 391, 431-432, etc.; or, at the very least, that the state of preservation of the buildings after the war of independence was extraordinary, e.g. Napier (1842) 370; d'Estourmel (1848) 95.

preservation of the Marbles that he sacrificed his career and his fortune for them',[201] seemed to believe this. He insisted that, had Elgin left the marbles in place, they would have been removed by someone else and, if not, they would have been 'exposed to a variety of more serious hazards'.[202] He proceeded to list these imaginary ills that could have befallen the marbles, one fanciful scenario after another—an underwhelming exercise in counterfactual history. The fact is, we know what happened to the marbles that Elgin left behind: they have survived.[203] There is no reason to believe that, if the other half of the frieze and the metopes and other removed sculptures had remained in place, they would not be in the Acropolis Museum with the marbles currently there.

What saved the remaining marbles was Greece gaining independence and putting a stop to the destruction. The new state imposed a ban on the export of antiquities.[204] Even before independence, Ioannis Capodistrias, the first Governor of Greece, prevented the French from removing archaeological finds from Olympia,[205] and Fauvel was denied permission to export the antiquities he had collected.[206] When the UK government proposed to repair at its expense the foundations of the Propylaea, the Greeks turned the offer down flat: they would rather repair them themselves,[207] since they had learnt to beware of the British even bearing gifts.[208] And when, from around the middle of the nineteenth century, various resident archaeology schools started to be established at Athens, the condition was imposed on them that what they discovered in their excavations must stay in the country.[209]

The Parthenon suffered by the removal of its marbles. There is strictly nothing to suggest that this was an act of rescue. This was stressed by Charles de Visscher, when he was a judge at the International Court of Justice (ICJ):

> It is very doubtful ... whether the arguments put forth can actually justify the irreparable damage resulting from [Elgin's] action. The fact is that the principle of the unity and integrity of a monument of such extraordinary artistic and historic value clearly outweighs any other consideration here. Neither the possibility of spoliation at the hands of foreigners, nor the likelihood of defacement or destruction of the monuments on the Acropolis ... had the dual character of certainty and imminence that might have justified so serious a step.[210]

---

[201] Merryman (1985) 1909.

[202] Merryman (1985) 1906, contrast 1909.

[203] See also Harold Nicolson, 'The Byron Curse Echoes Again', The New York Times (27 March 1949).

[204] See Chap. 2, text to 183.

[205] St Clair (1998) 319. See also Voudouri (2010) 458.

[206] St Clair (1998) 319.

[207] About (1863) 221-222.

[208] Similar comment in St Clair (1998) 320.

[209] St Clair (1998) 320.

[210] See de Visscher (1949) 828; cf Quatremère de Quincy (1836) 224-225, discussing Morosini ('Morosini had an excuse: it was from barbarians that he took this masterpiece. But you see that, by a false love of the arts, he ruined in one day what the barbarism of so many centuries had respected.

This is not to deny that some damage to the marbles in Athens did take place while they remained on the building. Photographs published in the *Illustrated London News* in 1929 comparing contemporary casts made by Walter Hege for the German Archaeological Institute in Athens and Elgin's old casts showed an unmistakable deterioration.[211] Even though, as mentioned earlier, casts are not a particularly reliable proof of the past condition of a surface and the moulding process that produced these casts was likely to have harmed the marbles, thus creating the damage that it also allowed to identify, the deterioration of some marbles is evident.

Damage was also suffered due to air pollution in Athens before the marbles were moved to the museum.[212] Fatally for this argument, as we have seen, London air too was polluted and, as early as 1845, the trustees of the British Museum were warned that the marbles were deteriorating from 'exposure to the London atmosphere, its smoke and dirt and the alterations of heated and damp air' as well as because of the coal-fired stoves used within the museum for heating.[213]

The effects of pollution by the Athens air appear to have now been removed. The laser cleaning programme of the Parthenon marbles and other sculptures at the Acropolis Museum was completed in June 2021.[214] It relied on the same purpose-built laser technology used to clean the west frieze in 2002–2005.[215] The laser cleaning made it possible to remove surface deposits safely without altering the historic patina.[216] Traces of tool marks and colour have been found in various parts.[217] Anthony Snodgrass commented on the 'sharpness in the Athens slabs':

> Looking at a depiction of two horsemen in Athens, ... he pointed to chisel marks and traces of colour in the crevices and folds of drapery, along with anatomical details such as veins on the horses' bellies. These are all missing from the London sculptures ... Professor Snodgrass said: 'The famous slab of two horsemen in the British Museum is very like the Athens one. Put them side by side and they make a striking comparison. Can we please stop having these extravagant claims about Elgin saving the sculptures? The west frieze is in better shape than anything in London, we can now see.[218]

So true it is, that in everything, *nothing is so dangerous as an ignorant friend*', author's translation, emphasis in original).

[211] Payne (2021) 57-58, figs 3.1-3.2; Jenkins (1990) 112.

[212] Karl E Meyer, 'Opinion – Editorial Notebook: Let Greece Have the Marbles', The New York Times (18 May 1997).

[213] Jenkins (2001) 4, 6.

[214] Acropolis Museum, 'Research and Conservation – New Technologies: Laser' https://theacropolismuseum.gr/en/new-technologies/laser.

[215] Frantzikinaki and others (2007). See also Acropolis Museum, 'Research and Conservation – New Technologies: Laser' https://theacropolismuseum.gr/en/new-technologies/laser; YSMA, 'Completed Interventions' https://www.ysma.gr/en/monuments/parthenon/completed-interventions/.

[216] Acropolis Museum, 'Research and Conservation – New Technologies: Laser' https://theacropolismuseum.gr/en/new-technologies/laser.

[217] Vlassopoulou (2006) 267; Vlassopoulou (2010) 220.

[218] Dalya Alberge, 'Sharp Relief of the Marbles Elgin Left Behind', The Times (25 November 2004).

But let us pause for a moment and suppose that the marbles were saved by Elgin. Would that justify their continued retention? To quote Christopher Hitchens, 'are there that many Lords or Commons who really take the view that, having saved the property of a neighbour in an emergency, one would be justified in annexing it for oneself?'[219]

6.3.1.3 The marbles are seen by more people in Bloomsbury than they would be in Athens

This is another flawed argument. If all museum exhibits should be displayed where they are seen by more people, then only a handful of museums would exist around the world. It is anyway estimated that fewer than three out of ten visitors to the British Museum actually step into the Duveen Gallery.[220] By contrast, we may assume that essentially every visitor to the Acropolis Museum visits the Parthenon Gallery.[221] If these estimations are correct and we take into account the number of international visitors, we find that the number of overseas visitors to the Duveen Gallery and the number of international visitors to the Acropolis Museum are comparable.[222]

Merryman took this argument to extremes. He talked of a 'distribution interest' as an 'international interest in the accessibility of cultural property to all people', which, for him, would argue in favour of a flow of art from art-rich countries to market countries.[223] He took the view that 'all of the works of a culture' do not 'belong at that culture's situs' and appeared to regret that '[c]riteria for an appropriate international distribution of the artifacts of a culture do not yet exist'.[224] It is difficult to understand in what sense world museums amassing other nations' cultural objects actually *distribute* works of art and make them accessible to all people. This is a two-edged argument. Maybe world museums should start to distribute some art—at least the art in their storerooms.

---

[219] Hitchens (2008) xx. See also Baynes (1843) 220 ('If we do not replace [the marbles] we act as an individual who, having taken part of his neighbour's property into his house to preserve it during a conflagration, should refuse to return it, when the flames were extinguished').

[220] Stewart (2001) 55.

[221] For a similar argument, see Robertson (2019) Chap. 5 (unnumbered page).

[222] To take an example from pre-covid visits, in 2017-2018, the British Museum had 3.7 million overseas visitors, British Museum, 'Report and Accounts for the Year Ended 31 March 2018' (2018) 27. If three out of ten visited the Duveen Gallery, this means that only 1.11 million overseas visitors saw the marbles. For the same year, the Acropolis Museum had 1.67 million visitors and it appears that about 70% of them were international visitors, Acropolis Museum, 'A Highlights Report June 2017-May 2018: Year Nine' (2018). If we take it for granted that all visitors to the Acropolis Museum visit the Parthenon Gallery, this means that about 1.17 million international visitors saw the marbles in the Acropolis Museum. In any case, the numbers are a bad argument about where the marbles should be.

[223] Merryman (1985) 1920.

[224] Merryman (1985) 1920-1921.

The basements of world museums are known to be full of objects that are never displayed. The British Museum makes no secret of the fact that at any one time only 1% of the *c* eight million objects in its collection is on public display in Bloomsbury.[225] While keeping 99% of a collection in storerooms may appear excessive, admittedly, any self-respecting museum must have its storerooms full. Not every drawing or pottery fragment is of interest to the average museum-goer, and there are only so many identical bottles, oil lamps, statuettes, what have you, that a museum can display at any one time without overwhelming its visitors. A lot of thinking must go into what to display and by the same token what not to display. The most beautiful and complete of the Parthenon marbles are on display in the British Museum, they belong to the privileged 1% of the collection. But how about the elegant if incomplete sandalled foot of a female figure, possibly Athena, from the Parthenon's west pediment, which is not on display? How about the architectural fragments from the Erechtheion (an anta capital and an architrave from the east porch, a marble coffer from the ceiling of the north porch, a fragment of the cornice) that are not on display?[226] Sure, these are fragments, not quite interesting as standalone museum exhibits. Is it in the British Museum storeroom or in Athens where most visitors would see them?

6.3.1.4 London is a safer home for the marbles than Athens

The argument that London is a safer home for the marbles has been pressed with a mix of contempt and condescension over the years, although—as we shall see later—it has ultimately been abandoned. The argument had been used from the very first to justify Elgin's actions and buttress his image as the saviour of the marbles. In 1844, when a set of *casts* was prepared (after persistent Greek requests, rather than as an attempt to salve the museum's figurative conscience), a requirement was imposed: the British Museum would send the casts on condition 'that some provision be made for their safekeeping'.[227] This, we are told, was 'an important consideration since there was little enough storage-space in Athens for the great quantity of sculptures that were being uncovered on the Acropolis, let alone for a substantial import of casts'.[228]

As recently as 1997, in a debate in the House of Lords, Woodrow Wyatt, a member of that house, voiced his concern thus: 'My Lords, is the Minister aware that it would be dangerous to return the marbles to Athens because they were under

---

[225] British Museum, Fact Sheet (2019) https://www.britishmuseum.org/sites/default/files/2019-10/fact_sheet_bm_collection.pdf. It appears that more than 100,000 Greek artefacts are kept in the museum's storerooms, see Hansard (2022a), intervention by Alfred Dubs.

[226] These are just some items of the Elgin collection that according to the museum's website are not on display as of September 2022. This information is accessible by consulting each item's individual page.

[227] Jenkins (1990) 107; About (1863) 221.

[228] Jenkins (1990) 107.

attack by Turkish and Greek fire in the Parthenon when they were rescued and the volatile Greeks might easily start hurling bombs around again?'[229] There are mixed in this argument a perception of modern Greeks as incapable of appreciating and protecting the masterpieces of their ancestors and the paraded superiority of the non-Greek speaker who can better appreciate and protect these same works. This attitude is not unique to the Parthenon case. One poignant comment by Greenfield tells us of 'the peculiar aberration of an avowed love and appreciation of art coupled with a contempt for the indigenous people from whom the art in question has sprung'.[230]

A few years later, when Greece hoped to obtain the marbles on the occasion of the return of the Olympic Games to the country, Anderson, then director of the British Museum, criticised Greece's storage facilities and the display of the marbles in Athens.

> There is urgent need in Athens of a proper building for displaying the many sculptures of the Parthenon and other treasures that are currently lumbered in store-rooms ... If symbolic gestures for 2004 are called for, there could be none better than Greece making sure that it properly displays what is already has.[231]

Merryman took this line of argument further. He wrote that 'objects that would be well-housed and preserved abroad' should not be 'allowed to deteriorate in warehouses or inadequately maintained and staffed museums or, often worse, at unprotected and unexcavated sites at home'.[232] There is no doubt that concerns about conservation and preservation are of the utmost importance. Excavated or open archaeological sites are particularly vulnerable and, unless appropriately protected, they risk decaying fast. The ancient cities in the Bay of Naples that fell victim to the explosion of Vesuvius in 79 AD are a good example of the need to balance excavation and conservation, since it is excavation itself that, by 'releasing the remnants of the past from the subterranean equilibrium that has preserved them', creates the need for conservation.[233] Common sense dictates that, only once conservation has been secured, should further excavation take place. However, the fact that a site, or part of a site, remains unexcavated is no reason to invite the market to take over. Besides, when one cares so much, one should dig into one's pockets and foot the excavation and preservation bill, just like the United Nations Educational, Scientific and Cultural Organization (UNESCO) and its member states do to protect the cultural heritage sites inscribed on the World Heritage List or on the List of World Heritage in Danger.[234]

---

[229] Hansard (1997).

[230] Greenfield (2007) 68.

[231] Imogen Tilden, 'Elgin Marbles Will Never Leave UK, Says Museum Chief', The Guardian (15 January 2002).

[232] Merryman (1985) 1889.

[233] Wallace-Hadrill (2006) 187.

[234] Convention Concerning the Protection of the World Cultural and Natural Heritage (World Heritage Convention) arts 11, 15.

But to return to Anderson's statement, before the new Acropolis Museum opened its doors in 2009, the finds from the Acropolis were displayed in a small dismal museum perched on the sacred rock that could do no justice to the treasure trove it held. In response to criticisms such as the one formulated by Anderson, Greece built the new Acropolis Museum, showing that it is prepared to take the necessary steps to dismantle all of the British Museum's arguments. So, while Anderson's assertion may have been true back then, now that the new Acropolis Museum is up and running beautifully, this is no longer a valid argument. Ultimately, as we have seen, when it comes to where the marbles are best protected, the British Museum has forfeited its claim to being a safer home.

6.3.1.5 The Parthenon marbles are part of Britain's cultural heritage

Merryman wrote that, even if the marbles 'are Greek in origin', over the time that they have been in the United Kingdom, they 'have become part of the British cultural heritage':

> The Elgin Marbles ... have entered British culture, help define the British to themselves, inspire British arts, give Britons identity and community, civilize and enrich British life, and stimulate British scholarship. While one may argue that in these terms the Greek claim is more (or less) powerful than that of the British, it is not unreasonable to perceive the two positions as roughly equivalent.[235]

It is unclear whether Merryman, himself an American, had consulted British people about this statement. His argument that the marbles serve as part of British national identity is at odds with this own theory of 'cultural internationalism', which condemns the attempt to inscribe cultural heritage in a nation and promotes the idea of shared cultural heritage.[236]

It is undeniable that the story of the acquisition of the Parthenon marbles is now part of British history and that the marbles have been in Britain for two centuries. But are the two positions 'roughly equivalent'? 'How does one weigh two centuries', as Jenifer Neils asked, 'against twenty-two?'[237] If the two positions are equivalent, why are the Parthenon marbles not on British passports as the Parthenon is on Greek passports? British passports include other elements of nation-building, such as Shakespeare and the Globe. Is it possible that the Parthenon with its abundance of symbolism matters to the Greeks as much as Shakespeare matters to the British?

A grand gesture of returning the marbles would more properly reflect British character. Byron and the many Britons who over the years have favoured the marbles' return to Athens would agree.[238] This was aptly captured in a letter

---

[235] Merryman (1985) 1916.

[236] See Sect. 6.3.2.

[237] Neils (2001) 243.

[238] Hitchens (2008) xvii.

published in The Telegraph in May 2022, in which the correspondent urged the marbles' return through taking into account the legacy of British culture:

> The Marbles are of much greater significance to the Greeks than they are to the British. In Athens they are a symbol of almost totemic significance. The return of the sculptures would be seen by history as a magnanimous gesture, reflecting the modern ethos of British culture instead of the mean rapaciousness of our past history. Make copies, give back the originals – for our future.[239]

6.3.1.6 The principle of repose

According to the so-called 'principle of repose', cultural property should remain where it is located, unless some overriding reason exists for it to move.[240] The principle could be used to refuse the loan of objects whose fragility makes them potentially unsuitable for transport.[241] In reality, it tends to be advocated by those who possess the cultural heritage of others and wish to resist repatriation.[242] Museum curators, who apply it as far as their own collections are concerned, often do not let it stand in the way of organising large exhibitions.[243] Neils has suggested that the correct application of a principle of repose would have been to maintain the Parthenon intact in 1801.[244]

6.3.1.7 The return of the marbles will be the end of world museums (floodgates argument)

In 1924, Harold Nicolson, then a junior clerk in the Foreign Office, suggested to the Labour prime minister, Ramsay MacDonald, that the government might make a gesture on the occasion of the centenary of Byron's death and return the caryatid removed from the Erechtheion or, if not the caryatid, at the very least a column. MacDonald replied that politics was 'the art of the possible' and that what Nicolson suggested was 'artless and impossible'.[245] Nicolson described MacDonald's reaction as follows: 'If we restored the single column, then why not restore the caryatid? And if we restored the caryatid, then we would be prejudicing our whole case and leaving ourselves with no justification at all for retaining the other and even more

---

[239] Alan Mole's letter to The Telegraph (23 May 2022).

[240] Neils (2001) 243.

[241] Neils (2001) 243.

[242] Neils (2001) 243; cf Merryman (1985) 1911.

[243] Neils (2001) 243.

[244] Neils (2001) 243.

[245] Harold Nicolson, 'The Byron Curse Echoes Again', The New York Times (27 March 1949).

valuable sculptures.'[246] To this, Nicolson replied that 'never, since the days of Lord Elgin, had any such justification existed'.[247]

This is the argument that the return of the marbles will be the thin end of the wedge ultimately resulting in the depletion of 'world' museum collections. The argument of the dissolution of universal museums has been defended by others, since MacDonald. Merryman relied on the case of the Parthenon marbles to argue that 'all of the great Western museums' (he gave as examples the Met, the British Museum, the Louvre, and the Hermitage) 'contain vast collections of works from other parts of the world' and stressed that, if 'works of foreign origin should be returned to their sources, as Third World nations increasingly demand in UNESCO and other international fora', the collections of these museums would be significantly reduced.[248] The assumption that all of the *great* museums are world museums is debatable. While no one would argue with the fact that world museums *are* generally great museums, some of the greatest museums hold specialised national or often regional collections. If one is interested in ancient Roman art from the Bay of Naples, the National Archaeological Museum of Naples (possibly to be 'complemented' in the future by smaller regional museums in the area) is the best. If people are passionate about Minoan art, they should probably visit the Heraklion Archaeological Museum. For Florentine Renaissance art, nothing tops the Uffizi Gallery. If a Londoner wishes to stroll into a Pre-Raphaelite art gallery, it will have to be Tate Britain—not the British Museum, not even the National Gallery. The assumption that there is something so special about world museums that makes it more important for the marbles too to be kept in a world museum than in the Acropolis Museum should not be taken as a given.

In a letter to the New York Times in 2002, Anderson defended the collections of what he termed 'international museums'. 'Once started', he wrote, 'the erosion of such collections could not begin and end with the Parthenon Sculptures, but would undermine the collections—and therefore the educational value—of international museums *the world over*'.[249] Only, it is not the case that Anderson's 'international museums' exist 'the world over', but in just a handful of countries. How about the perspective of the majority of countries that are not the United Kingdom, the United States, France, or Russia?

Irrespective of these arguments, the assumption of the haemorrhaging of world museums is a gross exaggeration.[250] Most museum exhibits were not acquired in the circumstances the Parthenon marbles were acquired. Most museum exhibits are 'portable', objects made for individual use, for the trade, 'to be bought and sold on

[246] Harold Nicolson, 'The Byron Curse Echoes Again', The New York Times (27 March 1949).
[247] Harold Nicolson, 'The Byron Curse Echoes Again', The New York Times (27 March 1949).
[248] Merryman (1985) 1895.
[249] Robert Anderson, 'Opinion: Great Museums' Mission' The New York Times (7 February 2002) (emphasis added).
[250] Neils (2001) 244.

the open market'.[251] Not so the Parthenon marbles. They are parts of a public building. Greece has made it abundantly clear that, while it is asking for the Parthenon marbles, it is not asking for all Greek antiquities.[252]

6.3.2 An Argument Apart: 'Cultural Nationalism' v 'Cultural Internationalism' (and Why It Is Both Misleading and Irrelevant)

In a 1986 article published in the *American Journal of International Law*, Merryman introduced what he called 'two ways of thinking about cultural property'.[253] The one he termed 'cultural nationalism' and the other 'cultural internationalism'.[254] His schematic design divided world opinion into two. On the one hand, he described UNESCO and the 1970 UNESCO Convention, countries rich in cultural heritage, and archaeologists as 'nationalist'.[255] On the other, he proclaimed himself, the 1954 Hague Convention,[256] apologists for 'encyclopaedic' museums, and a handful of market countries to be 'internationalist'. Merryman's theory of 'cultural internationalism' is deceptive in all kinds of ways, and it is rejected by the 143 states that have joined the 1970 UNESCO Convention.[257] These include the handful of market countries that Merryman described as 'internationalist', for they were not members of the 1970 UNESCO Convention in 1986.[258] However, for historical completeness, the theory will be briefly discussed.

According to Merryman, 'cultural nationalism' is the root cause of a country's refusal to export and trade its heritage.[259] He explained 'the basic cultural nationalist position' in the following terms: 'even though many "Greek" sculptures are in the British Museum and the Louvre beyond the reach of Greek laws, they remain

[251] Neils (2001) 244.

[252] See Chap. 5, text to nn 35-36. See also Celestine Bohlen, 'Greece Affirms Limits to Elgin Marble Claim', The New York Times (13 December 2002).

[253] Merryman (1986).

[254] Merryman reiterated his positions in later publications, see e.g. Merryman (1988); Merryman (2005).

[255] Merryman (1986); Merryman (2005).

[256] Merryman's distinction between the 1954 Hague Convention and the 1970 UNESCO Convention relies on an out-of-context reading of a recital in the preamble to the 1954 Hague Convention. In fact, the two conventions are aligned, in that they both protect cultural heritage in wartime and in peace respectively. The conventions are discussed in Sect. 9.2.1.

[257] See https://en.unesco.org/fighttrafficking/1970. See also Chap. 1, text to n 146.

[258] Compare Merryman (1986) 843 with the states listed as parties to the 1970 UNESCO Convention https://en.unesco.org/fighttrafficking/1970.

[259] It is interesting that he did not seem to draw the parallel with the fact that market countries too pass laws that prevent the deaccession of items in their collections.

Greek'.[260] For Merryman, the Parthenon marbles that line the walls of the British Museum should best be described as British.[261] The archaeological record disappears, the context is no longer important. The marbles in the British Museum become British. This is the logic of world museums. According to the 2002 Declaration on the Importance and Value of Universal Museums,

> The objects and monumental works that were installed decades and even centuries ago in museums throughout Europe and America were acquired under conditions that are not comparable with current ones. Over time, objects so acquired – whether by purchase, gift, or partage – have become part of the museums that have cared for them, and by extension part of the heritage of the nations which house them.[262]

Notice: 'purchase, gift, or partage' but not unlawful removal. To claim the Parthenon marbles as Greek is, in Merryman's view, to adopt an irredentist rhetoric, to become a cultural nationalist.

At the opposite end of the spectrum is Merryman's 'cultural internationalism' position, which regards the cultural heritage created in art-rich countries as belonging to all humanity and encouraging its export and trade. This Merryman explained as a way of thinking about cultural property as common cultural heritage, independent of place of 'origin or present location, independent of property rights or national jurisdiction'[263]—in other terms, independent of the historical record and context. Merryman, an art collector himself, favoured the free trade of cultural objects unrestrained by cooperation among states.[264] The theory's dominant rationale is commercial,[265] and it tends to minimise the archaeological destruction involved in the underlying activities that bring new material to the international market.[266] While Merryman described this pro-universal museum, pro-market bias as 'internationalist', others might prefer to see it as quite the opposite: nationalist[267] or, as an author described it, more akin to 'cultural imperialism'.[268]

In any event, Merryman's criticism of the 1970 UNESCO Convention's 'exclusive emphasis on nationalism'[269] is in conflict with reality: the Convention aims to stem the illicit traffic in cultural property, and to do so it encourages international

---

[260] Merryman (1988) 489-490.

[261] See also Bator (1982) 303, 307 ('The Elgin marbles are part of England's national patrimony. All such works of art are part of the national capital: They generate income (by attracting tourists, etc.) and they can produce social and psychological benefits for a country and its inhabitants', emphasis removed); Cuno (2011) xii.

[262] Declaration on the Importance and Value of Universal Museums (2002) https://bit.ly/36QkIyk.

[263] Merryman (1986) 831.

[264] Nafziger (2008) 202-203.

[265] Nafziger (2008) 203.

[266] Fincham (2013) 954-955, 1001. For a discussion of the destruction caused by the trade in unprovenanced antiquities, see Brodie (2006); Brodie (2004); Chippindale and Gill (2000).

[267] Nafziger (2008) 203.

[268] Prott (2005) 228 (emphasis removed).

[269] Merryman (1986) 850.

cooperation. Merryman, for his part, appeared to take exception to, for instance, the fact that the United States prosecutes smugglers.[270] The stopgap rhetoric of the 'cultural internationalism' argument never held any water and is now at last being abandoned.

6.3.3 *The Trustees' Statement: Current Arguments against Return*

The arguments of the British Museum have evolved over time and there is little doubt that, so long as the marbles remain there, they will keep evolving. They have included or include different justifications (Elgin saved the marbles, Elgin improved the arts in Britain, the Greeks actually imitated Elgin's example by removing the marbles to the museum,[271] the removal of the marbles was 'creative',[272] and so on) and they conscript Elgin's actions into the lawful-possession narrative.

This section draws on the arguments of the British Museum as expressed in the trustees' current statement about the Parthenon marbles. The statement is reproduced in the annex at the end of this book (Chap. 12). The statement focuses possibly as much on the Parthenon marbles as it does on the value of the British Museum—it attracts millions of visitors, entrance is free of charge, it lends widely, over 3.5 million objects from its collection are available to look at online,[273] it is a generous museum because it considers that the Acropolis Museum is a great museum too, and it showcases Greek art.[274] The statement starts by underlining the value of world museums. It continues with what it describes as a series of 'common misconceptions', although most of them are not misconceptions at all. These will now be considered in turn.

6.3.3.1 The British Museum as a 'world' museum

British culture secretary Wright told The Times in 2019: 'There is a huge cultural benefit to the world in having places in the world where people can see these things together'.[275] Take this statement out of context and one might be excused for thinking that Wright meant that the two halves of the Parthenon must be seen

---

[270] Merryman (1986) 851.

[271] Richard Morrison, 'Neil MacGregor: "There Is No Possibility of Putting the Elgin Marbles Back"', The Times (7 November 2014).

[272] Chapter 1, text to n 92.

[273] This leaves out more than half of the museum's collection, 4.5 million objects, which are neither online nor on public display, see text to n 225.

[274] See annex, 'The Parthenon Sculptures: The Trustees' Statement' (British Museum).

[275] David Sanderson, 'Minister Rules Out Return of Treasures', The Times (22 April 2019).

together. He did not. The trustees' statement explains that the British Museum 'tells the story of cultural achievement throughout the world' and that the 'Parthenon sculptures are a significant part of that story'. By praising the Parthenon marbles as part of 'the story of cultural achievement', the statement in fact only repeats a commonly accepted truth, although it creates the impression of magnanimity vis-à-vis Greece. The statement continues: 'The Museum is a unique resource for the world: the breadth and depth of its collection allow a global public to examine cultural identities and explore the complex network of interconnected human cultures.'

This is all very well as regards the overall value of the museum's collections and the museum's importance as an institution. But when it comes to the importance placed on individual parts of the collection, this argument does not work so well. While in the Acropolis Museum the remaining marbles are given pride of place, in the British Museum's 'story of cultural achievement', the marbles are no longer admired for themselves. In the Duveen Gallery, the marbles become little more than an example of Greek art that, when seen against the rest of the museum's collection, helps visitors experience the breadth and diversity of human creation and culture. Whatever the didactic value of their presence in a world museum, one could argue that the marbles can best be appreciated in a museum created in good part for them. In any case, it is unclear how one is to weigh the benefits of cultural heritage held in world museums against the loss to the culture that created it.[276] The credibility of the argument of the value of world museums is undercut by the fact that it is especially used as a defence against requests for repatriation.[277]

6.3.3.2 'Positive advantage and public benefit in having the sculptures divided between two great museums'

They say that the best defence is attack, and attack is what the British Museum seems to do with this argument. At least, it is otherwise difficult to understand where this statement comes from. To maintain that the Parthenon is best seen dismembered, its architectural fragments divided between the British Museum and the Acropolis Museum, is of course an absurd argument. Antoine Chrysostome Quatremère de Quincy said it back in 1796, when he argued against the spoliation of Italian art: *diviser c'est détruire* (to divide is to destroy).[278] But the British Museum seems to think it can turn such common sense on its head.

[276] O'Neill (2004) 199.

[277] O'Neill (2004).

[278] Quatremère de Quincy (1796) 20. Elsewhere, he discussed Morosini's vandalism: 'Do you not think you see Morosini stripping the pediment of the Parthenon in Athens to transport two figures to Venice? I ask you, what would these fragments mean, detached from their mass and their context?', Quatremère de Quincy (1836) 224-225 (author's translation).

The trustees explain that they 'firmly believe that there's a positive advantage and public benefit in having the sculptures divided between two great museums, each telling a complementary but different story'.[279] The narrative goes as follows. The Acropolis Museum makes it possible for the Parthenon marbles in Athens 'to be appreciated against the backdrop of Athenian history. The Parthenon sculptures in London are an important representation of ancient Athenian civilisation in the context of world history.' We've come full circle back to the world museum argument.[280]

However, once you start pulling on that thread, where do you stop? Would the trustees argue that Stonehenge too had better be divided in two? Or Westminster Abbey? St Paul's Cathedral? The Magna Carta? Or the Koh-i-Noor—'a diamond the size of a hen's egg',[281] whose property is, incidentally, also contested? *To divide is to destroy.*

The blow to the Acropolis Museum's claim to the missing half of the marbles is apparently mitigated by the patronising concession that the Acropolis Museum is a 'great' museum too, an attempt to stress what an even greater museum the British Museum is. Maybe the Acropolis Museum should state on its website that, while half of the marbles currently reside in another great museum, they should better return home.

The Parthenon marbles were part of a building. Both aesthetically and intellectually, they make little sense divided in two.[282] This is one of the reasons why states, including the United Kingdom, pass laws to protect the integrity of public monuments;[283] this is why the integrity of a site is made a condition for inscription on the World Heritage List under the World Heritage Convention;[284] and this is why the ICJ in the *Temple of Preah Vihear* case decided that the parts of the temple that Thailand had removed should be returned to Cambodia.[285] The most eloquent

---

[279] This line of argument was repeated by British Museum director Hartwig Fischer, in a letter to The Times in March 2020, see 'Letters to the Editor: Greeks Should be Glad we Have the Marbles', The Times (1 March 2020).

[280] This approach was further fleshed out in a recent statement by Hartwig Fischer: 'yes, these sculptures have been displaced, they have been taken from the place for which they were created and put in another context. So what is missing in Athens is present in London in a different context that triggers other kinds of thoughts and other types of creativity.' But he failed to explain what these 'other kinds of thoughts' and 'other types of creativity' are. In a similar statement, Ian Jenkins said: 'They are working here the way they should do, as a gift to the world from antiquity. They transcend their original function as ornaments and become art objects.' For the statements, see Kaya Burgess and Anthee Carassava, 'Auguste Rodin's Case for Elgin Marbles to Remain at British Museum', The Times (12 January 2018).

[281] Dalrymple and Anand (2016) 8.

[282] cf Neils (2001) 247.

[283] E.g. Planning (Listed Buildings and Conservation Areas) Act 1990; Ancient Monuments and Archaeological Areas Act 1979; Ancient Monuments Protection Act 1882.

[284] Operational Guidelines for the Implementation of the World Heritage Convention, WHC.21/01 (31 July 2021), paras 87-95.

[285] Chapter 7, text to nn 108-112.

answer probably came from Andrew Wallace-Hadrill, who, in a 2022 letter to The Times, declared:

> The key question is where they are displayed to their best advantage: separated from their provenance and from other fragments that physically join them, displayed inside-out and in the dull London light, or in view of the Parthenon, reconnected with adjoining fragments, displayed the right way round, and bathed in Mediterranean light? To me there is no choice.[286]

6.3.3.3 The marbles are 'a part of the world's shared heritage'

This argument echoes Merryman and his 'cultural internationalism' theory. The marbles are part of world cultural heritage and transcend national boundaries. But it is unclear why, even if the marbles are part of the world's shared heritage, which they certainly are, they must remain in the British Museum. The notion of shared cultural heritage has been adopted in order to ensure the protection of cultural property—not in order to identify where it should be located. If one takes the retentionist argument to its logical conclusion, the fact that the marbles are part of the world's shared heritage means that they belong equally to everyone, then they might as well be displayed in Athens—or better still they could rotate in exhibitions around the world. The argument that the marbles are 'a part of the world's shared heritage' does not support the British Museum's ownership argument or that the marbles should be located in Bloomsbury—rather the contrary. In 2004, the US Senate called on the United Kingdom to return the marbles to Greece 'in recognition that the Parthenon is part of the cultural heritage of the entire world and as such should be made whole'.[287]

6.3.3.4 Common misconceptions

The trustees' statement continues with a series of 'common misconceptions'. Some of them are not common at all but are an occasion for the museum to continue to create a good impression. As a rule of thumb, these 'common misconceptions' are statements unfavourable to the British Museum, which the trustees say are not true. They are the following:

---

[286] Andrew Wallce-Hadrill's letter to The Times, 'Times Letters: The Case for Returning the Elgin Marbles', The Times (12 January 2022).

[287] US Congress, Senate, S Con Res 134 'Expressing the sense of the Congress that the Parthenon Marbles should be returned to Greece', 108th Congress, 2nd session (22 July 2004). A similar plea asking for the return of the marbles to Greece has been repeated more recently, see Nick Allen and others, 'US Members of Congress Urge Britain to Return Elgin Marbles to Greece Next Year', The Telegraph (21 September 2020).

All of the Parthenon sculptures are in the British Museum

It is unclear why the trustees assume that anyone should think that all the Parthenon marbles are in the British Museum. However, presenting this as a 'common misconception' gives them the opportunity to claim that about half of the Parthenon's 'sculptures' are lost, for they have been destroyed in the course of the temple's long existence, while the 'sculptures' that still exist are dispersed in museums in a handful of cities, although the majority are divided between Athens and London. In fact, it is estimated that Greece and the United Kingdom between them hold over 98% of the surviving Parthenon sculptures in nearly equal halves.[288] That under 2% of the sculptures reside outside London, when London possesses practically 50%, is not a compelling argument against reunification. Moreover, five of these fragments have already been permanently returned to Greece: this is the case of a palm-sized foot from the north frieze repatriated by the University of Heidelberg in 2006; the restitution in 2022 of a bigger fragment previously housed in the Antonino Salinas Regional Archaeological Museum in Sicily, to which we will return; and latterly, in March 2023, the return of three fragments from the Vatican Museums—the head of a boy from the frieze, the head of a bearded man from a metope, and the chunk of a horse's head from a pediment.[289] There may also be something to be said about the ways in which these marbles were obtained. For example, the fragments in the Louvre were not detached from the walls of the Parthenon but were collected in the rubble.[290] Finally, if the 'sculptures' are thus divided between different museums, not all the *marbles* are in museums: the Parthenon still stands.

The Parthenon marbles in the British Museum were stolen

In order to contend that this is a misconception, the trustees' statement explains that Elgin 'acted with the full knowledge and permission of the legal authorities of the day in both Athens and London' and adds that his 'activities were thoroughly investigated by a Parliamentary Select Committee in 1816 and found to be entirely legal'. But did Elgin act with the 'full knowledge and permission' of the authorities in Constantinople? No one doubts that the corrupt local Ottoman officials in Athens were well aware of what was going on, but did the central Ottoman government know? And if the authorities in London knew what Elgin was doing, would 'knowledge and permission' of Elgin's actions in London render them lawful? Were Elgin's actions *thoroughly* investigated? Were they found to be *entirely legal*? The parliamentary select committee was never convened to examine the lawfulness of the marbles' acquisition, and its report remains silent on the matter. Nowhere does it state that Elgin's acquisition of the collection was lawful. The lawfulness of the marbles' acquisition has already been examined, and the marbles' removal and acquisition were shown to be unlawful.

---

[288] Snodgrass (2000), para 3.1.

[289] See Chap. 10, text to nn 66-67 and 130-134. On the return of the Vatican fragments, see Acropolis Museum, 'Permanent Reunification of Parthenon Fragments from the Vatican Museums to the Acropolis Museum' (Press release, 24 March 2023).

[290] See text to nn 179-180 and Chap. 2, text to n 150.

The British Museum has turned down the Greek government's request for a loan of the marbles
The trustees' statement makes it clear that Greece has 'never' asked the museum for a loan of the Parthenon marbles in the British Museum, only for their permanent removal to Athens. The trustees would consider 'any request for any part of the collection to be borrowed and then returned. The simple precondition required by the Trustees before they will consider whether or not to lend an object is that the borrowing institution acknowledges the British Museum's ownership of the object'. In 2019, it was reported that Greece had suggested a loan but made it clear that it would not sign an agreement 'ced[ing] its ownership'.[291]

This part of the statement continues with general declarations about what a generous lender the British Museum is, although what is at issue here is not the museum's generosity as a lender. Then the statement explains that 'any meaningful discussion' of a loan has been made impossible, because 'successive Greek governments have refused to consider borrowing or to acknowledge the Trustees (*sic*) ownership of the Parthenon sculptures in their care'.

The very idea of offering to loan unlawfully removed cultural heritage does nothing to take the heat out of the standoff. This is not a dispute about a loan but about the marbles' permanent return to Greece. Responding to Greece's request for the return of the marbles by discussing the possibility of a loan is irrelevant. George Osborne fell into the same contradiction when, writing in The Times in December 2021 in his capacity as chair of the British Museum, he referred to restitution claims in the following manner: 'Our response is not to be dismissive. We are open to lending our artefacts to anywhere who (*sic*) can take good care of them and ensure their safe return'.[292] A request for the return of an artefact is *not* a request for a loan. There is a deep contradiction in answering a request for return by discussing a loan. At any rate, why would the British Museum expect the Acropolis Museum or Greece to sign an agreement that stipulates that the British Museum owns the marbles, when precisely this alleged ownership is disputed?

The British Museum argues that it should keep the Parthenon marbles 'because there's nowhere to house them in Greece' and that Greece cannot care for them
This had been a long-standing argument of the British Museum, but with the opening of the new Acropolis Museum it was abandoned. The trustees explain that neither claim is true and that 'the British Museum doesn't argue this'. The museum does not argue this, and so it also fails to mention the failings in its own stewardship of the marbles. The trustees make polite noises applauding the display of the Parthenon marbles in the Acropolis Museum, but, when they mention that they create 'as full a picture as is now possible' of the Parthenon's original decorative scheme, they overlook the plain fact that the fullest picture will be made possible only when all the marbles are joined together.

---

[291] Mark Bridge and Anthee Carassava, 'Greece Can't Borrow Elgin Marbles until it Drops Claim', The Times (4 September 2019).

[292] George Osborne, 'It's Right to Be Proud of the British Museum', The Times (3 December 2021).

'The division of the Parthenon sculptures is a unique case. The sculptures can only be appreciated as a complete set'
Well, the division of the Parthenon sculptures *is* a unique case, for all the reasons already explained in the introduction. To argue that it is not a unique case, the trustees state that cultural objects have 'often' been 'divided and distributed through museums in many countries'. True, some of them have. But are they similar to the Parthenon? The trustees give the example of 'medieval and renaissance altarpieces'. We can assume that the trustees have in mind altarpiece panels separated and dispersed in different collections, such as Duccio's *Maestà* in Siena, which was intentionally disassembled in 1771 by its custodians, resulting in individual panels ending up in different countries across the world;[293] or Raphael's Colonna Altarpiece, which was made for a convent in Perugia and was later disassembled and sold piecemeal by the nuns when they ran into financial difficulties.[294] Even so, the temporary reunification at the Met of the main panel and the lunette of the altarpiece with the scenes from its predella, which had been separated in the seventeenth century, became an occasion for celebration and a special exhibition.[295] The Melun Diptych, by French court painter Jean Fouquet, is another dispersed altarpiece. The unification of the two main panels for an exhibition in Berlin in 2019 was described as 'a sensation' that offered 'viewers an exceptional aesthetic experience'.[296] There is no doubt that bringing together such panels and allowing the viewer to appreciate them for what they are, an ensemble, means that these pieces can be seen at their best.

Even so, is the separation of movable altarpiece panels in any way similar to hacking out of the Parthenon, a building, part of its structure? The analogy is contrived and it is inappropriate. The division of the Parthenon marbles can only be likened to the division of a building and a monument. Can we imagine the Sistine Chapel torn in two? God's outstretched hand and pointed finger separated from the hand of Adam receiving life in Michelangelo's famous fresco *The Creation of Adam*? In the Parthenon, even the statues are torn, as the politics of 'sculptural partition and annexation' cut through the *dramatis personae* in a single story.[297] The head of the pedimental figure of Iris is in Athens, but her headless torso is in London—it was, as we saw, one of the statues that were discovered in the process of being scrubbed in 1938. The front and middle part of the torso of Poseidon from the west pediment is in Athens, but the rear and upper part of his torso, including his shoulders and collarbones, are in London. Part of the thigh of Hermes (also from the

---

[293] Cooper (1965).

[294] Linda Wolk-Simon and Frank Dabell, 'Raphael at the Metropolitan: The Colonna Altarpiece' (2006) 63(4) The Metropolitan Museum of Art Bulletin 4. See also The National Gallery, 'Studying Raphael: Division of Altarpieces' https://www.nationalgallery.org.uk/research/research-resources/studying-raphael/studying-raphael-division-of-altarpieces.

[295] The Met, 'Raphael at the Metropolitan: The Colonna Altarpiece' (Press release, 19 May 2006).

[296] Staatliche Museen zu Berlin, 'Jean Fouquet. The Melun Diptych' (2018) https://www.smb.museum/en/exhibitions/detail/jean-fouquet-the-melun-diptych/.

[297] Christopher Hitchens, 'Opinion: A Home for the Marbles' The New York Times (18 June 2009).

west pediment) is in Athens, the remaining part of his surviving torso is in London.[298]

The statement of the trustees adds a misconception, which is that the marbles can 'only' be appreciated as a complete set. However, it is not that the marbles can 'only' be appreciated as a complete set, but rather that they can certainly be appreciated at an advantage as a complete set.

'The sculptures could be reunited on the Parthenon'

The trustees correctly point out that the marbles cannot be reunited on the Parthenon. As we have seen, the Greek authorities have removed almost all of the remaining pedimental sculptures, metopes, and frieze slabs to the Acropolis Museum, in the interest of conservation.[299] This and the fact that the Parthenon has in part been destroyed made former British Museum director, Neil MacGregor, remark that there is 'no possibility of recovering an artistic entity'.[300] That parts of the frieze and metopes have been destroyed cannot serve as an argument against the reunification of the marbles that do survive. It has been argued that, when incorporation into the original building is not possible, the next best means of restoration is 'archaeological reassembly which involves the placing of integral pieces of an ancient monument in as close proximity to each other as to make possible the optimum appreciation of the whole'.[301] Propinquity matters. Perhaps in the future some protective coating or other means that has not yet been devised will allow the marbles to return to the Parthenon. Until then, the marbles can be reunited in the Acropolis Museum in view of the Parthenon.

A solution would be for the British Museum to set up an outpost in Athens

This is another argument that assumes that the dispute is just about display. Maybe the debate *is* to a large extent about display. The main dispute is about where the marbles belong. In any event, the trustees reject this possibility, and the argument is fleshed out by once again singing the praises of world museums and the merits of dismembered cultural property. We read of the 'great public benefit to seeing the sculptures within the context of the world collection of the British Museum, in order to deepen our understanding of their significance within world cultural history', which is described as the 'ideal complement to the display in the Acropolis Museum'.

---

[298] This information is available on the website of the Acropolis Museum, https://theacropolismuseum.gr/en, in the description of the individual figures. E.g. for Poseidon, see https://theacropolismuseum.gr/en/parthenon-west-pediment-poseidon. In the Acropolis Museum, the original marbles are joined with plaster casts of the original parts in the British Museum (and in other museums), which makes the identification of the figures that are torn easy.

[299] See Chap. 2, text to nn 201-202.

[300] Richard Morrison, 'Neil MacGregor: "There Is No Possibility of Putting the Elgin Marbles Back"', The Times (7 November 2014).

[301] Greenfield (2007) 71-72.

UNESCO has offered to mediate but the British Museum has refused
It is unclear why the museum trustees believe this to be a misconception. Perhaps Lambert, former chair of the museum, did not write to UNESCO on 26 March 2015 refusing the offer to mediate? The commentary that accompanies this apparent 'misconception' is what Hitchens would have called 'a wriggling basket of red herrings'.[302] This part of the statement rehearses arguments made in the trustees' response to UNESCO following Greece's offer to mediate the dispute.[303] We find polite noises about the museum's 'long history of collaboration with UNESCO' and its admiration and support for UNESCO's work. If Merryman objected to the work of UNESCO, the British Museum 'admires' and 'supports' it. Then the trustees return to the arguments they invoked in that context and which have little to do with the mediation: the British Museum is not a governmental body (we will return to this question in Chap. 8); the museum trustees 'have a legal and moral responsibility to preserve and maintain all the collections in their care and to make them accessible to world audiences'; the trustees wish to 'strengthen existing good relations with colleagues and institutions in Greece, and to explore collaborative ventures directly between institutions, not on a government-to-government basis'. 'This is why', the statement continues, the trustees 'believe that UNESCO involvement isn't the best way forward. Museums holding Greek works, whether in Greece, the UK or elsewhere in the world, are naturally united in a shared endeavour to show the importance of the legacy of ancient Greece.' But isn't the British Museum's purpose to show ancient Greek culture as merely part of a history lesson, part of this 'story of cultural achievement throughout the world' to which the museum so endearingly clings? The statement further underlines the museum's commitment 'sharing the value of that legacy for all humanity'. These are beautiful words but what do they mean? How does the museum share the value of that legacy 'for all humanity'? More significantly, how do these words relate to the museum's refusal to mediate?

6.4 The Ban on Deaccession (British Museum Act 1963) and the Relevance of Domestic Legislation to International Law

The British Museum Act 1963, which we shall have the opportunity to discuss again in Chap. 8, provides the famous ban on deaccession. According to the Act, the trustees are not at liberty to dispose of objects vested in them as part of the museum's collections,[304] except if transferred to another British museum or gallery[305] or in one

[302] Hitchens (2008) xiii.

[303] See Sect. 5.3.2.

[304] British Museum Act 1963 s 3(4).

[305] British Museum Act 1963 s 9(1); Museums and Galleries Act 1992 s 6 and schedule 5.

of the following three situations: the object is a duplicate of another object in the museum's collection; the object, in the opinion of the trustees, was not made 'earlier than the year 1850, and substantially consists of printed matter of which a copy made by photography or a process akin to photography is held by the Trustees'; or the trustees consider that 'the object is unfit to be retained in the collections of the Museum and can be disposed of without detriment to the interests of students'.[306] The trustees may also dispose of an object in their collections 'if satisfied that it has become useless for the purposes of the Museum by reason of damage, physical deterioration, or infestation by destructive organisms'.[307]

The prohibition on the disposal of objects has been interpreted by the High Court of England and Wales in *Attorney General v Trustees of the British Museum.*[308] The case concerned a claim for the restitution of four Old Master drawings stolen by the Gestapo in 1939 and acquired by the British Museum a few years later.[309] The trustees wrote to the attorney general expressing the view that, if he were to sanction the return of the drawings, 'he would offer a straightforward solution to the ... case, in respect of which equity requires a swift solution'.[310] The attorney general did not oblige. He took the view that 'no moral obligation can justify a disposition by the trustees of an object forming part of the collections of the Museum' in breach of the British Museum Act 1963.[311] Accordingly, 'only legislation or a bona fide compromise' could allow the trustees to return the drawings.[312] The Holocaust (Return of Cultural Objects) Act 2009 4 years later opened the way for such objects to be returned, overriding the prohibition in the British Museum Act 1963 for Nazi looted artefacts. Another exception to the ban on deaccession had already been introduced with the Human Tissue Act 2004. Return of looted antiquities is patently not part of the above enumeration.

The British Museum then appears to be, in principle, unable to deaccession the Parthenon marbles, even if it wished to do so. When the trustees note that they have a 'legal' obligation to maintain the marbles in their collection, they are not entirely wrong. Formally, they would be within their rights to resist restitution, if removing the marbles from the British Museum is contrary to domestic law.[313] As

[306]British Museum Act 1963 s 5(1).

[307]'British Museum Act 1963 s 5(2). See further British Museum Policy: De-accession of Objects from the Collection' (2018) https://bit.ly/3Dm6zVR.

[308]*Attorney General v Trustees of the British Museum* [2005] EWHC (Ch).

[309]*Attorney General v Trustees of the British Museum* [2005] EWHC (Ch) [2], [5].

[310]*Attorney General v Trustees of the British Museum* [2005] EWHC (Ch) [6].

[311]*Attorney General v Trustees of the British Museum* [2005] EWHC (Ch) [45]; contrast *Re Snowden* [1970] EWHC (Ch) 700.

[312]*Attorney General v Trustees of the British Museum* [2005] EWHC (Ch) [46].

[313]Successive directors of the British Museum have invoked the fact that the museum is bound by deaccession legislation, see Imogen Tilden, 'Elgin Marbles Will Never Leave UK, Says Museum Chief', The Guardian (15 January 2002); 'Interview by Ioannis Andritsopoulos: Ta Nea's UK correspondent with the Director of the British Museum, Hartwig Fischer' (undated) https://bit.ly/3ruvyBL.

we have seen, this argument was also used by the UK government, which in rejecting the UNESCO mediation offer remarked that the trustees are prevented by law from deaccessioning objects in their collection.[314] In other words, the UK government invoked *domestic* law as an argument to decline the return of the marbles. However, it is well-established in international law that domestic law cannot serve as justification for a state's failure to perform its international obligations.[315] According to the International Law Commission's (ILC) Articles on State Responsibility, backed by 'a long line of authorities',[316] the characterisation of an act of a state 'as internationally wrongful is governed by international law' and 'is not affected by the characterisation of the same act as lawful by internal law'.[317] The commentary to this provision explains that an act of a state is 'internationally wrongful if it constitutes a breach of an international obligation, even if the act does not contravene the State's internal law—even if, under that law, the State was actually bound to act in that way'.[318] In plain terms, the British Museum could argue that it is bound by domestic law and cannot return the marbles because such an act would contravene domestic law. In contrast, the UK government could not prevent the return of the marbles, if international law requires it, with the argument that such an act would not conform to its domestic law. To set this ban aside, an enabling parliamentary act is necessary. However, the UK government has repeatedly dismissed the possibility of 'legislation that would enable permanent restitution from national institutions'.[319]

The suggestion has been made that the museum could take the view that the Parthenon marbles are 'unfit' to be displayed in its collections, taking into account the circumstances of their acquisition and the elements of the debate that overwhelmingly favour their return. There is reasonably broad agreement around the world that the marbles should be returned whether 'as a matter of law or conscience', making it unlikely that the trustees should be blamed for using their discretion under the British Museum Act 1963, were they to determine that the marbles are unfit to be retained and send them home.[320] Currently, this is an interpretation that neither the museum nor the government give to the term

---

[314] See Sect. 5.3.2.

[315] ILC Articles on State Responsibility art 3, also art 32. See also ILC Articles on State Responsibility, commentary, art 3, paras 1, 3-6, including examples from the case law; Vienna Convention on the Law of Treaties art 27, referring to performance of treaty obligations; Crawford (2013) 101.

[316] Crawford (2013) 101. See also ILC Articles on State Responsibility, commentary, art 3, paras 3-5.

[317] ILC Articles on State Responsibility art 3.

[318] See also ILC Articles on State Responsibility, commentary, art 3, para 1.

[319] E.g. Geraldine Kendall Adams, 'Culture Secretary Rules Out Restitution from National Museums', Museums Association (25 April 2019) https://bit.ly/3qyGy03. See further Hansard (2022b).

[320] Roger Michel's letter to The Times, 'Rules over Elgin Marbles', The Times (8 September 2022); Samantha Knights, as cited in Alex Marshall, 'As Europe Returns Artifacts, Britain Stays Silent', The New York Times (20 December 2021). See also Greenfield (2007) 103-104.

'unfit'.[321] According to the museum's policy on deaccessioning, the trustees would 'only' view an object in their collection as unfit to be retained 'if it was no longer useful or relevant to the Museum's purpose and if its retention would not be of benefit either to scholars or the general public, whether for display or research or any other purpose for which the Museum is established'.[322] As for the government, as we saw in Chap. 5, it used this element ('unfit') to argue that the British Museum could *not* deaccession the marbles.[323] The case law too appears to confirm this line of reasoning.[324] Even so, a further possibility exists. What if the trustees admitted that they do not have title to the marbles? In *Attorney General v Trustees of the British Museum*, the High Court reasoned that if the heirs of the original owner of the drawings established title to them, the drawings would 'never have been "part of the collections of the museum"', with the consequence that the ban on deaccessioning would not apply to them. To follow this statement to its logical conclusion, so long as Greece establishes title to the marbles, the British Museum is not prevented from deaccessioning them.[325]

6.5 Conclusion

This chapter has considered the marbles in the care of the British Museum. It opened with some controversial issues of stewardship. In particular, the first part of the chapter focused on the polychromy of the original Parthenon and the 1930s Duveen cleaning, which removed part of the historic patina and was suppressed for over half a century. The cleaning demolished one of the main arguments of the museum, that of the careful custodianship of the marbles. Next, the chapter engaged with the debate about the marbles' return. It considered and rejected the traditional positions in favour of the marbles' continued retention in the British Museum, Merryman's theory of 'cultural internationalism', and it addressed critically the arguments currently relied upon by the museum's trustees to resist the marbles' return. Finally, the chapter examined the ban on deaccession and argued that this is not an argument that can serve the UK government. The ban on deaccession makes it quasi-impossible for the trustees to return the marbles until there is an enabling act of parliament, except if

[321] However, see Greenfield (2007) 104, who mentions that some minor returns have taken place, although it is unclear under which section of the British Museum Act 1963.

[322] 'British Museum Policy: De-accession of Objects from the Collection' (2018) https://bit.ly/3Dm6zVR 3.5.

[323] See Chap. 5, text to n 55.

[324] In *Attorney General v Trustees of the British Museum* [2005] EWHC (Ch), the High Court could have taken the view that the return of the Nazi looted drawings could rely on the 'unfit' exception, but it did not.

[325] *Attorney General v Trustees of the British Museum* [2005] EWHC (Ch) [38]-[39]. See also Lewis (2016) 122-123.

they were to take the view that the marbles are 'unfit' to be retained in the museum's collections or admitted that they do not have title to them.

References

Edmond About, *La Grèce contemporaine* (5th edn, Hachette 1863)

Eleni Aggelakopoulou and Asterios Bakolas, 'What Were the Colors of the Parthenon? Investigation of the Entablature's Cornice Blocks' (2022) 140 Journal of Archaeological Science 105553

Paul M Bator, 'An Essay on the International Trade in Art' (1982) 34 Stanford Law Review 275

Charles Robert Baynes, *Notes and Reflections during a Ramble in the East: An Overland Journey from India, Visit to Athens, etc.* (Longman and others 1843)

Mary Beard, *The Parthenon* (Profile Books 2010)

British Museum, *A Description of the Collection of Ancient Marbles in the British Museum* (pt 6, British Museum 1830)

Neil Brodie, 'An Archaeologist's View of the Trade in Unprovenanced Antiquities' in Barbara T Hoffman (ed), *Art and Cultural Heritage: Law, Policy and Practice* (Cambridge University Press 2006)

Neil Brodie, 'Export Deregulation and the Illicit Trade in Archaeological Material' in Jennifer R Richman and Marion P Forsyth (eds), *Legal Perspectives on Cultural Resources* (AltaMira Press 2004)

Robert Browning, 'The Parthenon in History' in Christopher Hitchens, *The Parthenon Marbles* (first publication 1987, Verso 2008)

Christopher Chippindale and David WJ Gill, 'Material Consequences of Contemporary Classical Collecting' (2000) 104 (3) American Journal of Archaeology 463

Joan Breton Connelly, *The Parthenon Enigma: A Journey into Legend* (Head of Zeus 2014)

Frederick A Cooper, 'A Reconstruction of Duccio's Maestà' (1965) 47 (2) The Art Bulletin 155

James Crawford, *State Responsibility* (Cambridge University Press 2013)

James Cuno, *Who Owns Antiquity? Museums and the Battle over our Ancient Heritage* (Princeton University Press 2011)

William Dalrymple and Anita Anand, *Kohinoor: The Story of the World's Most Infamous Diamond* (De Juggernaut Books 2016)

M Delaroière, *Voyage en Orient* (Debécourt 1836)

Edward Dodwell, *A Classical and Topographical Tour through Greece* (vol 1, Rodwell and Martin 1819)

Mary Ann Eaverly, *Tan Men/Pale Women: Color and Gender in Archaic Greece and Egypt, A Comparative Approach* (University of Michigan Press 2013)

Jacob Epstein, *Let There Be Sculpture* (GP Putnam's Sons 1940)

Joseph d'Estourmel, *Journal d'un voyage en Orient* (vol 1, 2nd edn, Chapelet 1848)

Derek Fincham, 'The Parthenon Sculptures and Cultural Justice' (2013) 23 Fordham Intellectual Property, Media and Entertainment Law Journal 943

Elizabeth Key Fowden, 'The Parthenon Mosque, King Solomon, and the Greek Sages' in Maria Georgopoulou and Konstantinos Thanasakis (eds), *Ottoman Athens: Archaeology, Topography, History* (Gennadius Library of the American School of Classical Studies at Athens and Aikaterini Laskaridis Foundation 2019)

Elizabeth Key Fowden, 'The Parthenon, Pericles and King Solomon: A Case Study of Ottoman Archaeological Imagination in Greece' (2018) 42 (2) Byzantine and Modern Greek Studies 261

Katerina Frantzikinaki and others, 'The Cleaning of the Parthenon West Frieze by Means of Combined IR- and UV-Radiation' in Johann Nimmrichter, Wolfgang Kautek, and Manfred Schreiner (eds), Lasers in the Conservation of Artworks (Springer 2007)

Amerimni Galanos and Yanna Doganis, 'The Remnants of the Epidermis on the Parthenon' (2003) Studies in Conservation 48(1) 3
Jeanette Greenfield, *The Return of Cultural Treasures* (3rd edn, Cambridge University Press 2007)
Michael Greenhalgh, *Plundered Empire: Acquiring Antiquities from Ottoman Lands* (Brill 2019)
Hansard, 'House of Lords Parthenon Marbles Debate' (8 February 2022) (vol 818, Hansard 2022a)
Hansard, 'House of Lords National Heritage Act 1983 Debate' (13 October 2022) (vol 824, Hansard 2022b)
Hansard, 'House of Lords Debate' (19 May 1997) (vol 580, Hansard 1997)
Hansard, 'House of Lords Debate' (27 October 1983) (vol 444, Hansard 1983)
Evelyn B Harrison, '"Theseum" East Frieze: Color Traces and Attachment Cuttings' (1988) 57 (4) Hesperia 339
Francis Hervé, *A Residence in Greece and Turkey* (vol 1, Whittaker 1837)
Christopher Hitchens, *The Parthenon Marbles* (first publication 1987, Verso 2008)
John Cam Hobhouse, *A Journey Through Albania: And Other Provinces of Turkey in Europe* (vol 1, James Cawthorn 1813)
House of Commons, 'Culture, Media and Sport – Minutes of Evidence' (Culture, Media and Sport Committee Publications 8 June 2000)
Ian Jenkins, *The Parthenon Frieze* (British Museum 2002, reprinted 2019)
Ian Jenkins, 'Cleaning and Controversy: The Parthenon Sculptures 1811-1939' (2001) The British Museum Occasional Paper No 146
Ian Jenkins, 'Acquisition and Supply of Casts of the Parthenon Sculptures by the British Museum, 1835–1939' (1990) 85 The Annual of the British School at Athens 89
Ian Jenkins and A Middleton, 'Paint on the Parthenon Sculptures' (1988) 83 The Annual of the British School at Athens 183
OM Lewis, *The Mortgage on the Elgin Marbles* (High Tile Books 2016)
David Lindsay (aka Earl of Crawford), *The Crawford Papers* (ed John Vincent, Manchester University Press 1984)
Lucien Magne, *La conservation du Parthénon – Conférence faite le 31 mars 1905 à la Sorbonne* (Imprimerie nationale 1905)
Lucien Magne, *Le Parthénon: Études faites au cours de deux missions en Grèce (1894-1895)* (Imprimerie nationale 1895)
John Pentland Mahaffy, *Rambles and Studies in Greece* (2nd edn, Macmillan 1878)
Memorandum on the Subject of the Earl of Elgin's Pursuits in Greece (2nd edn, corrected, John Murray 1815)
Memorandum on the Subject of the Earl of Elgin's Pursuits in Greece (William Miller 1811)
John Henry Merryman, 'Cultural Property Internationalism' (2005) 12 International Journal of Cultural Property 11
John Henry Merryman, 'The Retention of Cultural Property' (1988) UC Davis Law Review 477
John Henry Merryman, 'Two Ways of Thinking about Cultural Property' (1986) 80 American Journal of International Law 831
John Henry Merryman, 'Thinking about the Elgin Marbles' (1985) 83 (8) Michigan Law Review 1881
Adolf Michaelis, *Ancient Marbles in Great Britain* (tr Charles Augustus Maude Fennell, Cambridge University Press 1882)
Marco del Monte and Cristina Sabbioni, 'A Study of the Patina Called "Scialbatura" on Imperial Roman Marbles' (1987) 32 (3) Studies in Conservation 114
James AR Nafziger, 'Cultural Heritage Law: The International Regime' in Centre for Studies and Research in International Law and International Relations (ed), *The Cultural Heritage of Mankin*d (Hague Academy of International Law, Brill 2008)
E Napier, *Excursions Along the Shores of the Mediterranean* (vol 2, Henry Colburn 1842)
Jenifer Neils, *The Parthenon Frieze* (Cambridge University Press 2001)
Mark O'Neill, 'Enlightenment Museums: Universal or Merely Global?' (2004) 2 (3) Museum and Society 190

Robin Osborne, 'The Viewing and Obscuring of the Parthenon Frieze' (1987) 107 Journal of Hellenic Studies 98
Emma M Payne, *Casting the Parthenon Sculptures from the Eighteenth Century to the Digital Age* (Bloomsbury 2021)
Lyndel V Prott, 'The International Movement of Cultural Objects' (2005) 12 International Journal of Cultural Property 225
Antoine Chrysostome Quatremère de Quincy, *Lettres sur l'enlèvement des ouvrages de l'art antique à Athenes et à Rome* (1836)
Antoine Chrysostome Quatremère de Quincy, *Lettres sur le préjudice qu'occasionneroient aux arts et à la science, le déplacement des monuments de l'art de l'Italie, le démembrement de ses écoles, et la spoliation de ses collections, galeries, musées, etc.* (1796)
Gisela MA Richter and Lindsley F Hall, 'Polychromy in Greek Sculpture' (1944) 2 (8) The Metropolitan Museum of Art Bulletin 233
Brunilde Sismondo Ridgway, *Prayers in Stone: Greek Architectural Sculpture* c *600-100 BCE* (University of California Press 1999)
Geoffrey Robertson, *Who Owns History? Elgin's Loot and the Case for Returning Plundered Treasure* (Biteback Publishing 2019)
David Rudenstine, 'Trophies for the Empire: The Epic Dispute Between Greece and England Over the Parthenon Sculptures in the British Museum' (2021) 39 Cardozo Arts and Entertainment Law Journal 377
Select Committee of the House of Commons, *Report on the Earl of Elgin's Collection of Sculptured Marbles* (Bulmer 1816)
Colin Simpson, *The Partnership: The Secret Association of Bernard Berenson and Joseph Duveen* (Bodley Head 1987)
AH Smith, 'Lord Elgin and his Collection' (1916) 36 Journal of Hellenic Studies 163
Anthony Snodgrass, 'The Integrity of the Monument and the Advantages of Re-uniting the London and Athens Marbles' (Annex B) in House of Commons, 'Culture, Media and Sport – Appendices to the Minutes of Evidence' (Culture, Media and Sport Committee Publications 18 July 2000)
William St Clair, *Who Saved the Parthenon?* (Open Book Publishers 2022)
William St Clair, *Lord Elgin and the Marbles* (Oxford University Press 1967, 1998, reprinted 2003)
William G Stewart, 'The Marbles: Elgin or Parthenon?' (2001) 6 Art Antiquity and Law 37
Charles de Visscher, *International Protection of Works of Art and Historic Monuments* (US Department of State 1949)
Christina Vlassopoulou, 'New Investigations into the Polychromy of the Parthenon' in Vinzenz Brinkmann, Oliver Primavesi, and Max Hollein (eds), Circumlitio*: The Polychromy of Antique and Mediaeval Sculpture* (Hirmer Verlag 2010)
Christina Vlassopoulou, 'The Conservation of the Parthenon West Frieze from the Archaeologist's Point of View' in Carol C Mattusch, AA Donohue, and Amy Brauer (eds), *Proceedings of the XVIth International Congress of Classical Archaeology Boston, August 23–26, 2003* (Oxbow Books 2006)
Daphne Voudouri, 'Law and the Politics of the Past: Legal Protection of Cultural Heritage in Greece' (2010) 17 International Journal of Cultural Property 547
Andrew Wallace-Hadrill, 'The Herculaneum Conservation Project: Introduction' (2006) 8 (4) Conservation and Management of Archaeological Sites 187
Hugh W Williams, *Travels in Italy, Greece and the Ionian Islands* (vol 2, Constable 1820)
Enoch Cobb Wines, *Two Years and a Half in the American Navy* (vol 2, Richard Bentley 1833)

Part II
Access to Dispute Settlement

Chapter 7
What Method of Dispute Settlement?

7.1 Introduction

Disputes between states are a fact of life in international relations, just as disputes between individuals are a fact of life in domestic legal orders.[1] International law provides means by which states can settle their disputes in a manner that does not endanger international peace and security.[2] States have the freedom to select the means by which they resolve their differences, being only limited by the obligation to resort to peaceful means.[3] Dispute settlement mechanisms are typically divided into two broad categories: on the one hand, diplomatic means, such as negotiations and mediation, which can also be described as 'soft' mechanisms, since they are not binding and the parties retain control of the process and outcome; on the other hand, legal or adjudicative means, namely arbitration and judicial settlement, which end with a binding decision handed down by arbitrators or judges.[4]

One way of making sense of the different dispute settlement mechanisms is to focus on four 'ideal' types, namely negotiations, mediation, arbitration, and judicial settlement, and to imagine them on a continuum.[5] As parties move along the continuum, from negotiations to judicial settlement, they increasingly lose flexibility and control over their dispute.[6] Flexibility and, by inference, diplomatic means are likely to be preferred by a party whose claim is political more than legal.[7]

---

[1] Merrills and de Brabandere (2022) 1.

[2] UN Charter art 2(3), also art 33. See also Convention for the Pacific Settlement of International Disputes (1907) art 1; UNGA Res 2625 (XXV) (24 October 1970) UN Doc A/*RES*/2625(XXV); UNGA Res 37/10 (15 November 1982) UN Doc A/RES/37/10 (Manila Declaration).

[3] Tomuschat (2012) 123.

[4] Peters (2003) 4.

[5] Salacuse (2007) 154.

[6] Salacuse (2007) 154-155.

[7] Merrills and de Brabandere (2022) 65.

C. Titi, *The Parthenon Marbles and International Law*,
https://doi.org/10.1007/978-3-031-26357-6_7

Contrariwise, the stronger a party's legal position, the less that party will be interested in keeping control over the dispute and the more it will be inclined to pursue legal means.[8] However, these constructs chiefly serve as heuristic devices and the reality of dispute settlement shows that the reasons that make a party pursue one dispute settlement mechanism instead of another are a lot more complex.[9] At any rate, despite how strong a party's legal claim, there is an argument to be made in favour of giving preference to diplomatic means.[10]

The chapter suggests that soft means of dispute settlement (notably, negotiations and mediation, in that order) are the most appropriate for the Parthenon marbles case. This is in line with the 1970 UNESCO Convention, which expressly provides that requests for the repatriation of objects 'shall be made through diplomatic offices'.[11] However, as discussed in Chap. 5, for 200 years, Greece has unavailingly sought a diplomatic resolution. As a consequence, even though diplomatic means are preferable if available, it is also appropriate to consider adjudicative dispute settlement options. This is important for one additional reason: whether Greece has access to adjudicative means of dispute settlement can have an impact on the United Kingdom's willingness to engage in diplomacy.

The chapter commences with the requirement of consent and then turns to the concrete dispute settlement means that may be available in the Parthenon marbles case. The chapter critically examines, on the one hand, diplomatic means of dispute settlement and, on the other, adjudicative means, focusing on the four 'ideal' dispute settlement options, and weighs their pros and cons. In doing so, the chapter does not aim to give a general account of the dispute settlement mechanisms that exist in international law, rather it considers those most relevant to the Parthenon marbles case. Next, the chapter addresses some selective practical issues with a bearing on the case, assessing in turn the requirement to exhaust local remedies, the possibility of an *ex aequo et bono* mandate, and the relief sought. Some of these issues are in fact matters of jurisdiction or admissibility. However, a choice was made to treat them in this chapter, as relevant factors when weighing the various dispute settlement options, rather than to examine them in the following chapter together with other jurisdictional and admissibility objections. The chapter argues that Greece does have access to adjudicative dispute settlement means, with an advisory proceeding before the International Court of Justice (ICJ) appearing as the most viable option, but insists that diplomacy is preferable by a long way.

---

[8] Tomuschat (2012) 123; Merrills and de Brabandere (2022) 70.

[9] E.g. Merrills and de Brabandere (2022) 69-73; Scott (2014).

[10] Peters (2003); Tomuschat (2012) 123.

[11] 1970 UNESCO Convention art 7(b)(ii). See also UNESCO, 'Operational Guidelines for the Implementation of the Convention on the Means of Prohibiting and Preventing the Illicit Import, Export and Transfer of Ownership of Cultural Property', adopted by Resolution 3.MSP 11 at the third Meeting of States Parties (18-20 May 2015), para 103 (discussed in Chap. 9, text to n 53).

7.2 Consent to Dispute Settlement

Consent is a *sine qua non* for accessing international dispute settlement mechanisms, both diplomatic and adjudicative. No state can be made to participate in international dispute settlement proceedings unless somewhere along the line it has agreed to do so. The principle derives from the concept of sovereignty,[12] which posits that legal rules can only bind states if they 'emanate from their own free will'.[13] Consent signifies the formal acceptance of the jurisdiction of an international court or tribunal, but it is not tantamount to *willingess* to submit to it when a particular dispute arises.[14] For this reason, the respondent often contests the jurisdiction of an international court or tribunal—less so where consent was given ad hoc and more so where consent was given in advance and in broad terms.[15] Consent legitimises the solution reached by diplomatic and legal means alike, although in the case of diplomatic means, and notably negotiations, this legitimacy could be tarnished by power disparities.[16] Consent functions differently in diplomatic and adjudicative means of dispute settlement.

Diplomatic means are quintessentially consensual in that the disputing parties must not only formally agree to pursue them but they must also substantively do so, engaging in the process in good faith from start to finish.[17] When resorting to diplomatic means, advance formal consent is not sufficient for the likely success of the proceeding. Since the disputing parties are obliged neither to reach a solution nor to comply with it, substantive consent is necessary for the duration of the proceeding and, since an eventual solution lacks binding force, even after the proceeding.[18]

Adjudicative proceedings also require the disputing parties' consent. No state can be compelled to appear before an international court or tribunal unless it has consented to its jurisdiction.[19] In arbitration, the requirement of consent is typically enshrined in arbitration rules that condition the tribunal's jurisdiction on the parties' written agreement to submit their dispute to arbitration.[20] For interstate arbitrations,

[12] Shaw (2017) vol 2, Chap. 9, para 154.

[13] *SS Lotus* (Judgment) PCIJ Series A No 10 (7 September 1927) 18.

[14] Fitzmaurice (1958) 86.

[15] Fitzmaurice (1958) 86.

[16] Peters (2003) 5.

[17] Titi (2019) 34-35.

[18] Titi (2019) 34-35.

[19] E.g. Lauterpacht (1933) 3-4; Fitzmaurice (1958) 66-129; Shaw (2017) vol 2, Chap. 9, para 154; Schreuer and others (2009) 190-253; Amerasinghe (2002) Chap. 3; Cogan (2008); Thirlway (2016) 35-42.

[20] E.g. Model Rules on Arbitral Procedure of the International Law Commission (ILC) (1958) preamble points 2, 4; Optional Rules for Arbitrating Disputes between Two States of the Permanent Court of Arbitration (PCA) (1992) art 1(1); ICSID Convention art 25(1).

consent can be given by means of a compromissory clause in a treaty or a *compromis*, an agreement to submit a specific dispute to arbitration.[21]

Similarly to arbitration, the ICJ has jurisdiction over disputes that states agree to refer to it.[22] States can decide to take future disputes in general or a particular dispute to the Court by treaty,[23] by signing a special agreement (*compromis*),[24] by concluding a framework agreement,[25] or by making a unilateral declaration accepting the Court's compulsory jurisdiction.[26] This latter type of declaration may be unconditional or qualified or limited in time.[27] It is up to states to decide if, and to what extent, they submit to the compulsory jurisdiction of the ICJ. Consent can also be given on the basis of the principle of *forum prorogatum*, whereby the prospective applicant state files an application inviting the respondent to accept the Court's jurisdiction over the dispute described in the application.[28] If the named respondent accepts the invitation, the Court's jurisdiction is founded.[29] In the case of the European Court of Human Rights, consent is given in the European Convention on Human Rights (ECHR) itself.[30] This means that all states that have signed and ratified the Convention have also consented to the Court's jurisdiction.

The fact that states need to give their (*voluntary*) consent in order to participate in dispute settlement proceedings does not mean that they may not agree to the '*compulsory*' jurisdiction of an international court or tribunal or that they may not commit to pursuing dispute settlement options in a particular order.[31] What matters is the states' *agreement* to do so. It is no wonder that the clause by virtue of which states give their consent to the compulsory jurisdiction of the ICJ is known as the '*optional* clause'.[32] An exception to this rule is that the pursuit of a particular type of dispute settlement may be imposed by a court to whose jurisdiction the parties have

---

[21] Ralston (1929) 49-53; Thirlway (2006); Butler (2006).

[22] Statute of the ICJ art 36(1).

[23] E.g. Convention on the Prevention and Punishment of the Crime of Genocide (1948) art IX; International Convention on the Elimination of All Forms of Racial Discrimination (1965) art 22; cf UN Convention against Transnational Organized Crime (2000) art 35(2). See further Shaw (2017) vol 2, Chap. 11, paras 176-177.

[24] Shaw (2017) vol 2, Chap. 11, para 175 and Chap. 9, para 155; Tomka (2002); Fitzmaurice (1958) 70-72.

[25] The framework agreement is a variation on the special agreement, and therefore it is not examined separately in this book. See Shaw (2017) vol 2, Chap. 11, para 178.

[26] Shaw (2017) vol 2, Chap. 9, para 155; Fitzmaurice (1958) 73-80; Merrills (2014) 8.

[27] Statute of the ICJ art 36(3).

[28] Shaw (2017) vol 2, Chap. 11, para 1.

[29] Shaw (2017) vol 2, Chap. 11, para 1. See also Fitzmaurice (1958) 80-86.

[30] ECHR section II.

[31] Cançado Trindade (2006) 266-269. E.g. Vienna Convention on Succession of States in respect of Treaties (1978) art 41; Agreement Governing the Activities of States on the Moon and Other Celestial Bodies (1979) art 15.

[32] Statute of the ICJ art 36(2). See Shaw (2017) vol 2, Chap. 12.

previously consented.[33] Finally, a question may be permitted as to whether states need to specifically consent to advisory proceedings before the ICJ when the request for an advisory opinion relates to a pending dispute between them. This particularity is discussed when the chapter considers the advisory jurisdiction of the ICJ.[34]

Even though Greece has sought to both negotiate with the United Kingdom and submit the Parthenon marbles dispute to mediation, there is nothing in international law to oblige the United Kingdom to engage in dispute settlement proceedings, unless it has previously consented to do so. The availability of any particular dispute settlement forum for the Parthenon marbles case must take the requirement of consent into account. Having considered consent in general, the chapter will now turn to the concrete options for settling the dispute.

7.3 Diplomatic Means

Diplomatic means seek a consensual solution to the dispute and therefore grant broad flexibility to the disputing parties. Their outcome, if successful, is not binding. This section reviews negotiations and mediation. The discussion on mediation also takes into account good offices and conciliation, which it treats as variations thereon.

7.3.1 Negotiations

Negotiations rely on direct exchanges between the disputing parties, without the involvement of a third party, in order to reach a commonly acceptable settlement of an existing or a potential dispute.[35] This makes negotiations a very flexible means of dispute settlement that can be used to resolve not only strictly speaking legal but also political disputes.[36] The ICJ has stressed the 'fundamental character' of this means of dispute settlement.[37] Negotiations are the most frequently resorted to method of dispute resolution and its advantages are deemed to be 'so great as to rule out the use of other methods'.[38] Yet, negotiations are not a panacea and, despite presenting 'the best prospect of a solution',[39] they are not always successful.[40] In general, if either of the disputing parties is unwilling to engage in a genuine dialogue with the other or if

[33] cf Collier and Lowe (1999) 22.

[34] See text to nn 122ff.

[35] Peters (2003) 4; UNCTAD (2010) xiv.

[36] United Nations (1992), para 22; cf Sect. 8.2.

[37] *North Sea Continental Shelf* (Judgment) [1969] ICJ Rep 3 [86].

[38] Merrills and de Brabandere (2022) 38; United Nations (1992), para 24.

[39] Merrills and de Brabandere (2022) 65.

[40] Cançado Trindade (2006) 232.

their respective positions are irreconcilable and there is no way to bridge them, negotiations have little prospect of success.[41]

For this reason, negotiations are typically not a precondition for accessing other means of dispute settlement,[42] and the availability of such other means as a potential complement to negotiations is desirable. Some treaties provide that if negotiations fail, the parties must turn to another method of dispute settlement.[43] Sometimes a judicial decision may direct the parties to initiate negotiations, such as in the *North Sea Continental Shelf* cases, where the ICJ required the parties to negotiate with a view to reaching an agreement on the delimitation of their continental shelf.[44] Contrariwise, in *Black Sea*, the ICJ assumed its jurisdiction precisely because the parties' negotiations had broken down.[45] In addition, nothing prevents the parties from engaging in negotiations while judicial proceedings are ongoing.[46]

Provision for negotiations is made in many an international convention,[47] including in treaties on the protection of cultural heritage.[48] Negotiations are the most frequently employed means of dispute resolution for restitution claims, and they sometimes result in bilateral agreements between countries or between countries and museums.[49] It was following a process of negotiation that Italy was able to sign bilateral agreements with the Boston Museum of Fine Arts, the Met, and the J Paul Getty Museum in California, by virtue of which it obtained the restitution of antiquities of suspicious provenance in exchange for loans of similar objects.[50] Negotiations between Germany and Turkey, following recommendations made by the Intergovernmental Committee for Promoting the Return of Cultural Property to its Countries of Origin or its Restitution in case of Illicit Appropriation (ICPRCP or

---

[41] Merrills and de Brabandere (2022) 85.

[42] E.g. see *Land and Maritime Boundary between Cameroon and Nigeria (Cameroon v Nigeria)* (Preliminary Objections Judgment) [1998] ICJ Rep 275 [56].

[43] For examples, see United Nations (1992), para 70.

[44] *North Sea Continental Shelf* (Judgment) [1969] ICJ Rep 3 [85]-[87], [101]. For other examples, see *Fisheries Jurisdiction (Federal Republic of Germany v Iceland)* (Merits Judgment) [1974] ICJ Rep 175 [67]; *Fisheries Jurisdiction (United Kingdom v Iceland)* (Merits Judgment) [1974] ICJ Rep ICJ 3 [75].

[45] *Maritime Delimitation in the Black Sea (Romania v Ukraine)* (Judgment) [2009] ICJ Rep 89 [21]. See also *Pulp Mills on the River Uruguay (Argentina v Uruguay)* (Judgment) [2010] ICJ Rep 14.

[46] E.g. *Application of the Interim Accord of 13 September 1995 (The Former Yugoslav Republic of Macedonia v Greece)* (Judgment) [2011] ICJ Rep 644 [57]; *Military and Paramilitary Activities in and against Nicaragua (Nicaragua v United States)* [1984] ICJ Rep 392 [106]; *United States Diplomatic and Consular Staff in Tehran* (Judgment) [1980] ICJ Rep 3 [37]; *Aegean Sea Continental Shelf (Greece v Turkey)* (Judgment) 1978 ICJ Rep 12 [29].

[47] E.g. UN Charter art 33; United Nations Convention on the Law of the Sea (UNCLOS) art 283; Understanding on Rules and Procedures Governing the Settlement of Disputes (Annex 2 of the Agreement Establishing the World Trade Organization – WTO) (DSU) art 4.

[48] E.g. UNESCO Convention on the Protection of the Underwater Cultural Heritage (2001) art 25; Convention on the Protection and Promotion of the Diversity of Cultural Expressions (2005) art 25.

[49] Chechi (2013) 188.

[50] Marie Cornu and Marc-André Renold (2010) 12.

Intergovernmental Committee) of the United Nations Educational, Scientific and Cultural Organization (UNESCO) over a timespan of more than 20 years, led to the return of the Boğazköy Sphinx from Germany to Turkey in 2011.[51] The sphinx, which used to guard a gate in Hattusa, the capital of the Hittites, was taken to Germany for restoration during World War I, but, instead of being returned to Turkey following the restoration, it was displayed in the Pergamon Museum.[52] It is put about that Germany's decision to return the sphinx was actually precipitated by Turkey's nonrenewal of a long standing licence that the German Archaeological Institute held to excavate in Turkey.[53]

Negotiations could also be used in the Parthenon marbles case and would be by far the most appropriate dispute settlement means. Chapter 5 has documented the initiatives taken in this respect over the course of 200 years, although it has also shown that, thus far, every attempt down that path has failed. Certainly, some negotiations only succeed after very long time spans, and the legal framework is now very different to what it was in the past, meaning that negotiations probably have their best chance of success.

7.3.2 *Mediation*

Shedding a layer of flexibility, mediation comes next as a possible dispute settlement option. Mediation is a negotiation facilitated by a third-party neutral, the mediator.[54] The role of the mediator has been described as that of bringing about a reconciliation of the parties' claims and 'appeasing the feelings of resentment which may have arisen between the states at variance'.[55] The presence of the third-party neutral removes the need for the disputing parties to confront each other directly.[56] Mediation is closely related to good offices and conciliation, which are briefly considered here.

Good offices lie between negotiations and mediation and are the mechanism with the lightest participation of a third party neutral.[57] The latter merely encourages the disputing parties to negotiate, resume negotiations, or simply helps them get

---

[51] E.g. ICPRCP, 'Final Report', 6th session, UN Doc 25 C/91 (16 June 1989), Recommendation no 2; ICPRCP, 'Report', 16th session, UN Doc CLT-2010/CONF.203/COM.16/5 (September 2010), Recommendation no 2. On the return, see https://en.unesco.org/news/germany-turkey.

[52] Susanne Güsten, 'Turkey Presses Harder for Return of Antiquities', The New York Times (25 May 2011).

[53] Susanne Güsten, 'Turkey Presses Harder for Return of Antiquities', The New York Times (25 May 2011).

[54] UNCTAD (2010) xix; Alberstein (2007) 334.

[55] Convention for the Pacific Settlement of International Disputes (1907) art 4.

[56] Tomuschat (2012) 125; Collier and Lowe (1999) 27.

[57] Lapidoth (2006), para 1.

together.[58] In principle, the third party does not participate in the exchanges between the disputing parties.[59] Yet in reality, the neutral may ultimately do more than just bring the disputing parties together and may take actively part in the resolution of the dispute, in which case his or her role could end up being that of a mediator.[60] For this reason, the term 'good offices' is routinely used as synonymous with mediation.[61] It is clear for example that UNESCO's encouragement of negotiations between Greece and the United Kingdom in relation to the return of the Parthenon marbles may be described as good offices.

Conciliation is a form of facilitated negotiation whose difference from mediation is one of degree: conciliation tends to be more formal than mediation.[62] Conciliation institutionalises the role of the third-party 'in a way comparable, but not identical', to arbitration.[63] The conciliator or conciliation commission is tasked with investigating the dispute and suggesting a solution to the parties.[64] This solution remains nonbinding.[65] Although there is something to be said about the different opportunities offered by these variations on mediation, the chapter does not discuss them separately, in light of their close proximity to mediation.

A number of international treaties,[66] including cultural heritage conventions,[67] provide for mediation, good offices, and conciliation. The 1970 UNESCO Convention establishes that at the request of at least two states parties to the Convention 'engaged in a dispute over its implementation, UNESCO may extend its good offices to reach a settlement between them'.[68] Some institutions, both at the national and international level, offer specialised mediation services for art disputes.[69] The UK Spoliation Advisory Panel resolves claims in relation to cultural property lost during the Nazi era and currently held in UK national or private collections.[70] The International Council of Museums (ICOM) and the World Intellectual Property Organization (WIPO) have collaborated in the development of a mediation process for disputes involving art and cultural heritage, 'including but not limited to return

[58] Lapidoth (2006), para 1.

[59] Collier and Lowe (1999) 27.

[60] United Nations (1992), para 102; Lapidoth (2006), para 2.

[61] Lapidoth (2006), para 2; Collier and Lowe (1999) 28.

[62] UNCTAD (2010) xiii, xix.

[63] Merrills and de Brabandere (2022) 104.

[64] Collier and Lowe (1999) 27; Merrills and de Brabandere (2022) 105.

[65] Collier and Lowe (1999) 27; Merrills and de Brabandere (2022) 115.

[66] E.g. UN Charter art 33; Convention for the Pacific Settlement of International Disputes (1907) art 4; DSU art 5.

[67] E.g. Hague Convention of 1954 art 22; Second Protocol to the Hague Convention of 1954 (1999) arts 35-36; UNESCO Convention on the Protection of the Underwater Cultural Heritage (2001) art 25(2); Convention on the Protection and Promotion of the Diversity of Cultural Expressions (2005) art 25 and annex.

[68] 1970 UNESCO Convention art 17(5).

[69] Chechi (2013) 192.

[70] See https://www.gov.uk/government/groups/spoliation-advisory-panel#contents.

and restitution, loan and deposit, acquisition, and intellectual property'.[71] ICOM-WIPO Art and Cultural Heritage Mediation is open to public and private parties, including states, museums, indigenous communities, and individuals.[72] A more recent initiative is the creation of the Court of Arbitration for Art (CAfA), a joint project of the Netherlands Arbitration Institute and Authentication in Art, for disputes in the wider art community.[73] CAfA provides a set of mediation rules and administers mediations, and, as its name reveals and as we will see in the following section, it also offers arbitration services.[74]

But international cultural heritage law's most prominent mediation and conciliation forum is a UNESCO body. The UNESCO Intergovernmental Committee is a permanent international body with an advisory role.[75] Its mandate is to assist states with disputes that fall outside the ambit of the existing non-retroactive conventions, notably those that relate to the return or restitution of cultural property of 'fundamental significance' for the requesting state and 'which has been lost as a result of colonial or foreign occupation or as a result of illicit appropriation'.[76]

According to its statutes, revised in 2005 to add mediation and conciliation to its mandate,[77] the UNESCO Intergovernmental Committee seeks to facilitate bilateral negotiations between states for the restitution or return of cultural property; to this effect, it may 'submit proposals with a view to mediation or conciliation';[78] the outcome of the mediation or conciliation process is not binding on the disputing states and, if it does not lead to the resolution of the issue, the case remains before the committee as unresolved.[79] The committee is also tasked with promoting multilateral and bilateral cooperation for the restitution or return of cultural property and fostering a public information campaign on the issue.[80] If institutional mediation or conciliation under the aegis of the UNESCO Intergovernmental Committee is relatively rare, UNESCO is active in offering its good offices, encouraging states

[71] See https://www.wipo.int/amc/en/center/specific-sectors/art/icom/.

[72] See https://www.wipo.int/amc/en/center/specific-sectors/art/icom/. For a discussion of ICOM-WIPO Art and Cultural Heritage Mediation, see Taşdelen (2016) 202-217.

[73] See https://www.cafa.world.

[74] See https://www.cafa.world.

[75] Statutes of the Intergovernmental Committee for Promoting the Return of Cultural Property to its Countries of Origin or its Restitution in case of Illicit Appropriation (ICPRCP Statutes), adopted by 20 C/Res 4/7.6/5 of the 20th session of the General Conference of UNESCO, Paris, 24 October-28 November 1978, art 1.

[76] ICPRCP Statutes arts 3(2) and 4.

[77] 33 C/Resolution 44, adopted by the General Conference of UNESCO at its 33rd session (October 2005).

[78] ICPRCP Statutes art 4(1).

[79] ICPRCP Statutes art 4(1).

[80] ICPRCP Statutes art 4.

to negotiate for the restitution and return of cultural objects, and raising awareness about the illicit traffic in cultural objects.[81]

Mediation has proved an effective means of dispute settlement for a number of cultural heritage disputes. One may instance the mediation between the Tasmanian Aboriginal Centre and the Natural History Museum in London, leading to the repatriation of the remains of seventeen Tasmanian Aboriginals previously held in the collection of the Natural History Museum.[82] The case is interesting to consider in relation to the Parthenon marbles dispute for, just as the British Museum is bound by the ban on deaccession, so was the Natural History Museum in relation to the remains of the Tasmanian Aboriginals prior to the adoption of the Human Tissue Act 2004. Section 47 of that act, which was passed in order to address this very issue, allows the deaccession of human remains, thus making the repatriation of the remains of the Tasmanian Aboriginals possible.

Mediation would be a well-suited method to settle the Parthenon marbles dispute but, as we saw in Chap. 5, the United Kingdom has rejected Greece's request to mediate the case under the auspices of the UNESCO Intergovernmental Committee.[83] However, as in the case of negotiations, the fact that Greece's attempts to mediate the Parthenon marbles case have failed does not mean that mediation is a non-starter and should be excluded as a possibility for the future. UNESCO continues to bring pressure to bear on the parties to reach a solution to the dispute by diplomatic means, and this may bear fruit at some point. In effect, mediation is appropriate when, especially in a long-standing dispute such as in the case of the Parthenon marbles, the legal framework changes, which can make either or both parties revise their position. In any case, mediation, just like negotiations, does not oblige the parties to reach a solution—ultimately, the parties can agree to disagree. Mediation can further encourage the parties to take into account nonlegal aspects of their dispute, such as ethical considerations, which could help them negotiate the difficult path to consensus.[84] These nonlegal aspects are particularly prominent in this case.

In short, Greece may be hard-pressed to convince the United Kingdom to engage in mediation, since the latter has already considered and rejected this option. However, mediation remains an appropriate means of dispute settlement for the Parthenon marbles case and, if it becomes a possibility in the future, it would certainly be worth exploring.

---

[81] See http://www.unesco.org/new/en/culture/themes/restitution-of-cultural-property/intergovernmental-committee/.

[82] Davies and Galloway (2008-9) 160; Natural History Museum, 'Agreement on Aboriginal Remains Reached' (Press release, 11 May 2007); Turnbull (2007). See also Gallagher (2010) 69-70.

[83] See Sect. 5.3.2.

[84] Cornu and Renold (2010).

7.4 Legal Means

In contrast with diplomatic means, legal or adjudicative dispute settlement methods delegate the decision about how to solve the dispute to a third party, an arbitrator or a judge. This decision is binding on the disputing parties. The flexibility and control over the proceeding that parties have when pursuing diplomatic means here in good part disappear. The ensuing discussion considers in turn arbitration and judicial settlement as possible legal avenues for the resolution of the Parthenon marbles case.

7.4.1 Arbitration

Although arbitration is less flexible than diplomatic means, still the disputing parties retain a considerable degree of autonomy.[85] They can choose the procedural rules according to which the arbitration will be conducted, the substantive law to be applied to their dispute, and the arbitrators.[86] In contrast with international courts with so-called 'permanent' judges, in arbitration disputes are usually heard by three-member tribunals[87] constituted ad hoc for the particular dispute.[88] Typically, each party appoints one arbitrator and the third arbitrator, who is the president of the tribunal, is appointed either jointly by the parties or by the two party-appointed arbitrators.[89]

Historically, arbitration was the preferred means for resolving interstate disputes,[90] although, ultimately, its popularity for this type of dispute declined in favour of judicial settlement.[91] However, arbitration did gain currency as a means of settling

[85] Böckstiegel (1997); Collier and Lowe (1999) 248.

[86] E.g. Veeder (2020); Böckstiegel (1997); Schreuer and others (2009) 475-489, 545-639; Kjos (2013) 68-80.

[87] A three-member panel is the default, e.g. see PCA Optional Rules for Arbitrating Disputes between Two States (1992) art 5; ICSID Convention art 37(2); Arbitration Rules of the United Nations Commission on International Trade Law (UNCITRAL) (2010/2013) art 7(1). Contrast European Convention for the Peaceful Settlement of Disputes (1957) art 20(2). In the alternative, an arbitral tribunal can be composed of an odd number of arbitrators.

[88] ILC Model Rules on Arbitral Procedure (1958) art 3; PCA Optional Rules for Arbitrating Disputes between Two States (1992) art 3; ICSID Convention art 37(1).

[89] PCA Optional Rules for Arbitrating Disputes between Two States (1992) art 5; European Convention for the Peaceful Settlement of Disputes (1957) art 20(2); ICSID Convention art 37; UNCITRAL Arbitration Rules (2010/2013) art 9; CAfA Arbitration Rules (2019) art 13(2)-(3). See further Schreuer and others (2009) 475-489; Bjorklund and others (2019) 4-8; Giorgetti (2019); Paulsson (2020).

[90] Ralston (1929) pt III; cf Westermann (1907); Bederman (2001) 8, n 14.

[91] Gray and Kingsbury (1992). See also Brower (2008) 265-266.

mixed disputes, notably between states and foreign investors.[92] Arbitration is occasionally provided for in cultural heritage conventions[93] and in agreements reached between states and museums. For instance, the agreement concluded in 2006 between the Italian Ministry of Cultural Heritage and Activities, the Sicilian Commission for Cultural and Environmental Heritage and Public Education, and the Met provides that if the parties cannot reach an amicable solution to a dispute, they can settle the matter 'in private by arbitration on the basis of the Rules of Arbitration and Conciliation of the International Chamber of Commerce'.[94] WIPO and CAfA, previously mentioned in relation to mediation, also administer arbitrations in art and cultural heritage disputes and have developed respective sets of procedural rules that can be used by the disputing parties.[95] However, until now, arbitration has only exceptionally been used for the settlement of cultural heritage disputes.[96]

In theory, the Parthenon marbles case could be resolved by arbitration. Currently, there is no treaty that enshrines the parties' consent to arbitrate the dispute. The European Convention for the Peaceful Settlement of Disputes of 1957, which provides for arbitration, is unavailable: not only has Greece not ratified it,[97] but also, since the dispute is, according to the argument presented in this book, an 'international legal dispute', it is excluded from arbitration; the Convention states that such disputes must be referred to the ICJ.[98] Greece and the United Kingdom could conclude a *compromis* agreeing to arbitrate the dispute.

In arbitration, the parties can select the law applicable to their dispute, and Greece would be likely to ensure that a prospective tribunal must resolve the dispute on the basis of international law only. In the contrary case, should the applicable law not be identified in the parties' agreement, the tribunal, which generally has the right to decide how to deal with unresolved procedural questions, could choose to apply English law to the dispute.

However, there is at present no indication that either Greece or the United Kingdom would agree to submit the dispute to arbitration. In addition, if Greece were to pursue adjudicative means, it would have reasons to prefer judicial settlement over arbitration. Greece may be at a disadvantage in arbitration as compared to

---

[92] For example, while the ICJ has dealt with under 200 disputes since 1948, investment arbitration tribunals have heard more than 1000 cases since 1987. For the ICJ cases, see https://www.icj-cij.org/en/list-of-all-cases. For the investment arbitrations, see https://investmentpolicy.unctad.org/investment-dispute-settlement.

[93] E.g. UNIDROIT Convention art 8(2).

[94] Agreement between the Italian Ministry of Cultural Heritage and Activities, the Sicilian Commission for Cultural and Environmental Heritage and Public Education, and the New York Metropolitan Museum of Art (21 February 2006) art 9.2.

[95] See https://www.wipo.int/amc/en/arbitration/ and https://www.cafa.world.

[96] Cornu and Renold (2010) 13; Roodt (2015) 191. The famous *Maria Altmann* arbitration, *Maria V Altmann and others v Austria*, arbitral award (15 January 2006), is precisely one of the exceptions.

[97] Council of Europe, 'Chart of signatures and ratifications: European Convention for the Peaceful Settlement of Disputes' https://bit.ly/3UblBWw (information correct as of November 2022).

[98] European Convention for the Peaceful Settlement of Disputes (1957) arts 1, 4, 19.

judicial settlement. A typical three-member arbitral tribunal that may be called upon to decide the dispute will normally be composed of one arbitrator appointed by Greece, one appointed by the United Kingdom, and a third arbitrator appointed with the agreement of the parties or by the two party-appointed arbitrators. Experience with arbitration, notably from the field of investment disputes, shows that party-appointed arbitrators tend to side with the interests of the party appointing them.[99] If both party-appointed arbitrators vote for their appointing state, the president of the tribunal, that is, the only arbitrator appointed by a neutral party or by agreement of the parties, may find himself or herself in a position, much like that of a sole arbitrator, where ultimately he or she is the one to take the decision. In such circumstances, assuming the disputing parties have selected their arbitrators with equal skill, they will have equal control over the arbitration. The case is different with judicial settlement, where the parties will have no such control over the process. In light of the nascent customary international law on returns and the support that Greece enjoys for the repatriation of the marbles within the United Nations, it is likely that the larger the panel that decides the dispute (and a large chamber is indeed probable in a court system), the more the odds will be in Greece's favour.

In short, the dispute could be decided in arbitration, if the parties drafted an arbitration agreement, although this possibility appears remote. If Greece decided to turn to adjudicative means of dispute settlement, it would be likely to prefer judicial settlement, because in arbitration the odds would not necessarily be in its favour. In addition, there are other compelling reasons why for this particular dispute a permanent court may be more appropriate than an ad hoc tribunal, notably in light of the dispute's importance and the need to clarify the law in this area. These reasons are addressed in the following section.

7.4.2 *Judicial Settlement*

Judicial settlement involves dispute resolution by permanent courts, and, like arbitration, it ends with a binding decision. This section focuses on the two courts that could conceivably be seized of the Parthenon marbles case: the ICJ and the European Court of Human Rights.

7.4.2.1 International Court of Justice

The ICJ is the principal judicial organ of the United Nations.[100] It is the only international court of general jurisdiction.[101] Its role is to decide, in accordance

---

[99] E.g. Paulsson (2010); van den Berg (2011).

[100] UN Charter art 92; Statute of the ICJ art 1.

[101] Merrills (2014) 8.

with international law,[102] contentious cases referred to it by states[103] and to give advisory opinions at the request of an authorised body.[104] The Court is composed of fifteen permanent judges, elected by the United Nations General Assembly (UNGA) and by the Security Council, for a renewable 9-year term.[105] Cases are typically decided by the full court, although with the agreement of the parties, a smaller chamber may be constituted.[106]

As a court of general jurisdiction, the ICJ has already decided a small number of disputes with a cultural heritage component.[107] Pride of place, for the purposes of the present discussion, goes to the *Temple of Preah Vihear* case, a dispute between Cambodia and Thailand concerning sovereignty over the territory surrounding the ruins of the Temple of Preah Vihear.[108] In its submissions, Cambodia had requested the Court to adjudge and declare that the temple was situated in Cambodian territory and that the artworks and parts of the monument that had been removed by the Thai authorities should be returned to Cambodia.[109] Having found that the temple of Preah Vihear was indeed situated in Cambodian territory, the Court concluded that Thailand was under an obligation to restore to Cambodia any sculptures, stelae, fragments of monuments, sandstone models, and ancient pottery that it had removed from the temple or the temple area, since the date of the occupation of the area by Thailand.[110] The Court was at pains to stress that Cambodia's request for restitution was 'implicit in, and consequential on, the claim of sovereignty itself'.[111] This means that appurtenances of a monument belong to the sovereign territory, otherwise stated, from the viewpoint of international law, they are immoveable.[112] This finding has a direct relevance to the Parthenon marbles case. As discussed in Chap. 4, if applied to the substance of the dispute, it means that the different parts

[102] Statute of the ICJ art 38(1).

[103] Statute of the ICJ arts 35-37.

[104] Statute of the ICJ art 65.

[105] Statute of the ICJ arts 3(1), 4(1), 13(1).

[106] Statute of the ICJ arts 25, 26(2), 29. See also Shaw (2017) vol 1, Chap. 6, para 96.

[107] *Case concerning the Temple of Preah Vihear (Cambodia v Thailand)* (Merits Judgment) [1962] ICJ Rep 6; *Request for Interpretation of the Judgment of 15 June 1962 in the* Case concerning the Temple of Preah Vihear (Cambodia v Thailand) *(Cambodia v Thailand)* (Judgment) [2013] ICJ Rep 281; *Certain Property (Liechtenstein v Germany)* (Preliminary Objections Judgment) [2005] ICJ Rep 6; *Application of the Convention on the Prevention and Punishment of the Crime of Genocide (Bosnia and Herzegovina v Serbia and Montenegro)* (Judgment) [2007] ICJ Rep 43; *Jurisdictional Immunities of the State (Germany v Italy: Greece intervening)* (Judgment) [2012] ICJ Rep 99.

[108] *Case concerning the Temple of Preah Vihear (Cambodia v Thailand)* (Merits Judgment) [1962] ICJ Rep 6.

[109] *Case concerning the Temple of Preah Vihear (Cambodia v Thailand)* (Merits Judgment) [1962] ICJ Rep 6, 11.

[110] *Case concerning the Temple of Preah Vihear (Cambodia v Thailand)* (Merits Judgment) [1962] ICJ Rep 6, 11, 37.

[111] *Case concerning the Temple of Preah Vihear (Cambodia v Thailand)* (Merits Judgment) [1962] ICJ Rep 6, 36.

[112] Greenfield (2007) 82. See Chap. 4, text to nn 119-120.

of the Parthenon removed while Greece was under Ottoman occupation still belong to the sovereign territory.[113]

In theory, the Parthenon marbles case could be decided by the ICJ in contentious proceedings. Both Greece and the United Kingdom accept the compulsory jurisdiction of the ICJ,[114] which means that in principle any of the two states is habilitated to submit a dispute involving the other to the Court. The current declaration of Greece recognising as compulsory the jurisdiction of the ICJ is not limited in time. However, the same cannot be said of the declaration of the United Kingdom, which restricts the scope of the Court's compulsory jurisdiction to disputes arising after 1 January 1987.[115] While the continued retention of the Parthenon marbles is the act giving rise to the continuing dispute, were the ICJ to consider as crucial the date when the facts leading to the dispute *first* arose,[116] the dispute would fall outside the compulsory jurisdiction of the ICJ. To remedy this *ratione temporis* limitation, Greece and the United Kingdom could negotiate a special agreement submitting the dispute to the ICJ. Alternatively, Greece could file an application inviting the United Kingdom to accept it, on the basis of the principle of *forum prorogatum*. However, neither state appears to be interested in a contentious proceeding. The United Kingdom treats the Greek claim for the marbles' return as a matter of 'debate', but it does not concede the existence of a dispute,[117] and Greece, concerned about the finality of a potentially adverse judgment, is unwilling to risk a contentious proceeding. Therefore, the last two options seem improbable as means by which to found the jurisdiction of the ICJ.

Yet there is another possibility. The ICJ may give its opinion on the fate of the Parthenon marbles by way of an advisory proceeding. According to the Charter of the United Nations (UN Charter), the UNGA or the Security Council may request an advisory opinion from the ICJ 'on any legal question'.[118] In addition, an advisory opinion may be sought by other UN organs and specialised agencies that the UNGA authorises to do so for 'legal questions arising within the scope of their activities'.[119]

---

[113] Chapter 4, text to nn 117-121.

[114] Respective declarations recognizing the jurisdiction of the Court as compulsory by Greece (14 January 2015) and the United Kingdom (22 February 2017).

[115] Respective declarations recognizing the jurisdiction of the Court as compulsory by Greece (14 January 2015) and the United Kingdom (22 February 2017). In fact, the temporal limitation is not the only reservation in the declaration of the United Kingdom. See Ulfstein (2023), who argues that a requirement for a notification to be made at least 6 months prior to the submission of a claim allows the United Kingdom to withdraw unilaterally from the Court's jurisdiction during that period, which means that 'the UK's declaration no longer meaningfully can be seen as compulsory'.

[116] *Certain Property (Liechtenstein v Germany)* (Preliminary Objections Judgment) [2005] ICJ Rep 6 [39]-[52]. See also Higgins (1997) 502; cf *Phosphates in Morocco* (Preliminary Objections Judgment) PCIJ Series A/B (14 June 1938).

[117] See Sect. 5.3.2.

[118] UN Charter art 96. See also Statute of the ICJ art 65(1).

[119] UN Charter art 96. See also Statute of the ICJ art 65(1).

In *Legality of the Threat or Use of Nuclear Weapons*, the ICJ found that it was unable to give an opinion when the World Health Organization (WHO) asked whether the threat or use of nuclear weapons is permitted under international law, since the question did not fall within the scope of the activities of the WHO.[120] But the Court accepted to give an opinion on the same matter when requested to do so by the UNGA.[121] An advisory proceeding has the peerless advantage that it avoids a head-on legal confrontation between Greece and the United Kingdom.

Since the Statute of the ICJ provides that the Court 'may' give an advisory opinion,[122] the ICJ has impressed on states the discretionary nature of its power to give advisory opinions.[123] However, according to the Court's established jurisprudence, a request for an advisory opinion must in principle be accepted, and 'only "compelling reasons" may lead the Court to refuse its opinion in response to a request falling within its jurisdiction'.[124] The Court has sometimes recognised that the exercise of its advisory jurisdiction should not 'have the effect of circumventing the principle that a State is not obliged to allow its disputes to be submitted to judicial settlement without its consent'.[125] Objections to the Court's advisory jurisdiction on the ground that proceedings bear on a pending dispute between states that have not consented to dispute settlement have been raised time and again.[126] But to the best of

[120] *Legality of the Threat or Use of Nuclear Weapons* (Advisory Opinion) [1996] ICJ Rep 66 [26].

[121] *Legality of the Threat or Use of Nuclear Weapons* (Advisory Opinion) [1996] ICJ Rep 226. See also Crawford (2019) 705.

[122] Statute of the ICJ art 65(1).

[123] *Legal Consequences of the Separation of the Chagos Archipelago from Mauritius in 1965* (Advisory Opinion) [2019] ICJ Rep 95 [63]; *Accordance with International Law of the Unilateral Declaration of Independence in Respect of Kosovo* (Advisory Opinion) [2010] ICJ Rep 403 [29]; *Legal Consequences of the Construction of a Wall in the Occupied Palestinian Territory* (Advisory Opinion) [2004] ICJ Rep 136 [44]; *Western Sahara* (Advisory Opinion) [1975] ICJ Rep 12 [23].

[124] *Legal Consequences of the Separation of the Chagos Archipelago from Mauritius in 1965* (Advisory Opinion) [2019] ICJ Rep 95 [65]. See also *Accordance with International Law of the Unilateral Declaration of Independence in Respect of Kosovo* (Advisory Opinion) [2010] ICJ Rep 403 [30]; *Legal Consequences of the Construction of a Wall in the Occupied Palestinian Territory* (Advisory Opinion) [2004] ICJ Rep 136 [44]; *Difference Relating to Immunity from Legal Process of a Special Rapporteur of the Commission on Human Rights* (Advisory Opinion) [1999] ICJ Rep 62 [29]; *Certain Expenses of the United Nations (Article 17, paragraph 2, of the Charter)* (Advisory Opinion) [1962] ICJ Rep 151, 155; *Judgments of the Administrative Tribunal of the ILO upon complaints made against the UNESCO* (Advisory Opinion) [1956] ICJ Rep 77, 86; *Interpretation of Peace Treaties with Bulgaria, Hungary and Romania (First Phase)* (Advisory Opinion) [1950] ICJ Rep 65, 71.

[125] *Legal Consequences of the Separation of the Chagos Archipelago from Mauritius in 1965* (Advisory Opinion) [2019] ICJ Rep 95 [85]; *Western Sahara* (Advisory Opinion) [1975] ICJ Rep 12 [33].

[126] E.g. *Legal Consequences of the Separation of the Chagos Archipelago from Mauritius in 1965* (Advisory Opinion) [2019] ICJ Rep 95; *Applicability of Article VI, Section 22, of the Convention on the Privileges and Immunities of the United Nations* (Advisory Opinion) [1989] ICJ Rep 177; *Legal Consequences for States of the Continued Presence of South Africa in Namibia (South West Africa) notwithstanding Security Council Resolution 276 (1970)* (Advisory Opinion) [1971] ICJ Rep

this author's knowledge, the Court has never refused to give an advisory opinion on that ground.[127] In reality, advisory opinions often do relate to specific disputes, and the disputing parties have not given their consent.[128] This has not failed to give a 'contentious aspect to advisory proceedings'.[129] In such cases, the question submitted to the Court sometimes refers to a 'situation' rather than to a 'dispute', e.g. the 'situation in Namibia'.[130]

Some authors argue that the states' consent is not even necessary in advisory proceedings.[131] The Court has explained that, in contrast with contentious cases, in advisory proceedings its opinion 'is only of an advisory character: as such, it has no binding force', 'even where the Request for an Opinion relates to a legal question actually pending between States'.[132] The Court has added for good measure that 'no State [. . .] can prevent the giving of an Advisory Opinion which the United Nations considers to be desirable in order to obtain enlightenment as to the course of action it should take'.[133] The purpose of an advisory opinion is not to settle a dispute between two or more states but to provide legal guidance to the organs and institutions that have asked for it.[134] So long as the request for an advisory opinion originates in a body authorised to make it, the Court is competent 'to give such opinion on any legal question arising within the scope of the activities of that body'.[135] Requests for opinions tend to relate to matters of special concern to the United Nations, and the fact that states express different legal views 'does not mean that, by replying to the request, the Court is dealing with a bilateral dispute'.[136] In such circumstances, 'the

16 [30]; *Western Sahara* (Advisory Opinion) [1975] ICJ Rep 12; *Interpretation of Peace Treaties with Bulgaria, Hungary and Romania (First Phase)* (Advisory Opinion) [1950] ICJ Rep 65, 71.

[127] Contrast *Status of Eastern Carelia* (Advisory Opinion) PCIJ Series B No 5 (23 July 1923).

[128] Crawford (2019) 704.

[129] Crawford (2019) 704.

[130] *Legal Consequences for States of the Continued Presence of South Africa in Namibia (South West Africa) notwithstanding Security Council Resolution 276 (1970)* (Advisory Opinion) [1971] ICJ Rep 16 [25].

[131] Lauterpacht (1958) 356-358; Conforti and Focarelli (2016) 428.

[132] *Interpretation of Peace Treaties with Bulgaria, Hungary and Romania (First Phase)* (Advisory Opinion) [1950] ICJ Rep 65, 71. See also *Applicability of Article VI, Section 22, of the Convention on the Privileges and Immunities of the United Nations* (Advisory Opinion) [1989] ICJ Rep 177 [31].

[133] *Interpretation of Peace Treaties with Bulgaria, Hungary and Romania (First Phase)* (Advisory Opinion) [1950] ICJ Rep 65, 71. See also *Applicability of Article VI, Section 22, of the Convention on the Privileges and Immunities of the United Nations* (Advisory Opinion) [1989] ICJ Rep 177 [31]; *Western Sahara* (Advisory Opinion) [1975] ICJ Rep 12 [39].

[134] *Legality of the Threat or Use of Nuclear Weapons* (Advisory Opinion) [1996] ICJ Rep 226 [15]; *Interpretation of Peace Treaties with Bulgaria, Hungary and Romania (First Phase)* (Advisory Opinion) [1950] ICJ Rep 65, 71.

[135] *Application for Review of Judgement No 158 of the United Nations Administrative Tribunal* (Advisory Opinion) [1973] ICJ Rep 172 [14].

[136] *Legal Consequences of the Separation of the Chagos Archipelago from Mauritius in 1965* (Advisory Opinion) [2019] ICJ Rep 95 [88]-[89]; *Legal Consequences of the Construction of a*

Court does not consider that to give the opinion requested would have the effect of circumventing the principle of consent by a State to the judicial settlement of its dispute with another State'.[137] The ICJ's Rules of Court expressly envisage the possibility of an advisory opinion on a legal question actually pending between two or more states.[138] Last, but certainly not least, states have already consented to advisory proceedings by becoming members of the United Nations and accepting the obligations contained in the UN Charter[139] and the Statute of the ICJ.[140]

An advisory proceeding in relation to the Parthenon marbles could be initiated by the UNGA or a specialised agency of the United Nations, namely UNESCO. The issue of the return and restitution of cultural property matters to both. The UNGA passes periodic resolutions on the return of cultural property.[141] The most recent at the time of writing is Resolution 76/16 on 'Return or restitution of cultural property to the countries of origin' of 2021.[142] This resolution, based on a Greek initiative, was co-sponsored by 110 other states,[143] the majority in the UNGA,[144] and adopted by consensus.[145] Although neither the UN Charter[146] nor practice[147] supply an unequivocal answer as to the required majority for the UNGA to request an advisory opinion, the adoption of Resolution 76/16 shows that such a majority (whether simple or two-thirds) can probably be obtained.[148] Besides, UNESCO, as a specialised agency of the United Nations,[149] may be authorised to request an advisory opinion on legal questions that fall squarely within the purview of its activities.

Wall in the Occupied Palestinian Territory (Advisory Opinion) [2004] ICJ Rep 136 [50]; *Western Sahara* (Advisory Opinion) [1975] ICJ Rep 12 [38]; *Legal Consequences for States of the Continued Presence of South Africa in Namibia (South West Africa) notwithstanding Security Council Resolution 276 (1970)* (Advisory Opinion) [1971] ICJ Rep 16 [34]; cf Gray (1987) 112, commenting that, rather than constituting 'a remedy for or against' the requesting body or agency, advisory opinions do actually tend to relate to 'a dispute or difference of opinion between different member states or groups of member states'.

[137] *Legal Consequences of the Separation of the Chagos Archipelago from Mauritius in 1965* (Advisory Opinion) [2019] ICJ Rep 95 [90].

[138] Rules of Court (ICJ) art 102(3).

[139] UN Charter art 4(1).

[140] Thirlway (2016) 62.

[141] See Chap. 10, n 98.

[142] UNGA Res 76/16 (6 December 2021) UN Doc A/RES/76/16.

[143] UNESCO, 'UN General Assembly Urges Continued Action to Stop Illicit Trafficking of Cultural Property' (6 December 2021).

[144] There are 193 UN members in total, see https://www.un.org/en/member-states/.

[145] UNESCO, 'UN General Assembly Urges Continued Action to Stop Illicit Trafficking of Cultural Property' (6 December 2021).

[146] UN Charter art 18.

[147] Shaw (2017) vol 1, Chap. 5, para 61.

[148] For a similar argument on the basis of the earlier UNGA resolution 73/130, see Geoffrey Robertson (2019) Chap. 6 (unnumbered page).

[149] Constitution of UNESCO art X in conjunction with UN Charter art 57.

If an advisory opinion is requested, the question may be phrased in terms that ensure both that the opinion can help clarify the law in this area and that it bears on the Parthenon marbles in particular. The United Kingdom may argue that such an opinion interferes with its right to consent to the jurisdiction of the Court. However, for the reasons explained above, such an objection is unlikely to be upheld.

From the viewpoint of international law, the ICJ would be an appropriate forum to pronounce on the Parthenon marbles. If, formally, there is no doctrine of binding precedent or *stare decisis* in international law,[150] and advisory opinions have no binding force in the first place,[151] how the dispute is resolved will have repercussions beyond the particular case. That an authoritative and appropriately constituted organ should clarify the state of customary international law on the return and restitution of cultural property would serve the interests of legal certainty, and none is better placed to do this than the ICJ. An eventual proceeding would attract a great deal of interest from third states, and judicial settlement with institutionalised third-party participation[152] would also be more appropriate than arbitration, where third-party intervention tends to be disallowed or is left to the discretion of the tribunal.[153]

In conclusion, although the possibility of contentious proceedings is remote, a request for an advisory opinion by the UNGA or UNESCO may be envisaged, and it could result in an opinion on the substance of the dispute. In advance, it is impossible to know whether a prospective advisory opinion would favour the marbles' return to Athens or not. However, it is this book's argument that the emerging customary international law favours the Greek claim and an advisory opinion of the ICJ would be likely to do so too.

7.4.2.2 European Court of Human Rights

The final forum that is conceivably a candidate to decide the Parthenon marbles dispute is the European Court of Human Rights. Part of the Council of Europe,[154] the European Court of Human Rights, is a regional human rights court that has overseen the application of the ECHR since the late 1950s.[155] Both Greece and the United Kingdom are members of the Council of Europe and, as such, they are contracting

[150] E.g. Statute of the ICJ art 59; Statute of the PCIJ art 59; Statute of the International Tribunal for the Law of the Sea (ITLOS) art 33(2). For a critical discussion, see e.g. Shaw (2017) vol 3, Chap. 27, paras 377A, 385, 390; Merrills (2014) 15-16; Guillaume (2011); Byers (1999) 120-126; cf Cohen (2015).

[151] See Sect. 7.5.3.

[152] See Shaw (2017) vol 3, Chap. 26 (in contentious proceedings) and Chap. 30, para 408 (in advisory proceedings); Torres Bernárdez (1995); Palchetti (2002); Jessup (1981); Wiik (2016); Van den Eynde (2019).

[153] E.g. PCA Optional Rules for Arbitrating Disputes between Two States (1992).

[154] On the Council of Europe, see https://www.coe.int/en/web/portal.

[155] Nussberger (2020) 3-15; Leach (2014) 410-412.

parties to the ECHR.[156] Since Greece and the United Kingdom are parties to the ECHR and its First Protocol, they have consented to the Court's jurisdiction and there is no need for a special agreement to submit the dispute to it. Some recent announcements to the effect that the United Kingdom may be leaving the ECHR[157] have not materialised, and the state continues to participate in the European system of human rights protection.

In contrast with the ICJ, the European Court of Human Rights, as a court of specialised jurisdiction, is only competent to hear human rights claims, notably those concerning alleged violations of rights enshrined in the ECHR and its protocols. This limits the scope of the legal arguments that can be submitted to it. Moreover, in contrast with its Inter-American counterpart, the European Court of Human Rights has not recognised the right of protection of cultural heritage as an active right, that is, a right that can support a claim as opposed to a defence.[158]

The ECHR allows for two types of claims: individual and interstate applications.[159] Pursuant to Article 34 of the ECHR, individual applications may be referred to the Court by 'any person, non-governmental organization or group of individuals' claiming to be a victim of a breach of the Convention. An individual application has already been submitted in relation to the Parthenon marbles. The *Syllogos ton Athinaion v United Kingdom* case was brought in 2015 by a Greek association constituted, inter alia, to ensure 'the protection and maintenance of the monuments and works of art connected with the history of Athens', relying on the United Kingdom's refusal to mediate in UNESCO.[160] The case, heard by a committee of three, including the British judge (but no Greek judge), was rejected on admissibility grounds.[161]

The second possibility is an interstate application. Pursuant to Article 33 of the ECHR, interstate cases may be brought by any contracting party for an alleged violation of the Convention. Few interstate cases have been decided by the European Court of Human Rights but their number is rising steadily.[162] Interstate cases are typically heard by a grand chamber of seventeen judges.[163] Although in individual applications the applicant must claim to be a victim of a violation of the Convention, states can refer to the Court 'any alleged breach' of the Convention.

---

[156] All Council of Europe members are required to become parties to the ECHR, see Council of Europe Res 1031 (1994).

[157] Adam Forrest, 'Liz Truss "Prepared to Withdraw" UK from European Convention on Human Rights', The Independent (13 July 2022).

[158] See Chap. 9, text to nn 73ff.

[159] ECHR arts 33-34.

[160] *Syllogos ton Athinaion v United Kingdom*, App no 48259/15, Decision (23 June 2016).

[161] *Syllogos ton Athinaion v United Kingdom*, App no 48259/15, Decision (23 June 2016).

[162] For a list, see https://www.echr.coe.int/Documents/InterState_applications_ENG.pdf.

[163] ECHR art 26(1). See Risini (2018) 51.

Two scenarios appear possible (at least in theory) and two related courses of action were put to Greece in 2015 by its erstwhile legal counsel.[164] Greece could file an application on behalf of all Greek citizens.[165] Alternatively, it was suggested that, as a sovereign state with legal personality, Greece could bring a claim on its own account for a violation of Article 1 of the First Protocol to the ECHR, which expressly protects not only natural but also 'legal' persons.[166] However, the viability of the latter option is doubtful as it seems to be controverted by the Court's case law. Let us consider it more closely. If Greece brought an individual (as opposed to an interstate) claim as a legal person under Article 34, its application would probably fail, since the Court has already held that states do not qualify to file an individual petition. In the 2020 decision in *Democratic Republic of the Congo v Belgium*, the Court had to determine whether the applicant state, which is not a contracting party to the ECHR and therefore cannot lodge an interstate application, might claim instead in its own right by filing an individual application under Article 34 of the ECHR.[167] According to the Court's jurisprudence, legal persons can only file individual petitions if they are nongovernmental organisations.[168] Since the Democratic Republic of the Congo could not qualify as a nongovernmental organisation, the Court rejected the application.[169]

There is of course another option, that is, Greece could invoke a violation of its own rights in an interstate application. However, even in that case, Greece would have trouble convincing the Court to uphold jurisdiction. In *Cyprus v Turkey*, the European Court of Human Rights determined that 'according to the very nature of the Convention, it is the individual, and not the State, who is directly or indirectly harmed and primarily "injured" by a violation of one or several Convention rights'.[170] For this reason, the Court ruled, 'if just satisfaction is afforded in an inter-State case, it should always be done for the benefit of individual victims'.[171] Latterly, this approach has been reinforced with the 2020 Grand Chamber decision in *Slovenia v Croatia*.[172] In that case, the Court rejected an interstate complaint in favour of a state-owned bank.[173] The Court clarified that there are two main types of interstate applications: 'those pertaining to general issues with a view to protecting

---

[164] Robertson, Palmer, and Clooney (2015) Chap. 6.

[165] Robertson, Palmer, and Clooney (2015) 118.

[166] First Protocol to the ECHR art 1(1). Also in Robertson, Palmer, and Clooney (2015) 120.

[167] *Democratic Republic of the Congo v Belgium*, App no 16554/19, Decision (6 October 2020) [12]-[15].

[168] *Democratic Republic of the Congo v Belgium*, App no 16554/19, Decision (6 October 2020) [16].

[169] *Democratic Republic of the Congo v Belgium*, App no 16554/19, Decision (6 October 2020) [17]-[21].

[170] *Cyprus v Turkey*, App no 25781/94, Just Satisfaction Judgment (12 May 2014) [46].

[171] *Cyprus v Turkey*, App no 25781/94, Just Satisfaction Judgment (12 May 2014) [46].

[172] *Slovenia v Croatia*, App no 54155/16, Decision (18 November 2020).

[173] *Slovenia v Croatia*, App no 54155/16, Decision (18 November 2020) [79].

the public order of Europe, and those where the applicant State complains of violations by another Contracting Party of the basic human rights of one or more clearly identified or identifiable persons'.[174] The Parthenon marbles case would probably match better the latter category, i.e. the applicant state should identify the persons victims of an alleged violation. The Court stressed that the ECHR is an instrument for the protection of human rights and drew on both *Cyprus v Turkey* and the ICJ Advisory Opinion of 28 May 1951[175] to hold that 'the particular logic of a human rights treaty is that the contracting States do not have any interest of their own'; rather, they should pursue 'the protection of the rights of individuals'.[176] The Court concluded that 'only individuals, groups of individuals and legal entities which qualify as "non-governmental organisations" within the meaning of Article 34 can be bearers of rights under the Convention, *but not a Contracting State* or any legal entity which has to be regarded as a governmental organisation'.[177] The foregoing shows, first, that Greece could not pursue an individual claim, and, second, that it could pursue an interstate dispute if it claimed in favour of all Greek citizens but not if it claimed on its own account, unless it could show that the claim related to the protection of 'the public order of Europe', which would be probably difficult to do.[178]

In any event, the Parthenon marbles case is a traditional interstate dispute, not one predominantly about human rights, and this author is sceptical about the appropriateness of an interstate claim in the European Court of Human Rights. The book returns to this topic, when examining the substantive law to be applied by the European Court of Human Rights in Chap. 9.

7.5 Practical Considerations

Having reviewed the available dispute settlement options, the chapter now addresses selective practical considerations that aid in weighing the pros and cons of different means of dispute settlement, and especially adjudicative means. Accordingly, the ensuing discussion focuses in turn on the exhaustion of local remedies, the appropriateness of an *ex aequo et bono* mandate, and the relief sought and the binding character of dispute settlement outcomes.

---

[174] *Slovenia v Croatia*, App no 54155/16, Decision (18 November 2020) [67].

[175] *Reservations to the Convention on Genocide* (Advisory Opinion) [1951] ICJ Rep 15, 23.

[176] *Slovenia v Croatia*, App no 54155/16, Decision (18 November 2020) [66].

[177] *Slovenia v Croatia*, App no 54155/16, Decision (18 November 2020) [66] (emphasis added).

[178] On the different interpretations of the term 'European public order' in the jurisprudence of the European Court of Human Rights, see Dzehtsiarou (2022).

7.5.1 *Exhaustion of Domestic Remedies*

In order to institute an international claim, it is sometimes necessary to exhaust the available judicial or administrative remedies in the respondent state's domestic legal system.[179] In the words of the ICJ in *ELSI*, 'the essence of the claim' must have 'been brought before the competent tribunals and pursued as far as permitted by local law and procedures, and without success'.[180] The rule is meant to give the state responsible for the alleged violation an opportunity to redress it within its own legal system, before international proceedings are instituted.[181] The following paragraphs consider the exhaustion of domestic remedies rule and its relevance to the Parthenon marbles case.

The exhaustion of local remedies is required under customary international law in the field of diplomatic protection, where the state claims for an indirect injury to one or more of its nationals (indirect claim).[182] A state may not bring an international claim in respect of an injured person, unless the latter has exhausted all local remedies.[183] However, the requirement to exhaust local remedies does not apply when the state claims directly for itself.[184]

But the nagging conundrum remains of how to distinguish between a direct and an indirect claim, since even claims for a direct injury may include elements of diplomatic protection.[185] In such cases, what matters is whether the claim's *preponderant* aim is to redress an injury to a national, or other physical person that the state is allowed to protect, *vel non*.[186] In *United States Diplomatic and Consular Staff in Tehran*, the ICJ found that Iran had violated the obligation it owed directly to the United States under international law to respect the inviolability of embassies and consulates, even if US diplomatic and consular staff had also suffered personal

---

[179] Shaw (2017) vol 3, Chap. 19, para 290. The obligation is limited to the state's *legal* remedies, e.g. administrative remedies of a discretionary nature are excluded, ILC, 'Second Report on Diplomatic Protection by Special Rapporteur John R Dugard', UN Doc A/CN.4/514 (28 February 2001), para 14.

[180] *Elettronica Sicula SpA (ELSI)* (Judgment) [1989] ICJ Rep 15 [59].

[181] *Interhandel (Switzerland v United States)* (Preliminary Objections Judgment) [1959] ICJ Rep 6, 27. For additional reasons, see Borchard (1916) 817–818.

[182] *Interhandel (Switzerland v United States)* (Preliminary Objections Judgment) [1959] ICJ Rep 6, 27; *Elettronica Sicula SpA (ELSI)* (Judgment) [1989] ICJ Rep 15 [50]. See further ILC, 'Second Report on Diplomatic Protection by Special Rapporteur John R Dugard', UN Doc A/CN.4/514 (28 February 2001), para 5.

[183] ILC Draft Articles on Diplomatic Protection art 14(1). See also *Avena and Other Mexican Nationals (Mexico v United States of America)* (Judgment) [2004] ICJ Rep 12 [40].

[184] Amerasinghe (2004) 146-168. See also ILC Draft Articles on Diplomatic Protection arts 14(3) and 16.

[185] Meron (1959) 85-86.

[186] ILC Draft Articles on Diplomatic Protection art 14(3) and commentary, art 14, para 11; ILC, 'Second Report on Diplomatic Protection by Special Rapporteur John R Dugard', UN Doc A/CN.4/514 (28 February 2001), paras 18-31; Meron (1959) 86;

injury.[187] In *Arrest Warrant of 11 April 2000*, both the Congo and one of its nationals (its foreign minister) had suffered injury, but the ICJ noted that the Congo did not invoke the personal rights of its national, rather it alleged the violation of the Congo's rights in light of the unlawfulness of the arrest warrant issued 'against a person who was at the time Minister for Foreign Affairs of the Congo'.[188] The Court concluded that the Congo had a direct legal interest in the claim and that it asserted a claim in its own name, therefore the requirement to exhaust local remedies did not apply.[189] The *Avena and Other Mexican Nationals* case was brought to the ICJ by Mexico in respect of 54 Mexican nationals who had been sentenced to death in the United States. The Court observed that violations of individual rights may entail the violation of the rights of the state and vice-versa.[190] This 'interdependence' between the rights of the state and the rights of individuals means that Mexico, in submitting a claim in its name, may 'request the Court to rule on the violation of rights which it claims to have suffered both directly and through the violation of individual rights'.[191] The Court found that the 'duty to exhaust local remedies does not apply to such a request'.[192] By contrast, in *Interhandel*, where Switzerland invoked a direct wrong out of an indirect injury to a national company, the ICJ relied on the fact that Interhandel had lost in litigation in the US court system and, having obtained certiorari from the US Supreme Court, could start all over again.[193] It concluded that the case was one of diplomatic protection and dismissed it on admissibility grounds, since local remedies had not been exhausted.[194]

If Greece instituted contentious before the ICJ, the above considerations would apply. Greece would be bringing a direct claim and the requirement to exhaust local remedies would be inapplicable. The situation would be similar, if Greece and the United Kingdom submitted the dispute to an arbitral tribunal. In the case of an advisory opinion of the ICJ, the requirement to exhaust local remedies is irrelevant, since the proceeding would no longer concern a bilateral dispute between Greece and the United Kingdom. Finally, we need to consider whether the requirement to

---

[187] *United States Diplomatic and Consular Staff in Tehran* (Judgment) [1980] ICJ Rep 3.

[188] *Arrest Warrant of 11 April 2000 (Democratic Republic of the Congo v Belgium)* (Judgment) [2002] ICJ Rep 3 [40].

[189] *Arrest Warrant of 11 April 2000 (Democratic Republic of the Congo v Belgium)* (Judgment) [2002] ICJ Rep 3 [40].

[190] *Avena and Other Mexican Nationals (Mexico v United States of America)* (Judgment) [2004] ICJ Rep 12 [40].

[191] *Avena and Other Mexican Nationals (Mexico v United States of America)* (Judgment) [2004] ICJ Rep 12 [40].

[192] *Avena and Other Mexican Nationals (Mexico v United States of America)* (Judgment) [2004] ICJ Rep 12 [40].

[193] *Interhandel (Switzerland v United States)* (Preliminary Objections Judgment) [1959] ICJ Rep 6, 27-29.

[194] *Interhandel (Switzerland v United States)* (Preliminary Objections Judgment) [1959] ICJ Rep 6, 27-29. For a criticism, see Crawford and Grant (2007), para 10.

exhaust domestic remedies would matter in the event of an interstate dispute in the European Court of Human Rights.

The exhaustion of domestic remedies is a requirement under the ECHR, including in the case of interstate applications.[195] If the purpose of the interstate dispute is to exercise diplomatic protection, local remedies must in principle be exhausted. According to the European Court of Human Rights in *Russia v Georgia*, the rule of the exhaustion of local remedies applies to interstate disputes, just as it does to individual claims, 'when the applicant State does no more than denounce a violation or violations allegedly suffered by "individuals" whose place, as it were, is taken by the State'.[196] Nonetheless, a number of exceptions have been carved out of the rule. For a start, in interstate disputes the exhaustion of local remedies rule is inapplicable when the applicant state alleges that it is legislation that violates the ECHR or its protocols.[197] Moreover, there is no need to exhaust local remedies if the applicant state alleges that a practice as such contravenes the ECHR or its protocols,[198] 'but does not ask the Court to give a decision on each of the cases put forward as proof or illustrations of that practice'.[199]

If Greece were to lodge an application with the European Court of Human Rights in order to assert its own direct claim, it would not be exercising diplomatic protection, and there would be no need to exhaust local remedies. However, as discussed above, this does not appear a likely scenario.[200] If Greece brought the claim to complain of an injury to all Greek citizens, it would be effectively exercising diplomatic protection. It would then appear that local remedies may need to be exhausted. Such a claim would be unlikely to be considered to fall under the exception of an application targeting an administrative practice, since the requirements for this type of claim do not match the facts. Yet it is possible that the exception of legislation may apply, since Greece could allege a continuing violation arising out of the two acts of parliament whose combined effect is the marbles' continued retention in the British Museum.[201]

In addition, another exception is relevant, and it concerns the futility of local remedies.[202] Pursuant to the International Law Commission's (ILC) draft Articles on

[195] ECHR art 35(1).

[196] *Georgia v Russia*, App no 38263/08, Decision (13 December 2011) [84].

[197] Risini (2018) 56.

[198] Such practice can be found to exist when the actions of the state occur repetitively and there is 'official tolerance', see *Georgia v Russia*, App no 38263/08, Decision (13 December 2011) [85]. See also *Georgia v Russia*, App no 13255/07, Merits Judgment (3 July 2014) [125]; *Cyprus v Turkey*, App no 25781/94, Judgment (10 May 2001) [99]; *Akdivar and others v Turkey*, App no 21893/93, Judgment (16 September 1996) [67].

[199] *Georgia v Russia*, App no 38263/08, Decision (13 December 2011) [85]. See also *Georgia v Russia*, App no 13255/07, Merits Judgment (3 July 2014) [125]; *Ireland v United Kingdom*, App no 5310/71, Judgment (18 January 1978) [159].

[200] Text to nn 164-178.

[201] See Sects. 6.4 and 8.3.2.

[202] Titi (2021) 96-98.

Diplomatic Protection, there is no need to exhaust local remedies if 'there are no reasonably available local remedies to provide effective redress, or the local remedies provide no reasonable possibility of such redress'.[203] The domestic remedies must be available not only in theory but also in practice.[204] The European Court of Human Rights too recognises the futility exception, albeit not in so many words. The Court has adopted a flexible approach to the application of the exhaustion of local remedies rule.[205] According to its established jurisprudence, the only remedies that need to be exhausted are those that are available and effective, which means not only that they must exist and be accessible and capable of providing redress, but also that they must have a reasonable prospect of success.[206] As previously discussed, English courts would be neither accessible nor capable of providing redress, even if Greece did bring a claim.[207] In short, even in the case of a dispute brought to the European Court of Human Rights, there would be no need to exhaust local remedies.

7.5.2 Ex aequo et bono*?*

Another issue to consider relates to the practical availability and appropriateness of an *ex aequo et bono* mandate, if an arbitration or contentious proceedings before the ICJ were pursued. The power to decide *ex aequo et bono*, conferred upon the adjudicative body only with the parties' agreement,[208] authorises a court or tribunal to reach—if appropriate—outside the law in order to decide 'on objective grounds of fair dealing and good faith'.[209] Two clarifications are necessary at the outset. First, *ex aequo et bono* jurisdiction does not rule out the application of law.[210] In effect, if the few instances in which tribunals decided on the basis of an *ex aequo et bono* mandate are anything to go by, adjudicators will generally not stray from positive law.[211]

[203] ILC Draft Articles on Diplomatic Protection art 15(a). For an example from arbitration, see *Affaire des forêts du Rhodope central (fond) (Grèce contre Bulgarie)* (1933) 3 RIAA 1405, 1420.

[204] ILC, 'Second Report on Diplomatic Protection by Special Rapporteur John R Dugard', UN Doc A/CN.4/514 (28 February 2001), para 17. See also *Cyprus v Turkey*, App no 25781/94, Judgment (10 May 2001) [99].

[205] *Ringeisen v Austria*, App no 2614/65, Merits Judgment (16 July 1971) [89]; *Lehtinen v Finland*, App no 39076/97, Decision (14 October 1999) (unnumbered page); *Gherghina v Romania*, App no 42219/07, Decision (9 July 2015) [87].

[206] *Sejdovic v Italy*, App no 56581/00, Merits and Just Satisfaction Judgment (1 March 2006) [46]; *Paksas v Lithuania*, App no 34932/04 Merits and Just Satisfaction Judgment (6 January 2011) [75]; *SAS v France*, App no 43835/11, Merits and Just Satisfaction Judgment (1 July 2014) [61]. See further d'Ascoli and Scherr (2007); Bernard Robertson (1990).

[207] See Sect. 5.6.

[208] E.g. Statute of the ICJ art 38(2).

[209] Hudson (1944) 103.

[210] Schreuer and others (2009) 635-636; Titi (2021) Chap. 7.

[211] Titi (2021) Chap. 7.

Second, the *ex aequo et bono* mandate is something quite distinct from the regular equitable considerations (or equity) that an international court or tribunal can apply anyway as part of international law.[212] Equity, as distinct from an *ex aequo et bono* mandate, is considered in Chap. 10.

States are generally reluctant to submit to *ex aequo et bono* adjudication. The ICJ has never decided *ex aequo et bono*, although a handful of arbitral tribunals have.[213] That states may regard the *ex aequo et bono* mandate with scepticism is easy to understand. This type of decision-making is sometimes seen as 'an act of goodwill and accommodation on the part of the State favoured by the law in force'.[214] *Ex aequo et bono* is likely to be sought when a party considers that the law in force is unjust and wishes to ensure that the equitable considerations favouring its claim prevail.[215] It is less probable that both disputing parties will be prepared for such a decision, which may clash with the legal rights of one of them.[216]

But states' disinclination to authorise a court or tribunal to decide *ex aequo et bono* does not mean that this type of adjudication is never appropriate. In fact, an *ex aequo et bono* decision may be useful in cases where the legal framework is not highly developed or is uncertain, where the issues at stake are very sensitive, and when what matters is not only to put an end to a dispute but also to reach a solution that is sustainable going forward.[217] Apropos the Parthenon marbles case, although a customary international law rule on the return of plundered cultural property is emerging, its contours are as yet unclear and have to be confirmed by an international court or tribunal. The dispute is certainly a matter of great sensitivity and a sustainable solution is needed.[218]

In practice, an *ex aequo et bono* authorisation in the Parthenon marbles case would enable an international court or tribunal to decide on the basis of the *debate*, although this does not mean that it would choose to do so. And even Merryman conceded that, were the matter to be determined 'on the basis of direct emotional appeal, the Marbles would go back to Greece tomorrow'.[219] Consequently, the United Kingdom would be unlikely to agree to endow a court or tribunal with *ex aequo et bono* authority.

An *ex aequo et bono* decision in the Parthenon marbles case would also be unlikely to help clarify and develop the international law on the return of cultural property, since future adjudicative bodies may reject the relevance of the most innovative equitable findings of an *ex aequo et bono* decision putting them down

---

[212]For a discussion, see Titi (2021) 154.

[213]Titi (2021) Chap. 7.

[214]Lauterpacht (1933) 321, 336.

[215]Sohn (1967) 333.

[216]Jennings (1967) 344. See further Dinstein (1986) 38.

[217]Titi (2021) 156.

[218]Fincham (2013) 1016.

[219]Merryman (1985) 1883.

to the particular nature of this mandate.[220] Concretely, this means that if a court or tribunal ordered the return of the Parthenon marbles to Athens on the basis of *ex aequo et bono* jurisdiction, the likelihood of other returns would be smaller than if a court or tribunal ordered their return under its regular jurisdiction.

Overall, it is doubtful that Greece would induce the United Kingdom to accept a type of dispute settlement that would be unlikely to favour the British side. However, as will become clear in Chap. 10, *ex aequo et bono* powers are not necessary to vindicate the Greek claim.

7.5.3 Relief Sought and Binding Force

The diplomatic means that Greece has pursued thus far in relation to the Parthenon marbles have sought the recovery of the missing marbles and their repatriation to Athens.[221] If Greece instituted adjudicative proceedings, their purpose would certainly be the same. Both diplomatic and adjudicative means may result in the return of the marbles, and restitution as a remedy is the focus of this section. The following paragraphs examine in turn the relief sought and the binding force of dispute settlement outcomes, commencing with diplomatic means and continuing with adjudicative means.

Restitution is the first kind of reparation available to a state that has been injured by an internationally wrongful act.[222] Reparation, according to the Permanent Court of International Justice (PCIJ) 'must, as far as possible, wipe out all the consequences of the illegal act and reestablish the situation which would, in all probability, have existed if that act had not been committed'.[223] This principle is now enshrined in the ILC Articles on State Responsibility, notably subject to the requirement that restitution is not materially impossible.[224] Only if restitution is impossible, should an international court or tribunal award compensation in its stead.[225] To return the marbles to the monument from which they were once torn is of course no longer possible, but what is possible is to return them to Athens to join their other half firmly ensconced in the new Acropolis Museum. The return or restitution of the marbles is the *only* remedy that Greece would seek and it would be certain to say so, to ensure that any other award, notably of compensation, would be *ultra petita*.

---

[220] Titi (2021) 156.

[221] See Chap. 5.

[222] ILC Articles on State Responsibility art 34. See also ILC Articles on State Responsibility, commentary, art 35, para 1. Contrast Gray (1987) 12-16.

[223] *Case Concerning the Factory at Chorzów (Claim for Indemnity)* (Merits) PCIJ Series A No 17 (13 September 1928) 47.

[224] ILC Articles on State Responsibility art 35. For a discussion, see Crawford (2013) 510-516.

[225] *Case Concerning the Factory at Chorzów (Claim for Indemnity)* (Merits) PCIJ Series A No 17 (13 September 1928) 47.

If diplomatic means are pursued, the return of the marbles is an available remedy. Certainly, the consensual nature of this type of dispute settlement does not guarantee that an agreement will actually be reached. If the parties do contrive a solution through diplomatic channels, the ensuing settlement agreement will not be binding, and compliance with it will depend on the parties' good will. That said, were Greece and the United Kingdom to successfully negotiate or mediate, there is no reason to assume that they would not respect the outcome of the proceeding.

Adjudicative means of dispute settlement result in principle in an arbitral or judicial decision, albeit one that is no longer consensual and typically pleases one party more than the other. In arbitration, a tribunal may have jurisdiction to award non-pecuniary relief, depending on the parties' arbitration agreement and any arbitration rules incorporated by reference into that agreement.[226] Arbitration rules are often silent on the possibility of awarding restitution or specific performance,[227] but, unless award of non-pecuniary relief is expressly prohibited, this silence is typically interpreted as permissive of such award.[228] Although tribunals usually award damages,[229] there are several examples in interstate arbitral practice of tribunals ordering non-pecuniary relief.[230]

As regards the ICJ, its remedial competence is enshrined in the Statute, which establishes that the Court's compulsory jurisdiction extends to legal disputes concerning 'the nature or extent of the reparation to be made for the breach of an international obligation'.[231] Disputing parties tend not to question the Court's competence to grant particular types of relief, except rarely in cases brought on the basis of compromissory clauses, and the ICJ has generally asserted its competence to award reparation.[232] The Court has ordered restitution or specific performance in a number of contentious cases,[233] including in the *Temple of Preah Vihear* dispute,[234] and it has clearly stated its opinion that non-monetary relief is appropriate in advisory proceedings.[235]

By this token, should the Court decide in favour of the Greek claim, it could order the return of the marbles to Greece. In contentious proceedings, such an order would be binding on the parties.[236] In advisory proceedings, technically the Court could not 'order' restitution, but it could still declare that it is of the opinion that the marbles

226 McKendrick and Maxwell (2013) 207.

227 E.g. PCA Optional Rules for Arbitrating Disputes between Two States (1992).

228 Schreuer (2004); McKendrick and Maxwell (2013) 209; Stephens-Chu (2014) 667.

229 Gray (1987) 11-16.

230 For examples, see Gray (1987) 12-16; Schreuer (2004) 327-329.

231 Statute of the ICJ art 36(2)(d). See also Brownlie (1996) 557. Contrast Gray (1987) 95.

232 Brownlie (1996) 558, 562.

233 Schreuer (2004) 326-327; Gray (1987) 96.

234 See text to nn 108-112.

235 E.g. *Legal Consequences of the Separation of the Chagos Archipelago from Mauritius in 1965* (Advisory Opinion) [2019] ICJ Rep 95.

236 Statute of the ICJ art 59.

should be returned to Greece. Although advisory opinions are not formally binding on the parties, except if provided so in an applicable convention,[237] in practice they are overwhelmingly persuasive.[238] Notably, the UNGA has been adopting resolutions in relation to advisory opinions issued at its request,[239] and, on at least one occasion, the International Tribunal for the Law of the Sea (ITLOS) has taken an ICJ advisory opinion to set the law, despite the fact that the state concerned has not 'complied' with it.[240] In short, pressure is put to bear on the state that is the addressee of an advisory opinion to comply with it. Despite non-compliance with the recent *Legal Consequences of the Separation of the Chagos Archipelago from Mauritius in 1965* advisory opinion,[241] the United Kingdom often abides by ICJ advisory opinions.[242] This gives reason to argue that, if the Court declared that it is of the opinion that the marbles should be returned to Greece, the United Kingdom would be likely to comply with that opinion.

Finally, the European Court of Human Rights could also grant the return of the marbles, if it found in favour of the Greek claim. Its decision would be binding.[243] In theory, the Court recognises the primacy of *restitutio in integrum*, although in practice it often opts for pecuniary compensation, including when restitution is

---

[237] E.g. Convention on the Privileges and Immunities of the Specialized Agencies (1949) art IX, section 32. See further Roberto Ago, 'Binding Advisory Opinions of the International Court of Justice' (1991) 85 American Journal of International Law 439; Thirlway (2016) 140.

[238] Shaw (2017) vol 3, Chap. 30, para 415; Thirlway (2016) 139; Oellers-Frahm (2012) 218.

[239] Oellers-Frahm (2012) 218.

[240] In relation to the advisory opinion in *Legal Consequences of the Separation of the Chagos Archipelago from Mauritius in 1965*, ITLOS held that, despite the fact that the United Kingdom has not withdrawn its administration from the Chagos Archipelago (see n 241), Mauritius has sovereignty over the archipelago, in accordance with the ICJ advisory opinion, *Dispute Concerning Delimitation of the Maritime Boundary between Mauritius and Maldives in the Indian Ocean (Mauritius/Maldives)* (Preliminary Objections Judgment) [2021] ITLOS Rep 1 [242]-[252].

[241] In *Legal Consequences of the Separation of the Chagos Archipelago from Mauritius in 1965*, the ICJ found the United Kingdom's continued administration of the Chagos Archipelago to be 'an unlawful act of a continuing character' and declared the United Kingdom to be 'under an obligation to bring an end' to this administration 'as rapidly as possible', *Legal Consequences of the Separation of the Chagos Archipelago from Mauritius in 1965* (Advisory Opinion) [2019] ICJ Rep 95 [177]-[178]. The UNGA issued a resolution 'demanding' that the United Kingdom comply with the advisory opinion within 6 months, UNGA Res 73/295 (22 May 2019) UN Doc A/RES/73/295, para 3. That deadline has expired and to date the United Kingdom has not complied with the advisory opinion. See UK Parliament, 'British Indian Ocean Territory', Statements UIN HCWS90 and UIN HLWS87 (5 November 2019) https://questions-statements.parliament.uk/written-statements/detail/2019-11-05/HCWS90 and https://questions-statements.parliament.uk/written-statements/detail/2019-11-05/hlws87 ('The UK has no doubt as to our sovereignty over the British Indian Ocean Territory (BIOT), which has been under continuous British sovereignty since 1814. Mauritius has never held sovereignty over the BIOT and the UK does not recognise its claim'); cf UK Parliament, 'British Indian Ocean Territory / Chagos Archipelago: Statement made on 3 November 2022 by James Cleverly', Statement UIN HCWS354 https://questions-statements.parliament.uk/written-statements/detail/2022-11-03/hcws354.

[242] Geoffrey Robertson (2019) Chap. 6.

[243] ECHR art 46.

possible and when a local law prevents a return to the *status quo ante*.[244] However, the Court could also ask the United Kingdom to amend its laws and return the marbles. The United Kingdom has a good record of compliance with the judgments of the European Court of Human Rights.[245] In short, the return of the marbles to Greece could be achieved by either diplomatic or legal means of dispute settlement, despite differences between them in relation to the binding character of respective decisions.

7.6 Conclusion

Sometimes it is not possible to remain above the fray. The Parthenon marbles dispute is so long-standing that it is now safe to say that it will not go away unless a solution is found. This chapter has considered the available dispute settlement options, inquiring in turn into diplomatic and adjudicative means. It stressed that it is the diplomatic means that are the most suitable to settle the Parthenon marbles case, although it noted their failure thus far. Turning to legal means, the chapter distinguished between arbitration and judicial settlement and suggested that, in this case, judicial settlement is the most appropriate of the two. In particular, the argument was made that the subject-matter of the dispute belongs to the general jurisdiction of the ICJ, which can—not only pronounce on the case but also—offer an authoritative interpretation of the customary international law on the return of cultural property unlawfully removed from its original context. Technically, it might be possible for the European Court of Human Rights to be pressed into service to decide the case in the course of an interstate proceeding. Both Greece and the United Kingdom are signatories to the ECHR and its First Protocol and have thus consented to the Court's jurisdiction. The requirement of consent may be more difficult to meet in relation to the contentious jurisdiction of the ICJ. However, there is another possibility, that of an advisory proceeding before the ICJ at the request of the UNGA or UNESCO. An advisory proceeding overcomes the eventual difficulties related to the consent requirement, it avoids a direct legal confrontation between Greece and the United Kingdom, and it still allows the ICJ, as a court of general jurisdiction, to pronounce on the state of the customary international law on the return or restitution of cultural property. The findings of this chapter will be complemented by an examination of matters of jurisdiction and admissibility and the substantive law to be applied by each court, topics that are addressed in Chaps. 8–10.

[244] E.g. *Papamichalopoulos and others v Greece*, App no 14556/89, Judgment (31 October 1995) [34]. For an analysis of *restitutio in integrum* under the ECHR, including its 'defective application', see Octavian Ichim, *Just Satisfaction under the European Convention on Human Rights* (Cambridge University Press 2015) 29-41.

[245] Council of Europe (Department for the Execution of Judgments of the European Court of Human Rights), 'Country Factsheet: United Kingdom' (last update at time of writing: 15 March 2021) https://rm.coe.int/1680709768.

References

Michael Alberstein, 'Forms of Mediation and Law: Cultures of Dispute Resolution' (2007) 22 (2) Ohio State Journal on Dispute Resolution 321

Chittharanjan Felix Amerasinghe, *Local Remedies in International Law* (2nd edn, Cambridge University Press 2004)

Chittharanjan Felix Amerasinghe, *Jurisdiction of International Tribunals* (Brill 2002)

Silvia d'Ascoli and Kathrin Maria Scherr, 'The Rule of Prior Exhaustion of Local Remedies in the International Law Doctrine and its Application in the Specific Context of Human Rights Protection' (2007) EUI Working Papers Law 2007/02

David J Bederman, *International Law in Antiquity* (Cambridge University Press 2001)

Albert Jan van den Berg, 'Dissenting Opinions by Party-Appointed Arbitrators in Investment Arbitration' in Mahnoush Arsanjani and others (eds), *Looking to the Future: Essays on International Law in Honor of W Michael Reisman* (Martinus Nijhoff 2011)

Andrea Bjorklund and others, 'Selection and Appointment of International Adjudicators: Structural Options for ISDS Reform' (2019) Academic Forum on ISDS Concept Paper 2019/11

Karl-Heinz Böckstiegel, 'The Role of Party Autonomy in International Arbitration' (1997) 52 (3) Dispute Resolution Journal 24

Edwin Montefiore Borchard, *The Diplomatic Protection of Citizens Abroad* (Banks Law 1916)

Charles H Brower II, 'The Functions and Limits of Arbitration and Judicial Settlement Under Private and Public International Law' (2008) 18 Duke Journal of Comparative and International Law 259

Ian Brownlie, 'Remedies in the International Court of Justice' in Vaughan Lowe and Malgosia Fitzmaurice (eds), *Fifty Years of the International Court of Justice* (Cambridge University Press 1996)

Nicholas Butler, 'Arbitration and Conciliation Treaties' (2006) Max Planck Encyclopedia of Public International Law

Michael Byers, *Custom, Power and the Power of Rules* (Cambridge University Press 1999)

Antônio Augusto Cançado Trindade, *A humanização do direito internacional* (Del Rey 2006)

Alessandro Chechi, 'Plurality and Coordination of Dispute Settlement Methods in the Field of Cultural Heritage' in Francesco Francioni and James Gordley (eds), *Enforcing International Cultural Heritage Law* (Oxford University Press 2013)

Jacob Katz Cogan, 'Competition and Control in International Adjudication (2008) 48 (2) Virginia Journal of International Law 411

Harlan Grant Cohen, 'Theorizing Precedent in International Law' in Andrea Bianchi, Daniel Peat, and Matthew Windsor (eds), *Interpretation in International Law* (Oxford University Press 2015)

John G Collier and Vaughan Lowe, *The Settlement of Disputes in International Law* (Oxford University Press 1999)

Benedetto Conforti and Carlo Focarelli, *The Law and Practice of the United Nations* (5th edn, Brill 2016)

Marie Cornu and Marc-André Renold, 'New Developments in the Restitution of Cultural Property: Alternative Means of Dispute Resolution' (2010) 17 International Journal of Cultural Property 1

James Crawford, *Brownlie's Principles of Public International Law* (9th edn, Oxford University Press 2019)

James Crawford, *State Responsibility* (Cambridge University Press 2013)

James Crawford and Thomas Grant, 'Local Remedies, Exhaustion of' (2007) Max Planck Encyclopedia of Public International Law

Chris Davies and Kate Galloway, 'The Story of Seventeen Tasmanians: The Tasmanian Aboriginal Centre and Repatriation from the Natural History Museum' (2008-9) 11 Newcastle Law Review 143

Yoram Dinstein, 'The Interaction of International Law and Justice' (1986) 16 Israel Yearbook on Human Rights 9

Kanstantsin Dzehtsiarou, *Can the European Court of Human Rights Shape European Public Order?* (Cambridge University Press 2022)
Derek Fincham, 'The Parthenon Sculptures and Cultural Justice' (2013) 23 Fordham Intellectual Property, Media and Entertainment Law Journal 943
Gerald Fitzmaurice, 'The Law and Procedure of the International Court of Justice, 1951-4: Questions of Jurisdiction, Competence and Procedure' (1958) 34 British Year Book of International Law 1
Steven Gallagher, 'Museums and the Return of Human Remains: An Equitable Solution?' (2010) 17 (1) International Journal of Cultural Property 65
Chiara Giorgetti, *The Selection and Removal of Arbitrators in Investor-State Dispute Settlement* (Brill 2019)
Christine Gray, *Judicial Remedies in International Law* (Oxford University Press 1987)
Christine Gray and Benedict Kingsbury, 'Developments in Dispute Settlement: Inter-State Arbitration Since 1945' (1992) 63 (1) British Yearbook of International Law 97
Jeanette Greenfield, *The Return of Cultural Treasures* (3rd edn, Cambridge University Press 2007)
Gilbert Guillaume, 'The Use of Precedent by International Judges and Arbitrators' (2011) 2 (1) Journal of International Dispute Settlement 5
Rosalyn Higgins, 'Time and the Law: International Perspectives on an Old Problem' (1997) 46 International and Comparative Law Quarterly 501
Manley O Hudson, *International Tribunals* (CEIP and Brookings Institution 1944)
Robert Jennings, 'General Course on Principles of International Law' (1967) 121 Recueil des cours 324
Philip Jessup, 'Intervention in the International Court' (1981) 75 American Journal of International Law 903
Hege Elisabeth Kjos, *Applicable Law in Investor-State Arbitration* (Oxford University Press 2013)
Ruth Lapidoth, 'Good Offices' (2006) Max Planck Encyclopedia of Public International Law
Philip Leach, 'The European System and Approach' in Scott Sheeran and Nigel Rodley (eds), *Routledge Handbook of International Human Rights Law* (Routledge 2014)
Hersch Lauterpacht, *The Development of International Law by the International Court* (Stevens and Sons 1958)
Hersch Lauterpacht, *The Function of Law in the International Community* (Oxford University Press 2012, original publication 1933)
Ewan McKendrick and Iain Maxwell, 'Specific Performance in International Arbitration' (2013) 1 (2) Chinese Journal of Comparative Law 195
Theodor Meron, 'The Incidence of the Rule of Exhaustion of Local Remedies' (1959) 35 British Year Book of International Law 83
John Merrills, 'The Place of International Litigation' in Natalie Klein (ed), *Litigating International Law Disputes: Weighing the Options* (Cambridge University Press 2014)
John Merrills and Eric de Brabandere, *Merrills' International Dispute Settlement* (Cambridge University Press 2022)
John Henry Merryman, 'Thinking about the Elgin Marbles' (1985) 83 (8) Michigan Law Review 1881
Angelika Nussberger, *The European Court of Human Rights* (Oxford University Press 2020)
Karin Oellers-Frahm, 'Article 96 UN Charter' in Andreas Zimmermann, Christian Tomuschat, and Karin Oellers-Frahm (eds), *The Statute of the International Court of Justice: A Commentary* (2nd edn, Oxford University Press 2012)
Paolo Palchetti, 'Opening the International Court of Justice to Third States: Intervention and Beyond' (2002) 6 Max Planck Yearbook of United Nations Law 139
Jan Paulsson, 'Appointment of Arbitrators' in Schultz and Ortino in Thomas Schultz and Federico Ortino (eds), *The Oxford Handbook of International Arbitration* (Oxford University Press 2020)
Jan Paulsson, 'Moral Hazard in International Dispute Resolution' (2010) 25 (2) ICSID Review 339
Anne Peters, 'International Dispute Settlement: A Network of Cooperational Duties' (2003) 14 (1) European Journal of International Law 1

Jackson Ralston, *International Arbitration from Athens to Locarno* (The Lawbook Exchange 1929)
Isabella Risini, *The Inter-State Application under the European Convention on Human Rights* (Brill 2018)
Bernard Robertson, 'Exhaustion of Local Remedies in International Human Rights Litigation – The Burden of Proof Reconsidered' (1990) 39 International and Comparative Law Quarterly 191
Geoffrey Robertson, *Who Owns History? Elgin's Loot and the Case for Returning Plundered Treasure* (Biteback Publishing 2019)
Geoffrey Robertson, Norman Palmer, and Amal Clooney, 'The Case for Return of the Parthenon Sculptures' (31 July 2015) (unpublished report, leaked on The Guardian website)
Christa Roodt, *Private International Law, Art and Cultural Heritage* (Elgar 2015)
Jeswald W Salacuse, 'Is There a Better Way? Alternative Methods of Treaty-Based, Investor-State Dispute Resolution' (2007) 31 Fordham International Law Journal 138
Christoph Schreuer, 'Non-Pecuniary Remedies in ICSID Arbitration' (2004) 20 (4) Arbitration International 325
Christoph Schreuer and others, *The ICSID Convention: A Commentary* (2nd edn, Cambridge University Press 2009)
Shirley Scott, 'Litigation versus Dispute Resolution through Political Processes' in Natalie Klein (ed), *Litigating International Law Disputes: Weighing the Options* (Cambridge University Press 2014)
Malcolm N Shaw, *Rosenne's Law and Practice of the International Court: 1920-2015* (5th edn, Brill 2017)
Louis Sohn, 'Arbitration of International Disputes *Ex Aequo et Bono*' in Pieter Sanders (ed), *International Arbitration Liber Amicorum for Martin Domke* (Martinus Nijhoff 1967)
Alper Taşdelen, *The Return of Cultural Artefacts: Hard and Soft Law Approaches* (Springer 2016)
Gisèle Stephens-Chu, 'Is it Always All About the Money? The Appropriateness of Non-Pecuniary Remedies in Investment Treaty Arbitration' (2014) 30 (4) Arbitration International 661
Hugh Thirlway, *The International Court of Justice* (Oxford University Press 2016)
Hugh Thirlway, 'Compromis' (2006) Max Planck Encyclopedia of Public International Law
Catharine Titi, *The Function of Equity in International Law* (Oxford University Press 2021)
Catharine Titi, 'Mediation and the Settlement of Investment Disputes: Between Utopia and Realism' in Catharine Titi and Katia Fach Gómez (eds), *Mediation in International Commercial and Investment Disputes* (Oxford University Press 2019)
Peter Tomka, 'The Special Agreement' in Nisuke Andåo, Edward McWhinney, and Rüdiger Wolfrum (eds), *Liber Amicorum: Judge Shigeru Oda* (vol 1, Kluwer Law International 2002)
Christian Tomuschat, 'Article 33 UN Charter' in Andreas Zimmermann and others (eds), *The Statute of the International Court of Justice: A Commentary* (2nd edn, Oxford University Press 2012)
Santiago Torres Bernárdez, 'L'intervention dans la procédure de la Cour internationale de Justice' (1995) 256 Recueil des cours 195
Paul Turnbull, 'Scientific Theft of Remains in Colonial Australia' (2007) 11 (1) Australian Indigenous Law Review 92
Geir Ulfstein, 'Farewell to Compulsory Jurisdiction' (2023) British Yearbook of International Law (advance online publication)
United Nations, *Handbook on the Peaceful Settlement of Disputes between States* (United Nations 1992)
United Nations Conference on Trade and Development (UNCTAD), *Investor-State Disputes: Prevention and Alternatives to Arbitration* (United Nations 2010)
Laura Van den Eynde, 'Amicus Curiae: European Court of Human Rights' (2019) Max Planck Encyclopedia of Public International Law
VV Veeder, 'Inter-State Arbitration' in Thomas Schultz and Federico Ortino (eds), *The Oxford Handbook of International Arbitration* (Oxford University Press 2020)
WL Westermann, 'Interstate Arbitration in Antiquity' (1907) 2 (5) Classical Journal 197
Astrid Wiik, *Amicus Curiae before International Courts and Tribunals* (Nomos and Hart Publishing 2016)

Chapter 8
Issues of Jurisdiction and Admissibility

8.1 Introduction

The eventual capacity of an international court or tribunal to pronounce on the Parthenon marbles inevitably affects our appreciation of the legal merits of the case. This does not contradict the argument advanced in Chap. 7, according to which diplomatic, as opposed to legal, means of dispute settlement are the most appropriate, with negotiations in particular appearing as the best candidate. After all, the legal merits of the case will matter even in a negotiation. This chapter addresses three broad topics that determine precisely the capacity of a dispute settlement body to examine the case. These are questions that, in one way or another, the debate has already raised, but they are also legal questions of jurisdiction and admissibility. They are the following. First, is the Parthenon marbles case or are the questions it raises political rather than legal and is that a bar to even evaluating it from the viewpoint of international law? Surely, if the case is political, an international dispute settlement body must decline jurisdiction? Second, who is responsible for the marbles' continued retention and eventual return? Can the dispute be resolved at the intergovernmental level or should the governments relegate the matter to the two museums? To wit, does the potential obligation to return the marbles fall on the British Museum or the UK government—or both? Last, is it not a little too late for Greece to assert its claim, seeing that the marbles have resided in the British Museum for over 200 years? In other words, what are the legal effects of the passage of time? The latter question will also give us the opportunity to consider some matters related to the merits. These three sets of questions are now answered in turn.

C. Titi, *The Parthenon Marbles and International Law*,
https://doi.org/10.1007/978-3-031-26357-6_8

8.2 Existence of a 'Legal' Dispute or Question

The jurisdiction of international courts and tribunals extends in principle to 'legal' disputes or questions.[1] We can infer from the Statute of the International Court of Justice (ICJ) that 'legal' disputes or questions revolve around treaty interpretation, any question of international law, the existence of a fact that, if confirmed, would breach an international obligation, and the reparation to be made 'for the breach of an international obligation'.[2] The ICJ is habilitated by its statute to decide legal disputes in contentious proceedings[3] or to give an advisory opinion on legal questions.[4] In *Western Sahara*, the ICJ observed that the questions that had been submitted to it were 'framed in terms of law' and raised 'problems of international law'.[5] Since they were 'susceptible of a reply based on law', the Court found them to be 'questions of a legal character'.[6] According to the Court's settled jurisprudence, mixed questions of law and fact are still 'legal'. In its advisory opinion in *Continued Presence of South Africa in Namibia*, the ICJ held that

> the contingency that there may be factual issues underlying the question posed does not alter its character as a 'legal question' as envisaged in Article 96 of the Charter [of the United Nations]. The reference in this provision to legal questions cannot be interpreted as opposing legal to factual issues. Normally, to enable a court to pronounce on legal questions, it must also be acquainted with, take into account and, if necessary, make findings as to the relevant factual issues.[7]

This statement was echoed and cited in the *Western Sahara* case, where the Court reiterated that, even if it has to establish some facts, before assessing them legally, 'a mixed question of law and fact is none the less a legal question'.[8] By the same token, the 'political aspects' of a question, which are so common in international relations, do not deny the question its 'legal' nature nor do they 'deprive the Court of a competence expressly conferred on it by its Statute'.[9] Whatever the political aspects

---

[1] Titi (2021) 158-159.

[2] Statute of the ICJ art 36(2).

[3] Statute of the ICJ art 36. See also UN Charter art 36(3).

[4] UN Charter art 96; Statute of the ICJ art 65(1).

[5] *Western Sahara* (Advisory Opinion) [1975] ICJ Rep 12 [15].

[6] *Western Sahara* (Advisory Opinion) [1975] ICJ Rep 12 [15]; *Legality of the Threat or Use of Nuclear Weapons* (Advisory Opinion) [1996] ICJ Rep 226 [13]; cf Kelsen (1952) 380-382.

[7] *Legal Consequences for States of the Continued Presence of South Africa in Namibia (South West Africa) notwithstanding Security Council Resolution 276 (1970)* (Advisory Opinion) [1971] ICJ Rep 16 [40].

[8] *Western Sahara* (Advisory Opinion) [1975] ICJ Rep 12 [17]. See also *Certain Property (Liechtenstein v Germany)* (Preliminary Objections Judgment) [2005] ICJ Rep 6 [25], referring to 'complaints of fact and law'.

[9] *Legality of the Threat or Use of Nuclear Weapons* (Advisory Opinion) [1996] ICJ Rep 226 [13].

of a question, the Court cannot deny its legal character, when it is asked to assess the lawfulness of the conduct of a state in light of international law.[10]

Is then the Parthenon marbles case legal and does it raise legal questions? As Hersch Lauterpacht, former judge at the ICJ, put it 'every international dispute is of a political character', and it is an understatement that only '*some* legal questions are political'.[11] The fact that Greece is pursuing diplomatic, as opposed to legal, means is firm evidence of its willingness not to escalate the case but in no way does it deprive it of its legal character. The questions raised by the Parthenon marbles case can be political, as they are ethical, aesthetic, and so on. But they are also legal. They are questions about sovereignty, ownership, and the new international law on the return of important cultural heritage.

8.3 Questions of Attribution: British Museum and UK Government (The Interstate Nature of the Dispute)

In 2021, the Intergovernmental Committee for Promoting the Return of Cultural Property to its Countries of Origin or its Restitution in case of Illicit Appropriation (ICPRCP or Intergovernmental Committee) of the United Nations Educational, Scientific and Cultural Organization (UNESCO) expressly recognised that 'the case has an intergovernmental character' and that the responsibility for the marbles' return falls on the UK government.[12] For its part, the UK government insists that it has no say in the matter and that it is something for the British Museum to decide. As we have seen, at the time of the purchase, the government tried to distance itself from Elgin's actions. However, both Elgin's ambassadorial rank and the fact that the UK government purchased the marbles—and that with full knowledge of the facts—would suffice to transform what may otherwise have been a private matter into an interstate case. The following paragraphs do not return to these aspects but consider instead two additional reasons why the case has an interstate nature. This section argues that as a public museum the British Museum can engage the responsibility of the state and, in any case, it is up to the UK government to allow deaccessioning.

[10] *Legality of the Threat or Use of Nuclear Weapons* (Advisory Opinion) [1996] ICJ Rep 226 [13]; *Accordance with International Law of the Unilateral Declaration of Independence in Respect of Kosovo* (Advisory Opinion) [2010] ICJ Rep 403 [27]; *Admission of a State to the United Nations (Charter, Art 4)* (Advisory Opinion) [1948] ICJ Rep 57, 61; cf *Application for Review of Judgement No 158 of the United Nations Administrative Tribunal* (Advisory Opinion) [1973] ICJ Rep 172 [14].

[11] Lauterpacht (1933) 161 (emphasis added).

[12] ICPRCP, 22nd session, 27-29 September 2021, ICPRCP/21/22.COM/Decisions, Decision 22. COM 6, para 7.

8.3.1 Attribution and State Responsibility

As an entity with legal personality, the state cannot perform all its activities without the involvement of intermediaries.[13] The process by which international law determines whether the conduct of a person or any intermediary is an 'act of state' and can engage the state's international responsibility is called 'attribution'.[14] Conduct attributed to the state is 'that of its organs of government, or of others who have acted under the direction, instigation or control of those organs', that is, as state agents.[15] A caveat is necessary: the rules of attribution under the international law of state responsibility should not be confused with rules of representation; they do not concern the power of an entity to make commitments on behalf of a state.[16]

The first kind of attribution that international law recognises is structural.[17] The acts or omissions of organs of state are considered conduct of the state, whatever the functions they exercise or the position they hold within the organisation of the state.[18] State organs are not only those of the central government but also those that exercise governmental authority 'of whatever kind or classification' and 'at whatever level in the hierarchy'.[19] An organ of state includes any person or entity on whom the internal law of the state confers this status.[20] If therefore the law of England and Wales describes the British Museum as an organ of state, which as we shall see it does, then the British Museum *will* be considered a state organ under international law. In reality, domestic law is not the be-all and end-all of the matter,[21] since international law recognises that state responsibility can also arise from the conduct of de facto organs.[22] The term 'de facto organs' covers the very persons or entities that are regarded as state organs under international law, even though municipal law does not formally grant them this status.[23] The state cannot evade responsibility for the conduct of its organs simply by denying them this status in its domestic law.[24] In any event, this is not the case of the British Museum, which is identified as a state organ under domestic law.

---

13 Kelsen (2005) 290; Crawford (2013) 113; Shaw (2021) 180-181; *German Settlers in Poland* (Advisory Opinion) PCIJ Series B No 6 (10 September 1923) 22.

14 Crawford (2013) 113.

15 ILC Articles on State Responsibility, commentary, pt one, Chap. II, commentary, para 2.

16 Dolzer, Kriebaum, and Schreuer (2022) 314.

17 Crawford (2013) 127.

18 ILC Articles on State Responsibility art 4(1).

19 ILC Articles on State Responsibility, commentary, art 4, paras 6, 8.

20 ILC Articles on State Responsibility art 4(2).

21 ILC Articles on State Responsibility, commentary, art 4, para 11.

22 Crawford (2013) 124-126.

23 Palchetti (2017), para 1.

24 ILC Articles on State Responsibility, commentary, art 4, para 11.

The second kind of attribution international law recognises is functional.[25] If a person or entity is empowered by domestic law to exercise governmental authority and is actually acting in that capacity, its conduct will be attributable to the state.[26] In determining whether the conduct of an entity engages the international responsibility of the state under the functional criterion, one must take into account not only the type of authority the entity in question exercises but other elements too, such as the manner in which the powers have been conferred on it, 'the purposes for which they are to be exercised', and 'the extent to which the entity is accountable to government' for the exercise of these powers.[27] So long as the conduct of an entity relates to the exercise of governmental powers that domestic law authorises, this conduct will be attributable to the state.[28] Therefore, even if there were any doubt as to the formal status of the British Museum as a state organ under the structural criterion, if the museum acted as a state organ, its conduct would still be attributable to the state.

The third kind of attribution is based on the element of control: even when there is no attribution under the previous criteria, the actions of a person or entity will be attributed to the state, when that person or entity acts on the instructions or under the control of the state.[29]

Let us now turn to the British Museum. As a non-departmental public body (NDPB),[30] the British Museum is formally part of the state.[31] Therefore the structural criterion is satisfied and we need look no further: the British Museum is a state organ and its conduct is attributable to the state. But even if domestic law did not expressly describe the British Museum as a state organ, as an NDPB, the British Museum carries out governmental functions.[32] NDPBs operate at arm's length from ministers.[33] That said, they are no strangers to 'the process of national government' and, although not part of a government department, it is precisely a government department that typically sets the 'strategic framework' and the minister is accountable to parliament for the NDPB.[34] Like other NDPBs, the British Museum was

---

[25] Crawford (2013) 127.

[26] ILC Articles on State Responsibility art 5.

[27] ILC Articles on State Responsibility, commentary, art 5, para 6.

[28] ILC Articles on State Responsibility art 5. See further Crawford (2013) 126-132.

[29] ILC Articles on State Responsibility art 8; ILC Articles on State Responsibility, commentary, art 8; Crawford (2013) Chap. 5.

[30] See British Museum, 'Governance' https://www.britishmuseum.org/about-us/governance.

[31] United Kingdom, Cabinet Office, 'Public Bodies Handbook - Part 1, Classification of Public Bodies' (2016) 5; Glossary of public sector information and re-use terms, The National Archives 2015 https://www.nationalarchives.gov.uk/documents/information-management/glossary-of-psi-re-use-terms.pdf 4.

[32] United Kingdom, Cabinet Office, 'Public Bodies Handbook - Part 1, Classification of Public Bodies' (2016) 13.

[33] United Kingdom, Cabinet Office, 'Public Bodies Handbook - Part 1, Classification of Public Bodies' (2016) 13.

[34] United Kingdom, Cabinet Office, 'Public Bodies Handbook - Part 1, Classification of Public Bodies' (2016) 13.

established by act of parliament,[35] and it is directly accountable to the Department for Digital, Culture, Media, and Sport. Even then if the structural criterion were not satisfied, the functional criterion would be, and the British Museum's conduct would still be attributable to the UK government.

But let us go to extremes and assume that the British Museum did not have the status of a state organ under domestic law and did not exercise governmental functions. The British Museum receives funding from the Department for Digital, Culture, Media, and Sport, known as grant-in-aid.[36] In the 2020/2021 financial year (April 2020 to March 2021), this funding amounted to £65.4 million grant-in-aid.[37] With a total expenditure of £76.6 million for the same financial year, grant-in-aid covered more than 85% of the museum's expenditure.[38]

But it is not only that the state controls the purse strings. The majority of the museum's trustees are appointed by the executive. The British Museum comprises twenty-five trustees, of whom fifteen are appointed by the prime minister, one is appointed by the crown, four are appointed by the secretary of state for digital, culture, media, and sport[39] on the nominations of the presidents of the Royal Society, the Royal Academy, the British Academy, and the Society of Antiquaries of London, and five are appointed by the trustees of the British Museum.[40] The director is appointed by the trustees with the prime minister's approval, and his salary is determined by the Treasury.[41] As for the chair, he is elected by the board of trustees from among its members.[42] The current chair, Osborne, is a former Chancellor of the Exchequer. His 2021 appointment was announced amid growing concern that government is 'trying to manipulate the governance of Britain's national museums'

[35] An Act for the Purchase of the Museum, or Collection of Sir Hans Sloane, and of the Harleian Collection of Manuscripts; and for providing One General Repository for the better Reception and more convenient Use of the said Collections; and of the Cottonian Library, and of the Additions thereto, 1753: 26 George 2 c 22 (British Museum Act 1753).

[36] Grant-in-aid is '[a] sum of money provided to an organisation to be applied in general support for the objectives of that organisation. A payment by a government department – usually referred to as the "sponsor department" – to finance all or part of the costs of the body in receipt of the grant in aid. Grant in aid is paid where the government has decided, subject to Parliamentary controls, that the recipient body should operate at arm's length', Government Grants Definitions https://assets.publishing.service.gov.uk/government/uploads/system/uploads/attachment_data/file/654680/2017-09-27_Grant_Definitions.pdf.

[37] British Museum, 'Report and Accounts for the Year Ended 31 March 2021' (2021) 15, 39.

[38] British Museum, 'Report and Accounts for the Year Ended 31 March 2021' (2021) 15, 39.

[39] British Museum, 'Board of Trustees' https://www.britishmuseum.org/about-us/governance.

[40] British Museum Act 1963 s 1(1).

[41] British Museum Act 1963 s 6.

[42] British Museum, 'Board of Trustees' https://www.britishmuseum.org/about-us/governance.

in order to align it with ministerial agendas.[43] Government has shown an avowed interest in the composition of museum boards.[44]

The 'arm's length' approach is meant to allow national museums a certain margin of independence from the relevant ministry and shield them from succumbing to pressure. An example that springs to mind, though arguably unlikely to be repeated in the United Kingdom today, is that of the Soviet art sales under Stalin in the late 1920s and early 1930s in order to increase liquidity. The sales depleted the Hermitage collection and brought Dutch, Italian and Spanish old masters to the United States.[45]

In reality, the arm's length model is being put to the test time and again. It is said that, typically, the body directs its arm, and 'all that is gained by an arm's length is a certain notion of removal of directly traceable control'.[46] But control is there. Consider the September 2021 letter from the culture secretary Dowden on contested heritage sent to a number of top UK publicly funded museums, stating in no uncertain terms that

> the Government *does not support the removal of statues or other similar objects*. . . . I would expect Arm's Length Bodies' approach to issues of contested heritage to be consistent with the Government's position. . . . The significant support that you receive from the taxpayer is an acknowledgement of the important cultural role you play for the entire country. It is imperative that you continue to act impartially, in line with your publicly funded status, and not in a way that brings this into question. This is especially important as we enter a challenging Comprehensive Spending Review, in which all government spending will rightly be scrutinised.[47]

The meaning of 'impartially' in this context is not obvious. The letter essentially asked national museums to toe the line and ensure that their policies match government targets or else the government might tighten the purse strings. It is difficult to act 'impartially' (or independently) in such circumstances, which confirms that the British Museum would be an organ of state, even if domestic law did not already grant it that status, and even if it did not function as a state organ. It operates under the direction and control of the state, a fact further stressed by the topic to which we will now turn: the ban on deaccession.

---

[43] Mark Brown, 'George Osborne Appointed Chair of British Museum', The Guardian (24 June 2021); Dan Hicks, 'Does George Osborne at the British Museum Signal a Dangerous Blow to the Arts?' (25 June 2021) https://bit.ly/3MypOiQ.

[44] E.g. Oliver Dowden, 'Comment: We Won't Allow Britain's History to Be Cancelled', The Telegraph (15 May 2021). For a similar comment, see Dan Hicks, 'Does George Osborne at the British Museum Signal a Dangerous Blow to the Arts?' (25 June 2021) https://bit.ly/3MypOiQ.

[45] Williams (1979).

[46] Charlotte Higgins, 'An Atmosphere of Threat Lingers over the Arts – and it's Created by the Government', The Guardian (6 December 2021).

[47] Letter from the Culture Secretary Oliver Dowden on HM Government Position on Contested Heritage INT2020/19838/DC (22 September 2020) https://www.gov.uk/government/publications/letter-from-culture-secretary-on-hm-government-position-on-contested-heritage (emphasis in original).

8.3.2 The Ban on Deaccession Revisited

There is an additional compelling reason why the continued retention of the marbles in the British Museum is attributable to the UK government. The fact of the matter is that, in principle, even had the British Museum wished to return the marbles to Greece, it would not be allowed to do so, unless it used the loophole of the 'unfit' object. However, this is not how either the government or the museum have interpreted the term 'unfit'.[48] Thus far, the marbles' return appears to have been made almost impossible under English law. The British Museum Act 1816 vested the marbles in the trustees of the museum 'in perpetuity'. The British Museum Act 1963 prevents the museum from deaccessioning them. Ultimately, it is the government that must take the decision to return the marbles.

The matter of deaccessioning and whether it should be decided by government or museums was raised in October 2022 in a debate in the House of Lords, with a question brought by Vaizey.[49] Although nominally the question concerned whether the government intended to review the National Heritage Act 1983, which prevents other museums from deaccessioning but not the British Museum, in reality, the debate it opened also concerned the British Museum Act 1963, as well as the new Charities Act 2022. The Charities Act 2022 will allow museum trustees to deaccession items in their collections on ethical grounds.[50] The relevant sections of the act were due to be implemented in autumn 2022, but their commencement is now delayed; the sections are officially 'under further consideration prior to commencement'.[51] Even under that act, deaccessioning of highly valued cultural objects will not only depend on the museum but will also require the approval of the Charity Commission, the attorney general, or a court.[52] In the debate, the government's answer was that there were no plans to amend the National Heritage Act 1983.

The idea that the decision on deaccessioning should lie with government has previously been supported by MacGregor. Discussing whether museums can retain cultural objects obtained in colonial times (he steered clear of the topic of the marbles) in a context of extreme power inequality, he argued that this is a question to be answered *by governments* and that museum curators do not have the competence to do so.[53] This is a far cry from—indeed, a turnaround on—what he said in an internal memo in 2002: 'I shall urge the Secretary of State to be extremely firm on the point that discussions be held only between museums. If once HM Government intervenes in a matter of this sort, the precedents for Egypt, Iraq, Nigeria etc. become

[48] But see Chap. 6, text to nn 320-325.

[49] Hansard (2022).

[50] See Chap. 10, text to nn 206-209.

[51] Charities Act 2022 s 41(4). See also UK Government, Guidance, 'Charities Act 2022: Implementation Plan' (updated 14 October 2022).

[52] Charities Act 2022 s 16(1).

[53] MacGregor (2021) 191-192.

uncontrollable.'[54] There is of course a different view, and that is that if museum directors 'are responsible enough to be appointed, then surely they should be considered responsible enough to make decisions on the return of objects'.[55]

In the case of the Parthenon marbles, as things stand, the UK government needs to take a legal step before the British Museum can deaccession them. That said, the museum's approach of washing its hands of the repatriation debate is unhelpful: museums too have a responsibility and the British Museum becomes increasingly isolated in its point-blank refusal to genuinely consider requests for repatriations.

8.3.3 Attribution to the UK Government

The British Museum and the UK government have passed the buck to each other in order to refuse the repatriation of the Parthenon marbles. In November 2021, when the Greek prime minister, Mitsotakis, raised the issue of the Parthenon marbles' return during an official state visit to the United Kingdom, the British prime minister, Johnson, 'reiterated the United Kingdom's long-standing position that this matter is one for the trustees of the British Museum'.[56] However, as we have seen, this is *not* primarily a matter for the trustees of the British Museum, who, even had they wished to deaccession the Parthenon marbles, would have some difficulty doing so before the UK government reviews the applicable legislation to that effect. Things may change with the new Charities Act 2022, as and when section 16, whose commencement is currently delayed, comes into force.

In conclusion, as this part of the chapter has shown, responsibility for the return of the marbles rests both with the British Museum and the UK government. However, the museum (which admittedly has shown no appetite for returning the marbles) does in principle need enabling legislation to be legally able to deaccession them and repatriate them to Athens. The only possible conclusion then is that the *primary* responsibility lies at the moment of writing with the UK government.

[54] Chris Hastings, 'Revealed: How Rowdy Schoolboys Knocked a Leg off one of the Elgin Marbles', The Telegraph (15 May 2005).

[55] Hansard (2022).

[56] UK Government, 'PM meeting with PM Mitsotakis of Greece: 16 November 2021' (Press release, 16 November 2021).

8.4 Legal Effects of the Lapse of Time (including Issues related to the Merits)

It is said that our understanding of the 'legitimacy' of the British Museum's possession of the marbles 'rests on two uneasy principles: the idea that a great deal of time has passed, and that long possession, even if it was illicit, creates a superior legal and moral right to the British retention of the sculptures'.[57] The passage of time alone does not make a bad title good. But it does mean that the objection might be raised that it has been too long for Greece to now be able to pursue the return of the marbles.

In contrast with municipal legal systems, international law contains no statute of limitations and lays down no fixed time-bars for bringing a claim.[58] This simple truth was recognised by Merryman, although he appeared to confound the standing of the dispute under *international* and *national* law.[59] Merryman expressed the view that the lapse of time 'inevitably has an effect, and all legal systems recognize this fact in rules of prescription'.[60] He added that, although international law has of course no statute of limitations, 'the same considerations apply'.[61] Then he turned his attention to the national level and argued that 'the Greeks have lost any right of action they might have had for the recovery of the Marbles before an English court', since under English law, the dispute would be time-barred.[62] He thus appeared to contend that Greece's claim *under international law* is barred, because the time limit of the English statute of limitations has expired.[63]

There is no prescription in international law in the way that we understand prescription in domestic legal systems. That Greece did not resort to English courts in the early nineteenth century, at a time when it was not even an independent state, is irrelevant to its capacity to pursue the return of the marbles under international law today. International law does not impose time-bars for bringing a claim but it recognises some circumstances in which a claim may become inadmissible. To

---

[57] Fincham (2013) 1001.

[58] *Certain Phosphate Lands in Nauru (Nauru v Australia)* (Preliminary Objections Judgment) [1992] ICJ Rep 240 [32]; *Gentini* (1903) 10 RIAA 551, 558; ILC Articles on State Responsibility, commentary, art 45, para 9.

[59] Merryman (1985) 1900-1901.

[60] Merryman (1985) 1900.

[61] Merryman (1985) 1900.

[62] Merryman (1985) 1901.

[63] Strictly speaking, Merryman did not actually say this. However, this is the received impression when one reads his article. Another author has interpreted Merryman's argument to be precisely this, that because Greece did not respect the English statute of limitations, it has lost its right to bring the claim to an international court, see Robertson (2019), Chap. 5 (unnumbered page).

understand these circumstances, we must turn to four interrelated concepts: waiver, estoppel, acquiescence, and extinctive prescription.[64]

However, before we do, two clarifications are necessary. First, while prescription under domestic law the way Merryman discussed it (that is, as a matter of compliance with procedural rules for bringing claims) would be a matter of jurisdiction and admissibility, under international law, the concepts that are the focus of this section would not necessarily function as jurisdictional or admissibility objections. In fact, some of them would be matters of substance to be joined to the merits. It is certain, for example, that acquiescence or estoppel will not affect the ICJ's discretion to exercise its advisory jurisdiction but, if relevant, they may and should be addressed with the merits. They could even form part of the question put to the Court. For instance, the Court could be asked to give an opinion on whether the passage of time means that Greece has abandoned its claim to the marbles. The Court would then examine such a question as a matter of substance.

The second clarification concerns human rights proceedings. Exceptionally, the fact that the removal of the marbles occurred more than two centuries ago, may prevent a particular court, the European Court of Human Rights, from assuming jurisdiction. Article 35 of the European Convention on Human Rights, which that court is bound to apply, imposes a time limit of 4 months for bringing a claim, applicable both to individual and interstate claims.[65] Despite the continued retention of the marbles, it is unclear whether the Court would accept to hear the case. In individual disputes, the European Court of Human Rights has recognised that, when the alleged violation constitutes a continuing situation and no local remedies are available, the time limit does not run.[66] Yet the same Court has stressed the duty of diligence in pursuing a claim, even in the case of continuing violations.[67] In *Syllogos ton Athinaion v United Kingdom*, which was an *individual* application for the return of the Parthenon marbles, the Court observed that, since the marbles' removal had taken place 'some 150 years before the Convention was drafted and ratified by the respondent State, the applicant's complaints would appear to be inadmissible as incompatible *ratione temporis* with the provisions of the Convention'.[68] But then the Court added that '[e]ven assuming that the continued retention of the Marbles constitutes a continuing act', it would have to dismiss the claim on different

[64] Despite the confident distinction sometimes drawn in the literature, which also informs this section for heuristic purposes, these are overlapping concepts.

[65] E.g. *Slovenia v Croatia*, App no 54155/16, Decision (18 November 2020) [40].

[66] E.g. *Varnava and others v Turkey*, App nos 16064/90-16073/90, Judgment (Merits and Just Satisfaction) (18 September 2009) [159]; *Iordache v Romania*, App no 6817/02 Judgment (14 October 2008) [50].

[67] E.g. *Sokolov and others v Serbia*, App no 30859/10 and others, Decision (14 January 2014) [31]-[36]; *Varnava and others v Turkey*, App nos 16064/90-16073/90, Judgment (Merits and Just Satisfaction) (18 September 2009) [159]-[172]; cf *Syllogos ton Athinaion v United Kingdom*, App no 48259/15, Decision (23 June 2016).

[68] *Syllogos ton Athinaion v United Kingdom*, App no 48259/15, Decision (23 June 2016).

grounds.[69] In conclusion, an application to the European Court of Human Rights may still be possible, but it may also prove to be time-barred.

Bearing in mind that this is the exception and that it would have no impact on the capacity of other dispute settlement bodies, including the ICJ, to consider the case, let us now turn to the rule and the four concepts of waiver, estoppel, acquiescence, and extinctive prescription.

8.4.1 Waiver

Expression of the principle of consent,[70] a waiver is the renunciation by an injured state of a right or claim.[71] If an injured state validly waives a right or claim, it is prevented from invoking the international responsibility of the state that allegedly injured it.[72] Although some of the case law has insisted on the need for the waiver to be express,[73] it is often accepted that a waiver may also be inferred from state conduct on condition that it be unequivocal (implied waiver).[74] It is, however, unclear how an implied waiver is to be distinguished from the closely-related concept of acquiescence and whether an attempt to even draw a distinction between the two is necessary.[75] Given the overlap between implied waiver and acquiescence and the fact that acquiescence will be considered below (see Sect. 8.4.3), it is sufficient to note that Greece has not waived its right to the missing marbles nor has it waived its claim.

[69] *Syllogos ton Athinaion v United Kingdom*, App no 48259/15, Decision (23 June 2016).

[70] ILC Articles on State Responsibility, commentary, art 45, para 2.

[71] Crawford (2013) 70.

[72] ILC Articles on State Responsibility art 45.

[73] *Certain Norwegian Loans (France v Norway)* (Preliminary Objections Judgment) [1957] ICJ Rep 9, 26 ('Abandonment cannot be presumed or inferred; it must be declared expressly').

[74] ILC Articles on State Responsibility, commentary, art 45, para 5. However, contrast para 6, where the only possibility envisaged is that of an 'explicit' waiver. See also Crawford (2013) 71; Tams (2010) 1038; *Affaire de l'indemnité russe (Russie, Turquie)* (1912) 11 RIAA 421, 446; *Certain Phosphate Lands in Nauru (Nauru v Australia)* (Preliminary Objections Judgment) [1992] ICJ Rep 240 [13], where the Court eventually rejected the objection based on an implied waiver [72]; *Armed Activities on the Territory of the Congo (Democratic Republic of the Congo v Uganda)* (Judgment) [2005] ICJ Rep 168 [293] ('waivers or renunciations of claims or rights must either be express or unequivocally implied from the conduct of the State alleged to have waived or renounced its right'), where the Court also eventually rejected the objection based on the alleged waiver [293].

[75] Crawford (2013) 72, 559; Tams (2010) 1044.

8.4.2 Estoppel

Estoppel is an expression of the Latin slogan *non concedit venire contra factum proprium*; it is a prohibition of contradicting one's behaviour.[76] This is a consequence of the need for consistency and predictability in international legal relations.[77] International law protects a state's legitimate expectations that the conduct of another state has created.[78] Yet estoppel does not protect *all* legitimate expectations.[79] In order for a representation made by a state to give rise to legitimate expectations, it must be clear and unequivocal, unconditional, and voluntary; it must emanate from a competent authority; the state to which the representation was made must have relied on it in good faith; and this reliance must have caused it some prejudice.[80] According to dissenting Judge Spender in the *Temple of Preah Vihear* case,

---

[76]Titi (2021) 165. See also *Case Concerning the Factory at Chorzów* (Claim for Indemnity – Merits) PCIJ Series A No 17 (13 September 1928) 31; *Legal Status of Eastern Greenland (Denmark v Norway)* (Judgment) PCIJ Series A/B No 53 (5 April 1933) 69-71.

[77]MacGibbon (1958) 468-469; Franck and Sughrue (1993) 566; Wagner (1986) 1779; Brown (1996) 384.

[78]Cottier and Müller (2007), para 1; Kolb (2006) 833; *Delimitation of the Maritime Boundary in the Bay of Bengal (Bangladesh/Myanmar)* (Judgment) [2012] ITLOS Rep 4 [124].

[79]Brown (1996) 397-398.

[80]Titi (2021) 165-168; Bowett (1957) 188-194; Cottier and Müller (2007), para 3; Das (1997) 611; contrast MacGibbon (1958) 473-475. For some of the case law, see *Aguilar-Amory and Royal Bank of Canada claims (Great Britain v Costa Rica)* (1923) 1 RIAA 369 (*Tinoco* case) 383-384; *Case concerning the payment of various Serbian Loans issued in France*, PCIJ Series A No 20 (12 July 1929) 39; *Legal Status of Eastern Greenland (Denmark v Norway)* (Judgment) PCIJ Series A/B No 53 (5 April 1933) 72; *Delimitation of the Maritime Boundary in the Bay of Bengal (Bangladesh/Myanmar)* (Judgment) [2012] ITLOS Rep 4 [124]; *Delimitation of the Maritime Boundary in the Gulf of Maine Area* (Judgment) [1984] ICJ Rep 246 [130]; *Case concerning the Temple of Preah Vihear (Cambodia v Thailand)* (Separate Opinion Fitzmaurice) [1962] ICJ Rep 52, 63; *Land, Island and Maritime Frontier Dispute (El Salvador/Honduras), Application to Intervene* (Judgment) [1990] ICJ Rep 92 [63]; *North Sea Continental Shelf* (Judgment) [1969] ICJ Rep 3; *Case concerning the Arbitral Award made by the King of Spain on 23 December 1906* (Judgment) [1960] ICJ Rep 192, 195-213 (relying on both estoppel and acquiescence); *Barcelona Traction, Light and Power Company* (Judgment) [1964] ICJ Rep 6, 24-25; *Flegenheimer* (1958) 14 RIAA 327, 381-382; *Chagos Marine Protected Area Arbitration (Mauritius v United Kingdom)*, PCA Case No 2011-03, Award, 18 March 2015 [435]ff. Estoppel has also been addressed in numerous investment awards, e.g. *Amco Asia Corporation and others v Indonesia*, ICSID Case No ARB/81/1, Decision on Jurisdiction, 25 September 1983 [47.5]-[47.6]; *Pope & Talbot v Canada*, UNCITRAL, Interim Award, 26 June 2000 [111]; *Canfor Corporation and others v United States*, UNCITRAL, Order of the Consolidation Tribunal, 7 September 2005 [168]; *Duke Energy International Peru Investments No 1 v Peru*, ICSID Case No ARB/03/28, Award, 18 August 2008 [231], [249]-[250]; *Yukos Universal (Isle of Man) v Russia*, PCA Case No 2005-04/AA227, Interim Award on Jurisdiction and Admissibility, 30 November 2009 [287]-[288]; *Nova Scotia Power Incorporated v Venezuela*, PCA Case No 2009-14, Award on Jurisdiction, 22 April 2010 [141]-[143]; *Mobil Exploration and Development Argentina and Mobil Argentina v Argentina*, ICSID Case No ARB/04/16, Decision on Jurisdiction and Liability, 10 Apr 2013 [228]; *Mamidoil Jetoil Greek Petroleum Products v Albania*, ICSID Case No ARB/11/24, Award, 30 March 2015 [469]; *Vestey*

> the principle operates to prevent a State contesting before the Court a situation contrary to a clear and unequivocal representation previously made by it to another State, either expressly or impliedly, on which representation the other State was, in the circumstances, entitled to rely and in fact did rely, and as a result that other State has been prejudiced or the State making it has secured some benefit or advantage for itself.[81]

Judge Spender reasoned that there had been no 'clear and unequivocal representation', nor was there any evidence of detriment in that case.[82] That said, the Court's reasoning in *Temple of Preah Vihear* relied on both estoppel and acquiescence,[83] and acquiescence does not in fact require a clear and unequivocal representation nor does it require detriment.

So can an estoppel objection be raised against the Greek claim? Greece has not made a clear and unequivocal representation to the United Kingdom that it will not ask for the marbles, and it has not created a legitimate expectation in the United Kingdom to that effect. The opposite is true. Greece has shown by every means at its disposal that it will not stop asking for the marbles. Even in the hypothetical case that it had made such a representation, the element of detrimental reliance on the representation would be missing. The requirements for an objection based on estoppel are not met.

8.4.3 Acquiescence

Expression of yet another Latin slogan, '*qui tacet consentit*', acquiescence stands for the proposition that silence or inaction in circumstances that require some kind of reaction creates legal effects.[84] Although acquiescence is implied in the passage of

Group v Venezuela, ICSID Case No. ARB/06/4, Award, 15 April 2016 [257]; *Pac Rim Cayman v El Salvador*, ICSID Case No ARB/09/12, Award, 14 October 2016 [8.47]; *UAB E energija (Lithuania) v Latvia*, ICSID Case No ARB/12/33, Award, 22 December 2017 [532]; *Chevron Corporation and Texaco Petroleum Corporation v Ecuador*, PCA Case No 2009-23, Second Partial Award on Track II, 30 August 2018 [7.88]-[7.114]; *Oded Besserglik v Mozambique*, ICSID Case No ARB (AF)/14/2, Award, 28 October 2019 [426].

[81] *Case concerning the Temple of Preah Vihear (Cambodia v Thailand)* (Separate Opinion Spender) [1962] ICJ Rep 101, 143-144.

[82] *Case concerning the Temple of Preah Vihear (Cambodia v Thailand)* (Separate Opinion Spender) [1962] ICJ Rep 101, 142.

[83] Titi (2021) 166.

[84] MacGibbon (1954) 143; Antunes (2006), para 6; Titi (2021) 168. See further *Fisheries Case (United Kingdom v Norway)* (Judgment) (1951) ICJ Rep 116, 139; *Grisbådarna (Norway v Sweden)*, PCA Case No 1908-01, Award, 23 October 1909, 6-7. Acquiescence has also been considered in investment arbitrations in relation to investors' alleged failure to object to regulatory changes affecting their investment, e.g. *Ronald Lauder v Czech Republic*, Final Award, 3 September 2001 [271]-[273]; *Siemens v Argentina*, ICSID Case No ARB/02/8, Award, 17 January 2007 [306]; *MCI Power Group and New Turbine v Ecuador*, ICSID Case No. ARB/03/6, 31 July 2007 [302]; *Joseph C Lemire v Ukraine*, ICSID Case No ARB/06/18, Dissenting Opinion Voss (Award), 1 March 2011 [153]-[161]; *AES Corporation and Tau Power v Kazakhstan*, ICSID Case No

time, in reality, it is the conduct of the state whose silence or inaction is relevant that gives rise to acquiescence.[85] The mere lapse of time is not enough.[86] What matters is that the state fails to assert a claim over time, although in the circumstances some action, the assertion of the claim, would have been called for.[87]

Acquiescence can function as a form of estoppel or waiver, where silence or inaction is viewed as a representation to the effect that a state has waived a right or claim.[88] Although sometimes the distinction drawn between acquiescence and estoppel stresses that acquiescence is a unilateral act, while estoppel requires detrimental reliance by another state,[89] in reality, the dividing line between the two concepts is not as clear-cut.[90]

To take just one example from the case law, in the *Temple of Preah Vihear* case, the ICJ considered acquiescence to decide on the sovereignty of the territory surrounding the temple. Thailand had contended that a map published on behalf of a mixed delimitation commission that showed the temple to be in Cambodia had no binding character and that Thailand had never accepted it or, if it did accept it, it was on the basis of a 'mistaken belief' that the map corresponded correctly to the watershed line.[91] The Court found that, although when initially published the map was not binding, Thailand's subsequent conduct showed that it accepted the boundary drawn on the map.[92] In other words, Thailand had acquiesced to the frontier line that situated the temple in Cambodia.[93]

Greece never did acquiesce to the removal of the marbles nor has it acquiesced in the British Museum's or the United Kingdom's ownership of the marbles. As we saw in Chap. 6, this fact is readily admitted by the trustees of the British Museum when they explain why they cannot loan the marbles to Greece.[94] Greece has not stopped

---

ARB/10/16, Award, 1 November 2013 [235]-[237]; *NextEra Energy Global Holdings and NextEra Energy Spain Holdings v Spain*, ICSID Case No. ARB/14/11, Decision on Jurisdiction, Liability and Quantum Principles, 12 March 2019 [269].

[85] Crawford (2019) 408; Crawford (2013) 559.

[86] Crawford (2013) 559-562.

[87] Crawford (2013) 559. See also *Fisheries Case (United Kingdom v Norway)* (Judgment) (1951) ICJ Rep 116, 139; ILC Articles on State Responsibility, commentary, art 45, paras 6, 9, 11.

[88] *Case concerning the Temple of Preah Vihear (Cambodia v Thailand)* (Separate Opinion Fitzmaurice) [1962] ICJ Rep 52, 62-63; MacGibbon (1954) 147; Schwarzenberger (1955) 257; Bowett (1957) 199-202; Wagner (1986) 1783; Franck (1993) 68; Titi (2021) 169.

[89] Crawford (2019) 408. See also *Gulf of Maine Delimitation of the Maritime Boundary in the Gulf of Maine Area* (Judgment) [1984] ICJ Rep 246 [130].

[90] Titi (2021) 169; Tams (2010) 1045; Antunes (2006), paras 6, 23; cf *Gulf of Maine Delimitation of the Maritime Boundary in the Gulf of Maine Area* (Judgment) [1984] ICJ Rep 246 [129].

[91] *Case concerning the Temple of Preah Vihear (Cambodia v Thailand)* (Merits Judgment) [1962] ICJ Rep 6, 21.

[92] *Case concerning the Temple of Preah Vihear (Cambodia v Thailand)* (Merits Judgment) [1962] ICJ Rep 6, 21 and 32-33.

[93] Titi (2021) 170.

[94] See Sect. 6.3.3.4.

asking for the marbles. Its claim has come to be regarded as 'perennial', including by the UK government.

8.4.4 Extinctive Prescription

Extinctive prescription results from unreasonable delay in the presentation of a claim, when this delay causes a disadvantage to the respondent.[95] In *Certain Phosphate Lands in Nauru*, the ICJ recognised that delay on the part of an applicant state may render a claim inadmissible.[96] However, for this to happen, the mere passage of time is not enough.[97] Since international law does not specify a particular time limit for bringing a claim, it is 'for the Court to determine in the light of the circumstances of each case whether the passage of time renders an application inadmissible'.[98] That means that the parallel with limitation periods in domestic law, such as the one drawn by Merryman, is inaccurate, since domestic law does lay down specific time limits.[99] In international law, extinctive prescription may only bar a claim if the delay has actually caused prejudice or 'procedural unfairness' to the defendant.[100] This was endorsed in *Stevenson* in the following passage.

> When a claim is internationally presented for the first time after a long lapse of time, there arise both a presumption and a fact. The presumption, more or less strong according to the attending circumstances, is that there is some lack of honesty in the claim, either that there was never a basis for it or that it has been paid. The fact is that by the delay in making the claim the opposing party – in this case the Government – is prevented from accumulating the evidence on its part which would oppose the claim, and on this fact arises another presumption that it could have been adduced. In such a case the delay of the claimant, if it did not establish the presumption just referred to, would work injustice and inequity in its relation to the respondent Government.[101]

Where neither prejudice nor procedural unfairness to the respondent are shown to have resulted from the lapse of time, the claim is unlikely to be held inadmissible on that ground.[102] For extinctive prescription to apply then, the following cumulative conditions must be met: there must have been negligence on the part of the claimant;

[95] Wouters and Verhoeven (2008), para 4; King (1934); Institut de droit international (1925).

[96] *Certain Phosphate Lands in Nauru (Nauru v Australia)* (Preliminary Objections Judgment) [1992] ICJ Rep 240 [32].

[97] Crawford (2013) 561.

[98] *Certain Phosphate Lands in Nauru (Nauru v Australia)* (Preliminary Objections Judgment) [1992] ICJ Rep 240 [32].

[99] Crawford (2013) 561.

[100] Crawford (2013) 561. See also *Gentini* (1903) 10 RIAA 551, 558; cf ILC Articles on State Responsibility, commentary, art 45, paras 6-11, discussing the effects of the lapse of time in the context of *acquiescence*.

[101] *Stevenson* (1903) 9 RIAA 385, 386.

[102] Crawford (2013) 562.

this negligence must have led to an unreasonable delay in presenting a claim (if a state brings a claim in a timely manner but then delays pursuing it, there is no extinctive prescription); and the respondent suffers a disadvantage.[103] Long lapse of time creates a presumption of negligence, but this presumption is rebuttable.[104] Extinctive prescription is not admitted when the respondent has a record of the facts.[105] The respondent must be placed at a disadvantage *in establishing its defence*,[106] so that if there is 'a clear record of the facts, or if the facts are admitted', there can be no prescription.[107] This is in line with the rationale of the plea of prescription, which has been described as finding 'its foundation in the highest equity – the avoidance of possible injustice to the defendant'.[108] The objection of the lapse of time is rejected if the respondent fails to prove that it suffered any prejudice,[109] for example when the contested actions have been the object of public and parliamentary scrutiny from the first, as in the case of the acquisition of the Parthenon marbles, and therefore the defendant state has been 'in a position to collect and preserve evidence' relating to the claim.[110]

When considering the Parthenon marbles case in light of these conditions, it becomes immediately obvious that extinctive prescription cannot be relevant to it. For a start, the assumption of delay is incorrect. Chapter 5 has documented Greece's unrelenting demands for the return of the marbles in the course of the 200 years since Elgin removed them from the Acropolis. Greece presented its claim for the first time soon after acquiring its independence. The 'absence of a record of facts' is not true either. First, we have the select committee report and numerous surviving letters and historical accounts. Second, the UK government could not in good faith invoke the absence of a record of facts, such as due to the impossibility of talking to witnesses, since in 1816, the parliamentary select committee drafted its report showing disregard for such witnesses, including the account offered by its own ambassadors who succeeded Elgin. Similarly, the statement that the lapse of time means that 'no documents, in particular the various firmans, exist in the original'[111] is moot: the various firmans did not exist in the original even at the

[103] King (1934) 87; Hobér (2001) 285, 334.

[104] King (1934) 89.

[105] King (1934) 88. See also *Tagliaferro case (of a general nature)* (1903) 10 RIAA 592, 593.

[106] King (1934) 90; Wouters and Verhoeven (2008), para 6. See also *Case of John H Williams v Venezuela* (Decision of the Commissioner, Mr Little) (1885) 29 RIAA 279, 291-292; *Case of Ann Eulogia Garcia Cadiz (Loretta G Barberie) v Venezuela* (Opinion of the Commissioner, Mr Findlay) (1885) 29 RIAA 293, 298; *Case of Amos B Corwin v Venezuela (The schooner Mechanic case)* (Decision of the Commissioner, Mr Little) (1885) 29 RIAA 260, 269.

[107] King (1934) 90. See also *Case of John H Williams v Venezuela, decision of the Commissioner, Mr Little* (1885) 29 RIAA 279, 292.

[108] *Gentini* (1903) 10 RIAA 551, 558.

[109] ILC Articles on State Responsibility, commentary, art 45, para 8.

[110] ILC Articles on State Responsibility, commentary, art 45, para 8.

[111] This statement is made in Neils (2001) 240. However, this does not prevent that author from taking an unambiguous position in favour of the marbles' restitution, ibid Chap. 8.

time of events—the principal witnesses were unable to produce them for the select committee investigation. Finally, there is nothing to show that the UK government is placed at a disadvantage, procedural or other, even if there had been a delay. In short, the argument that the claim is time-barred is untenable.

8.5 Conclusion

Under the heading of jurisdiction and admissibility, this chapter has reviewed three crucial topics. It has determined that the case of the Parthenon marbles, while certainly being political, is also legal and raises legal questions. In light of this, it makes sense to move beyond the debate and view the case through the prism of international law. The chapter considered the rules of attribution of state responsibility and showed that, just as UNESCO's ICPRCP stated in 2021, the case is intergovernmental in nature. There are many reasons for this, but this chapter focused on two: the British Museum's status as an NDPB and therefore as an organ of state whose conduct is attributable to the United Kingdom and the fact that the UK government needs to pass legislation to allow the British Museum to deaccession the marbles. Finally, the chapter assessed the legal effects of the passage of time, seeing that the marbles have now been in the British Museum for so long. It examined waiver, estoppel, acquiescence, and extinctive prescription and found that none of them are relevant to the Parthenon marbles case, meaning that Greece has not legally lost its capacity to assert its claim for the return of the marbles under international law.

References

Nuno Sérgio Marques Antunes, 'Acquiescence' (2006) MaxPlanckEPIL

DW Bowett, 'Estoppel before International Tribunals and its Relation to Acquiescence' (1957) 33 British Yearbook of International Law 176

Christopher Brown, 'A Comparative and Critical Assessment of Estoppel in International Law' (1996) 50 University of Miami Law Review 369

Thomas Cottier and Jörg Paul Müller, 'Estoppel' (2007) Max Planck Encyclopedia of Public International Law

James Crawford, *Brownlie's Principles of Public International Law* (9th edn, Oxford University Press 2019)

James Crawford, *State Responsibility* (Oxford University Press 2013)

Hans Das, 'Estoppel et l'acquisescement' (1997) 30 Revue belge de droit international 607

Rudolf Dolzer, Ursula Kriebaum, and Christoph Schreuer, *Principles of International Investment Law* (3rd edn, Oxford University Press 2022)

Derek Fincham, 'The Parthenon Sculptures and Cultural Justice' (2013) 23 Fordham Intellectual Property, Media and Entertainment Law Journal 943

Thomas Franck, 'Fairness in the International Legal and Institutional System' (1993) 240 Recueil des cours 9

Thomas Franck and Dennis Sughrue, 'The International Role of Equity-as-Fairness' (1993) 81 Georgetown Law Journal 563

Hansard, 'House of Lords National Heritage Act 1983 Debate' (13 October 2022) (vol 824, Hansard 2022)

Kaj Hobér, *Extinctive Prescription and Applicable Law in Interstate Arbitration* (Iustus Förlag 2001)

Institut de droit international, 'La prescription libératoire en droit international public' (Rapporteurs Nicolas Politis and Charles de Visscher) (1925) 32 Yearbook of the Institut de droit international 1.

Hans Kelsen, *Pure Theory of Law* (tr Max Knight, 2nd edn, The Lawbook Exchange 1967, 2005)

Hans Kelsen, *Principles of International Law* (first published 1952, Lawbook Exchange 1959)

BE King, 'Prescription of Claims in International Law' (1934) 15 British Year Book of International Law 82

Robert Kolb, 'General Principles of Procedural Law' in Andreas Zimmermann and others (eds), *The Statute of the International Court of Justice: A Commentary* (Oxford University Press 2006)

Hersch Lauterpacht, *The Function of Law in the International Community* (Oxford University Press 2012, original publication 1933)

IC MacGibbon, 'Estoppel in International Law' (1958) 7 (3) International and Comparative Law Quarterly 468

IC MacGibbon, 'The Scope of Acquiescence in International Law' (1954) 31 British Year Book of International Law 143

Neil MacGregor, *À monde nouveau, nouveaux musées* (Hazan Louvre éditions 2021)

John Henry Merryman, 'Thinking about the Elgin Marbles' (1985) 83 (8) Michigan Law Review 1881

Jenifer Neils, *The Parthenon Frieze* (Cambridge University Press 2001)

Paolo Palchetti, 'De facto Organs of a State' (2017) Max Planck Encyclopedia of Public International Law

Geoffrey Robertson, *Who Owns History? Elgin's Loot and the Case for Returning Plundered Treasure* (Biteback Publishing 2019)

Georg Schwarzenberger, 'The Fundamental Principles of International Law' (1955) 87 Recueil des cours 195

Malcolm N Shaw, *International Law* (9th edn, Cambridge University Press 2021)

Christian J Tams, 'Waiver, Acquiescence, and Extinctive Prescription' in James Crawford and others (eds), The Law of International Responsibility (Oxford University Press 2010)

Catharine Titi, *The Function of Equity in International Law* (Oxford University Press 2021)

Megan Wagner, 'Jurisdiction by Estoppel in the International Court of Justice' (1986) 74 California Law Review 1777

Robert C Williams, 'The Quiet Trade: Russian Art and American Money' (1979) 3 (1) The Wilson Quarterly 162

Jan Wouters and Sten Verhoeven, 'Prescription' (2008) Max Planck Encyclopedia of Public International Law

Part III
The Law Applicable to the Substance of the Dispute

Chapter 9
Treaty Law

9.1 Introduction

International courts make decisions on the basis of law and, in particular, international law. Article 38 of the Statute of the International Court of Justice (ICJ) lays out the recognised sources of international law, which include treaty law, international custom, and general principles of law.[1] This part of the book focuses on two sources of international law and their relevance to the Parthenon marbles case. In particular, this chapter examines treaty law, while the chapter that follows turns to customary international law.

This chapter starts by enquiring into three international conventions that address the protection and return of unlawfully removed cultural property. It argues that these conventions are very important but that they do not apply directly to the Parthenon marbles case. Even so, the fact that the United Kingdom has recently joined two of the three conventions is significant, for it evidences the country's 'softening' towards the return of unlawfully removed cultural property. These conventions need to be taken into account when examining the new customary international law on returns. Next, the chapter reviews the protection of property and cultural heritage in the European human rights system, with a focus on the right

[1]The enumeration of sources in Article 38 of the Statute of the ICJ is no longer regarded as exhaustive or complete, Greenwood (2008); Pellet and Müller (2019) 851-864. Some authors argue that the decisions of international organisations are themselves sources of international law, e.g. Pellet and Müllet (2019) 857-861. This book will not consider whether the 2021 decision of the Intergovernmental Committee for Promoting the Return of Cultural Property to its Countries of Origin or its Restitution in case of Illicit Appropriation (ICPRCP or Intergovernmental Committee) of the United Nations Educational, Scientific and Cultural Organization (UNESCO) discussing the United Kingdom's 'obligation' to return the marbles (ICPRCP, 22nd session, 27-29 September 2021, ICPRCP/21/22.COM/Decisions, Decision 22.COM 6, para 7) is international law, as a decision emanating from an international organisation. Instead, it will take it into account when examining customary international law in Chap. 10.

C. Titi, *The Parthenon Marbles and International Law*,
https://doi.org/10.1007/978-3-031-26357-6_9

to the protection of property and the right to cultural identity that the European Court of Human Rights might be called upon to apply. However, the relevance of the European human rights system is not evident, since this book finds that, contrary to what has been suggested by Greece's erstwhile legal counsel, human rights law is not a promising avenue to pursue the return of the Parthenon marbles. In addition to the jurisdictional hurdles identified in Chaps. 7 and 8 for bringing claims to the European Court of Human Rights, that Court's jurisprudence gives little support to the idea of cultural rights as active rights, except perhaps if brought under the ambit of the right to the protection of property.

9.2 Protection of Cultural Property

States have been concluding international treaties that protect cultural heritage. Three of them in particular are relevant to the return and restitution of cultural property: the Hague Convention of 1954 and, especially, its First Protocol on the return of cultural heritage removed during an armed conflict or from an occupied territory, the 1970 UNESCO Convention, and the 1995 UNIDROIT Convention. All three conventions have already been mentioned but they are considered here in more detail. While the former two have a large membership, the UNIDROIT Convention, which is perhaps the most far-reaching, still lags behind. An added disadvantage that narrows the impact of the three conventions is their prospective character. The ensuing paragraphs will consider these conventions in turn. The analysis is not meant to be exhaustive but focused on the most important provisions for our purposes.

9.2.1 The Conventions

9.2.1.1 The Hague Convention of 1954 and its Protocols

The fundamental principles underlying the Hague Convention of 1954 are generally seen as reflective of customary international law on the protection of cultural property in war and occupation.[2] The Convention, adopted in the wake of World War II, establishes the dual need to safeguard and respect cultural property.[3] Safeguarding requires preparation in peacetime for the protection of cultural property in the event of an armed conflict.[4] Respect for cultural property is a broader and

---

[2] E.g. see Nahlik (1967) 145-148; Gioia (2001) 26; Roger O'Keefe (2006) 336-338; Scovazzi (2011) 356.

[3] Hague Convention of 1954 art 2.

[4] Hague Convention of 1954 art 3.

more significant commitment. The Convention stipulates the contracting parties' obligation to respect cultural property situated in the territory of any contracting party.[5] It requires parties to refrain from using cultural property and its surroundings for purposes that are likely to 'expose it to destruction or damage' in the event of a conflict, as well as to refrain from acts of hostility directed against such property.[6] This same requirement of respect imposes on contracting parties a duty to 'prohibit, prevent and, if necessary, put a stop to any form of theft, pillage or misappropriation of, and any acts of vandalism directed against, cultural property';[7] an obligation to refrain from taking reprisals against such property[8] and from requisitioning movable cultural property.[9] The Convention does not only apply to situations of armed conflict but also to cases of occupation, whether partial or total, and irrespective of whether the occupation meets with armed resistance.[10]

The First Protocol to the 1954 Hague Convention imposes on states the obligation to return cultural property removed during an armed conflict or from an occupied territory and stipulates that such property can 'never be retained as war reparations'.[11] Contracting parties to the First Protocol undertake to prevent the exportation of cultural property from a territory they occupy during an armed conflict.[12] They also commit to take into their custody cultural property directly or indirectly imported from an occupied territory.[13] At the close of hostilities, each contracting party must return any such cultural property to the territory previously occupied.[14] The Protocol further addresses the return of cultural heritage deposited abroad for protection during hostilities. Such property left in safekeeping with a contracting party during a conflict must, at the end of hostilities, be returned to the territory from which it came.[15] The provision is said to have been inspired by the dispute about some national treasures evacuated from Poland at the beginning of World War II that would not find their way home until about 20 years later.[16] It calls to memory Hammersley's 1816 plea in the UK parliament that the Parthenon marbles should be kept together and returned, without question, to Athens when so requested.[17]

The Second Protocol to the Convention goes further in that it stipulates expressly that an occupying force must 'prohibit and prevent' the 'illicit export, other removal

[5]Hague Convention of 1954 art 4.

[6]Hague Convention of 1954 art 4(1).

[7]Hague Convention of 1954 art 4(3).

[8]Hague Convention of 1954 art 4(4).

[9]Hague Convention of 1954 art 4(3).

[10]Hague Convention of 1954 arts 5 and 18(2).

[11]First Protocol to the Hague Convention of 1954 s I.

[12]First Protocol to the Hague Convention of 1954 s I(1).

[13]First Protocol to the Hague Convention of 1954 s I(2).

[14]First Protocol to the Hague Convention of 1954 s I(3).

[15]First Protocol to the Hague Convention of 1954 s II(5).

[16]Roger O'Keefe (2006) 199-200; Toman (1996) 338.

[17]See Chap. 1, text to nn 128-130.

or transfer of ownership of cultural property'.[18] The occupier must in principle also not allow any archaeological excavations to take place.[19] If, exceptionally, such excavations do take place, they must 'be carried out in close cooperation with the competent national authorities of the occupied territory'.[20]

Almost all 134 member states of the 1954 Hague Convention have also signed its First Protocol.[21] The Second Protocol has a narrower membership,[22] but it is both about half a century younger than the Convention and First Protocol, and its membership will certainly increase further. That said the obligation to return plundered cultural heritage is a corollary of the customary international law rule on the prohibition of plunder in times of war and, arguably, occupation.[23] Both Greece and

[18]Second Protocol to the Hague Convention of 1954 (1999) art 9(1)(a).

[19]Second Protocol to the Hague Convention of 1954 (1999) art 9(1)(b).

[20]Second Protocol to the Hague Convention of 1954 (1999) art 9(2).

[21]As of 1 January 2023, 111 states are parties to the First Protocol, see UNESCO, 'The Hague Convention: States Parties' https://en.unesco.org/protecting-heritage/convention-and-protocols/states-parties.

[22]The Second Protocol has a membership of 86, see UNESCO, 'The Hague Convention: States Parties' https://en.unesco.org/protecting-heritage/convention-and-protocols/states-parties.

[23]The customary law nature of the prohibition of plunder in wartime is not examined in this book. On this, see Séfériadès (1932); Nahlik (1967) 89; Kowalski (2001) 61ff; Roger O'Keefe (2006) 336-343; Francioni (2012) 8-15, 25; Scovazzi (2018) 2. On the prohibition of plunder in wartime as a rule of customary international law already in existence in the early eighteenth century, see Chap. 4, text to n 114. Elements that are often discussed in support of the customary law nature of the prohibition of plunder in wartime include: the 1813 *Marquis de Someruelas* (various spellings) case, where the Vice-Admiralty Court of Halifax held that paintings that had been captured as a war prize should be restored to their rightful owner. The case is discussed in Merryman (1996); the return of Napoleon's loot; Lincoln's 1863 Lieber code, a military manual governing the conduct of the Union Army in the American Civil War, which required that '[c]lassical works of art . . . must be secured against all avoidable injury, even when they are contained in fortified places whilst besieged or bombarded', Instructions for the Government of Armies of the United States in the Field, General Orders, No 100 (24 April 1863) art 35; the 1871 statement in the House of Commons by the then British prime minister, William Ewart Gladstone, in relation to objects taken from Maqdala during the 1868 British expedition to Abyssinia, that he 'deeply regretted that those articles were ever brought from Abyssinia, and could not conceive why they were so brought. . . . [H]e deeply lamented, for the sake of the country, and for the sake of all concerned, that those articles, to us insignificant, though probably to the Abyssinians sacred and imposing symbols, or at least hallowed by association, were thought fit to be brought away by a British Army. . . . If those articles were acquired it should be . . . with the view of their being held only until they could be restored', Hansard (1871) cc 949-951; the Hague Convention of 1899 (II) with Respect to the Laws and Customs of War on Land and annexed Regulations (Regulations art 56 prohibiting the seizure and destruction of historical monuments and works of art) and the Hague Convention (IV) of 1907 with Respect to the Laws and Customs of War on Land and annexed Regulations; Treaty of Versailles (1919) arts 238, 245, 247, and similar clauses on restitution in peace treaties that followed; the Inter-Allied Declaration against Acts of Dispossession Committed in Territories under Enemy Occupation or Control (London, 5 January 1943); Charter of the International Military Tribunal, Agreement for the Prosecution and Punishment of the Major War Criminals of the European Axis (1945) art 6(b); Geneva Convention relative to the Protection of Civilian Persons in Time of War (1949) art 33; the restitution of Nazi looted artefacts; Statute of the International

the United Kingdom are contracting parties to the Convention and its two protocols. The fact that the United Kingdom is a recent contracting party (since 2017) only serves to underline that its policy in relation to the protection of cultural property is evolving. While this does not mean that the United Kingdom would not have adhered to these principles before 2017, since they are broadly reflective of customary international law, it underlines its willingness to openly embrace them.

9.2.1.2 The 1970 UNESCO Convention

The 1970 UNESCO Convention applies to cultural property that each state designates as important, including objects found in archaeological excavations or products of archaeological discoveries and 'elements of artistic or historical monuments or archaeological sites which have been dismembered'.[24] The Convention regards the coerced export and transfer of cultural property arising from foreign occupation as 'illicit', making it clear that such property too is subject to repatriation.[25]

The Convention recognises that 'the illicit import, export and transfer of ownership of cultural property' impoverish the cultural heritage of art-rich countries and that international co-operation is one of the most efficient means of protecting cultural property.[26] To this end, the contracting parties undertake the obligation to 'oppose such practices', including by making 'the necessary reparations'.[27] States undertake to create and maintain 'national services' for the protection of cultural

---

Criminal Tribunal for the Former Yugoslavia (1993) art 3 and the case law of that tribunal, which has ruled that the willful destruction of cultural property is a criminal act in accordance with customary international law, see Francioni (2012) 11; Rome Statute of the International Criminal Court (1998) art 8(2). See also UNSC resolutions, such as UNSC Res 1483 (22 May 2003) UN Doc S/RES/1483(2003), para 7, concerning actions to facilitate the safe return to Iraq of cultural property unlawfully removed from the country since 1990 – for other examples, see Chap. 10, n 101. The customary law nature of the obligation to return art plundered during wartime in the past and even more recently does not, however, find universal acceptance, e.g. see Carducci (2020) 195, arguing that, since states decided to address the issue of restitution during an armed conflict in the First Protocol to the 1954 Hague Convention, instead of in the main Convention, given that separate ratifications were needed, 'seems to confirm that in 1954 the international community of States' did not consider that customary international law 'firmly established and clearly imposed [on them] a well-defined obligation to return cultural property removed during an armed conflict'. However, this argument is not convincing. It is suggested that, since some of the 'proposed obligations implicated private-law rights of ownership', with which some states did not wish to interfere, it was thought preferable to address them in a separate instrument, Roger O'Keefe (2006) 197. See also Toman (1996) 336ff. In any event, as discussed above, almost all states parties to the Hague Convention are also now parties to the First Protocol.

[24] 1970 UNESCO Convention art 1. See also art 4.

[25] 1970 UNESCO Convention art 11.

[26] 1970 UNESCO Convention art 2(1).

[27] 1970 UNESCO Convention art 2(2).

heritage.[28] The functions of these 'services' include the establishment of national inventories of protected property and 'a list of important public and private cultural property whose export would constitute an appreciable impoverishment of the national cultural heritage'; promoting the establishment of technical and scientific institutions, such as museums, libraries, and laboratories, for the preservation of cultural heritage; and the supervision of archaeological excavations, ensuring the preservation of cultural heritage in situ.[29] States must endow the 'national services' with adequate funds to enable them to meet the obligations arising out of the Convention.[30] States parties further commit to take the necessary measures to prevent their museums and 'similar institutions' from acquiring illegally exported cultural property that has originated in another contracting state, as well as to inform such other state when an offer is made of cultural property that has been illegally removed from its territory.[31] States undertake to 'prohibit the import of cultural property stolen from a museum or a religious or secular public monument or similar institution' in another contracting party and, at the request of the state of origin, they commit to 'take appropriate steps to recover and return any such cultural property'.[32]

The Convention further requires states parties to prevent the transfer of ownership of cultural property likely to encourage illicit imports or exports of such property; to facilitate 'the earliest possible restitution of illicitly exported cultural property to its rightful owner'; to 'admit actions for recovery of lost or stolen items of cultural property'; and to 'recognize the indefeasible right of each State Party . . . to classify and declare certain cultural property as inalienable which should therefore ipso facto not be exported' and facilitate its recovery if it has been exported.[33]

The Convention has not escaped criticism mainly on account of its narrow scope. For a start, it covers only specific kinds of illicit removal, notably acquisitions of cultural property by museums and 'similar institutions'[34] and thefts from museums, religious or secular public monuments, and 'similar institutions', on condition that the property in question has been 'documented as appertaining to the inventory of that institution'.[35] Thefts of cultural property from individuals or unlawfully excavated cultural property do not in principle fall within the scope of the Convention.[36] Moreover, the Convention is not self-executing, which means that to implement it national legislation is required. Its obligations can be described as 'soft', to the extent that the Convention lacks an enforcement mechanism and only provides for

[28] 1970 UNESCO Convention art 5.

[29] 1970 UNESCO Convention art 5.

[30] 1970 UNESCO Convention art 14.

[31] 1970 UNESCO Convention art 7(a).

[32] 1970 UNESCO Convention art 7(b).

[33] 1970 UNESCO Convention art 13.

[34] 1970 UNESCO Convention art 7(a).

[35] 1970 UNESCO Convention art 7(b)(i).

[36] Scovazzi (2011) 374.

diplomatic action.[37] Finally, as we will discuss in Sect. 9.2.2, it is not retroactive. That said, if the Parthenon marbles case fell into the temporal scope of the Convention, its provisions would be directly applicable. Both Greece and the United Kingdom are parties to the 1970 UNESCO Convention.[38] In this case too, the United Kingdom is a relatively recent member (since 2002).

9.2.1.3 The UNIDROIT Convention

The UNIDROIT Convention was adopted to complement and improve on the 1970 UNESCO Convention. In contrast with the latter, it is self-executing, that is, there is no need for implementing legislation. The Convention applies directly to claims for the restitution of stolen and illegally exported cultural property.[39] The UNIDROIT Convention states unambiguously that the possessor of a *stolen* cultural object must return it.[40] For the purposes of the Convention, 'unlawfully excavated or lawfully excavated but unlawfully retained' cultural objects are to be regarded as stolen.[41] In contrast then with the 1970 UNESCO Convention, the UNIDROIT Convention expressly covers the products of unlawful archaeological excavations. The Convention reserves a distinct treatment for *illegally exported* (as opposed to stolen) cultural objects. Member states are entitled to request the courts or other competent authorities of other member states to order the return of a cultural object that has been illegally exported from their territory.[42] However, unlike stolen objects, which must be returned in all cases, a few conditions have to be met before illegally exported objects can be returned. The requesting state must show that the removal of the cultural property in question impairs significantly any one of a number of interests, including the preservation of the property or of its context, 'the integrity of a complex object', or the preservation of scientific or historical information.[43] Alternatively, the requesting state can establish that the property has 'significant cultural importance' for it.[44]

Like the 1970 UNESCO Convention, the UNIDROIT Convention is not retroactive (see Sect. 9.2.2). The relevance of the UNIDROIT Convention is currently limited by its narrow (54-strong) membership, from which major market countries are still missing.[45] This could change in the future, as the Convention's membership

[37] 1970 UNESCO Convention art 7(b)(ii).

[38] See https://en.unesco.org/fighttrafficking/1970.

[39] UNIDROIT Convention art 1.

[40] UNIDROIT Convention art 3(1).

[41] UNIDROIT Convention art 3(2).

[42] UNIDROIT Convention art 5(1).

[43] UNIDROIT Convention art 5(3).

[44] UNIDROIT Convention art 5(3).

[45] See https://www.unidroit.org/instruments/cultural-property/1995-convention/status/.

basis seems to be increasing steadily.[46] As of the time of writing, the United Kingdom is not a member of the UNIDROIT Convention.

9.2.2 Temporal Remit and Impact of the Conventions

In principle, the three conventions and the protocols to the 1954 Hague Convention apply prospectively only. Therefore, they are not directly relevant to the Parthenon marbles case or to other disputes that arose before their entry into force. That international treaties are not in principle retroactive is stated in the Vienna Convention on the Law of Treaties of 1969. Accordingly, a treaty does 'not bind a party in relation to any act or fact which took place or any situation which ceased to exist before the date of the entry into force of the treaty with respect to that party', except if 'a different intention appears from the treaty or is otherwise established'.[47] That said, this provision expressly stipulates the non-retroactivity rule for situations that have 'ceased to exist' before the entry into force of the treaty in question. While the removal of the Parthenon marbles as an act that took place in the past would not be covered, their continued retention in the British Museum, arguably, might be.

In any event, while the direct applicability of the 1954 Hague Convention and its protocols may be questioned, since these instruments do not contain an express non-retroactivity clause, the dominant interpretation does not regard them as retroactive, even in relation to situations that have not ceased to exist. As for the 1970 UNESCO Convention and the UNIDROIT Convention, they expressly establish a temporal limitation. The 1970 UNESCO Convention provides for the recovery and return of illicit cultural property imported after the Convention's entry into force for both states concerned.[48] The critical date is not that of the theft but the date on which the stolen or illicitly exported cultural property enters the territory of a state party to the Convention.[49] But there is certainly nothing in the 1970 UNESCO Convention to prevent a state from applying its provisions to objects removed prior to 1970.[50] On the contrary, the Convention provides unequivocally that nothing in it shall be interpreted so as to prevent member states from concluding and implementing agreements for the restitution of cultural property removed before the Convention's entry into force for the states concerned.[51] In addition, the Convention does not in

[46] In the last five and a half years (March 2017-August 2022), seventeen new states ratified or acceded to the UNIDROIT Convention. This is an increase of over 45% compared to the Convention's pre-2017 membership, see https://www.unidroit.org/instruments/cultural-property/1995-convention/status/.

[47] Vienna Convention on the Law of Treaties (1969) art 28. See also *Ambatielos case (Jurisdiction) (Greece v United Kingdom)* (Preliminary Objection Judgment) [1952] ICJ Rep 27, 40.

[48] 1970 UNESCO Convention art 7.

[49] 1970 UNESCO Convention art 7.

[50] Prott (2012) 4; Bator (1982) 378.

[51] 1970 UNESCO Convention art 15.

any way legitimise unlawful transactions that took place prior to its entry into force.[52] Its operational guidelines expressly encourage states 'to find a mutually acceptable agreement which is in accordance with the spirit and the principles of the Convention, taking into account all the relevant circumstances' in relation to objects unlawfully removed before the Convention's entry into force for any of the states concerned.[53] The requirement to take into account all relevant circumstances is significant in that it points to equity.[54] In Australia, the legislation implementing the 1970 UNESCO Convention does not apply temporal limitations but regards as unlawful the import of a protected cultural object, so long as its export from a foreign country was prohibited by a local law relating to cultural property, irrespective of when the export took place.[55] In the United States, despite a statement at the time of ratification to the effect that the 1970 UNESCO Convention is understood not to be retroactive,[56] the National Stolen Property Act (NSPA)[57] and the Archaeological Resources Protection Act (ARPA)[58] *are* retroactive. In this sense, they are appropriate as vehicles for foreign countries to seek the repatriation of unlawfully removed cultural heritage that makes its way into the United States.[59] In a joint declaration made by Italy and Libya on 4 July 1998, Italy pledged to return 'all manuscripts, archives, documents, artefacts and archaeological pieces transferred to Italy during and after the Italian occupation of Libya in accordance with the [1970 UNESCO Convention]'.[60] What is significant about this statement is that it contains the commitment of the two signatories to apply the 1970 UNESCO Convention retrospectively, covering events potentially going back to 1911. The statement is reported to have formed the basis of the Italian decree that paved the way for the return of the statue of Cyrene to Libya, an artefact that, as we shall see, had been taken to Italy in 1915.[61]

[52] UNESCO, 'Operational Guidelines for the Implementation of the Convention on the Means of Prohibiting and Preventing the Illicit Import, Export and Transfer of Ownership of Cultural Property', adopted by Resolution 3.MSP 11 at the third Meeting of States Parties (18-20 May 2015), para 102.

[53] UNESCO, 'Operational Guidelines for the Implementation of the Convention on the Means of Prohibiting and Preventing the Illicit Import, Export and Transfer of Ownership of Cultural Property', adopted by Resolution 3.MSP 11 at the third Meeting of States Parties (18-20 May 2015), para 103.

[54] See Sect. 10.3.1.

[55] Protection of Movable Cultural Heritage Act 1986 (Act No 11, 1986, as amended up to Act No 61, 2016) s 14. The Act is interpreted to apply to objects imported into Australia after the country's accession to the 1970 UNESCO Convention, see Forrest (2004) 620; Prott (2012) 4.

[56] See https://bit.ly/3NDoITc.

[57] 18 USC §§ 2314ff.

[58] 16 USC 88 470aa-470mm.

[59] Vitale (2009) 1861; Januszkiewicz (2015) 366.

[60] Unofficial English translation, see https://bit.ly/38GGcyV.

[61] See Chap. 10, text to n 65.

The UNIDROIT Convention too, while in principle prospective,[62] expressly affirms that 'in no way' does it confer 'any approval or legitimacy upon illegal transactions of whatever kind' that may have taken place before its entry into force.[63] Nor does it affect the right of a state or other person to claim on the basis of other remedies that may be available outside the framework of the Convention for the restitution or return of cultural objects stolen or illegally exported prior to its entry into force.[64] Provisions such as this were introduced precisely so as not to prejudice eventual requests for restitution or return of important cultural objects that many contracting states had lost prior to the entry into force of the conventions.[65]

It would then be a mistake to assume that, to the extent that the conventions are not retroactive, they are irrelevant to the return of cultural heritage unlawfully removed from its original context prior to their adoption. That the opposite is true is obvious from the sea change that cultural heritage law has undergone latterly. The Conventions have encouraged the examination of the provenance of cultural objects.[66] This process was put in train as soon as the 1970 UNESCO Convention entered into force, as museums and local governments started to incorporate it into their acquisitions policies, including in countries, such as the United Kingdom, where the Convention was not as yet binding.[67] In many cases, 1970 is used as the cut-off date to indicate 'acceptable' provenance.[68] The Conventions have also certainly prompted at least some of the numerous returns of cultural objects unlawfully removed from their original context prior to their entry into force, which we will consider in the next chapter. Last, and certainly not least, the Conventions have helped change attitudes by reducing tolerance towards illicit removals of cultural property and are therefore relevant to the emergence of the new rule of customary international law on the return of unlawfully removed cultural property.

9.3 Human Rights Law

9.3.1 The European Convention on Human Rights

The protection of cultural property is often understood to form part of international human rights safeguards.[69] Even so, the concrete relevance of human rights

[62] UNIDROIT Convention art 10(1) and (2).

[63] UNIDROIT Convention preamble and art 10(3).

[64] UNIDROIT Convention art 10(3).

[65] Prott (1996) 68-69.

[66] Fincham (2013) 962.

[67] Patrick O'Keefe (1998) 20.

[68] Brodie (2006); Prott (2012) 3; Gerstenblith (2013).

[69] E.g. Hausler (2020) 209-213; United Nations Human Rights Council (UNHRC) Res 37/17 (19 March 2018) UN Doc A/ HRC/37/L.30, para 1; UNHRC (2016), para 34, discussing the

instruments to the Greek claim for the return of the Parthenon marbles is not immediately evident. This topic is considered since it has been suggested that Greece could submit a claim under Article 1 of the First Protocol to the European Convention on Human Rights (ECHR) for a violation of the right to the peaceful enjoyment of one's possessions and under Article 8 of the ECHR for a breach of a right to cultural identity.[70]

The European Court of Human Rights has taken into account the right to the protection of cultural heritage as a passive right, that is, as a state defence.[71] Accordingly, it regards the protection of cultural property as a legitimate aim that the state can pursue when it interferes with individual rights.[72] So, in *Beyeler v Italy*, the Court held that the state's control over the art market is such 'a legitimate aim' to safeguard the state's 'cultural and artistic heritage' and established that 'the national authorities enjoy a certain margin of appreciation in determining what is in the general interest of the community'.[73] However, the Court has not for the moment recognised the right to the protection of cultural heritage as an active right giving rise to a claim.[74]

This approach is to be contrasted with the jurisprudence of the Inter-American Court of Human Rights, which has admitted a 'concept of property in indigenous communities'[75] and has interpreted the right to property[76] not only as an individual

---

'intentional destruction of cultural heritage sites, objects and monuments' as undermining 'numerous human rights, including the right to freedom from discrimination; the right to freedom of thought, conscience and religion; and the right to take part in cultural life, including the right to maintain and develop the cultural practices of one's choice, and to access cultural heritage including one's own history, and the right to freedom of artistic expression and creativity'; UNHRC (2010), para 3.

[70] Robertson (2019) preface and Chap. 6 (unnumbered pages).

[71] Titi (2017) 552.

[72] European Court of Human Rights (2017), para 78.

[73] *Beyeler v Italy*, App no 33202/96, Merits Judgment (5 January 2000) [112]. For other examples, see *Debelianovi v Bulgaria*, App no 61951/00, Merits and Just Satisfaction Judgment (29 March 2007); *Kozacioğlu v Turkey*, App no 2334/03, Merits and Just Satisfaction Judgment (19 February 2009) [53]-[54], [64], [82]; *Ehrmann and SCI VHI v France*, App no 2777/10, Decision (7 June 2011); cf *Syllogos ton Athinaion v United Kingdom*, App no 48259/15, Decision (23 June 2016).

[74] Titi (2017) 552.

[75] E.g. *Awas Tingni Mayagna (Sumo) Indigenous Community v Nicaragua*, Judgment, Inter-American Court of Human Rights Series C No 79 (31 August 2001) [149]; *Moiwana Community v Suriname*, Judgment (Preliminary Objections, Merits, Reparations and Costs), Inter-American Court of Human Rights Series C No 124 (15 June 2005) [131]; *Saramaka People v Suriname*, Judgment, Inter-American Court of Human Rights Series C No 172 (28 November 2007) [118]ff; cf the American Declaration on the Rights of Indigenous Peoples, adopted in 2016, which provides specifically for redress through restitution with respect to indigenous peoples' 'cultural, intellectual, religious, and spiritual property taken without their free, prior, and informed consent or in violation of their laws, traditions, and customs', American Declaration on the Rights of Indigenous Peoples, AG/RES 2888 (XLVI-0/16) art XIII.

[76] American Convention on Human Rights art 21.

but also as a communal right.[77] This strain of jurisprudence of the Inter-American Court of Human Rights is also interesting in that the Court perceives human rights treaties as living instruments 'whose interpretation must adapt to the evolution of the times and, specifically, to current living conditions'.[78] The Court is also inclined to take into account not only binding legal instruments but soft law too, such as recommendations, significantly extending the scope of human rights protection.[79] This is not the case of the European Court of Human Rights.

9.3.2 Right to Property

The right to property is protected under Article 1 of the First Protocol to the ECHR, which establishes the right of every person to the 'peaceful enjoyment' of their possessions.[80] According to the same article, '[n]o one shall be deprived of his possessions except in the public interest and subject to the conditions provided for by law and by the general principles of international law'.[81] The state retains the right to 'enforce such laws as it deems necessary to control the use of property in accordance with the general interest'.[82]

Cultural property has already formed part of the jurisprudence of the European Court of Human Rights in relation to violations of the right to property. In *Catholic Archdiocese of Alba Iulia v Romania*, which arose out of the state's failure to return to the owner association a historical library and an astronomical museum despite a 14-year-old restitution order, the European Court of Human Rights stressed the cultural and historical value of the disputed property.[83] It found that the state's prolonged failure to implement the restitution order and the uncertainty this created for the applicant association was particularly difficult to understand in light of the property's cultural and historical importance.[84] For the Court, the latter should have called for rapid action in order to ensure its preservation and its use in the public

[77] Francioni (2013) 18.

[78] *Awas Tingni Mayagna (Sumo) Indigenous Community v Nicaragua*, Judgment, Inter-American Court of Human Rights Series C No 79 (31 August 2001) [146].

[79] Barelli (2009) 980.

[80] First Protocol to the ECHR art 1(1).

[81] First Protocol to the ECHR art 1(1).

[82] First Protocol to the ECHR art 1(2).

[83] *Catholic Archdiocese of Alba Iulia v Romania*, App no 33003/03, Judgment (25 September 2012) [87]-[88].

[84] *Catholic Archdiocese of Alba Iulia v Romania*, App no 33003/03, Judgment (25 September 2012) [97].

interest.[85] The Court concluded that there had been a violation of Article 1 of the First Protocol.[86]

In the case of the Parthenon marbles, the retention of the fifteen metopes, half of the original surviving frieze, and the seventeen pedimental figures in Bloomsbury, in addition to parts of other buildings from the Acropolis, including a caryatid from the Erechtheion, interferes with the integrity of the very monuments from which they were taken and, as a consequence, it interferes with Greece's full enjoyment of these monuments.[87] By the same token, the marbles' retention amounts to a deprivation of Greece's 'possessions'.[88] Strictly speaking, according to the argument presented in Chap. 7, Greece could not in fact invoke a violation of 'its' right to property but rather a breach of the right of all Greek citizens to enjoy this public property.

The United Kingdom could still be entitled to keep the marbles, if it proved that this served a legitimate public or general interest,[89] probably by relying on the value of world museums. If the United Kingdom established that the interference did serve the general interest, it would also have to prove that the retention of the marbles strikes a 'fair balance' between the requirements of the protection of Greece's property and the general interest of the community.[90] The Court would conduct a proportionality analysis, since 'there must be a reasonable relationship of proportionality between the means employed and the aims pursued'.[91] Given that the claim would be based on the continued retention of the marbles, this relationship would need to exist at the time the case is decided rather than at the time of the marbles' initial removal.[92] It is argued that 'the balancing of material factors' would favour Greece's claim.[93] In conclusion, if the practical and jurisdictional hurdles are passed, a claim under Article 1 of the First Protocol would have some chances of success.

---

[85] *Catholic Archdiocese of Alba Iulia v Romania*, App no 33003/03, Judgment (25 September 2012) [97].

[86] *Catholic Archdiocese of Alba Iulia v Romania*, App no 33003/03, Judgment (25 September 2012) [98].

[87] Robertson, Palmer, and Clooney (2015) 120-123.

[88] On deprivation of property under the ECHR, see European Court of Human Rights (2022), paras 94-100; Rainey, Wicks, and Ovey (2017) 560.

[89] European Court of Human Rights (2022), paras 129-140.

[90] *Beyeler v Italy*, App no 33202/96, Merits Judgment (5 January 2000) [107]; *Sporrong and Lönnroth v Sweden*, App nos 7151/75 and 7152/75, Merits Judgment (23 September 1982) [69]. See also First Protocol to the ECHR art 1(2).

[91] *'Bulves' AD v Bulgaria*, App no 3991/03, Merits and Just Satisfaction Judgment, 22 January 2009 [62]; *Phillips v United Kingdom*, App no 41087/98, Merits and Just Satisfaction Judgment (5 July 2001) [51]; European Court of Human Rights (2022), paras 141-190.

[92] Robertson, Palmer, and Clooney (2015) 126.

[93] Robertson, Palmer, and Clooney (2015) 127-128.

9.3.3 Right to Cultural Identity?

It has also been suggested that Greece could submit an interstate claim under Article 8 of the ECHR in respect of a right to cultural identity.[94] The provision establishes the right to respect for one's 'private and family life'.[95] States should not interfere with the exercise of this right except 'in accordance with the law' and if 'necessary in a democratic society in the interests of national security, public safety or the economic wellbeing of the country, for the prevention of disorder or crime, for the protection of health or morals, or for the protection of the rights and freedoms of others'.[96] According to the settled jurisprudence of the European Court of Human Rights, the state has a 'positive obligation' to set in place a framework that ensures the respect of Article 8 of the ECHR.[97] Since the European Court of Human Rights has recognised the right of minority and ethnic communities to their identity,[98] the argument has been advanced that cultural identity should also be protected, so as to include 'the right to the return of such an iconic symbol of a people's cultural identity as the Parthenon Sculptures'.[99]

However, the Court's jurisprudence thus far does not seem to justify such optimism. In an obiter in *Syllogos ton Athinaion v United Kingdom*, which as we have seen was an individual claim brought by a Greek association for the return of the marbles, the Court rejected the idea that 'Article 8 gives rise to a general right to protection of cultural heritage' of the nature contended in the case.[100] More recently, in *Ahunbay and others v Turkey*, the petitioners complained against the construction of a dam that put at risk an archaeological site.[101] The Court held that cultural heritage rights are intrinsic to the specific status of the individuals who claim them, that is, the only such established rights are those of minority and indigenous groups to access and enjoy their culture.[102] But the Court did not find a 'European consensus', not even a tendency among the member states of the Council of Europe,

---

[94]Robertson (2019) preface and Chap. 6 (unnumbered page).

[95]ECHR art 8(1).

[96]ECHR art 8(2).

[97]E.g. *Bărbulescu v Romania*, App no 61496/08, Merits and Just Satisfaction Judgment (5 September 2017) [108], [114]-[115]; *Craxi v Italy (No 2)*, App no 25337/94, Merits and Just Satisfaction Judgment (17 July 2003) [68]-[76]; *Benediktsdóttir v Iceland*, App no 38079/06, Decision (16 June 2009) (unnumbered paragraphs).

[98]E.g. *Chapman v United Kingdom*, App no 27238/95, Merits Judgment (18 January 2001); *Ciubotaru v Moldova*, App no 27138/04, Merits and Just Satisfaction Judgment (27 April 2010).

[99]Robertson, Palmer, and Clooney (2015) 131.

[100]*Syllogos ton Athinaion v United Kingdom*, App no 48259/15, Decision (23 June 2016).

[101]*Ahunbay and others v Turkey*, App no 6080/06, Decision (29 January 2019).

[102]*Ahunbay and others v Turkey*, App no 6080/06, Decision (29 January 2019) [23]-[24].

that would allow us to infer that the ECHR recognises 'an individual universal right to the protection of one or another cultural heritage', as was requested in the case.[103]

9.4 Conclusion

International treaties protect cultural heritage and in certain cases provide mechanisms that allow such heritage to be returned to where it was taken from, when it has been unlawfully removed. This chapter considered in turn the conventions that focus on the protection and return of cultural heritage, notably the 1954 Hague Convention and its two protocols, the 1970 UNESCO Convention, and the UNIDROIT Convention. The chapter observed that the first two conventions have a large membership and that both Greece and the United Kingdom are parties to them. However, the conventions are not retroactive and do not therefore apply directly to the Parthenon marbles case. Even so, their significance should not be overlooked: as the following chapter will argue, they contribute to changing attitudes and show the commitment of states to the restitution of unlawfully removed cultural heritage. The chapter further examined the protection of property and a potential right to cultural identity under the ECHR as the legal basis for the return of the Parthenon marbles. However, while the violation of a right to property claim might have some possibility of success, the chapter found that the jurisprudence of the European Court of Human Rights does not confirm the view that the Court recognises a right to cultural identity as an active right. This, also in light of the analysis in Chaps. 7 and 8, including the time-limitations for bringing a claim under the ECHR, leads to the conclusion that the human rights claim does not have good chances of success.

References

Mauro Barelli, 'The Role of Soft Law in the International Legal System: The Case of the United Nations Declaration on the Rights of Indigenous Peoples' (2009) 58 International and Comparative Law Quarterly 957

Paul M Bator, 'An Essay on the International Trade in Art' (1982) 34 Stanford Law Review 275

Neil Brodie, 'The Effect of an Artefact's Provenance on its Saleability' (2006) 19 Culture Without Context 4

Guido Carducci, 'The Role of UNESCO in the Elaboration and Implementation of International Art, Cultural Property, and Heritage Law' in Anne-Marie Carstens and Elizabeth Varner (eds), *Intersections in International Cultural Heritage Law* (Oxford University Press 2020)

European Court of Human Rights, *Guide on Article 1 of Protocol No. 1 to the European Convention on Human Rights: Protection of Property* (Council of Europe/European Court of Human Rights 2022)

[103] *Ahunbay and others v Turkey*, App no 6080/06, Decision (29 January 2019) [25] (author's translation).

European Court of Human Rights, *Cultural Rights in the Case-law of the European Court of Human Rights* (Council of Europe/European Court of Human Rights 2011, updated 2017)

Derek Fincham, 'The Parthenon Sculptures and Cultural Justice' (2013) 23 Fordham Intellectual Property, Media and Entertainment Law Journal 943

Craig Forrest, 'Australia's Protection of Foreign States' Cultural Heritage' (2004) 27 (3) UNSW Law Journal 605

Francesco Francioni, 'Plurality and Interaction of Legal Orders in the Enforcement of Cultural Heritage Law' in Francesco Francioni and James Gordley (eds), *Enforcing International Cultural Heritage Law* (Oxford University Press 2013)

Francesco Francioni, 'The Evolving Framework for the Protection of Cultural Heritage in International Law' in Silvia Borelli and Federico Lenzerini (eds), *Cultural Heritage, Cultural Rights, Cultural Diversity* (Martinus Nijhoff 2012)

Patty Gerstenblith, 'The Meaning of 1970 for the Acquisition of Archaeological Objects' (2013) 38 (4) Journal of Field Archaeology 364

Andrea Gioia, 'The Development of International Law relating to the Protection of Cultural Property in the Event of Armed Conflict: The Second Protocol to the 1954 Hague Convention' (2001) 11 (1) Italian Yearbook of International Law 25

Christopher Greenwood, 'Sources of International Law' (2008) http://legal.un.org/avl/pdf/ls/greenwood_outline.pdf

Hansard, 'Abyssinian War House of Commons Debate: Motion for an Address' (30 June 1871) (vol 207, Hansard 1871)

Kristin Hausler, 'The UN Security Council, the Human Rights Council, and the of Cultural Heritage' in Anne-Marie Carstens and Elizabeth Varner (eds), *Intersections in International Cultural Heritage Law* (Oxford University Press 2020)

Katarzyna Januszkiewicz, 'Retroactivity in the 1970 UNESCO Convention: Cases of the United States and Australia' (2015) 41 (1) Brooklyn Journal of International Law 329

Wojciech W Kowalski, 'Restitution of Works of Art pursuant to Private and Public International Law' (2001) 288 Recueil des cours 11

John Henry Merryman, 'The Marquis de Somerueles: Vice-Admiralty Court of Halifax, Nova Scotia Stewart's Vice-Admiralty Reports 482 (1813)' (1996) 5 International Journal of Cultural Property 319

Stanisław Nahlik, 'La protection internationale des biens culturels en cas de conflit armé' (1967) 120 Recueil des cours 62

Patrick J O'Keefe 'Museum Acquisitions Policies and the 1970 UNESCO Convention' (1998) 50 (1) Museum International 20

Roger O'Keefe, *The Protection of Cultural Property in Armed Conflict* (Cambridge University Press 2006)

Alain Pellet and Daniel Müller, 'Article 38' in Andreas Zimmermann, Christian Tomuschat and Karin Oellers-Frahm (eds), *The Statute of the International Court of Justice: A Commentary* (3rd edn, Oxford University Press 2019)

Lyndel V Prott, 'Strengths and Weaknesses of the 1970 Convention: An Evaluation 40 Years after its Adoption', Background paper, second edition, for participants in the Second Meeting of States Parties to the 1970 Convention, UNESCO, 20-21 June 2012

Lyndel V Prott, 'UNESCO and UNIDROIT: A Partnership against Trafficking in Cultural Objects' (1996) 1 Uniform Law Review 59

Bernadette Rainey, Elizabeth Wicks, and Clare Ovey, *Jacobs, White, and Ovey: The European Convention on Human Rights* (7th end, Oxford University Press 2017)

Geoffrey Robertson, *Who Owns History? Elgin's Loot and the Case for Returning Plundered Treasure* (Biteback Publishing 2019)

Geoffrey Robertson, Norman Palmer, and Amal Clooney, 'The Case for Return of the Parthenon Sculptures' (31 July 2015) (unpublished report, leaked on The Guardian website)

Tullio Scovazzi, 'Repatriation and Restitution of Cultural Property: Relevant Rules of International Law' in Claire Smith (ed), *Encyclopedia of Global Archaeology* (Springer 2018)

Tullio Scovazzi, '*Diviser c'est détruire*: Ethical Principles and Legal Rules in the Field of Return of Cultural Property' (2011) 94 (2) Rivista di diritto internazionale 341

S Sériadès, 'La question du rapatriement des « Marbres d'Elgin » considérée plus spécialement au point de vue du droit des gens' (1932) 10 Revue de droit international 52

Catharine Titi, 'International Dispute Settlement in Cultural Heritage Law and in the Protection of Foreign Investment: Is Cross-Fertilisation Possible?' (2017) 8 (3) Journal of International Dispute Settlement 535

Jiri Toman, *The Protection of Cultural Property in the Event of Armed Conflict* (Dartmouth and UNESCO Publishing 1996)

UNHRC, 'Report of the Special Rapporteur in the Field of Cultural Rights' UN Doc A/ 71/ 317 (9 August 2016)

UNHRC, 'Report of the Independent Expert in the Field of Cultural Rights, Ms Farida Shaheed, submitted pursuant to Resolution 10/23 of the Human Rights Council' UN Doc A/HRC/14/36 (22 March 2010)

Katherine D Vitale, 'The War on Antiquities: United States Law and Foreign Cultural Property' (2009) 84 (4) Notre Dame Law Review 1835

Chapter 10
Customary International Law

10.1 Introduction

Customary international law expresses the principle that 'the way things have always been done becomes the way things *must* be done'.[1] International custom is the 'soul' of international law,[2] for, as James Crawford remarked, 'international law is a customary law system, despite all the treaties'.[3] In contrast with the fragmented and changeable treaty law, which is only binding on states parties to a given treaty, international custom is in principle applicable to—and binding on—all states, whether or not they have participated in its creation.[4] When there is no binding international treaty, a dispute is governed by customary international law.[5] This does not mean that international custom has no role to play when an international treaty is applicable,[6] nor does it mean that treaties are irrelevant to it—some may reflect customary international law, and others may be useful for the determination of its norms.[7]

The debate about the role of customary international law in the protection of cultural heritage is not new, but it has typically been approached from angles that are not directly relevant to the Parthenon marbles case. As we have seen, the prohibition of plunder and the return of cultural heritage removed during an armed conflict are generally regarded as forming part of customary international law.[8] But there is some resistance to the idea that removals from an occupied territory fall under the scope of

---

[1] Thirlway (2019) 60 (emphasis in original).

[2] I am thankful to Mauro Politi for this wonderfully evocative description.

[3] Crawford (2014) 57.

[4] Thirlway (2019) 61, 63.

[5] *Continental Shelf (Libya/Malta)* (Judgment) [1985] ICJ Rep 13 [26].

[6] Pellet and Müller (2019) 902.

[7] *Continental Shelf (Libya/Malta)* (Judgment) [1985] ICJ Rep 13 [26].

[8] See Chap. 9, text to n 23.

C. Titi, *The Parthenon Marbles and International Law*,
https://doi.org/10.1007/978-3-031-26357-6_10

the customary law rule, although this book has argued that they do.[9] There is also disagreement about whether Greece at the time of the removals was an occupied territory or in a state of *debellatio*, which some will regard as more akin to peace.[10] There is a discussion about other aspects of the customary international law on the protection of cultural heritage, such as whether there is a prohibition of the exploitation of weakness for cultural gain, an obligation to preserve the cultural context, and a duty of cooperation.[11] Authors have recognised that some such obligations apply beyond treaty law.[12] Even so, when it comes to the existence of a customary law rule on the return of cultural property unlawfully removed in situations other than armed conflict, that is, in peace or even occupation, legal scholars have often shown circumspection. Tullio Scovazzi, for instance, recognised that the law increasingly favours returns, an evolution that 'deserves to be strengthened for evident moral and cultural reasons'.[13] He even argued that the ethical and 'cultural principles that dictate the restitution are being progressively transformed into legal rules' but stopped short of concluding that this trend has 'reached the final stage when a body of new customary rules on restitution of cultural properties is definitely created'.[14]

This book takes a different view. It argues that a new customary international law on the return of unlawfully removed cultural heritage is actually emerging, although its precise contours are yet to be determined. Despite the lingering doubt about whether the rule is already in existence, this chapter recognises that what the customary international law is today can only be determined in retrospect and argues that the rule seems to already exist. The Parthenon marbles case falls squarely within the scope of this rule, which imposes on states a duty to return cultural heritage unlawfully removed from its original context, with no reference to the political situation in the sovereign territory at the time of the removal. The chapter presents a second argument in favour of the marbles' repatriation, relying on equity and 'cultural justice'. Irrespective of the nascent customary international law rule on returns, equity, itself a source of international law, plainly and unambiguously requires the repatriation of the marbles to Athens.

[9] See Sect. 4.5.1 and Chap. 9, text to n 23.

[10] See Sect. 4.5.1.

[11] Scovazzi (2018) 5-6; Francioni (2012).

[12] Scovazzi (2018) 5-6; Francioni (2012).

[13] Scovazzi (2011) 394.

[14] Scovazzi (2018) 6. See also Francioni (2012) 25.

10.2 Return of Important Cultural Property

Let us then consider the emerging rule on the return of cultural property unlawfully removed from its original context. This section starts by describing how customary international law is created and identified, and it continues by examining whether customary international law's constitutive elements, that is, state practice and acceptance as law (*opinio iuris*), support the existence of a norm on the return of cultural property. This part of the chapter also reviews the contribution of museums to the creation of such a norm.

10.2.1 Custom Formation and Identification

Customary international law is notoriously difficult to identify. 'The problem with establishing customary international law', explained Crawford, 'is that it seems impossible'.[15] Some guidance, however, is offered in Article 38 of the Statute of the International Court of Justice (ICJ), which describes international custom as 'evidence of a general practice accepted as law'.[16] For the establishment then of a customary international law norm two requirements must be met: there must be general practice, and this practice must be accepted as law (*opinio iuris*).[17] The ICJ has confirmed that '[n]ot only must the acts concerned amount to a settled practice, but they must also be such, or be carried out in such a way, as to be evidence of a belief that this practice is rendered obligatory by the existence of a rule of law requiring it'.[18]

Practice, the first element of customary international law, must be general, in the sense that it must be widespread and representative, as well as uniform and consistent.[19] However, uniformity and consistency of practice are generally in the eye of

[15] Crawford (2014) 57.

[16] ICJ Statute art 38(1)(b).

[17] See also ILC, 'Conclusions on Identification of Customary International Law' (2018), conclusion 2; Crawford (2019) 24-27; Pellet and Müller (2019) 904-905; Byers (1999) 130; Mendelson (1998); Villiger (1997) 61; Ferrari Bravo (1985) 243.

[18] *North Sea Continental Shelf* (Judgment) [1969] ICJ Rep 3 [77]. See also *Continental Shelf (Libya/Malta)* (Judgment) [1985] ICJ Rep 13 [27].

[19] ILC, 'Conclusions on Identification of Customary International Law' (2018), conclusion 8; *Colombian-Peruvian Asylum* (Judgment) [1950] ICJ Rep 266, 276 (discussing the need for 'a constant and uniform usage practised by the States in question'); *Right of Passage over Indian Territory* (Merits Judgment) [1960] ICJ Rep 6, 40 ('constant and uniform practice'); *North Sea Continental Shelf* (Judgment) [1969] ICJ Rep 3 [74] (practice should be 'extensive and virtually uniform in the sense of the provision invoked'); *Fisheries Jurisdiction (United Kingdom v Iceland)* (Joint Separate Opinion Forster, Bengzon, Jiménez de Aréchaga, Nagendra Singh and Ruda) [1974] ICJ Rep 45 [16] ('State practice must be common, consistent and concordant'); *Delimitation of the Maritime Boundary in the Gulf of Maine Area* (Judgment) [1984] ICJ Rep 246 [111] ('a sufficiently

the beholder, 'a matter of appreciation' rather than hard science.[20] What is required is substantial uniformity of practice.[21] Unanimity of practice is not required, 'either in the sense that all States must have been shown to have participated in it, or in the sense that there is evidence that the *opinio,* the view that it is a binding custom, is held by all States'.[22] On the authority of the ICJ, for the emergence of a rule of customary international law, the conduct of states does not have to be 'in absolutely rigorous conformity' with the rule; conformity 'in general' is sufficient,[23] meaning that 'some inconsistencies and contradictions are not necessarily fatal to a finding of "a general practice"'.[24] No particular duration is required.[25] If the practice is repeated with frequency, the element of consistency may be satisfied more rapidly than if the practice is infrequent.[26]

Inaction too may count as practice, provided that it is deliberate, that is, the state must be conscious of the fact that it abstains from acting.[27] Inaction constitutive of state practice can be difficult to prove, since silence can mean any number of different things from tacit agreement (e.g. this is the presumption in acquiescence) to lack of interest in the matter.[28] Tolerance of a practice, evidenced through the state's failure to react over a period of time, may show acceptance as law; however, for inaction to have this probative effect, some reaction must have been called for, such as because the practice was detrimental to the state's interests.[29] By the same token, the state must have been 'in a position to react', meaning that it must have been aware of the practice and it must have had the opportunity to react.[30]

extensive and convincing practice'); *Maritime Delimitation and Territorial Questions between Qatar and Bahrain* (Merits Judgment) [2001] ICJ Rep 40 [205].

[20] Crawford (2019) 22.

[21] Crawford (2019) 22-23. See further *North Sea Continental Shelf* (Judgment) [1969] ICJ Rep 3 [74].

[22] Thirlway (2019) 67; Ferrari Bravo (1985) 246; Lachs (1980) 175.

[23] *Military and Paramilitary Activities in and against Nicaragua (Nicaragua v United States)* (Merits Judgment) [1986] ICJ Rep 14 [186].

[24] ILC, 'Conclusions on Identification of Customary International Law' (2018), conclusion 8.

[25] ILC, 'Conclusions on Identification of Customary International Law' (2018), conclusion 8; cf Cheng (1965).

[26] Thirlway (2019) 74. See further *North Sea Continental Shelf* (Judgment) [1969] ICJ Rep 3 [74].

[27] ILC, 'Conclusions on Identification of Customary International Law' (2018), conclusion 6 and commentary para 3.

[28] Crawford (2019) 23; Thirlway (2019) 73; Baka (2022).

[29] ILC, 'Conclusions on Identification of Customary International Law' (2018), conclusion 10 and commentary para 8; Dumberry (2016) 309-321; Lepard (2010) 171-217. See further *Military and Paramilitary Activities in and against Nicaragua (Nicaragua v United States)* (Merits Judgment) [1986] ICJ Rep 14 [188]; *Legality of the Threat or Use of Nuclear Weapons* (Advisory Opinion) [1996] ICJ Rep 226 [70]; cf *SS Lotus* (Judgment) PCIJ Series A No 10 (7 September 1927) 28, where the PCIJ held that, for abstention from action to be significant, it must be based on the state's perception that it has a duty to abstain.

[30] ILC, 'Conclusions on Identification of Customary International Law' (2018), conclusion 10, commentary para 8.

Awareness does not need to be proved but will often be assumed such as because of the publicity of a certain practice.[31]

The second, the subjective, element of customary international law, acceptance as law, presents a trickier conundrum. This lies at the core of the chronological paradox in the formation of customary international law, since acceptance as law presupposes that, for new customary norms to come into existence, states 'must believe that those rules already exist, and that their practice, therefore, *is* in accordance with law'.[32] In other words, 'in order for a norm to become a part of international law, it must already be a part of international law'.[33] This means that new customary international law norms are only ever created, if states mistakenly believe that they already exist.[34] International courts and tribunals have repeatedly acknowledged this process. In order to avoid the assumption that states are deceived into believing that they have a legal obligation to act as they do, an alternative approach to acceptance as law is to examine state practice 'to see whether there emerges a pattern such as would emerge if States had been acting under the constraint of law'.[35]

A relevant, if partly unresolved question, is whose practice and whose acceptance as law is required for the creation of customary international law.[36] For instance, for cultural heritage law, are only the practice and acceptance as law of market states relevant? The ICJ has recalled that practice must include the participation of states 'whose interests were specially affected'.[37] In the case of the return of cultural property, it is both the interests of market countries and those of source countries that are affected. The states whose acceptance as law matters are those that engage in relevant practice and those in a position to react to it.[38]

Evidence of practice and of acceptance as law may take many forms, which include diplomatic correspondence, treaty practice, legislation, executive and administrative acts, including claims before national and international courts, resolutions adopted by organs of the UN, notably the General Assembly, and at intergovernmental conferences, decisions of national and international courts, public statements made by a state or on behalf of a state, official publications, press releases, legal

[31] ILC, 'Conclusions on Identification of Customary International Law' (2018), conclusion 10, commentary para 8.

[32] Byers (1999) 130-133, especially 130 (emphasis in original); see also Crawford (2014) 67.

[33] Dahlman (2012) 332. See also Dumberry (2016) 302-305; Lepard (2010) 112-121; Kammerhofer (2004) 534-535.

[34] Crawford (2014) 78.

[35] Allot (1971) 103. See also Crawford (2014) 76, 78.

[36] Thirlway (2019) 68.

[37] *North Sea Continental Shelf* (Judgment) [1969] ICJ Rep 3 [73].

[38] *Military and Paramilitary Activities in and against Nicaragua (Nicaragua v United States)* (Merits Judgment) [1986] ICJ Rep 14 [207]; ILC, 'Conclusions on Identification of Customary International Law' (2018), conclusion 9, commentary para 5.

opinions of government advisers, and official legal manuals.[39] While there is a clear overlap between the forms that practice and acceptance as law may take,[40] some forms are more likely to be useful for the identification of practice and others for the identification of acceptance as law. For instance, acceptance as law is particularly likely to be embodied in statements.[41] That said, it is now generally accepted that practice too comprises both physical and verbal conduct.[42] It is not only how states act that matters but the statements they make too count towards practice.[43] In fact, we need to consider a diverse range of materials, that is, 'what States say, what they do, and what they say about what they do'.[44] If a state engages in unlawful conduct but still seeks to justify it by using legal arguments, the justification could carry more weight than the conduct itself.[45] According to the ICJ in *Military and Paramilitary Activities in and against Nicaragua*, if state conduct appears to be incompatible with a rule but the state defends it 'by appealing to exceptions or justifications contained within the rule itself, then whether or not the State's conduct is in fact justifiable on that basis, the significance of that attitude is to confirm rather than to weaken the rule'.[46] As we will see, this is what the United Kingdom does with respect to the Parthenon marbles: it explains their continued retention with the argument that they were lawfully removed.

Despite the overlap between state practice and acceptance as law, both must be shown to exist.[47] This does not exclude that the same act can serve both as evidence of state practice *and* acceptance as law, since it is broadly conceded that evidence of acceptance as law needs to be obtained from state practice.[48] But it does mean that two distinct enquiries into practice and into acceptance as law are necessary,

[39] ILC, 'Conclusions on Identification of Customary International Law' (2018), conclusions 6 and 10; Shaw (2021) 68-70; Crawford (2019) 21-22; Pellet and Müller (2019) 906-907, 911; Treves (2019) 144-145; Guzman (2005) 151-153.

[40] Thirlway (2015) 502; Titi (2021) 123.

[41] ILC, 'Conclusions on Identification of Customary International Law' (2018), conclusion 10, commentary para 3.

[42] ILC, 'Conclusions on Identification of Customary International Law' (2018), conclusion 6.

[43] ILC, 'Conclusions on Identification of Customary International Law' (2018), conclusion 6, commentary para 2; Wood and Sender (2020), para 6; cf d'Aspremont (2014).

[44] Wood and Sender (2020), para 6.

[45] Wood and Sender (2020), para 6. See also *Military and Paramilitary Activities in and against Nicaragua (Nicaragua v United States)* (Merits Judgment) [1986] ICJ Rep 14 [207].

[46] *Military and Paramilitary Activities in and against Nicaragua (Nicaragua v United States)* (Merits Judgment) [1986] ICJ Rep 14 [186].

[47] ILC, 'Conclusions on Identification of Customary International Law' (2018), conclusion 3.

[48] ILC, 'Conclusions on Identification of Customary International Law' (2018), conclusion 3, commentary para 8; Crawford (2014) 69; Lepard (2010) 122-139; Mendelson (1998) 206-207; Dumberry (2016) 309-321; Klabbers (2009) 187; Kammerhofer (2004) 526; Byers (1999) 136-141; Thirlway (2015) 502; Koskenniemi (2011) 56; Titi (2021) 123.

irrespective of overlaps in the material used as evidence for the one and for the other.[49]

Finally, when assessing evidence in order to ascertain the existence of general practice and its acceptance as law one needs to consider the nature and context of the norm and of the evidence for it.[50] For example, when examining domestic laws as evidence of practice, the manner of their interpretation and application may have greater significance than the text itself.[51] Or, national court decisions will not be of a very great importance, if they remain unenforced or have been reversed by parliament on account of their incompatibility with international law.[52] By the same token, not all statements made by state organs matter equally: carefully planned remarks will generally matter more than casual comments or those made 'in the heat of the moment'.[53] At the time when the United States ratified the 1970 UNESCO Convention, it made a declaration to the effect that it understood the Convention not to be retroactive.[54] This declaration, made 40 years ago, will not negate the evidence of subsequent consistent US practice of returning stolen or looted cultural artefacts irrespective of whether they were removed before or after the entry into force of the 1970 UNESCO Convention. Or, the fact that the Greek government, having been advised to start legal action because the marbles should be returned to Athens, inter alia, as a matter of customary international law,[55] still insists on appealing to the United Kingdom's good will, calling the return of the marbles an 'ethical' and 'political' issue in order to avoid a head-on legal confrontation with the United Kingdom, cannot be taken as evidence of contrary practice. As we have seen, international legal disputes are also political anyway.[56] Greece has made it clear that the marbles are too important to risk the uncertainty of judicial proceedings and prefers to pursue a solution through diplomatic means.[57] This is also in line with the Operating Guidelines for the Implementation of the 1970 UNESCO Convention.[58] It

---

[49] ILC, 'Conclusions on Identification of Customary International Law' (2018), conclusion 3, commentary para 8.

[50] ILC, 'Conclusions on Identification of Customary International Law' (2018), conclusion 3; *Case concerning rights of nationals of the United States of America in Morocco* (Judgment) [1952] ICJ Rep 176, 200.

[51] ILC, 'Conclusions on Identification of Customary International Law' (2018), conclusion 3, commentary para 5.

[52] ILC, 'Conclusions on Identification of Customary International Law' (2018), conclusion 3, commentary para 5.

[53] ILC, 'Conclusions on Identification of Customary International Law' (2018), conclusion 3, commentary para 5.

[54] For the declarations and reservations to the 1970 UNESCO Convention, see https://bit.ly/3NDoITc.

[55] Robertson (2019) preface.

[56] See Sect. 8.2. See further Lauterpacht (1933) 161.

[57] Liz Alderman, 'Greece Rules Out Suing British Museum Over Elgin Marbles', The New York Times (14 May 2015).

[58] Chapter 9, text to n 53.

should not lead to the conclusion that Greece does not consider that the return of the marbles is required by international law—in fact, Greece clearly sees the return of the marbles as its legal right.

10.2.2 Widespread and Representative State Practice

There is ample evidence of state practice on returns that take place despite the fact that they fall outside the coverage of the non-retroactive conventions. The introduction to this book has already documented some state practice, such as the return of thousands of manuscripts from Denmark to Iceland between 1971 and 1997[59] and the 1990 successful replevin action brought by Cyprus and the Greek-Orthodox Church of Cyprus in *Autocephalous Greek-Orthodox Church v Goldberg* in the United States.[60] The latter case bears similarities to the Parthenon marbles case, for the stolen Byzantine mosaics that were the object of the replevin action had been stolen from an occupied territory, a Cypriot church after the 1974 Turkish invasion of the island. Numerous examples of returns until 2007 are discussed in Greenfield's *The Return of Cultural Treasures*.[61] In this section, we will consider additional evidence of state practice, focusing on more recent returns.

Some countries have had more opportunity to engage in relevant state practice. This is the case of the United States, a big art market with major world museums, and Italy, a country particularly rich in art. For example, in 2021, the United States repatriated two carved decorative lintels, originally part of ancient Thai temples. The lintels had been stolen and illegally exported over 50 years earlier. They were repatriated after the City and County of San Francisco agreed to their forfeiture to the United States with a view to their return to Thailand.[62]

Italy has been at the forefront of efforts to both restore looted cultural property and to actively pursue the recovery of antiquities and other cultural property unlawfully removed from its territory.[63] Earlier Italian examples include the return of the Lion of Judah and the Axum Obelisk to Ethiopia.[64] In 2008, Italy repatriated to Libya the headless statue of the Venus of Cyrene, a Roman copy of a now-lost Hellenistic work, which had been discovered by Italian troops in 1913 and

[59] See Chap. 1, text to nn 160-161.

[60] *Autocephalous Greek-Orthodox Church of Cyprus and Cyprus v Goldberg*, 717 F Supp 1374 (SD Ind 1989), aff'd 917 F.2d 278 (7th Cir 1990). See Chap. 1, text to nn 153-159.

[61] Greenfield (2007).

[62] US Department of Justice, US Attorney's Office, Northern District of California, 'United States Successfully Negotiates the Return of Two Thai Religious Relics Reported Stolen by Thailand and Displayed at San Francisco Asian Art Museum' (10 February 2021); 'Thailand welcomes back stolen artefacts after San Francisco forfeiture', Reuters (31 May 2021).

[63] E.g. see Scovazzi (2014); Nicole Winfield, 'Italy Sending Parthenon Fragment to Athens in Nudge to UK', Bloomberg (5 January 2022).

[64] Pankhurst (1999); 'Obelisk Returned to Ethiopia after 68 Years', The Guardian (20 April 2005).

transported to Italy in 1915, at a time when Italy had unilaterally annexed Libya.[65] Interestingly, Libya did not then exist as an independent state but was under occupation, much like Greece at the time when Elgin's agents were at work on the Parthenon.

An Italian return that speaks volumes to the Parthenon marbles dispute is that of a small fragment from the Parthenon's east frieze, depicting the foot of the goddess Artemis. The fragment, which permanently joined the Parthenon frieze in 2022, had been in the possession of Robert Fagan, the former British consul in Sicily, and was later sold to the University of Palermo by his widow.[66] How the fragment came to be in Fagan's possession is, frankly, anyone's guess.[67] One of the conceivable explanations is that it went astray from the Elgin collection, although there is no firm evidence to support this—or any other—version.

A big chunk of returns concerns the restitution of Nazi looted art, including antiquities illegally excavated, stolen, or otherwise removed by the Nazis.[68] In France, at least 140 such restitutions have been recorded.[69] Two of the most recent are those of the Gustav Klimt painting *Rose Bushes under Trees*, previously held at the Musée d'Orsay, and *Le Père* by Marc Chagall.[70] Another recent restitution of Nazi looted art, this time by Italy, is that of *Lot with His Two Daughters Serving Him Drinks*, a painting by Nicolas Poussin.[71] In 2021, the Dresden State Art Collection, which as its name reveals is a public museum, returned to the grandchildren of Jules

---

[65] Scovazzi (2009) 355.

[66] Nicole Winfield, 'Italy Sending Parthenon Fragment to Athens in Nudge to UK' Bloomberg (5 January 2022).

[67] Nicole Winfield, 'Italy Sending Parthenon Fragment to Athens in Nudge to UK' Bloomberg (5 January 2022).

[68] E.g. see Milton Esterow, 'New Research Tracks Ancient Artifacts Looted by the Nazis', The New York Times (18 January 2022), reporting the restitution of more than 13,000 items to Greece by the Pfahlbau Museum in Unteruhldingen and 26 antiquities from the University of Graz in Austria. See also 'Stolen Antiquities Return to Greece from Austria', GTP Headlines (23 November 2017). See also Chap. 1, text to nn 147-152.

[69] Projet de loi n° 4632 relatif à la restitution ou la remise de certains biens culturels aux ayants droit de leurs propriétaires victimes de persécutions antisémites (enregistré à la Présidence de l'Assemblée nationale le 3 novembre 2021), exposé des motifs. This bill has now become law, Loi n° 2022-218 du 21 février 2022 relative à la restitution ou la remise de certains biens culturels aux ayants droit de leurs propriétaires victimes de persécutions antisémites, JORF of 22 February 2022.

[70] French Ministry of Culture, 'Restitution du tableau de Gustav Klimt, Rosiers sous les arbres, aux ayants droit de Nora Stiasny' (Press release, 23 March 2022); French Ministry of Culture, 'Restitution du tableau de Marc Chagall, Le Père, aux ayants-droit de David Cender' (Press release, 1 April 2022). See also Loi n° 2022-218 du 21 février 2022 relative à la restitution ou la remise de certains biens culturels aux ayants droit de leurs propriétaires victimes de persécutions antisémites, JORF of 22 February 2022.

[71] Tessa Solomon, 'Nazi-Looted Poussin Painting Found in Italy, Returned to Owners' ARTnews (1 April 2021). For a discussion of the return of Nazi looted art until 2007, see Greenfield (2007) 282-299.

Strauss Nicolas de Largillière's *Portrait of a Lady as Pomona*, which had been sold under duress in 1941.[72]

A more recent wave of returns and announced returns, concerns art, especially African art, removed as a result of colonialism or foreign occupation.[73] For instance, Belgium has started a process of revising its collections with a view to returning to the Democratic Republic of the Congo 84,000 museum artefacts acquired by the country during the colonial era.[74] A joint Belgian-Congolese expert commission is expected to classify artefacts intro three categories: looted objects, which should be returned immediately to the Democratic Republic of the Congo; cultural objects legitimately acquired, which can remain in Belgium; and objects with unclear provenance.[75] The latter are expected to remain in Belgium but their legal status will change to allow deaccessioning.[76] Burundi and Rwanda will also likely be concerned by Belgian restitutions.[77] Thomas Dermine, Belgium's state secretary for science policy, described the move towards the return of objects acquired in colonial times as 'important and highly symbolic', because it acknowledges that 'the colonial regime as a political model implies a form of domination that is fundamentally unequal and influences the terms of exchange'.[78] A Belgian law adopted in the summer of 2022 put into effect the new policy.[79] The law covers specifically defined objects held in federal scientific establishments that were acquired between 1885 and the independence of the state of origin.[80] Interestingly, the decision to restore the objects in question will be based on the 'illegitimate' (as opposed to 'unlawful') character of the acquisition, which, however, is described as an acquisition of an

[72]Dresden State Art Collection, 'The Staatliche Kunstsammlungen Dresden (Dresden State Art Collections) restitute the "Portrait of a Lady as Pomona" by Nicolas de Largillière from the holdings of the Gemäldegalerie Alte Meister (Old Masters Picture Gallery)' (28 January 2021) https://bit.ly/3NdNNE8. In 2022, the Strauss family sold the painting at auction for US $1.23 million, Sotheby's, 'Master Paintings & Sculpture Part I' (27 January 2022) https://bit.ly/3GAtRJd.

[73]See also MacGregor (2021) 194.

[74]Camille Gijs, 'Belgium Takes Small Step toward Returning Artifacts to Congo', Politico (17 February 2022).

[75]Catherine Hickley, 'Belgium Plans to Hand Back Colonial Loot to DR Congo', The Art Newspaper (24 December 2021).

[76]Catherine Hickley, 'Belgium Plans to Hand Back Colonial Loot to DR Congo', The Art Newspaper (24 December 2021).

[77]'Restitution policy of the Royal Museum for Central Africa' https://www.africamuseum.be/en/about_us/restitution (information correct as of November 2022).

[78]Catherine Hickley, 'Belgium Plans to Hand Back Colonial Loot to DR Congo', The Art Newspaper (24 December 2021).

[79]Loi reconnaissant le caractère aliénable des biens liés au passé colonial de l'État belge et déterminant un cadre juridique pour leur restitution et leur retour, 3 July 2022 (Moniteur belge 28 September 2022).

[80]Loi reconnaissant le caractère aliénable des biens liés au passé colonial de l'État belge et déterminant un cadre juridique pour leur restitution et leur retour, 3 July 2022 (Moniteur belge 28 September 2022) art 3.

object under duress or by violence.[81] Since the adoption of the law, a draft bilateral agreement has been sent to the Democratic Republic of the Congo proposing the constitution of the joint expert commission.

In the Netherlands, a 2020 government advisory report recommended the unconditional return of looted cultural heritage to its countries of origin.[82] In response to the report, the government undertook to return unconditionally any cultural objects stolen from a former Dutch colony. It also agreed that cultural objects stolen from other colonies or those that are 'of particular cultural, historic or religious significance to a country, may also be eligible for return'.[83] In 2022, Germany and Nigeria signed an agreement transferring ownership to Nigeria of more than 500 Benin bronzes from the collection of the Ethnological Museum in Berlin.[84] According to the German government, additional agreements affecting the collections of other museums are to be concluded.[85] Other countries are following suit. For example, Austria is looking into returning artefacts acquired in colonial times. Although Austria itself was not a colonial power, many items were acquired by Austrian merchants.[86]

Human remains are also increasingly the object of restitutions. The return of the remains of the Tasmanian aboriginals previously held in the Natural History Museum in London has already been discussed.[87] More recent restitutions include Germany's return to Namibia of the remains of Herero and Nama people, victims of the Namibian genocide,[88] and the repatriation of Hawaiian remains held in German and Austrian museums and university collections since the nineteenth and early

---

[81] Loi reconnaissant le caractère aliénable des biens liés au passé colonial de l'État belge et déterminant un cadre juridique pour leur restitution et leur retour, 3 July 2022 (Moniteur belge 28 September 2022) art 4(1).

[82] 'Summary of Report Advisory Committee on the National Policy Framework for Colonial Collections' (in English) (7 October 2020) https://www.raadvoorcultuur.nl/documenten/adviezen/2020/10/07/summary-of-report-advisory-committee-on-the-national-policy-framework-for-colonial-collections. The full report is available (in Dutch) here https://dutchculture.nl/en/news/Report-Advisory-Committee-National-Policy-Framework-Colonial-Collections.

[83] Government of the Netherlands, 'Government: Redressing an Injustice by Returning Cultural Heritage Objects to their Country of Origin' (29 January 2021) https://bit.ly/3Gbr7Ss.

[84] 'Germany Signs Deal to Give Ownership of Benin Bronzes to Nigeria', Reuters (25 August 2022); Catherine Hickley, 'And So it Begins: Germany and Nigeria Sign Pre-accord on Restitution of Benin Bronzes', The Art Newspaper (15 October 2021); see also Alex Marshall, 'Germany Sets Out Plans to Return Benin Bronzes', The New York Times (30 April 2021).

[85] 'Germany Signs Deal to Give Ownership of Benin Bronzes to Nigeria', Reuters (25 August 2022). Another example of a recent return by Germany is that of the repatriation to Namibia of a fifteenth century Portuguese stone cross removed during colonial times, 'Germany to Return Portuguese Stone Cross to Namibia', BBC News (17 May 2019).

[86] Catherine Hickley, 'Austria Takes First Step to Return Artefacts from Colonial Era', The Art Newspaper (7 January 2022); Austrian Ministry of Arts, Culture, Civil Service and Sport, 'Österreichische Bundesmuseen im kolonialen Kontext: Staatssekretärin Mayer richtet Fachgremium ein' (20 January 2022).

[87] See Chap. 7, text to n 82.

[88] 'Germany Returns Skulls of Namibian Genocide Victims', BBC News (29 August 2018).

twentieth centuries.[89] Germany's culture minister, Claudia Roth stated unambiguously that '[h]uman remains from colonial contexts have no place in our museums and universities' and their return is 'a priority'.[90]

To these returns, we must add the repatriation of archival material, including a case that is not properly speaking a return. In 1990, the United Kingdom sent to Australia an original copy of the Commonwealth of Australia Constitution Act (1900), technically a piece of UK legislation, without unlawful removal involved.[91] The constitution was formerly to be kept in the Public Records Office and was deaccessioned with the Australian Constitution (Public Record Copy) Act 1990.[92]

National court decisions can also be relied upon as evidence of state practice. US court decisions are leading with returns,[93] but they are not the only ones. In the Supreme Court of Ireland, Chief Justice Finlay recognised that it is now 'universally accepted ... that one of the most important national assets belonging to the people is their heritage and knowledge of its true origins and the buildings and objects which constitute keys to their ancient history'.[94] Therefore, 'a necessary ingredient of sovereignty in a modern State ... is and should be an ownership by the State of objects which constitute antiquities of importance which are discovered and which have no known owner'.[95] More recently, this statement has been cited approvingly by the English Court of Appeal.[96] This line of case law seems to follow in the lines of

[89] Catherine Hickley, 'Native Hawaiians Collect Ancestors' Skulls from European Museums', The New York Times (10 February 2022).

[90] 'Germany and Austria repatriate 19th-century ancestral human remains to Hawaii', Euronews (11 February 2022). Contrast Loi reconnaissant le caractère aliénable des biens liés au passé colonial de l'État belge et déterminant un cadre juridique pour leur restitution et leur retour, 3 July 2022 (Moniteur belge 28 September 2022) art 3(1).

[91] Magnusson (2007) 8-9.

[92] Australian Constitution (Public Record Copy) Act 1990, c 17, s 1. There have also been numerous treaties providing for the return of archival material, for a discussion see Greenfield (2007) 392.

[93] E.g. *United States v Hollinshead*, 495 F.2d 1154 (9th Cir 1974), concerning the successful prosecution of the Californian art dealer Clive Hollinshead for transporting into the United States a stolen Guatemalan stela; *United States v McClain*, 545 F.2d 988 (5th Cir 1977) and *United States v McClain*, 593 F.2d 658 (5th Cir 1979), concerning the defendants' conviction for conspiracy to receive, conceal and/or sell stolen goods in contravention of the National Stolen Property Act (NSPA), 18 USC §§ 2314, 2315. On this case law, see also Greenfield (2007) 163, noting its significance for the return of cultural heritage, since 'criminal law was being brought to bear on illicit export of foreign cultural property'; *United States v Bernstein* case, No CR-82-00019-A (ED Va 5 March 1982), in relation to the prosecution for a false customs declaration of David Bernstein after US customs officials seized pre-Columbian objects he was importing. As a result of the prosecution, numerous pre-Columbian objects were returned from the United States to Peru before US enactment of implementing legislation to put the 1970 UNESCO Convention into effect; *Autocephalous Greek-Orthodox Church of Cyprus and Cyprus v Goldberg*, 717 F Supp 1374 (SD Ind 1989), aff'd 917 F.2d 278 (7th Cir 1990); cf *David Cassirer and others v Thyssen-Bornemisza Collection Foundation*, 596 US_(2022).

[94] *Webb v Ireland* [1988] IR 353, 383.

[95] *Webb v Ireland* [1988] IR 353, 383.

[96] *Iran v Barakat Galleries Limited* (2007) EWCA Civ 1374.

the seminal ICJ judgment in the *Temple of Preah Vihear* case, where the Court held that ownership was tied to territorial sovereignty and that the artefacts removed from the temple should be returned.[97]

State practice is also evidenced by numerous resolutions of the United Nations General Assembly (UNGA) on the return or restitution of cultural property to their countries of origin.[98] Under the Charter of the United Nations (UN Charter), the General Assembly is mandated to 'make recommendations' in order to encourage 'the progressive development of international law and its codification'.[99] It is in this light that its recommendations must be understood. As we have seen, the most recent UNGA resolution on the return of cultural property was supported by 111 states and adopted by consensus.[100]

---

[97] *Case concerning the Temple of Preah Vihear (Cambodia v Thailand)* (Merits Judgment) [1962] ICJ Rep 6. Interestingly, a similar argument for movable property had been made by Castlereagh, when arguing in favour of the return of Napoleon's loot: 'upon what principle deprive France of her late territorial acquisitions, and preserve to her the spoliations appertaining to those territories, which all modern conquerors have invariably respected as inseparable from the country to which they belonged?', Note delivered by Viscount Castlereagh to the Allied Ministers, and placed upon their Protocol, Paris, 11 September 1815, reprinted in von Martens (1818) 608.

[98] E.g. UNGA Res 76/16 (6 December 2021) UN Doc A/RES/76/16; UNGA Res 73/130 (24 December 2018) UN Doc A/RES/73/130; UNGA Res 70/76 (9 December 2015) UN Doc A/RES/70/76; UNGA Res A/67/L.34 (5 December 2012) UN Doc A/67/L.34; UNGA Res 64/78 (7 December 2009) UN Doc A/RES/64/78; UNGA Res 61/52 (4 December 2006) UN Doc A/RES/61/52; UNGA Res 58/17 (3 December 2003) UN Doc A/RES/58/17; UNGA Res 56/97 (14 December 2001) UN Doc A/RES/56/97; UNGA Res 54/190 (17 December 1999) UN Doc A/RES/54/190; UNGA Res 52/24 (25 November 1997) UN Doc A/RES/52/24; UNGA Res 50/56 (11 December 1995) UN Doc A/RES/50/56; UNGA Res 48/15 (2 November 1993) UN Doc A/RES/48/15; UNGA Res 46/10 (22 October 1991) UN Doc A/RES/46/10; UNGA Res 44/18 (6 November 1989) UN Doc A/RES/44/18; UNGA Res 42/7 (22 October 1987) UN Doc A/RES/42/7; UNGA Res 40/19 (21 November 1985) UN Doc A/RES/40/19; UNGA Res 38/34 (25 November 1983) UN Doc A/RES/38/34; UNGA Res 36/64 (27 November 1981) UN Doc A/RES/36/64; UNGA Res 35/127 and 35/128 (11 December 1980); UNGA Res 34/64 (29 November 1979) UN Doc A/RES/34/64; UNGA Res 33/50 (14 December 1978); UNGA Res 32/18 (11 November 1977); UNGA Res 31/40 (30 November 1976); UNGA Res 3391 (XXX) (19 November 1975) UN Doc A/RES/3391(XXX); UNGA Res 3187 (XXVIII) (18 December 1973) UN Doc A/RES/3187(XXVIII). See also United Nations Declaration on the Rights of Indigenous Peoples (UNGA Res 61/295 (13 September 2007) UN Doc A/RES/61/295), providing for redress through effective means that 'may include restitution' (arts 11(2) and 28(1)). The resolution, initially adopted by a majority of 144 states in favour, was later endorsed unanimously by 182 states, including notably by all four states that had initially voted against it, UN Office of the High Commissioner for Human Rights, 'Outcome Document of the Durban Review Conference' (24 April 2009), para 73. See also https://www.un.org/development/desa/indigenouspeoples/declaration-on-the-rights-of-indigenous-peoples.html.

[99] UN Charter art 13(1)(a).

[100] Chapter 7, text to nn 142-145.

Evidence of state practice can also be found in resolutions of the United Nations Security Council (UNSC),[101] domestic legislation,[102] multilateral international or regional treaties,[103] bilateral treaties, executive agreements, and memoranda of understanding,[104] declarations by states and organs of the state,[105] and activities

[101] In contrast with the resolutions passed by the UNGA, which concern the return of cultural property in general, the resolutions of the UNSC relate to cultural property removed especially in times of armed conflict, including when it is trafficked by terrorist groups, e.g. UNSC Res 2347 (24 March 2017) UN Doc S/RES/2347(2017); UNSC Res 2199 (12 February 2015) UN Doc S/RES/2199(2015); UNSC Res 1483 (22 May 2003) UN Doc S/RES/1483(2003).

[102] E.g. (Australia) Protection of Movable Cultural Heritage Act 1986 (Act No 11, 1986, as amended up to Act No 61, 2016) s 14; (United States) National Stolen Property Act (NSPA), 18 USC §§ 2314, 2315; Archaeological Resources Protection Act (ARPA), 16 USC 88 470aa-470mm, see also Greenfield (2007) 164; United States Code: Importation of Pre-Columbian Monumental or Architectural Sculpture or Murals, 19 USC §§ 2091-2095 (Suppl 2 1970).

[103] Convention on the Protection of the Arch[a]eological, Historical, and Artistic Heritage of the American Nations of the Organization of American States (1976) AG/RES.210 (VI-O/76) (Convention of San Salvador) arts 10-13. Pursuant to the Convention, states parties undertake to adopt measures to 'prevent and curb the unlawful exportation, importation, and removal of cultural property, as well as those necessary for the *return* of such property to the state to which it belongs in the event of its removal' (art 10, emphasis added). For another example, see Central American Convention for the Restitution and Return of Archaeological, Historical and Artistic Objects (signed in Guatemala in 1995) arts 1-2.

[104] E.g. Treaty of Cooperation between the United States of America and the United Mexican States Providing for the Recovery and Return of Stolen Archaeological, Historical and Cultural Properties (17 July 1970); Agreement between the United States of America and the Republic of Peru for the Recovery and Return of Stolen Archaeological, Historical and Cultural Properties (14 September 1981); Agreement between the United States of America and the Republic of Guatemala for the Recovery and Return of Stolen Archaeological, Historical and Cultural (21 May 1984); Agreement between the Government of Canada and the Government of the United States of America concerning the Imposition of Import Restrictions on Certain Categories of Archaeological and Ethnological Material (10 April 1997); Memorandum of Understanding between the Government of the United States of America and the Government of the Republic of Cyprus concerning the Imposition of Import Restrictions on Pre-Classical and Classical Archaeological Objects (16 July 2002); Memorandum of Understanding between the Government of the United States of America and the Government of the Republic of Ecuador concerning the Imposition of Import Restrictions on Categories of Archaeological and Ethnological Material of Ecuador (22 May 2019). According to UNESCO, by January 2022, China had signed 23 bilateral agreements to facilitate the return and restitution of cultural property and fight against illicit trafficking, UNESCO, 'China Celebrates Second International Day against Illicit Trafficking in Cultural Property' (19 January 2022) https://bit.ly/3GtfruD. These include a memorandum of understanding with the United States, Memorandum of Understanding between the United States of America and China (14 January 2009). Another example is the Joint Declaration made by Italy and Libya on 4 July 1998, reported to form the basis of the Italian decree that paved the way for the return of the statue of Cyrene to Libya. For the Italian decree, see Scovazzi (2009) 355. See further the more recent Treaty of Friendship, Partnership, and Cooperation between the Great Socialist People's Libyan Arab Jamahiriya and the Republic of Italy, which provides for the return to Libya of manuscripts and artefacts removed by Italy during the colonisation period (without mention of the 1970 UNESCO Convention) (ibid, art 10).

[105] E.g. (Argentina) Statement by President Cristina Fernandez de Kirchner in favour of returns with an indirect criticism of 'the great museums of the world', where one can see 'pieces from Greece, Syria, Egypt, Asia and even Latin America, and which have not been returned', see 'Argentina to

within (other) international organisations, including the United Nations Educational, Scientific and Cultural Organization (UNESCO).[106] Notable in the latter context are the decisions and recommendations of the Intergovernmental Committee for Promoting the Return of Cultural Property to its Countries of Origin or its Restitution in case of Illicit Appropriation (ICPRCP or Intergovernmental Committee). These decisions and recommendations concern the return of both cultural property in general and the Parthenon marbles in particular and include a 2021 decision, which shall be discussed later in this chapter.[107] The ICPRCP was established precisely in order to assist with the repatriation of cultural property that 'has a fundamental significance from the point of view of the spiritual values and cultural heritage of the people of a Member State or Associate Member of UNESCO and which has been lost as a result of colonial or foreign occupation or as a result of illicit appropriation', that is, cultural property that in principle falls outside the scope of the 1970 UNESCO Convention.[108] To these instances of state practice, we must add the declarations and recommendations of international forums on the return of cultural property, such as those held in South Korea, Greece, China, and Turkey between

Restore 4,000 Artefacts to Ecuador and Peru', BBC News (23 August 2015); (China) Statement by the Chinese President, Xi Jinping, in favour of returns of cultural property in general and of the Parthenon marbles in particular, on the occasion of his 2019 visit to Greece, Iliana Magra, 'In Struggle Over Parthenon Marbles, Greece Gets Unexpected Ally: Xi Jinping', The New York Times (13 November 2019); (Italy) '"Fagan" Parthenon Fragment Has Been Permanently Returned to Greece', Neos Kosmos (7 June 2022), quoting Italian culture minister, Dario Franceschini, who described Italy as being 'at the forefront of applying in practice the principle of the return of cultural property'; (Mexico) Mexican Government, Foreign Affairs-Culture, 'Mexican Government Holds a Forum on the Return and Restitution of Cultural Property' (Press release, 29 August 2022) https://bit.ly/3CcOH0F, reporting various statements; (Scotland) National Museums Scotland, 'Procedure for Considering Requests for the Permanent Transfer of Collection Objects to Non-UK Claimants' (2021), which outlines the criteria and management of requests for the permanent transfer of objects to claimants outside the United Kingdom. National Museums Scotland https://bit.ly/3fmFCtt. National Museums Scotland is another non-departmental public body (NDPB), see National Museums Scotland Framework Document https://www.nms.ac.uk/media/1163485/nms-framework-agreement-2018.pdf; (United States) US Congress, Senate, S Con Res 134 'Expressing the sense of the Congress that the Parthenon Marbles should be returned to Greece', 108th Congress, 2nd session (22 July 2004).

[106] E.g. UNESCO, 'Operational Guidelines for the Implementation of the Convention on the Means of Prohibiting and Preventing the Illicit Import, Export and Transfer of Ownership of Cultural Property', adopted by Resolution 3.MSP 11 at the third Meeting of States Parties (18-20 May 2015), paras 102-103, encouraging states to apply the spirit of the 1970 Convention to requests for the return of unlawfully removed cultural property that does not enter into the temporal remit of the Convention, see Chap. 9, text to n 53.

[107] See text to nn 178-180.

[108] Statutes of the Intergovernmental Committee for Promoting the Return of Cultural Property to its Countries of Origin or its Restitution in case of Illicit Appropriation (ICPRCP Statutes), adopted by 20 C/Res 4/7.6/5 of the 20th session of the General Conference of UNESCO, Paris, 24 October-28 November 1978, arts 3(2), 4.

2011 and 2015, to the extent that they involve state participation;[109] and, arguably, even the legal opinions of government advisers.[110]

A question to consider is whether international treaties, such as the 1970 UNESCO Convention, that are not retroactive count as state practice or whether, by not being retroactive, they in fact constitute contrary state practice. As we have seen, the conventions have encouraged the return of cultural property unlawfully removed prior to their entry into force, despite not being retroactive. The conventions show the commitment of states to the restitution of unlawfully removed cultural property and they too progressively codify customary international law in the field of return. For this reason, it is suggested that such instruments in fact count as state practice and what matters is how they are applied.

Similarly, we should take into account the very numerous returns that take place irrespective of whether they fall within the scope of the 1970 UNESCO Convention, such as because they are decided on the basis of local criminal laws without necessary reference to the international legal framework.[111] We should also include returns of items that were looted in wartime when such returns are not ostensibly based on the law of war, such as the return from Chile to Peru in 2007 of almost 4000 books that Chilean soldiers had removed from the National Library of Peru in 1881, 126 years earlier, during the War of the Pacific;[112] and returns that we may qualify as 'domestic'. The Stone of Destiny, the coronation stone of Scottish kings (popularly known as the 'Stone of Scone') removed to England from Scotland in 1296 was

---

[109] E.g. Ancient Olympia Recommendation (2013), especially para 12 making express reference to the return of the Parthenon marbles. For the international forums, see UNGA Res 70/76 (9 December 2015) UN Doc A/RES/70/76, para 7.

[110] E.g. (France) Felwine Sarr and Bénédicte Savoy, 'Rapport sur la restitution du patrimoine culturel africain. Vers une nouvelle éthique relationnelle' (November 2018); cf (United Kingdom) 'Report of the Ministerial Advisory Panel on Illicit Trade' (Department for Culture, Media, and Sport 2000).

[111] E.g. the 2022 confiscation by the New York police of 27 looted ancient Greek, Roman, and Egyptian artefacts from the Met for restitution to Italy and Egypt, Tom Mashberg and Graham Bowley, 'Investigators, Citing Looting, Have Seized 27 Antiquities from the Met', The New York Times (2 September 2022); Italian court decisions or restitution resolutions asking for the return of stolen or looted or unlawfully exported objects, such as in relation to the so-called Getty bronze (bought by the US museum in the 1970s), see Gaia Pianigiani, 'Italian Court Rules Getty Museum Must Return a Prized Bronze', The New York Times (4 December 2018); Elisabetta Povoledo, 'Italy Still Wants the Getty Bronze, and Perhaps More', The New York Times (24 May 2019); James Imam, 'Italy Passes Restitution Resolution amid Renewed Calls for Return of the "Victorious Youth" Bronze from Getty Museum', The Art Newspaper (19 July 2021); for an earlier detailed account, see Fincham (2014); and a 2022 ruling by a Naples court that a Roman marble copy of *The Doryphoros* (a bronze by the Greek artist Polykleitos) bought by the Minneapolis Institute of Art (Mia) in the 1980s had been illegally excavated in the 1970s, see Benjamin Sutton, 'Italian Court Calls for Restitution of Ancient Marble Statue from Minneapolis Institute of Art', The Art Newspaper (30 March 2022); Elisabetta Povoledo, 'Italy Says Ancient Statue in US Museum Was Stolen, Not Lost at Sea', New York Times (20 May 2022).

[112] Scovazzi (2011) 364.

returned home 700 years later, in 1996.[113] Between 1982 and 2001, Denmark returned to Greenland around 35,000 archaeological and ethnographic items that had been removed during the colonial period.[114] Other returns within countries concern the restitution of cultural property to indigenous peoples.[115]

In conclusion, the foregoing discussion, including examples given in previous chapters, supports the argument that there is sufficient evidence of state practice that is widespread and representative.

10.2.3 Uniform and Consistent State Practice?

But is this state practice also uniform and consistent? For one, not all returns are the same. Some are ordered by an international judgment, such as in the *Temple of Preah Vihear* case'[116] others are the result of a national judgment, such as in *Autocephalous Greek-Orthodox Church v Goldberg*,[117] an arbitral award, such as in *Maria Altmann v Austria*,[118] mediation, negotiations, and so on. In some cases, return has been accomplished through a long-term deposit, and in others it comes under the guise of a 'gift'. However, ultimately, the act that matters is the return.

More troubling than the manner of return is the question of contrary state practice. Despite the numerous returns, many—indeed most—items stubbornly remain in foreign museums. What does it mean, for example, that France allows the return of some African objects, but not of all the rest? States have taken measures to allow the return of Nazi looted art, human remains and, increasingly, art removed in colonial times or as a result of occupation. But we can then ask whether general state practice is limited to these types of items and whether classical antiquities are excluded. It is certainly true that Italy and the United States have been returning antiquities, yet other states have not. For example, Germany is willing to return its Benin bronzes but how about the Pergamon Altar or the Nefertiti bust?

No one claims that all items should be repatriated. The nascent rule concerns only important cultural property. In Belgium too, the new policy that encourages the return to Africa of artefacts looted in colonial times focuses on 'specific items that

---

[113]Michael White, 'From the Archive, 4 July 1996: Stone of Scone Going Home after 700 Years', The Guardian (4 July 2015).

[114]Gabriel (2009).

[115]E.g. (United States) Native American Graves Protection and Repatriation Act (NAGPRA) 1990; National Museum of the American Indian Act (NMAIA), 20 USC §80q (Public Law 101-185), as amended by the NMAIA Amendment of 1996 (Public Law 104-278); cf American Declaration on the Rights of Indigenous Peoples, AG/RES 2888 (XLVI-0/16) art XIII.

[116]*Case concerning the Temple of Preah Vihear (Cambodia v Thailand)* (Merits Judgment) [1962] ICJ Rep 6.

[117]*Autocephalous Greek-Orthodox Church of Cyprus and Cyprus v Goldberg*, 717 F Supp 1374 (SD Ind 1989), aff'd 917 F.2d 278 (7th Cir 1990).

[118]*Maria V Altmann and others v Austria*, arbitral award (15 January 2006).

have the highest symbolic value'.[119] The Parthenon marbles are not just any Greek antiquities in a foreign museum. They are *par excellence* the 'high-profile' items that fall within the scope of the nascent rule. Not all antiquities will have to be returned under the new legal framework. Returns are selective and concern objects of particular significance to the requesting state.

It is difficult to put all cultural objects in the same basket. To appreciate why one item is returned and another is not, we need to understand the particular circumstances of the case (e.g. has the state of origin asked for the particular heritage? under what conditions was the cultural property acquired?) and we need to consider the statements governments make when they decide whether to return items. The fact that a state refuses to return artefacts with the argument that they were lawfully acquired (irrespective of whether they in fact were) is not a bar to the emergence of a customary law rule concerning *unlawfully* removed items. It appears that some years ago an informal request was made by Greece for the return of the Venus de Milo, now in the Louvre, and the French response was that the statue had been lawfully obtained.[120] The fact that an item is not returned precisely with the argument that it was lawfully acquired gives all the more reason to suggest that, had it been *un*lawfully acquired, the state would give it back. The National Museum of Denmark in Copenhagen too, probably in an attempt to forestall or discourage prospective requests, claims that the heads of a centaur and a Lapith youth it holds from south metope IV (the metope itself is in the British Museum) were 'bought' in Athens by one of Morosini's naval officers, after they bombarded the Parthenon.[121] That said, not all examples of state practice on returns concern unlawful removals. However, if returns occur when the initial acquisition was not unlawful, a fortiori they must happen when it actually was.

The statements that states make about keeping objects matter. The fact alone that a state refuses to return cultural heritage does not contradict general practice if either the state invokes exceptions to the rule or such conduct is considered by other states to violate international law.[122] And there is often a very long distance between what a state considers to be right (an eventual return) and the extent to which it is willing to comply with this obligation. It is probably in this light that we can also interpret the fact that sometimes the repatriation of objects is announced but then legislatures delay putting it into practice.

It is suggested that state practice on returns is not only widespread and representative but also uniform and consistent. It concerns especially unlawfully removed

[119] Catherine Hickley, 'Belgium Plans to Hand Back Colonial Loot to DR Congo', The Art Newspaper (24 December 2021).

[120] Greenfield (2007) 111-112.

[121] National Museum of Denmark https://samlinger.natmus.dk/as/asset/39613 and https://samlinger.natmus.dk/as/asset/39607 (in Danish). But see Chap. 2, text to n 151.

[122] *Military and Paramilitary Activities in and against Nicaragua (Nicaragua v United States)* (Merits Judgment) [1986] ICJ Rep 14 [186].

heritage often of significant importance to the host state and returns are decided on a case-by-case basis.

10.2.4 Do Museums Contribute to State Practice? (and Some Reflections on Museum Practice)

Although non-state actors do not generally contribute to state practice, the conduct of museums is often relevant for customary international law. It is broadly accepted that only practice attributable to the state matters for the formation of customary international law.[123] Therefore, practice is to be drawn from the conduct of the organs of state that exercise legislative, executive, judicial, or other functions.[124] National or public museums are themselves organs of state and can contribute to general practice for the purposes of the creation of customary international law.

That said, the conduct of non-state actors can still be relevant when assessing state practice.[125] Non-state actors can contribute *indirectly* to the formation of customary international law, such as by 'stimulating or recording' practice and acceptance as law.[126] Non-state actors can lobby states and induce them to behave in a certain way.[127] Or, their conduct may be used as evidence of their compliance with state practice. In addition, the actions of non-state actors may be 'acknowledged' and 'adopted' by states and so become state conduct.[128] Non-state actors can also contribute to the formation of customary international law when they establish 'a particular rule of behaviour' against which states do not protest, thus showing agreement with the rule.[129] In other words, states' attitude towards museum practice, such as tolerance of returns, may count as state practice.

Often what qualifies as museum practice in a narrow sense is tied to conduct attributable to the state, irrespective of whether the museum is actually a public museum, since returns require a certain collaboration between states and museums. This is the case, for example, when a museum repatriates an object because the state has ordered it to do so. A remarkable example of close collaboration between a

---

[123] ILC, 'Second Report on Identification of Customary International Law by Special Rapporteur Michael Wood', UN Doc A/CN.4/672 (22 May 2014), para 34; Mendelson (1998) 203; Dinstein (2007) 266; Villiger (1997) 16-17; d'Aspremont (2011) 430; Dumberry (2016) 118-125; cf ILC, 'Conclusions on Identification of Customary International Law' (2018), conclusion 4.

[124] ILC Articles on State Responsibility art 4(1); cf ILC, 'Conclusions on Identification of Customary International Law' (2018), conclusion 5.

[125] ILC, 'Conclusions on Identification of Customary International Law' (2018), conclusion 4.

[126] ILC, 'Conclusions on Identification of Customary International Law' (2018), conclusion 4, commentary para 8; Mendelson (1998) 203; Dinstein (2007) 266-268; Roberts (2001) 775.

[127] Mendelson (1998) 203.

[128] ILC Articles on State Responsibility art 11.

[129] On the role of state silence or inaction, see text to nn 27-31.

museum, regional government, and central government is that of the previously-mentioned permanent return to Athens, in January 2022, of a small fragment of the Parthenon frieze, which started as an agreement for a time-limited deposit between Sicily's Antonino Salinas Regional Archaeological Museum in Palermo and the Acropolis Museum. From the start, the idea was that the piece would return to Athens permanently (*sine die*).[130] As of June 2022, with the agreement of the central Italian government, the fragment has been permanently returned to Athens and has joined the east frieze in the Acropolis Museum.[131] While approval of the central Italian government was pending, Alberto Samonà, Sicily's councillor for culture, emphasised the 'very strong symbolic value' of the return of this 'small but significant fragment'.[132] He situated the Italian return within the broader context of the calls for restitution of the Parthenon marbles and described it as Italy's 'response to the international debate'.[133] His comments were backed by the Italian culture minister, Dario Franceschini, who voiced his 'great appreciation' for the initiative of the Sicilian regional government.[134]

Another relevant example is that of a dispute brought to the ICPRCP that resulted in the return to Tanzania of a Makonde mask held in the privately owned collection of the Barbier-Mueller Museum in Geneva. The mask had been stolen at a time when Switzerland was not yet party to the 1970 UNESCO Convention. The Swiss authorities acted as facilitator in the negotiations that took place with the museum owner.[135]

An interesting yet distinct question, not directly relevant to state practice, is whether some form of museum practice on returns may be said to have developed. We have already seen that in 2002 a number of world museums signed the Declaration on the Importance and Value of Universal Museums, which took the view that 'objects acquired in earlier times must be viewed in the light of different sensitivities

---

[130] Acropolis Museum, 'The First Return of a Parthenon Sculpture from Abroad to the New Acropolis Museum' (10 January 2022) https://www.theacropolismuseum.gr/en/exhibition-programs/first-return-parthenon-sculpture-abroad-new-acropolis-museum; Moira Lavelle, 'How a Small Marble Foot Has Put More Pressure on the British Museum to Return the Elgin Marbles', The Independent (16 January 2022); Nick Squires, 'Italian Handover of Elgin Marbles Fragment Puts Pressure on UK to Follow Suit', The Telegraph (2 January 2022); Gordon Rayner, '"Momentum is Building" for UK to Give Back Elgin Marbles, Claims Greek PM', The Telegraph (7 January 2022); Nicole Winfield, 'Italy Sending Parthenon Fragment to Athens in Nudge to UK' Bloomberg (5 January 2022).

[131] '"Fagan" Parthenon Fragment Has Been Permanently Returned to Greece', Neos Kosmos (7 June 2022).

[132] Rebecca Ann Hughes, 'Italy Returns Parthenon Sculpture to Greece amid Calls for Reunification of Marbles' Forbes (5 January 2022).

[133] Rebecca Ann Hughes, 'Italy Returns Parthenon Sculpture to Greece amid Calls for Reunification of Marbles' Forbes (5 January 2022).

[134] Nick Squires, 'Italian Handover of Elgin Marbles Fragment Puts Pressure on UK to Follow Suit', The Telegraph (2 January 2022).

[135] ICPRCP, 'Secretariat Report', 16th session, UN Doc CLT-2010/CONF.203/COM.16/2 (July 2010), para 4.

and values, reflective of that earlier era'.[136] As noted in that earlier discussion, the statement referred to acquisitions made by purchase, partage, or as a gift and did not thus concern illicit removals.[137] The declaration recognised that each call for repatriation should be decided on its own merits.[138] It was signed by a non-representative list of eighteen museums—although the British Museum does not appear to have been one of the signatories,[139] information leaked to the press indicated that the statement was a response to a 'call for help' from MacGregor, then director of the British Museum, who faced strong lobbying for the repatriation of the Parthenon marbles.[140] If this was a response to a call for help, it showed very scant support, since most museums rejected it.[141] The declaration has not shielded world museums from repatriations: it is contradicted and discredited by the practice, including the long list of restitutions, that have followed it.

Some years earlier, the International Council of Museums (ICOM) had adopted a resolution that supported the UNESCO Intergovernmental Committee and urged museums 'to initiate dialogues with an open-minded attitude concerning requests for the return of cultural property'.[142] Almost 1000 delegates are reported to have voted in favour of the resolution, with ten abstentions, and no votes against.[143] ICOM's 2017 Code of Ethics for Museums recognises museum collections' potentially 'strong affinities with national, regional, local, ethnic, religious or political identity' and that it is important for museum policies to be 'responsive to this situation'. Accordingly, the code includes two provisions on return and restitution, expanding on the commitments made earlier:

> 6.2 Return of Cultural Property
>
> Museums should be prepared to initiate dialogue for the return of cultural property to a country or people of origin. This should be undertaken in an impartial manner, based on scientific, professional and humanitarian principles as well as applicable local, national and international legislation, in preference to action at a governmental or political level.
>
> 6.3 Restitution of Cultural Property

---

[136] Declaration on the Importance and Value of Universal Museums (2002) https://bit.ly/36QkIyk.

[137] See Chap. 6, text to n 262.

[138] Declaration on the Importance and Value of Universal Museums (2002) https://bit.ly/36QkIyk.

[139] The available information is contradictory with many authors suggesting that the British Museum actually was a signatory, e.g. see Greenfield (2007) 86. However, see the website of the Hermitage Museum, where the British Museum is not listed among the signatories https://bit.ly/3nEUmEN.

[140] Celestine Bohlen, 'Major Museums Affirm Right to Keep Long-Held Antiquities', The New York Times (11 December 2002).

[141] According to 2019 data, there are about 55,000 museums around the world, De Gruyter Saur (2019). While most museums were simply not signatories, some openly criticised the declaration. A strong criticism came from Mark O'Neill, Head of Glasgow Museums, see O'Neill (2004). For other criticisms from within the museum world, see Greenfield (2007) 88.

[142] Stewart (2001) 48.

[143] Stewart (2001) 48.

> When a country or people of origin seeks the restitution of an object or specimen that can be demonstrated to have been exported or otherwise transferred in violation of the principles of international and national conventions, and shown to be part of that country's or people's cultural or natural heritage, the museum concerned should, if legally free to do so, take prompt and responsible steps to cooperate in its return.

ICOM's 2019 guidelines on deaccessioning suggest a number of reasons for which a museum 'might consider' deaccessioning an object. These include possession of an object that is 'inconsistent with applicable law or *ethical principles*, e.g., the object was, or may have been, stolen or illegally exported or imported, or the object may be subject to other legal claims for return or restitution'.[144] Indirectly, the guidelines encourage the return of not only unlawfully but also unethically acquired objects.

Despite differences between museums, it is possible to identify trends. These often, although not always, take their cue from government and changes in state laws. Examples include the Met's 1993 decision to return to Turkey the Lydian Hoard, acquired by the museum between 1966 and 1970, as part of an out-of-court settlement;[145] and the Met's repatriation of the Euphronios krater, discussed in the introduction,[146] which was said to signal a shift in world museum attitudes in relation to art-rich countries whose works of art these museums display.[147] More recently, in the context of the 2022 confiscation by the New York police of 27 looted ancient Greek, Roman, and Egyptian artefacts, the Met expressed its full support of the Manhattan district attorney's office investigations and stressed that its collecting policies have become more rigorous in recent decades since the acquisition of these items.[148] In 2021, the Smithsonian's National Museum of the American Indian returned a pre-Inca breastplate, known as the *Sol de Soles*, to Peru. The object had been in the museum's collection for more than a century.[149] Museums and university collections have returned colonial human remains to Australia and Eskimo skeletal remains to Greenland.[150]

Several returns concern African artefacts, including the Benin bronzes. In its published restitution policy, the Belgian Royal Museum for Central Africa in Tervuren, home to a sizeable collection of African artefacts, discusses with approval the new Belgian legal framework for the repatriation of cultural objects 'related to colonisation'.[151] In 2020, top museums in the Netherlands too backed the advisory

---

[144] ICOM (2019) (emphasis added).

[145] Kaye and Main (1995) 150; Greenfield (2007) 420, 423; Alessandro Chechi, Anne Laure Bandle, and Marc-André Renold, 'Lydian Hoard: Turkey and Metropolitan Museum of Art', Platform ArThemis (undated) https://bit.ly/39H3KnM.

[146] Chapter 1, text to nn 168-169.

[147] Fincham (2013) 958.

[148] Tom Mashberg and Graham Bowley, 'Investigators, Citing Looting, Have Seized 27 Antiquities from the Met', The New York Times (2 September 2022).

[149] Nora McGreevy, 'A Golden Symbol of National Identity Returns to Peru' Smithsonian Magazine (24 June 2021).

[150] Magnusson (2007) 9; cf text to nn 87-90 and Chap. 7, text to n 82.

[151] 'Restitution policy of the Royal Museum for Central Africa' https://www.africamuseum.be/en/about_us/restitution (information correct as of November 2022).

report proposing the creation of a legal structure to allow the return of tens of thousands of cultural objects removed by force from former Dutch colonies.[152] It was sometime later that the Dutch government agreed to the unconditional return of cultural objects that had essentially been stolen.[153] As we have seen, German museums too are starting to return their Benin bronzes.[154]

In 2021, the Met announced that it will be sending a few objects to Nigeria;[155] the University of Aberdeen and Jesus College Cambridge returned other objects;[156] and the Boston Museum of Fine Arts has acknowledged that its Benin bronzes should be repatriated.[157] As of October 2022, the Smithsonian National Museum of African Art in Washington DC is repatriating its Benin bronzes.[158] Earlier that year, the Smithsonian Institution's new policy became effective, authorising its museums to return looted or *unethically* acquired objects.[159] The Smithsonian prides itself on the new policy and sees it as providing leadership: 'The Smithsonian is this amazing wonder—this gift not just to the country but to the world', Lonnie Bunch III, secretary of the Smithsonian, told The New York Times. 'Smithsonian will be the place people point to, to say "This is how we should share our collections and think about ethical returns"'.[160]

Other museums stress the importance of their provenance research. The Boston Museum of Fine Arts has a webpage dedicated to returned artefacts.[161] The National Gallery of Art in Washington DC provides a searchable database of its collection and information on each item's provenance and exhibition history.[162] The Met has a webpage on provenance research, discussing in particular Nazi looted artworks and some restitutions of objects to their 'rightful owners'.[163] A new 2022 law in the State

[152] Daniel Boffey, 'Dutch Museums Vow to Return Art Looted by Colonialists', The Guardian (8 October 2020).

[153] See text to nn 83 and 168.

[154] See text to nn 84-85.

[155] Helen Stoilas, 'The Met will Return Two Benin Bronzes to Nigeria', The Art Newspaper (9 June 2021).

[156] Catherine Hickley, 'Smithsonian Museum of African Art Removes Benin Bronzes from Display and Plans to Repatriate them', CNN (5 November 2021).

[157] Ted Loos, 'A Long Way Home for "Looted" Art Is Getting Shorter', The New York Times (27 April 2022).

[158] Hannah McGivern, 'Trove of Benin Bronzes in US Museum Collections Repatriated to Nigeria', The Art Newspaper (11 October 2022).

[159] Smithsonian Institution, 'Collections Management' (Smithsonian Directive 600, 12 May 2022); see also Matt Stevens, 'In a Nod to Changing Norms, Smithsonian Adopts Policy on Ethical Returns', The New York Times (3 May 2022).

[160] Matt Stevens, 'In a Nod to Changing Norms, Smithsonian Adopts Policy on Ethical Returns', The New York Times (3 May 2022).

[161] Boston Museum of Fine Arts, 'Ownership Resolutions' https://www.mfa.org/collections/provenance/ownership-resolutions.

[162] See https://www.nga.gov/collection.html.

[163] The Met, 'Provenance Research Project' https://www.metmuseum.org/about-the-met/policies-and-documents/provenance-research-project.

of New York requires museums to disclose which artworks on display were stolen by the Nazis.[164]

There is an inclination to examine provenance—or at least to be vocal about examining provenance—and to allow for a discussion of returns. We can of course query whether all museums engage in these activities in good faith. We must not forget that museums are directly affected by returns, and we cannot expect them to rejoice at having to part with objects in their collections.

Ultimately, it is as yet unclear whether some form of museum practice is emerging that actually imposes on museums a duty to return unlawfully or unethically acquired cultural property. The official discourse tends to be that some items may have to be returned. But whether states need to keep museums honest or whether museums change their provenance and restitution policies of their own accord, the *state* practice is there.

10.2.5 Acceptance as Law (opinio iuris)

The second element of customary international law is acceptance of state practice as law. This book suggests that the state practice on returns is motivated by a sense of legal right or obligation. Acceptance as law is evident in numerous statements made by states. This is how we should understand Macron's 2017 declaration that African cultural heritage '*can't* just be in European private collections and museums'.[165] In 2019, a representative of the Chinese government stated that looted Chinese artefacts, including some that were removed in the nineteenth century, 'should' be returned to China. Allowing such items to be auctioned, he observed, runs 'counter to the underlying spirit of relevant international treaties and UN resolutions' and it is the 'responsibilit[y]' of every state to encourage the restitution of cultural heritage.[166] In 2021, US Attorney Anderson declared that '[t]he United States is committed to returning stolen relics to nations seeking to preserve their heritage'. 'We will use all our power', he added, 'including civil forfeiture, to ensure that *misappropriated* cultural items are returned to their *rightful* owners'.[167] At about the same time, the Dutch government, addressing returns of colonial objects,

---

[164] Taylor Dafoe, 'A New Law Requires New York Museums to Indicate If Artworks on View Passed Through Nazi Hands', Artnet News (12 August 2022).

[165] Anna Codrea-Rado, 'Emmanuel Macron Says Return of African Artifacts Is a Top Priority', The New York Times (29 November 2017) (emphasis added).

[166] Lucy Hornby, 'China Calls for Return of Art Treasures from Abroad', Reuters (17 November 2009).

[167] US Department of Justice, US Attorney's Office, Northern District of California, 'United States Successfully Negotiates the Return of Two Thai Religious Relics Reported Stolen by Thailand and Displayed at San Francisco Asian Art Museum' (10 February 2021) https://www.justice.gov/usao-ndca/pr/united-states-successfully-negotiates-return-two-thai-religious-relics-reported-stolen (emphasis added).

announced: 'Because of the imbalance of power during the colonial era, cultural objects were—effectively—often stolen. The government is keen to help *rectify* this historic injustice by returning cultural heritage objects to their country of origin and by strengthening international cooperation in this area.' According to the minister of education, culture, and science, Ingrid van Engelshoven, '[t]here is *no place* in the Dutch State Collection for cultural heritage objects that were acquired through theft. If a country wants them back, we will give them back.'[168]

Domestic laws too can provide evidence of acceptance as law. For example, the explanatory statement prefacing the 2021 French bill (now law) on the restitution of some Nazi looted art referred, among others, to the 'need' to return the stolen artworks; the 'commitment' made by 44 states, including France, through the adoption of the 1998 Washington Principles, to 'facilitate restitutions, and find "just and equitable" solutions for the families concerned'; and the fact that France has in place 'a genuine public policy of restitution' of Nazi-spoiled artworks and is 'anxious to move forward in the path of reparation'.[169]

Acceptance as law is further obvious in UNGA resolutions, such as Resolution 3187 (XXVIII) on 'Restitution of works of art to countries victims of expropriation' of 1973, which affirms that 'the prompt restitution to a country of its *objets d'art*, monuments, museum pieces, manuscripts and documents by another country, without charge, ... constitutes *just reparation* for damage done'.[170] Recent UNGA resolutions have addressed the return or restitution of cultural property while noting with approval a 2018 resolution of the United Nations Human Rights Council (UNHRC),[171] according to which 'the organized looting, smuggling and theft of and illicit trafficking in cultural property ... are contrary to international law'.[172]

National court decisions too can provide evidence of acceptance as law. In Italy, a 2008 judgment of the Council of State, Italy's highest administrative court, upheld a ministerial decree (and an earlier judgment rendered by the Regional Administrative Tribunal of Lazio) ordering the return of the statue of the Venus of Cyrene to Libya. The judgment held that the obligation to return looted artefacts removed during occupation or colonisation is imposed by customary international law.[173] Accordingly, Italy's obligation to return the Venus of Cyrene to Libya was based primarily

[168]Government of the Netherlands, 'Government: Redressing an Injustice by Returning Cultural Heritage Objects to their Country of Origin' (29 January 2021) https://bit.ly/3Gbr7Ss (emphasis added).

[169]Projet de loi n° 4632 relatif à la restitution ou la remise de certains biens culturels aux ayants droit de leurs propriétaires victimes de persécutions antisémites (enregistré à la Présidence de l'Assemblée nationale le 3 novembre 2021) (author's translation).

[170]UNGA Res 3187 (XXVIII) (18 December 1973) UN Doc A/RES/3187(XXVIII), para 1 (emphasis added).

[171]UNHRC Res 37/17 (22 March 2018).

[172]UNGA Res 76/16 (6 December 2021) UN Doc A/RES/76/16, recitals; UNGA Res 73/130 (24 December 2018) UN Doc A/RES/73/130, recitals.

[173]Scovazzi (2009); Chechi (2008) 160-164.

on customary international law.[174] The Council of State also held that ownership of cultural objects cannot be established through prescription.[175] In other words, the passage of time does not make a bad title good. The Council added that military occupation was not a prerequisite for the application of the customary international rule on the return cultural property.[176]

In *Autocephalous Greek-Orthodox Church v Goldberg*, a concurring judge in the Supreme Court of Indiana in the United States declared:

> a short cultural memory is not an adequate justification for participating in the plunder of the cherished antiquities that play important roles in the histories of foreign lands. The UNESCO Convention and the Cultural Property Implementation Act constitute an effort to instill respect for the cultural property and heritage of all peoples. The mosaics before us are of great intrinsic beauty. They are the virtually unique remnants of an earlier artistic period and should be returned to their homeland and their rightful owner. This is the case not only because the mosaics belong there, but as a reminder that greed and callous disregard for the property, history and culture of others cannot be countenanced by the world community or by this court.[177]

References to the return of cultural property to its 'rightful' owners or to the return of 'plundered', 'stolen', or 'unlawfully exported' cultural property do not need an additional mention of a legal obligation; the obligation is reflected in the common legal opprobrium attaching to terms such as 'stolen' or 'unlawfully exported' cultural property.

Activities within international organisations provide additional evidence of acceptance as law. In September 2021, an ICPRCP decision recognised the United Kingdom's 'obligation' to return the marbles,[178] the word 'obligation' plainly expressing acceptance as law. Additionally, the decision referred to 'the legitimate *and rightful* demand of Greece'.[179] It was adopted unanimously by the 22 members of the Intergovernmental Committee elected from the UNESCO member states, that is, Argentina, Armenia, Benin, Cameroon, Canada, Democratic People's Republic of Korea, Ecuador, Egypt, Greece, Guatemala, Guinea, India, Iraq, Italy, Japan, Mali, Mexico, Pakistan, Moldova, Republic of Korea, and Zambia.[180]

---

[174] Scovazzi (2009); Chechi (2008) 160-164; Visconti (2021) 568.

[175] Scovazzi (2009) 358.

[176] The Council of State reasoned that the obligation to restore looted cultural objects was the result of the interplay of the prohibition of the use of force and the principle of self-determination of peoples, Scovazzi (2009) 358; Chechi (2008) 164.

[177] *Autocephalous Greek-Orthodox Church of Cyprus and Cyprus v Goldberg*, 917 F.2d 278 (7th Cir 1990) (Concurring opinion Cudahy).

[178] ICPRCP, 22nd session, 27-29 September 2021, ICPRCP/21/22.COM/Decisions, Decision 22. COM 6, para 7. See also Chap. 5, text to n 62.

[179] ICPRCP, 22nd session, 27-29 September 2021, ICPRCP/21/22.COM/Decisions, Decision 22. COM 6, para 7 (emphasis added).

[180] On unanimity, see ICPRCP Rules of Procedure rule 8.3. A video of the session is available on UNESCO's website https://events.unesco.org/event?id=69990611&lang=1033.

Last, and certainly not least, acceptance as law is also evident 'when States act in conformity with a treaty provision by which they are not bound',[181] such as when they return cultural heritage that does not fall within the scope of the 1970 UNESCO Convention; and acceptance as law is evident in the absence of reaction to the numerous returns that increasingly take place around the world.

Yet is all state practice accompanied by evidence of acceptance as law? Sometimes there may even be indications that a state is trying to present the return as a one-off case, shying away from creating a legal obligation that will bind it in the future. This is in particular the case when a state declares that the return does not create a precedent or when it labels the return a 'gift' (*ex gratia*). When in 2004 the US Senate tried to impress upon the United Kingdom that it 'should' return the marbles, it also proclaimed this to be intended as 'a gesture of good will', which 'would set no legal precedent, nor in any other way affect the ownership or disposition of other objects in museums in the United States or around the world'.[182] Similarly, it was said that, according to the French government, 'a handful of high-profile returns, to Senegal and the Republic of Benin, should not create a legal precedent leading to further restitution'.[183]

The fear of creating a precedent is that of the slippery slope leading to an unstoppable wave of restitutions. The fact that some items are returned, a decision taken in light of the specific circumstances of the case, must not create an expectation that everything else will be returned too. The disclaimer about the non-creation of a legal precedent is meant to ensure that the state will not have to repatriate just any item in the future and it cannot gainsay that the specific return that does take place is accompanied by acceptance as law.

The fact that a return is labelled a 'gift' may too appear to call into question acceptance as law. It must, however, be put in perspective, especially in light of contradicting evidence that shows that calling the return a 'gift' is a way of saving face. The 'gift' approach does not necessarily contradict the creation of customary international law. Usually, the assumption here is that the state does not concede the unlawful nature of the initial removal. When states repatriate cultural property, most often they use the neutral term 'return', rather than 'restitution'; they do not admit that an unlawful act may have taken place. It is this book's argument that these apparent exceptions to the rule do not negate the existence of *opinio iuris* and that, to the extent that there is state practice, this state practice does seem to be accepted as law.

---

[181] ILC, 'Conclusions on Identification of Customary International Law' (2018), conclusion 9, commentary para 4.

[182] US Congress, Senate, S Con Res 134 'Expressing the sense of the Congress that the Parthenon Marbles should be returned to Greece', 108th Congress, 2nd session (22 July 2004).

[183] Barnaby Phillips, 'Western Museums Are Starting to Return Colonial-era Treasures', The Economist (Online extra) (27 October 2021).

10.2.6 Is the United Kingdom a Persistent Objector?

According to the theory or principle of the persistent objector, even if a rule of customary law has emerged, a state may still exempt itself from its application, if it objected to the rule during its formation and for so long as it continues to object.[184] The authority generally given for the concept of persistent objector is the *Fisheries (United Kingdom v Norway)* case,[185] which however concerned particular, as opposed to general, customary international law.[186] Particular customary international law is often regional in nature and 'applies only among a limited number of States'.[187] It is certain that particular international law cannot bind states that have not themselves accepted it as law.[188] Although the endorsement of the concept of persistent objector by the International Law Commission (ILC) could appear to settle the matter, its relevance is contradicted by some ICJ judgments. Notably, in the *North Sea Continental Shelf* cases, the ICJ held that customary international law rules, 'by their very nature, must have equal force for all members of the international community, and cannot therefore be the subject of any right of unilateral exclusion exercisable at will by any one of them in its own favour'.[189] The concept of persistent objector is controversial, and it has not escaped severe criticism.[190] It is not the purpose of this book to evaluate the theory of persistent objector. In case it is accepted, we must consider whether the United Kingdom is a persistent objector to the emerging customary rule concerning the return of unlawfully removed cultural property and therefore whether it is not bound by it and would not be obliged to return the marbles.

The United Kingdom (alongside Japan and Russia)[191] sometimes appears to be reluctant to return objects. To take an early example, in the 1970s, the wooden Taranaki panels, Maori panels which had been illegally exported from New Zealand, turned up at an impending auction at Sotheby's in London. At the time, neither New Zealand nor the United Kingdom was party to the 1970 UNESCO Convention. Although New Zealand reacted at once, the English courts failed to forfeit the antiques to the New Zealand government, and that despite the fact that they had

[184] ILC, 'Conclusions on Identification of Customary International Law' (2018), conclusion 15; Crawford (2019) 26; Fitzmaurice (1957) 99-101; Stein (1985); Thirlway (2019) 99-102.

[185] *Fisheries Case (United Kingdom v Norway)* (Judgment) (1951) ICJ Rep 116, 131. See also *Colombian-Peruvian Asylum* (Judgment) [1950] ICJ Rep 266, 277-278.

[186] For a discussion, see Abi-Saab (1987) 180-181; D'Amato (2010).

[187] ILC, 'Conclusions on Identification of Customary International Law' (2018), conclusion 16.

[188] ILC, 'Conclusions on Identification of Customary International Law' (2018), conclusion 16 and commentary paras 6-7.

[189] *North Sea Continental Shelf* (Judgment) [1969] ICJ Rep 3 [63].

[190] Schachter (1982) 292-293; Charney (1985); Conforti (1988) 74-77; Tomuschat (1993) 284–290; Kelly (2000); Kelly (2017); D'Amato (2010); Dumberry (2010); Dumberry (2016) 392-405; cf Petersen (2017); Olivier Barsalou (2006).

[191] Greenfield (2007) 279-280 and Chap. 6. As of the time of writing, neither state is party to the UNIDROIT Convention, but both are party to the 1970 UNESCO Convention.

been illegally exported. The panels were ultimately returned home after they were sold to New Zealand by the heirs of the Swiss art collector who possessed them.[192] Yet since that time, the United Kingdom has joined the 1970 UNESCO Convention and, progressively, the law and attitudes have been evolving.

For a start, the policy unfavourable to repatriations is contradicted by the returns that do take place (see Sect. 10.2.2) and by the policies of devolved governments, e.g. Scotland.[193] In addition, even when the United Kingdom deflects restitution claims, it tends to do so with the argument that it lawfully owns the objects in question.[194] This is the very reason it refuses to return the Parthenon marbles—this and the fact, of course, that it insists that it has no say in the matter, since this is something for the British Museum to decide. As for the British Museum, it stresses that it is prevented from returning the marbles by the British Museum Act 1963. Already back in 1983, almost 20 years before the United Kingdom became a party to the 1970 UNESCO Convention, the UK observer to the ICPRCP had remarked that 'the fact that the United Kingdom does not accept the principle of the return of cultural property *except in cases of illegal acquisition* does not mean that we are opposed in principle to the return of objects'.[195] This possibly means that the United Kingdom is for the time being a persistent objector to the return of *lawfully* removed artefacts—but this is a distinct question. In the case of the Benin bronzes, the British Museum describes them as 'spoils of war' that it received 'as a donation'.[196] The museum adds that its collection of Benin bronzes 'only grew to its current size following the acquisition of major private collections'.[197] Although the museum does not mention lawful acquisition, the implication is clear: the museum suggests that it is justified in keeping the bronzes because they were either donated or sold to it. The government itself relegates decision-making to the museum.

Yet not all British museums consider that their retention of the Benin bronzes is lawful. The Horniman Museum and Gardens in south east London, which like the British Museum is a non-departmental public body (NDPB), announced in 2022 that it has agreed to return ownership of its 72 Benin bronzes to Nigeria.[198] It appears that the museum's decision was subject to approval by the Charity Commission,[199] a

[192] Greenfield (2007) 142-148; Elizabeth Fraccaro, Alessandro Chechi, and Marc-André Renold, 'Case Note: Maori Panels – New Zealand and Ortiz Heirs' Platform ArThemis (November 2018) https://bit.ly/3MVGW2i.

[193] See n 105.

[194] E.g., see Sri Lankan artefacts and manuscripts, Greenfield (2007) 133-134.

[195] Greenfield (2007) 229 (emphasis added).

[196] British Museum, 'Benin Bronzes' https://bit.ly/3E0DP7A.

[197] British Museum, 'Benin Bronzes' https://bit.ly/3E0DP7A.

[198] Horniman Museum and Gardens, 'Horniman to Return Ownership of Benin Bronzes to Nigeria' (7 August 2022) https://www.horniman.ac.uk/story/horniman-to-return-ownership-of-benin-bronzes-to-nigeria/#.

[199] Hansard (2022).

non-ministerial government department accountable to parliament.[200] According to that museum's restitution and repatriation policy,

> occasions will arise when it will be appropriate to enter into discussions with stakeholders about the potential restitution or repatriation of cultural objects and human remains which are in [the collection of the Horniman] and were acquired by force or other forms of duress, by theft, or were communal property which was acquired from a person not authorised to give it. Each discussion will be held on a case by case basis . . .[201]

In 2022, the Victoria and Albert Museum (V&A), another NDPB, returned the marble head of a Greek god to Turkey, where it was reattached to the third-century AD sarcophagus to which it belonged.[202] The repatriation of the head, which is reported to have been in storage at the V&A, resolves a case that had been pending for almost 90 years.[203] That said, this transfer is in fact a long-term loan, since the V&A, like the British Museum, is prevented from deaccessioning items in its collection except on a very limited number of grounds.[204] In 2022, Tristram Hunt, director of the V&A, called for the law on deaccessioning to be changed.[205] The new Charities Act 2022, which was briefly discussed in Chap. 8, will make it easier for museums to deaccession items, if they are under a 'moral obligation' to do so.[206] Although the commencement of the relevant sections of the act is currently delayed,[207] as and when these become effective, they will expressly make it possible for museums with statutory bans on deaccessioning to return items in their collections.[208] The new provisions will reverse *Attorney General v Trustees of the British Museum*, which did not recognise that a 'moral obligation' is sufficient justification for deaccessioning.[209] This means that not only unlawful but also unethical acquisitions may result in return. In short, there is firm evidence that the United Kingdom's 'objections' are weakening, and it is doubtful, even if we accept the theory of persistent objector, that the United Kingdom is a persistent objector.

---

[200] See https://www.gov.uk/government/organisations/charity-commission/about#who-we-are.

[201] Horniman Museum and Gardens, 'Restitution and Repatriation Policy' (March 2021), point 6.1.

[202] Martin Bailey, 'Victoria and Albert Museum Returns—and Reattaches—a Third-century Marble Head of Greek God Taken from Turkey' The Art Newspaper (1 July 2022).

[203] Martin Bailey, 'Victoria and Albert Museum Returns—and Reattaches—a Third-century Marble Head of Greek God Taken from Turkey' The Art Newspaper (1 July 2022).

[204] National Heritage Act 1983 s 6.

[205] Angelica Villa, 'Victoria & Albert Museum Director Decries "Unsatisfactory" UK Law Barring Deaccessioning', ARTnews (5 July 2022); Jo Lawson-Tancred, 'A New UK Law Gives Museums Unprecedented Power to Deaccession Art and Repatriate Objects in Their Collections' Artnet News (27 September 2022).

[206] Charities Act 2022 ss 15, including s 331A(3), and 16.

[207] See Chap. 8, text to n 51.

[208] Charities Act 2022 ss 15, including s 331A, and 16.

[209] See Chap. 8, text to nn 308-312.

10.2.7 The New Customary Law on Return

Societies change, the mores and ethics of the time evolve, and law changes in consequence. So does customary international law. The formation of customary international law has been treated on analogy with the progressive creation of a road across empty land. At the beginning, the tracks are uncertain, there is no path. But as time wears on, 'for some reason of common utility', users begin to follow the same route until a path becomes clear. The path in turn gives way to a road and, ultimately, the road becomes the only recognised route, although it is impossible to know when exactly the transformation took place.[210]

Today's customary international law cannot necessarily be determined today. While a rule may undergo a long gestation period, at some juncture comes the transition from state practice that is not yet binding as customary international law to state practice that reflects a binding rule of law, and this transition—the metamorphosis of the chrysalis into a butterfly[211]—is 'instantaneous'.[212] But to identify the moment of the transition is not an exact science, and it is only in retrospect that we can even hope to confirm that it has actually taken place. As Crawford pointed out, we should abandon 'the idea that we could write a textbook definitively stating what international law was on a specific day . . . We simply cannot tell what the law is on a specific day except after the fact'.[213]

The law on the return of unlawfully removed cultural property has been evolving. There is no consensus at this moment on whether the chrysalis has metamorphosed into a butterfly, but it may be that it already has. State practice accepted as law seems to confirm that especially unlawfully removed cultural property of particular importance to the state of origin increasingly makes its way back home and the reason for this is a sense of legal obligation. Very new developments show that the law on returns will progressively also concern unethically removed cultural property. There are exceptions to the rule but these can be explained precisely as exceptions that do not invalidate the rule. Whether or not the exceptions are justified is a distinct question. For example, some items do not return because the country of origin is said to be unable to look after its collections. It has been suggested that in some cases there can be 'no confidence that returned artefacts would be safely retained by recipient institutions. Irrespective of the means by which such artefacts came to be currently held by museums, curators are bound to apply the criterion of continued preservation and exhibition'.[214] Yet, it is unclear that even arguments such as these are going to hold in the future. The retention of other items is justified with the claim that they do not have a particular significance for their state of origin. It has been

[210] See de Visscher (1957) 149.

[211] Pellet and Müller (2019) 919.

[212] Thirlway (2019) 76-77; Cheng (1965).

[213] Crawford (2014) 81. See also *Legal Consequences of the Separation of the Chagos Archipelago from Mauritius in 1965* (Advisory Opinion) [2019] ICJ Rep 95 [142]-[143].

[214] Greenfield (2007) 128-129.

argued, for instance, that the Rosetta Stone is not unique: other stelae have been found with the same bilingual decree inscribed in hieroglyphs, demotic (the everyday ancient Egyptian script), and ancient Greek. The significance of *this* particular stone is that it made it possible for the French Egyptologist Jean-François Champollion to decipher Egyptian hieroglyphs. The stone has been said to be of at least as much value to the English (or, the devil's advocate might suggest, the French) as to Egypt.[215] In other cases, such as when it comes to the Parthenon marbles, states resist return with the claim that the objects were lawfully acquired. Finally, there is a very long distance between what countries consider right and what they are prepared to do.

10.3 Equity

As a principle of customary international law with, among others, a gap-filling and corrective function, equity is especially apt for application in situations where the legal framework is incomplete or uncertain.[216] Demands for 'cultural justice' confirm equity's particular relevance to international cultural heritage law.[217] The following paragraphs consider two applications of equity to the Parthenon marbles' case.

10.3.1 The Importance of the Context (Equity as Individualised Justice)

To apply equity as individualised justice is to do 'justice in the concrete case', taking into account 'the relevant "factual matrix" of that case'.[218] Equity as individualised justice does not affect the overarching legal framework but adapts it before applying it to the individual case,[219] in order to reach a decision that 'is just and fair for that case'.[220] As a form of individualised justice, equity is circumstance-specific, that is, it requires us to take into account the relevant circumstances of the particular case.[221]

[215] Robertson (2019) (unnumbered page).

[216] See Titi (2021) in general and, for a discussion of equity as a source of international law, 113-135.

[217] Fincham (2012).

[218] *Continental Shelf (Tunisia/Libya)* (Separate Opinion Jiménez de Aréchaga) [1982] ICJ Rep 100 [24]. For a discussion of equity as individualised justice, see Titi (2021) 71-73.

[219] See de Visscher (1972) 4.

[220] *Continental Shelf (Tunisia/Libya)* (Separate Opinion Jiménez de Aréchaga) [1982] ICJ Rep 100 [25].

[221] Titi (2021) 71-73 and *passim*; Lachs (1993) 326.

Relevant circumstances include those surrounding the removal of the contested cultural property (lawfulness, legitimacy, etc.), its context (historical, archaeological, architectural, etc.), the importance of the contested cultural property to the requesting state, the passage of time (including questions of acquiescence—no one would argue, for instance, that Egyptian obelisks brought to Rome by the early emperors should be returned to Egypt 2000 years later or that the horses of San Marco, with their own sad history of repeated looting, should now be removed from Venice), the cultural heritage protection record of the requesting state, and potentially its political context (e.g. there is a general unwillingness to repatriate cultural heritage to a country run by a military dictatorship).[222] If we apply these criteria to the Parthenon marbles case, we would probably find that the marbles should be returned to Athens. The elements we would take into account include the conditions of their removal; the destruction caused to the Parthenon by Elgin's men; the criticisms that were made at the time; the importance of the Parthenon; the significance of the marbles to the state of origin and the insistence with which it has clamoured for them over the years; the careless conditions under which these, the most beautiful of the Parthenon slabs, were stored and cleaned in the British Museum; the fact that the majority of British people favour their return; that they are part of a building and are thus legally immoveable; and the demands around the world for their return, from the US Senate to the majority of states in the UNGA, that make their continued retention an aberration.

10.3.2 Equity and the Evolution of Law

'Law must be stable and yet it cannot stand still', wrote Roscoe Pound. 'Hence all the thinking about law has struggled to reconcile the conflicting demands of the need of stability and of the need of change'.[223] Nowhere is this tension between stability and change so palpable as in the struggle between the strict application of law and equity.[224] Law has a tendency to become rigid.[225] Societal imperatives tend to be a step ahead of the law and, although new law tries to close the gap, this constantly reopens.[226] It is said that the happiness of a society rests on the promptness with which this gap is closed.[227] One of the functions of equity relates precisely to the need to narrow this gulf, in order to remedy the disjunction between the law as it is and the law as it should be.[228]

[222] Scovazzi (2020) 161-162; Risvas (2020) 294.

[223] Pound (1923) 1.

[224] Titi (2021) 74.

[225] Denning (1952) 1.

[226] Sumner Maine (1897) 24. See further Watt (2009) 10.

[227] Sumner Maine (1897) 24.

[228] E.g. see Megarry and Baker (1966) 5-6.

If Elgin had removed the marbles today, he would have fallen foul of the law in all kinds of ways. Not only would his actions have violated the 1970 UNESCO Convention, but he would also be liable to imprisonment under the law of England and Wales.[229] When the Dealing in Cultural Objects (Offences) Act 2003 was introduced, the Department for Culture, Media, and Sport made the following declaration:

> A new offence designed specifically to combat traffic in unlawfully removed cultural objects will assist in maintaining the integrity of buildings, structures and monuments . . . *worldwide* by reducing the commercial incentive to those involved in the looting of such sites. *It will send a strong signal that the Government is determined to put a stop to such practices.*[230]

Is this statement to be taken to mean that the government is determined to put a stop to such practices when they happen now but that it does not mind if they happened in the past? It is argued that an intertemporal application of international law and notably of the 1970 UNESCO Convention would allow the return of the marbles.

Intertemporal law concerns the application of international norms in time.[231] It is not substantive law but a technique that allows us to identify the applicable law.[232] According to Max Huber's famous dictum in the 1928 *Island of Palmas* arbitration, 'a juridical fact must be appreciated in the light of the law contemporary with it';[233] the creation of a right is subject to the law in force at the time of its creation, and its continued existence must follow the evolution of law.[234] In other words, while the removal of the marbles is subject to the law of the early nineteenth century, their continued retention in the British Museum must be viewed in light of contemporary international law and the obligations the latter imposes on states in relation to unlawfully removed cultural heritage. Derek Fincham has already argued that 'cultural justice' requires the application of the modern legal framework to the Parthenon marbles dispute.[235] Nonlegal scholars have expressed incomprehension at international lawyers' apparent inability to solve the case. Neils, possibly thinking of Merryman, wrote: 'While legal scholars would like to apply modern instruments, like the statute of limitations, to the issue of repatriation, they find the application of other modern international laws' (we can think here of the non-retroactive conventions) 'to be inadmissible'.[236] Although Huber's dictum has given rise to

---

[229] Dealing in Cultural Objects (Offences) Act 2003 s 1(3).

[230] Department for Culture, Media, and Sport, 'Dealing in Tainted Cultural Objects – Guidance on the Dealing in Cultural Objects (Offences) Act 2003' (January 2004) 3 (emphasis added).

[231] *Sovereignty over Pedra Branca/Pulau Batu Puteh, Middle Rocks and South Ledge (Malaysia/Singapore)* (Declaration Bennouna) [2008] ICJ Rep 128 [2]; Institut de Droit International (1975) first recital; Linderfalk (2011) 148; Kotzur (2008), para 1.

[232] Thirlway (1989) 130; Wheatley (2021) 487.

[233] *Island of Palmas case (Netherlands, USA)* (1928) 2 RIAA 829, 845.

[234] *Island of Palmas case (Netherlands, USA)* (1928) 2 RIAA 829, 845. See also Higgins (1997) 516.

[235] Fincham (2013).

[236] Neils (2001) 242.

controversy and criticism,[237] intertemporal law has been accepted by international courts and tribunals,[238] and to rely on it in this case would be in accordance with equity.

10.4 Conclusion

Societies change before the law does. The ethics of collecting and retaining cultural property have been evolving. The law is inevitably changing in consequence. States—and museums—return cultural items that were unlawfully acquired in the past, regardless of whether they are obliged to do so under the non-retroactive conventions. They do so without reference to the political situation that obtained in the country of origin at the time of the removal (war, peace, occupation). Increasingly, cultural heritage acquired under unethical conditions starts to be returned too. The chapter has argued that the growing number of returns has translated into a nascent customary international law rule that appears to be supported by general practice motivated by a sense of legal obligation. What was acceptable in the past, no longer is. States start to face up to old wrongs and redress them. The chapter has shown that even the United Kingdom does not object to the new customary international law rule, although when it comes to the Parthenon marbles, it still has a hard decision to make, that is, to send the marbles home. Finally, the chapter argued that equity (or 'cultural justice') favours the marbles' return, irrespective of the new customary law rule. Doing individualised justice by taking into account the specific circumstances of the case or relying on intertemporal law to apply the modern legal framework and especially the 1970 UNESCO Convention to the case would be sufficient to restore the marbles to Athens.

References

Georges Abi-Saab, 'Cours général de droit international public' (1987) 207 Recueil des cours 15

Philip Allott, 'Language, Method and the Nature of International Law' (1971) 45 British Yearbook of International Law 79

Anthony D'Amato, 'The Concept of Special Custom in International Law (2010) Northwestern University School of Law Faculty Working Paper 116

Jean d'Aspremont, 'Customary International Law as a Dance Floor: Part II' EJIL: Talk! (15 April 2014)

Jean d'Aspremont, 'Conclusion: Inclusive Law-making and Law-enforcement Processes for an Exclusive International Legal System' in Jean d'Aspremont (ed), *Participants in the*

[237] E.g. Jessup (1928) 740; Higgins (1997) 516-518. See also Elias (1980) 286; Wheatley (2021) 488.

[238] Higgins (1997).

International Legal System: Multiple Perspectives on Non-State Actors in International Law (Routledge 2011)
Anna Irene Baka, 'The Logic of Absence in Customary International Law: An Open-System Approach' in Panos Merkouris, Jörg Kammerhofer and Noora Arajärvi (eds), *The Theory, Practice, and Interpretation of Customary International Law* (Cambridge University Press 2022)
Olivier Barsalou, 'La doctrine de l'objecteur persistant en droit international public' (2006) 19 (1) Revue québécoise de droit international 1
Luigi Ferrari Bravo, 'Méthodes de recherche de la coutume internationale dans la pratique des États' (1985) 192 Recueil des cours 233
Michael Byers, *Custom, Power and the Power of Rules* (Cambridge University Press 1999)
Jonathan Charney, 'The Persistent Objector Rule and the Development of Customary International Law' (1985) 56 British Yearbook of International Law 1
Alessandro Chechi, 'The Return of Cultural Objects Removed in Times of Colonial Domination and International Law: The Case of the Venus of Cyrene' (2008) 18 (1) Italian Yearbook of International Law 159
Bin Cheng, 'United Nations Resolutions on Outer Space: "Instant" International Customary Law?' (1965) Indian Journal of International Law 23
Benedetto Conforti, 'Cours général de droit international public' (1988) 212 Recueil des cours 11
James Crawford, *Brownlie's Principles of Public International Law* (9th edn, Oxford University Press 2019)
James Crawford, *Chance, Order, Change – The Course of International Law* (Brill 2014)
Christian Dahlman, 'The Function of *Opinio Juris* in Customary International Law' (2012) 81 Nordic Journal of International Law 327
Alfred Denning, 'The Need for a New Equity' (1952) 5 (1) Current Legal Problems 1
Yoram Dinstein, 'The Interaction between Customary International Law and Treaties' (2007) 322 Recueil des cours 250
Patrick Dumberry, *The Formation and Identification of Rules of Customary International Law in International Investment Law* (Cambridge University Press 2016)
Patrick Dumberry, 'Incoherent and Ineffective: The Concept of Persistent Objector Revisited' (2010) 59 International Law and Comparative Law Quarterly 779
TO Elias, 'The Doctrine of Intertemporal Law' (1980) 74 American Journal of International Law 285
Derek Fincham, 'Transnational Forfeiture of the Getty Bronze' (2014) 32 Cardozo Arts and Entertainment Law Journal 471
Derek Fincham, 'The Parthenon Sculptures and Cultural Justice' (2013) 23 Fordham Intellectual Property, Media and Entertainment Law Journal 943
Derek Fincham, 'Justice and the Cultural Heritage Movement' (2012) 20 Virginia Journal of Social Policy and Law 43
Gerald Fitzmaurice, 'The General Principles of International Law Considered from the Standpoint of the Rule of Law' (1957) 92 Recueil des cours 3
Francesco Francioni, 'The Evolving Framework for the Protection of Cultural Heritage in International Law' in Silvia Borelli and Federico Lenzerini (eds), *Cultural Heritage, Cultural Rights, Cultural Diversity* (Martinus Nijhoff 2012)
Mille Gabriel, 'The Return of Cultural Heritage from Denmark to Greenland' (2009) 61 Museum International 30
Jeanette Greenfield, *The Return of Cultural Treasures* (3rd edn, Cambridge University Press 2007)
De Gruyter Saur, *Museums of the World 2019* (26th edn, De Gruyter Saur 2019)
Andrew Guzman, 'Saving Customary International Law' (2005) 27 Michigan Journal of International Law 115
Hansard, 'House of Lords National Heritage Act 1983 Debate' (13 October 2022) (vol 824, Hansard 2022)

Rosalyn Higgins, 'Time and the Law: International Perspectives on an Old Problem' (1997) 46 International and Comparative Law Quarterly 501
ICOM, *Guidelines on Deaccessioning of the International Council of Museums* (ICOM 2019)
Institut de Droit International, 'The Intertemporal Problem in Public International Law' (Rapporteur Max Sørensen) (1975)
Philip C Jessup, 'The Palmas Island Arbitration' (1928) 22 American Journal of International Law 735
Jörg Kammerhofer, 'Uncertainty in the Formal Sources of International Law' (2004) 15 European Journal of International Law 523
Lawrence M Kaye and Carla T Main, 'The Saga of the Lydian Hoard Antiquities: From Uşak to New York and Back again' in Kathryn W Tubb (ed), *Antiquities: Trade or Betrayed – Legal, Ethical and Conservation Issues* (Archetype 1995)
J Patrick Kelly, 'Customary International Law in Historical Context: The Exercise of Power without General Acceptance' in Brian Lepard (ed), *Reexamining Customary International Law* (Cambridge University Press 2017)
J Patrick Kelly, 'The Twilight of Customary International Law' (2000) 40 Virginia Journal of International Law 449
Jan Klabbers, *An Introduction to International Institutional Law* (2nd edn, Cambridge University Press 2009)
Martti Koskenniemi, *The Politics of International Law* (Bloomsbury 2011)
Markus Kotzur, 'Intertemporal Law' (2008) Max Planck Encyclopedia of Public International Law
Manfred Lachs, 'Equity in Arbitration and in Judicial Settlement of Disputes' (1993) 6 (2) Leiden Journal of International Law 323
Manfred Lachs, 'The Development and General Trends of International Law in Our Time' (1980) 169 Collected Courses of The Hague Academy of International Law 9
Hersch Lauterpacht, *The Function of Law in the International Community* (Oxford University Press 2012, original publication 1933)
Brian Lepard, *Customary International Law* (Cambridge University Press 2010)
Ulf Linderfalk, 'The Application of International Legal Norms over Time: The Second Branch of Intertemporal Law' (2011) 58 (2) Netherlands International Law Review 147
Neil MacGregor, *À monde nouveau, nouveaux musées* (Hazan Louvre éditions 2021)
Magnus Magnusson, 'Introduction to the Second Edition' in Jeanette Greenfield, *The Return of Cultural Treasures* (3rd edn, Cambridge University Press 2007)
Georg Friedrich von Martens, *Nouveau recueil de traités d'alliance, de paix, de trêve, de neutralité, de commerce, de limites, d'échange etc. et de plusieurs autres actes: 1814-1815* (vol 2, Librairie de Dieterich 1818)
RE Megarry and PV Baker, *Snell's Principles of Equity* (26th edn, Sweet and Maxwell 1966)
Maurice H Mendelson, 'The Formation of Customary International Law' (1998) 272 Recueil des cours 155
Jenifer Neils, *The Parthenon Frieze* (Cambridge University Press 2001)
Mark O'Neill, 'Enlightenment Museums: Universal or Merely Global?' (2004) 2 (3) Museum and Society 190
Richard Pankhurst, 'Ethiopia, the Aksum Obelisk, and the Return of Africa's Cultural Heritage' (1999) 98 African Affairs 229
Alain Pellet and Daniel Müller, 'Article 38' in Andreas Zimmermann, Christian Tomuschat and Karin Oellers-Frahm (eds), *The Statute of the International Court of Justice: A Commentary* (3rd edn, Oxford University Press 2019)
Niels Petersen, 'The Role of Consent and Uncertainty in the Formation of Customary International Law' in Brian Lepard (ed), *Reexamining Customary International Law* (Cambridge University Press 2017)
Roscoe Pound, *Interpretations of Legal History* (Cambridge University Press 1923)

Michail Risvas, 'Underwater Cultural Heritage in Africa and Questions of Immunity, State Ownership and Succession: What Role for Equity?' (2020) 35 International Journal of Marine and Coastal Law 264

Anthea Roberts, 'Traditional and Modern Approaches to Customary International Law: A Reconciliation' (2001) 95 (4) American Journal of International Law 757

Geoffrey Robertson, *Who Owns History? Elgin's Loot and the Case for Returning Plundered Treasure* (Biteback Publishing 2019)

Oscar Schachter, 'International Law in Theory and Practice' (1982) 178 Recueil des cours 9

Tullio Scovazzi, 'The Restitution of Illicitly Exported Cultural Properties: Recent Italian Cases' (2020) 64 (1) Pravovedenie 156

Tullio Scovazzi, 'Repatriation and Restitution of Cultural Property: Relevant Rules of International Law' in Claire Smith (ed), *Encyclopedia of Global Archaeology* (Springer 2018)

Tullio Scovazzi, 'The Trend Towards the Restitution of Cultural Properties: Some Italian Cases' in Denis Alland and others (eds), *Unity and Diversity of International Law* (Brill 2014)

Tullio Scovazzi, '*Diviser c'est détruire*: Ethical Principles and Legal Rules in the Field of Return of Cultural Property' (2011) 94 (2) Rivista di diritto internazionale 341

Tullio Scovazzi, 'The Return of the Venus of Cyrene' (2009) 14 Art Antiquity and Law 355

Malcolm N Shaw, *International Law* (9th edn, Cambridge University Press 2021)

Ted L Stein, 'The Approach of the Different Drummer: The Principle of the Persistent Objector in International Law' (1985) 26 Harvard International Law Journal 457

William G Stewart, 'The Marbles: Elgin or Parthenon?' (2001) 6 Art Antiquity and Law 37

Henry Sumner Maine, *Ancient Law* (16th edn, John Murray 1897)

Hugh Thirlway, *The Sources of International Law* (2nd edn, Oxford University Press 2019)

Hugh Thirlway, 'Human Rights in Customary Law' (2015) 28 Leiden Journal of International Law 495

Hugh Thirlway, 'Law and Procedure of the International Court of Justice 1960–1989: Part One' (1989) 60 British Yearbook of International Law 1

Catharine Titi, *The Function of Equity in International Law* (Oxford University Press 2021)

Christian Tomuschat, 'Obligations Arising for States without or against their Will' (1993) 241 Recueil des cours 195

Tullio Treves, 'The Expansion of International Law' (2019) 398 Recueil des cours 9

Mark Villiger, *Customary International Law and Treaties* (2nd end, Kluwer Law International 1997)

Arianna Visconti, 'Between "Colonial Amnesia" and "Victimization Biases": Double Standards in Italian Cultural Heritage Law' (2021) 28 International Journal of Cultural Property 551

Charles de Visscher, *De l'équité dans le règlement arbitral ou judiciaire des litiges de droit international public* (Pedone 1972)

Charles de Visscher, *Theory and Reality in Public International Law* (Princeton University Press 1957)

Gary Watt, *Equity Stirring* (Hart Publishing 2009)

Steven Wheatley, 'Revisiting the Doctrine of Intertemporal Law' (2021) 41 (2) Oxford Journal of Legal Studies 484

Michael Wood and Omri Sender, 'State Practice' (2020) Max Planck Encyclopedia of Public International Law

Part IV
Time Future

Chapter 11
Conclusion: Homecoming

... and when all of that time is fully discovered it will prove to have been already known.

Michael Ondaatje, *The English Patient* (1992)

The time has come for the Parthenon marbles that form part of the Elgin collection in the British Museum to return home. Taking into account the evolution of international law on the protection of cultural heritage, this is the only viable way forward. This book has considered the case of the Parthenon marbles in the British Museum in light of the international legal framework for the protection of cultural property and has shown that contemporary international law requires the marbles' return to Greece on a number of distinct legal grounds. Elgin never had any permission to strip the Parthenon of its pedimental sculptures, metopes, or frieze slabs, and this 'acquisition' was unlawful, a fact confirmed at the time by the British ambassador, Adair, and repeated by Elgin himself in an 1811 letter to the then prime minister, Perceval. It was by means of bribes to the local Ottoman officials, and without the knowledge of the Sublime Porte, that Elgin removed the marbles, at a time when corruption was a crime punishable under English law. As the occupying force, the Ottomans would have anyway been legally unable to dispose of the Parthenon marbles and, as the International Court of Justice (ICJ) has confirmed in the *Temple of Preah Vihear* case, public monuments belong to the sovereign territory in perpetuity.

When Elgin, finding himself in dire financial circumstances, decided to sell his collection to the UK government, a parliamentary select committee was called upon to rubber-stamp the purchase. The committee conducted an investigation that can be described as perfunctory at best. The testimony of crucial witnesses was ignored, the evidence of corruption was brushed aside, and the admission that Elgin did not possess the marbles lawfully was conveniently forgotten. In part because the unlawfulness was a known fact, the UK government tried to disassociate itself from Elgin's actions. It purchased the marbles from Elgin, and it passed an act of parliament vesting their curation in the British Museum, apparently hoping to correct in this manner the flaw in the legal title. This may have been a useful trick under English

C. Titi, *The Parthenon Marbles and International Law*,
https://doi.org/10.1007/978-3-031-26357-6_11

law, but under international law, ownership of the marbles never passed. However, their possession did. By 1817, they were in the British Museum, which thus became the 'possessor' of the marbles.

Knowing that ownership of the marbles could not pass is one thing. Successfully claiming the marbles' return is another. While a diplomatic approach to the return of the marbles to Greece is preferable, understanding the legal merits of the dispute has a direct impact on the parties' willingness to negotiate and the concessions they are prepared to make. In this book, the enquiry into the legal merits of the case focused on how it would be received by two dispute settlement bodies, the European Court of Human Rights and, especially, the ICJ. The analysis revealed that an advisory proceeding before the ICJ could achieve the return of the marbles to Greece.

In contrast with what is often argued, the book has shown that the dispute about the return of the Parthenon marbles has an interstate character. Not only was Elgin a British ambassador and the UK government purchased the marbles, but as a non-departmental public body (NDPB), the British Museum is an organ of state whose conduct is attributable to the United Kingdom, in accordance with the international law of state responsibility. Moreover, before the British Museum can deaccession the marbles, the UK government needs, in principle, to pass enabling legislation. For all these reasons, the case cannot be dismissed as a conundrum that only concerns the two museums. It is, first and foremost, an intergovernmental case. Despite the passage of time since the marbles' removal, Greece has not lost the capacity to assert its claim for their return. Its persistent requests for the marbles over two uninterrupted centuries have ensured that the claim is not time-barred and that the objections of waiver, estoppel, acquiescence, and extinctive prescription cannot be successfully raised against it.

As to the substantive law applicable to the case, international treaties are of limited direct relevance. Human rights law and, especially, the European Convention on Human Rights appear ill-adapted to what is essentially a dispute about sovereignty and cultural heritage. Cultural heritage treaties have their own limitations. However, equity can come to the claim's legal aid, either by allowing the application of the modern legal framework for the protection and return of cultural heritage to the case (intertemporal law) or by calling for individualised justice to be done taking into account all relevant circumstances.

More crucially, a distinct legal argument was presented in this book in favour of the marbles' return to Greece, relying on the evolution of the ethics of retaining cultural property. States increasingly return such property when it has been unlawfully acquired, regardless of whether the non-retroactive cultural heritage conventions are applicable. Sometimes states return unethically acquired cultural property too. The examination of state practice and acceptance as law, customary international law's constitutive elements, consolidated one of the book's overarching arguments, that is, that customary international law on the return of unlawfully removed cultural heritage of particular significance has reached an inflection point. A new rule is emerging that requires the return of the Parthenon marbles to Athens, and even the United Kingdom does not object to this rule.

Although the book has focused on the Parthenon marbles, the relevance of its findings about the new legal framework for the return of cultural property stretches beyond this case. The Parthenon marbles are not the only contested items in world museum collections. Nevertheless, it would be a mistake to see the Parthenon marbles case as the tip of the iceberg that will lead to the depleting of world museums. The fear of a slippery slope is only partly justified. This is so for a number of reasons. If the Parthenon marbles are returned because they have been unlawfully removed, this return will have no impact on items held by world museums *lawfully*. Although there are a great many other disputes about the return of cultural heritage, not all of them concern unlawfully, or even unethically, removed cultural property. That said, some of them certainly do. It is sometimes suggested that, in order to prevent the 'emptying' of its collections, the United Kingdom could decide to return the Parthenon marbles as a 'gift'—thus no binding precedent would arise requiring the return of other objects. But as we have seen, whether one names the return a 'restitution' or a 'gift', the law has already moved forward. It is not the repatriation of the Parthenon marbles that will create a legal precedent. Precedents already exist. They form the basis of the new customary international law, with its widespread and consistent state practice adopted out of a sense of legal right or obligation. A number of objects, falling within the scope of the nascent customary international law rule, will have to be returned.

Still, some disputes will be barred, such as if the states of origin have waived their claim. Other cases will concern individual objects made for the trade, rather than parts of a monument. The Parthenon marbles case after all *is* in many respects a truly unique case. Another relevant fact that helps put things in perspective is that the requests for return are not as numerous as it is often imagined. In a debate in the House of Lords in October 2022, the example of the Victoria and Albert Museum (V&A) was discussed. The V&A holds in its collections over 2.7 million items but has 'received' only nine 'restitution cases' in over 20 years.[1] The mass exodus of antiquities and other artefacts from world museums (the apprehension that when you start pulling on the thread of restitution, world museums will be left with, frankly, nothing) is not borne out by the facts.

Yet it would also be naïve to assume that the new legal framework will have no impact on world museums and their way of doing business going forward. In 2006, MacGregor, then director of the British Museum, made an unfortunate and short-lived prediction, when he announced hopefully: 'Repatriation is yesterday's question'.[2] This proved to be more wishful thinking than a prescient look into the future. Certainly, the question of repatriation has been raised in the past, but this does not make it yesterday's question. Repatriation is very much today's question.

---

[1] Hansard (2022).

[2] Charlotte Higgins, 'Into Africa: British Museum's Reply to Ownership Debate', The Guardian (13 April 2006).

Is this then the beginning of the 'dismantling' of world museum collections, as Osborne seems to fear?[3] World museums are not without resources, but it is essential to go with the times. At the very least, if museums are to embrace this brave new world, they have to make every effort to publish an inventory of their collections and research their provenance.[4] Many museums have already recognised this need. This is not the beginning of the end for world museums but the beginning of a new era, one that requires an honest assessment of the past, reliance on collaborative projects (something that the British Museum is particularly proud of doing), and, probably, a greater focus on temporary exhibitions (less about 'owning', more about displaying). If museums do not embrace this new world, they will find themselves increasingly isolated, until states make it their business to keep them honest. Either one goes with the times, or one is surpassed by them—much like the British Museum was made to remove Sloane's bust, place it in a glass cabinet and label Sloane a slave-owner, despite its initial resistance.

As for the Parthenon marbles, they belong in Athens. So long as they remain in London there may be some corner of the British Museum that is forever Greece,[5] but the time has come when even the British Museum will not be able to hold on to them. The retentionists' arguments honed over two centuries simply cut no ice today. '[W] hat was acceptable during the age of empire', wrote Rudenstine, 'must give way to the demands of an ever-shrinking world that aspires to the rule of law'.[6] It is no longer possible to cling to looted treasures removed from their original context unlawfully. We are at a turning point, and the pressure on states and museums to return such items is increasing fast.

So what next? Greece will continue to campaign for the return of the marbles, even if it does not seek the initiation of advisory proceedings before the ICJ. Many options seem possible for a voluntary return of the marbles. The UK government could repeal or amend the British Museum Act 1816 and the British Museum Act 1963. Or, it could pass a law allowing the trustees of the British Museum to deaccession items in their collections, when they regard themselves as being under a moral obligation to do so. In both cases, the museum's trustees would then need to deaccession the marbles and return them to Greece. The commencement of the relevant provisions of the Charities Act 2022, as and when it comes, will be a step in the right direction. That said, even under that act, the decision to deaccession treasures above a certain value threshold will not depend solely on museum trustees but will also require the approval of the Charity Commission, the attorney general, or a court. The simplest option for the return of the marbles would be to directly transfer

---

[3] Cristina Ruiz, 'As Infrastructure Crumbles, British Museum Plans to Fix Parthenon Marbles Gallery Next', The Art Newspaper (3 November 2022).

[4] That much was admitted in MacGregor (2021) 196.

[5] Allusion is made here to Rupert Brooke's, poem *The Soldier*, ('If I should die, think only this of me: / That there's some corner of a foreign field / That is for ever England'), which has a poignant feel to it, given the poet's own sad end in Greece during World War I.

[6] Rudenstine (2002) 471.

them by statute: parliament could pass an act transferring the marbles to Greece. Although as an NDPB, the British Museum is meant to operate at arm's length from government, as we have seen, government does take important decisions affecting NDPBs. Indeed, the British Museum and other major national museums in the United Kingdom are currently prevented from deaccessioning items in their collections precisely because the arm's length model still reserves for parliament the decision on deaccessioning. A recent claim by the British Museum that '[a]ll decisions relating to collections are taken by the Museum's trustees' is inaccurate.[7] But the museum's trustees also have a responsibility, and there are things they can do. They could take the view, for instance, that the Parthenon marbles are unfit to be kept in their collections. Although this would be contrary to the dominant interpretation of the deaccessioning provisions in the British Museum Act 1963, British support for the marbles' return is so strong that the trustees could hardly be criticised for doing so.

Yet, at the moment of writing, the trustees are concerned about returns dismantling the museum and are delighted instead to discuss loans. All of the trustees? This is unclear, as rumours have a minority of trustees waver. The impetus for return will change if, when appointing trustees in the future, the UK government chooses individuals who embrace the new ethics of collecting, in accordance with the new international law.

Despite this resistance to the idea of return, there is little doubt that the Parthenon marbles in the British Museum will be going home. This is not to foretell the future but to understand the past and the present. As a New York Times opinion article written some 20 years ago put it, '[m]useums around the world fear establishing a precedent that would cause a broad new look at the legal status of their own antiquities. But that look has already begun.'[8] The process for the return of the Parthenon marbles has already begun. It began when attitudes towards the retention of illicit cultural property started to change. It began when tolerance towards the retention of unlawfully, and even unethically, acquired cultural property started to decrease. It began when international law started to evolve mirroring these shifts in attitude. The clock is ticking at last and, the question about the return of the Parthenon marbles is no longer *whether*. It is rather *when*.

---

[7] Vivienne Chow, 'The UK Has Rejected UNESCO's Call on British Authorities to Reassess Their Position on the Contested Parthenon Marbles', Artnet News (5 October 2021).

[8] 'Opinion: Return the Parthenon Marbles', The New York Times (2 February 2002).

References

Hansard, 'House of Lords National Heritage Act 1983 Debate' (13 October 2022) (vol 824, Hansard 2022)
Neil MacGregor, *À monde nouveau, nouveaux musées* (Hazan Louvre éditions 2021)
David Rudenstine, 'Lord Elgin and the Ottomans: The Question of Permission' (2002) 23 (2) Cardozo Law Review 449

Chapter 12
Annex: The Parthenon Sculptures—The Trustees' Statement (British Museum)

© 2022 The Trustees of the British Museum

The position of the Trustees of the British Museum

The British Museum tells the story of cultural achievement throughout the world, from the dawn of human history over two million years ago, until the present day. The Parthenon sculptures are a significant part of that story.

The Museum is a unique resource for the world: the breadth and depth of its collection allow a global public to examine cultural identities and explore the complex network of interconnected human cultures. The Trustees lend extensively all over the world and over 4.5 million objects from the collection are available to study online. The Parthenon sculptures are a vital element in this interconnected world collection. They're a part of the world's shared heritage and transcend political boundaries.

The Acropolis Museum allows the Parthenon sculptures that are in Athens (about half of what survives from the ancient world) to be appreciated against the backdrop of Athenian history. The Parthenon sculptures in London are an important representation of ancient Athenian civilisation in the context of world history. Each year millions of visitors, free of charge, admire the artistry of the sculptures and gain insight into how ancient Greece influenced—and was influenced by—the other civilisations that it encountered. The Trustees firmly believe that there's a positive advantage and public benefit in having the sculptures divided between two great museums, each telling a complementary but different story.

Common misconceptions

All of the sculptures from the Parthenon are in the British Museum
This is incorrect. About half of the sculptures from the Parthenon are lost, having been destroyed over the 2500 years of the building's history. The sculptures that remain are found in museums in six countries, including the Louvre and the Vatican, though the majority is divided roughly equally between Athens and London.

C. Titi, *The Parthenon Marbles and International Law*,
https://doi.org/10.1007/978-3-031-26357-6_12

The Parthenon sculptures now in the British Museum were stolen
This isn't true. Lord Elgin, the British diplomat who transported the sculptures to England, acted with the full knowledge and permission of the legal authorities of the day in both Athens and London. Lord Elgin's activities were thoroughly investigated by a Parliamentary Select Committee in 1816 and found to be entirely legal. Following a vote of Parliament, the British Museum was allocated funds to acquire the collection.

The Greek government has asked for a loan of the sculptures which has been turned down by the British Museum
The Trustees have never been asked for a loan of the Parthenon sculptures by Greece, only for the permanent removal of all of the sculptures in its care to Athens. The Trustees will consider (subject to the usual considerations of condition and fitness to travel) any request for any part of the collection to be borrowed and then returned. The simple precondition required by the Trustees before they will consider whether or not to lend an object is that the borrowing institution acknowledges the British Museum's ownership of the object. In 2014 the Museum lent the pediment sculpture of the river-god Ilissos to the State Hermitage Museum in St Petersburg, Russia, on the anniversary of that museum's foundation. The Trustees frequently lend objects from the collection to museums all around the world, including Greece. The Museum lends thousands of objects to hundreds of museums worldwide each year.

The Trustees' policy and their willingness to consider loans to Athens has been made clear to the Greek government, but successive Greek governments have refused to consider borrowing or to acknowledge the Trustees ownership of the Parthenon sculptures in their care. This has made any meaningful discussion on the issue virtually impossible.

The British Museum argues that the sculptures in their collection should remain in London because there's nowhere to house them in Greece and that the Greek authorities can't look after them
Neither of these claims is true, and the British Museum doesn't argue this. The Trustees argue that the sculptures on display in London convey huge public benefit as part of the Museum' worldwide collection. Our colleagues in Athens are, of course, fully able to conserve, preserve and display the material in their care. We admire the display in the Acropolis Museum, in which the Parthenon sculptures are complemented by casts of all of those in London and elsewhere, creating as full a picture as is now possible of the original sculptural decoration of the temple.

The division of the Parthenon sculptures is a unique case. The sculptures can only be appreciated as a complete set
This isn't so. Europe's complex history has often resulted in cultural objects, such as medieval and renaissance altarpieces from one original location being divided and distributed through museums in many countries. Bringing the Parthenon sculptures back together into a unified whole is impossible. The complicated history of the Parthenon meant that by 1800 about half of the sculptures had been lost or destroyed.

The sculptures could be reunited on the Parthenon
This isn't possible. Though partially reconstructed, the Parthenon is a ruin. It's universally recognised that the sculptures that still exist could never be safely returned to the building: they're best seen and conserved in museums. For this reason, all the sculptures that remained on the building have now been removed to the Acropolis Museum, and replicas are now in place.

The matter could be solved by the British Museum setting up an outpost in Athens
The Trustees of the British Museum believe that there's a great public benefit to seeing the sculptures within the context of the world collection of the British Museum, in order to deepen our understanding of their significance within world cultural history. This provides the ideal complement to the display in the Acropolis Museum. Both museums together allow the fullest appreciation of the meaning and importance of the Parthenon sculptures and maximise the number of people that can appreciate them.

UNESCO have offered to mediate on the issue but the British Museum has refused
The British Museum has a long history of collaboration with UNESCO and admires and supports its work. However, the British Museum isn't a government body. The Trustees have a legal and moral responsibility to preserve and maintain all the collections in their care and to make them accessible to world audiences. The Trustees want to strengthen existing good relations with colleagues and institutions in Greece, and to explore collaborative ventures directly between institutions, not on a government-to-government basis. This is why we believe that UNESCO involvement isn't the best way forward. Museums holding Greek works, whether in Greece, the UK or elsewhere in the world, are naturally united in a shared endeavour to show the importance of the legacy of ancient Greece. The British Museum is committed to playing its full part in sharing the value of that legacy for all humanity.

Correction to: Introduction

Correction to:
Chapter 1 in: C. Titi, *The Parthenon Marbles and International Law*,
https://doi.org/10.1007/978-3-031-26357-6_1

The amounts "£21902" and "£2.52 million" were incorrect in the initially published version of this chapter, which has now been corrected.

The updated version of the chapter can be found at
https://doi.org/10.1007/978-3-031-26357-6_1

C. Titi, *The Parthenon Marbles and International Law*,
https://doi.org/10.1007/978-3-031-26357-6_13

9783031263569